THE SEMINAR OF
JACQUES LACAN

BOOK III

By Jacques Lacan

TELEVISION

THE SEMINAR OF JACQUES LACAN BOOK I

THE SEMINAR OF JACQUES LACAN BOOK II

THE SEMINAR OF JACQUES LACAN BOOK III

THE SEMINAR OF JACQUES LACAN BOOK VII

ECRITS: A SELECTION

FEMININE SEXUALITY

THE FOUR FUNDAMENTAL CONCEPTS
OF PSYCHO-ANALYSIS

THE SEMINAR OF

JACQUES LACAN

Edited by Jacques-Alain Miller

BOOK III

The Psychoses 1955–1956

TRANSLATED WITH NOTES BY

Russell Grigg

W · W · NORTON & COMPANY

NEW YORK LONDON

Originally published in French as
Le Seminaire, Livre III, Les Psychoses
by Editions du Seuil, Paris, 1981 and

First American edition 1993
First published as a Norton paperback 1997

Library of Congress Cataloging-in-Publication Data

Lacan, Jacques, 1901–1981
[Psychoses. English]
The psychoses / translated with notes by Russell Grigg. —1st
American ed.
p. cm. —(The Seminar of Jacques Lacan : bk. 3)
Translation of: Les psychoses.
Includes bibliographical references.

1. Psychoses. 2. Psychoses—Patients—Language. 3. Schreber,
Daniel Paul, 1842–1911. Denkwürdigkeiten eines Nervenkranken.
I. Grigg, Russell. II. Title. III. Series: Lacan, Jacques, 1901–
Séminaire de Jacques Lacan. English ; bk. 3.
BF173.L14613 1988 bk. 3
[RC512]
150.19'5 s—dc20
[616.89] 92-28360

ISBN: 978-0-393-31612-4

W. W. Norton & Company, Inc.
500 Fifth Avenue, New York, NY 10110
W. W. Norton & Company Ltd.
10 Coptic Street, London WC1A 1PU

CONTENTS

Translator's note vii
Abbreviations ix

INTRODUCTION TO THE QUESTION OF THE PSYCHOSES

I Introduction to the question of the psychoses 3
II The meaning of delusion 16
III The Other and psychosis 29
IV "I've just been to the butcher's" 44

THEMATICS AND STRUCTURE OF THE PSYCHOTIC PHENOMENON

V On a god who does not deceive and one who does 59
VI The psychotic phenomenon and its mechanism 73
VII The imaginary dissolution 89
VIII The symbolic sentence 102
IX On nonsense and the structure of God 117
X On the signifier in the real and the bellowing-miracle 130
XI On the rejection of a primordial signifier 143

ON THE SIGNIFIER AND THE SIGNIFIED

XII The hysteric's question 161
XIII The hysteric's question (II): *What is a woman?* 173
XIV The signifier, as such, signifies nothing 183
XV On primordial signifiers and the lack of one 196
XVI Secretaries to the insane 206

XVII Metaphor and metonymy (I): "His sheaf was neither miserly nor spiteful" 214
XVIII Metaphor and metonymy (II): Signifying articulation and transference of the signified 222
XIX An address: Freud in the century 231

THE ENVIRONS OF THE HOLE

XX The appeal, the allusion 247
XXI The quilting point 258
XXII "Thou art the one who wilt follow me" 271
XXIII The highway and the signifier "being a father" 285
XXIV "Thou art" 295
XXV The phallus and the meteor 310

Bibliography 324
Index 329

TRANSLATOR'S NOTE

This is a translation of the seminar that Lacan delivered to the Société Française de Psychanalyse over the course of the academic year 1955–56. The original French text is the third in a series of Lacan's seminars, beginning in 1953, that is being edited by Jacques-Alain Miller.

I have been mindful of James Strachey's translations of Freud in the *Standard Edition*. On the whole it has been possible to avoid major divergences from Strachey, the two exceptions being to render *"investissement"* as "investment" rather than "cathexis" and *"pulsion"* as "drive" rather than "instinct." In this I follow the practice adopted by the translators of Seminars I and II and by Stuart Schneiderman in *Returning to Freud: Clinical Psychoanalysis in the School of Lacan* (New Haven: Yale University Press, 1980).

The translation of this seminar is faced with one further complication arising from the fact that it deals extensively with Schreber's *Memoirs of My Nervous Illness*. Schreber's terms have often been rendered differently in the English translation of the *Memoirs*, in the *Standard Edition* version of Freud's case history, and in Lacan's article, "The question preliminary to any possible treatment of psychosis," in *Ecrits: A Selection*. This has, on a very small number of occasions, required some explanation, which will be found in the footnotes.

I should add that I have diverged in two major ways from the translations of Seminars I and II.

First, the terms *"signification"* and *"sens,"* which appear in Seminars I and II as "signification" and "meaning" respectively, have been translated as "meaning" and "sense." I am following the practice of Stuart Schneiderman here, for essentially the same reason he gives: there seems little reason to resort to the archaism of the English "signification" when there are two common English terms that will do adequate service.

Secondly, the term *"méconnaissance"* is rendered as "misrecognition," instead of "failure to recognize" or "misunderstanding." The latter term has to be reserved for "*malentendu,*" while there are contexts in which the first does not capture the appropriate meaning.

I have followed Seminars I and II in indicating the distinction, a significant one in the original, between "*moi*" and "*ego*" by putting "ego" in roman when "*moi*" appears in the original and in italics when "*ego*" has been used.

Finally, the numbers in the margin of this translation refer to the pagination of the French edition published by *Editions du Seuil* in 1981. It is hoped that this practice will assist those who, while needing to refer to the English edition, are in a position to consult the original.

I wish to thank Jacques-Alain Miller for the assistance and advice he gave me while I was preparing this translation. I am also grateful to the editor at W. W. Norton, Susan Barrows Munro, for her encouragement and patience in helping me to bring this long and sometimes difficult translation to publication.

Many very helpful comments were made by Kerry Murphy and Rosemary Sorensen, who both generously read an entire draft of the manuscript. I owe them gratitude for invaluable suggestions on ways to improve the style of the translation. Dominique Hecq, with her sensitivity to the idiom of both languages, gave me sound advice on a number of difficult points.

Finally, I would like to record my thanks to Deakin University for its support while I was engaged on this work.

Russell Grigg
Geelong, Australia
June 1992

ABBREVIATIONS

Mem	D. P. Schreber, *Memoirs of My Nervous Illness,* translated and edited with introduction, notes, and discussion by Ida MacAlpine & Richard Hunter, with a new introduction by Samuel M. Weber, Cambridge, MA: Harvard University Press, 1988. Originally published as *Denkwürdigkeiten eines Nervenkranken,* Leipzig: Oswald Mutze, 1903. Page numbers refer to the pagination of the original German edition, noted in the margin of the English translation.
SE	Sigmund Freud, *Standard Edition of the Complete Psychological Works of Sigmund Freud* (24 volumes), translated and edited by James Strachey in collaboration with Anna Freud, assisted by Alix Strachey and Alan Tyson, London: The Hogarth Press and the Institute of Psycho-Analysis; New York: Norton, 1953–74.
GW	Sigmund Freud, *Gesammelte Werke* (18 volumes), Frankfurt: S. Fischer Verlag.
Sem	Jacques Lacan, *The Seminar of Jacques Lacan,* Books I and II, New York: Norton, 1988.
E	Jacques Lacan, *Ecrits,* Paris: Seuil, 1966. Where there are two numbers, separated by a slash, /, the first number refers to the page number in the French edition, the second to the page number in *Ecrits: A Selection,* translated by Alan Sheridan, New York: Norton, 1977.

Freud-Fliess	*The Complete Letters of Sigmund Freud to Wilhelm Fliess 1887–1904*, translated and edited by Jeffrey Moussaieff Masson, Cambridge, MA: Harvard University Press, 1985
Origins	Sigmund Freud, *The Origins of Psycho-Analysis. Letters to Wilhelm Fliess, Drafts and Notes 1887–1902*, edited by Marie Bonaparte, Anna Freud, and Ernst Kris, translated by Eric Mosbacher and James Strachey, introduction by Ernst Kris, New York: Basic Books, 1954.

INTRODUCTION TO THE QUESTION OF THE PSYCHOSES

I 11

Introduction to the question of the psychoses

SCHIZOPHRENIA AND PARANOIA
M. DE CLÉRAMBAULT
THE MIRAGES OF UNDERSTANDING
FROM *VERNEINING* TO *VERWERFUNG*
PSYCHOSIS AND PSYCHOANALYSIS

This year the question of the psychoses begins.

I say the *question* because one can't speak straightaway of their *treatment*, as was announced in the initial notice, and still less of the treatment of psychosis *in Freud*, for he never spoke of it, except by allusion.

We shall start with Freud's theory and assess what it contributes to the issue, but we shall not fail to introduce the notions we have developed over the past years, nor to deal with all the problems that the psychoses raise for us *today*. Clinical and nosographic problems first. I've been thinking that all the benefit analysis might produce with respect to them hasn't yet been fully extracted. Problems of treatment, too, which our work for this year ought to lead into – this is our aim.

Thus it's not by chance that I initially gave what we shall finish with as our title. Let us say it was a lapsus, a significant lapsus.

1

I would like to stress one primary, self-evident truth – the least noticed as is always the case.

In what has been done, is done, and is now in the course of being done
concerning treatment of the psychoses the schizophrenias are much more 12
readily explored than the paranoias, a much more lively interest is taken in them, and greater results are expected from this. Why then does paranoia, on the contrary, have a rather privileged position for Freudian doctrine – that of a knot, but also of a resistant nucleus?

It might take us a long time to answer that question, but it will remain just below the surface of our approach.

Of course, Freud wasn't unaware of schizophrenia. The movement involving this concept's development was contemporary with him. But while he recognized, admired, and even encouraged the work of the Zurich school and put analytic theory into relation with what was being constructed around Bleuler, he kept his distance nevertheless. He was initially and essentially interested in paranoia. And, to give you straightaway a reference point that you can return to, I remind you that at the end of the observation on the Schreber case, which is his major text concerning the psychoses, Freud traces out a watershed, as it were, between paranoia on the one hand and on the other everything he would like, he says, to be called paraphrenia, which exactly covers the field of the schizophrenias.[1] This is a necessary reference point for the intelligibility of everything we shall subsequently have to say – for Freud the field of the psychoses divides in two.

What does the term *psychosis* cover in the field of psychiatry? Psychosis is not dementia. The psychoses, if you like – there is no reason to deny oneself the luxury of this word – correspond to what has always been called and legitimately continues to be called *madness*. This is the domain Freud divides in two. He did not go in for much more nosology than this on the subject of psychosis, but on this point he is quite clear, and given the status of its author we cannot neglect this distinction.

In this respect, as sometimes happens, Freud is not absolutely in step with his time. Is he way behind it? Is he way ahead of it? There lies the ambiguity. At first sight he is way behind it.

I can't recount to you here the history of paranoia since it made its first appearance with a psychiatrist disciple of Kant at the beginning of the nineteenth century,[2] but let me tell you that at its maximum extension in German psychiatry it covered almost all forms of madness – seventy percent of the ill in asylums bore the label of paranoia. Everything we call psychosis or madness was paranoia.

In France the word *paranoia,* at the time it was introduced into nosology – this was very late, a matter of some fifty years – was identified with something
13 thing fundamentally different. A paranoiac – at least until the thesis of a certain Jacques Lacan attempted to stir up people's minds,[3] which was limited to a small circle, to the small circle that matters, which means that nobody talks of paranoiacs as they used to before – a paranoiac was a nasty person, an intolerant one, a bad-humored type, proud, mistrustful, irritable, and who overestimated himself. This feature formed the foundation of paranoia – when the paranoiac was far too paranoid, he would end up deluding. It was less a question of a conception than of a clinical picture, moreover a very fine one.

[1] "Psycho-Analytic Notes on an Autobiographical Account of a Case of Paranoia (Dementia Paranoides)," SE 12:75–76.

[2] R. A. Vogel is generally credited with having introduced the term into modern usage in 1764.

[3] Jacques Lacan, *De la psychose paranoïaque dans ses rapports avec la personnalité.*

This is roughly where things stood in France, without my distorting anything, after the publication of M. Génil-Perrin's work on the paranoid constitution, which had spread the characterological notion of anomaly of the personality, essentially made up of what one may well describe – the book's style bears the mark of this inspiration – as the perverse structure of character.[4] Like all perverts, it sometimes happens that the paranoiac goes beyond the limits and falls into that frightful madness, the unbounded exaggeration of his unfortunate character.

That outlook can be described as psychological, psychologizing, or even as psychogenetic. All the formal references to an organic base, to temperament for example, don't change a thing – it's really a psychological genesis. Something is defined and assessed at a certain level, and its development follows uninterrupted with an autonomous coherence that is self-sufficient in its own field. This is why, in a word, it's a question of psychology, despite the author's own explicit rejection of this point of view.

In my thesis I tried to promote another view. I was certainly still a young psychiatrist then, and I had been introduced to psychiatry largely through the works, the direct teaching, and, I would even be so bold as to say, the intimacy of someone who played a very important role in French psychiatry of that period, M. de Clérambault, whose personality, action, and influence I call to mind in this introductory discussion.[5]

For those among you who have only an approximate knowledge of his work – and there must be some – M. de Clérambault is supposed to have been the fierce defender of an extreme organicist conception. That was certainly the explicit design of his theoretical statements. However, I do not believe they give a correct perspective – either on the influence of his personality and teaching or on the true range of his discoveries. 14

His work has, independently of its theoretical aims, a concrete clinical value – there are a considerable number of clinical syndromes that Clérambault located in a completely original manner and that have since then been

[4] See Georges Génil-Perrin, *Les Paranoïaques*, specially pt. 2, "La constitution paranoïaque."

[5] Gaëten Gatian de Clérambault (1872–1934), Psychiatrist-in-charge at the Special Infirmary for the Insane of the Paris Prefecture of Police from 1920 to 1934, sought to describe the psychoses on the basis of a common element, the *syndrome of mental automatism*, on the grounds that delusion underlies all the different forms in which psychosis appears. He claimed that the disturbances from which delusions stem, which he called *elementary phenomena*, are of purely organic origin; not being part of the subject's own thought processes, they impose themselves upon the subject's mind from without. These phenomena include thought-echoes, verbal enunciations of actions, and various forms of hallucination. See de Clérambault, "Psychoses à base d'automatisme."

In 1966 Lacan, describing de Clérambault as his "only master in psychiatry," observed that "his mechanistic ideology . . . seems to me, in its grasp of the subjective text, to be closer to what can be constructed as a structural analysis than does any other clinical effort in French psychiatry." "De nos antécédents," E, 65.

integrated into the heritage of psychiatric experience. He made precious, original contributions which have never been taken up since. I have in mind his studies on psychosis caused by toxic substances. In a word, in the realm of the psychoses Clérambault remains absolutely indispensable.

The notion of mental automatism is apparently brought into focus in Clérambault's work and teaching by his concern to demonstrate the fundamentally *anideational* [*anidéique*], as he put it, character of the phenomena that manifest themselves in the development of psychosis. What this means is *that which doesn't correspond to a train of thought,* but unfortunately this doesn't make much more sense than the master's discourse does. This reference point is supposedly located, then, in terms of being understandable. The initial reference to understanding serves to decide exactly what it is that introduces a breach and appears as unintelligible.

Here we have an assumption that it would be an exaggeration to describe as naive, since surely none is more commonly held – and still, I fear, by you, or at least many among you. The major progress in psychiatry since the introduction of this movement of investigation called psychoanalysis has consisted, or so it's believed, in restoring meaning to the chain of phenomena. This is not false in itself. But what is false is to imagine that the sense in question is what we understand. What we are supposed to have learned once again, as is thought everywhere in medical quarters, the expression of psychiatrists' *sensus commune,* is to understand patients. This is a pure mirage.

The notion of understanding has a very clear meaning. It's a source that, under the name of *relation of understanding,* Jaspers has made the pivot of all so-called general psychopathology.[6] It consists in thinking that some things are self-evident, that, for example, when someone is sad it's because he doesn't have what his heart desires. Nothing could be more false—there are people who have all their heart desires and are still sad. Sadness is a passion of quite another color.

I would like to insist on this. When you give a child a smack, well! it's understandable that he cries – without anybody's reflecting that it's not at all obligatory that he should cry. I remember a small boy who whenever he got
15 a smack used to ask – *Was that a pat or a slap?* If he was told it was a slap he cried, that belonged to the conventions, to the rules of the moment, and if it was a pat he was delighted. But this isn't the end of the matter. When one gets a smack there are many other ways of responding than by crying. One can return it in kind, or else turn the other cheek, or one can also say – *Hit me, but listen!* A great variety of possibilities offer themselves, which are

[6] See Karl Jaspers, "Meaningful Connections," "*Verständliche Zusammenhänge,*" chap. 5 of his *General Psychopathology*.

neglected in the notion of relation of understanding as it's spelled out by M. Jaspers.

Before next time you can refer to his chapter entitled "Meaningful Connections." Its inconsistencies soon appear – this is the value of a sustained discourse.

Understanding is evoked only as an ideal relation. As soon as one tries to get close to it, it becomes, properly speaking, ungraspable. The examples that Jaspers takes as the most apparent – his reference points, with which he very quickly and inevitably confuses the notion itself – are ideal references. But what is striking is that in his own text he cannot, despite all the art he puts into sustaining this mirage, avoid giving precisely the examples that have always been refuted by the facts. For example, since suicide demonstrates a tendency towards decline, towards death, it seems that each and every one of us could say – but only if one sets out to get us to say it – that it more readily takes place at the decline of nature, that is during autumn. Yet it has been known for a long time that many more people commit suicide in spring. That is neither more nor less understandable. Surprise at there being more suicides in spring than autumn can only be based on this inconsistent mirage called the relation of understanding – as if there were anything that could ever be grasped in this order!

One is led to think then that psychogenesis is to be identified with the reintroduction of this celebrated relation into a relationship with the object of psychiatry. This is in fact very difficult to conceive, because it's literally inconceivable but, like all things that are not well grasped, or captured in a real concept, it remains a latent assumption, one that has been latent throughout all the changes in the complexion of psychiatry over the last thirty years. Well, if that is what psychogenesis is, I say – because I think that most of you are by now capable of grasping it, after two years of teaching on the symbolic, the imaginary and the real, and I also say it for those who aren't yet up to it – that the great secret of psychoanalysis is that there is no psychogenesis. If that is what psychogenesis is, there is precisely nothing that
could be further from psychoanalysis in its whole development, its entire 16
inspiration and its mainspring, in everything it has contributed, everything it has been able to confirm for us in anything we have established.

Another way of expressing things, one that goes much further, is to say that the psychological is, if we try to grasp it as firmly as possible, the ethological, that is, the whole of the biological individual's behavior in relation to his natural environment. There you have a legitimate definition of psychology. There you have an order of real relations, an objectifiable thing, a field with quite adequately defined boundaries. But to constitute an object of science, one must go a little bit further. It has to be said of human psychology what Voltaire used to say about natural history, which was that it's not as natural as all that and that, frankly, nothing could be more anti-natural.[7] Everything that in human behavior belongs to the psychological order is subject to such profound anomalies and constantly presents such obvious paradoxes that the problem arises of knowing what needs to be introduced in order for a cat to find its kittens.

If one forgets the landscape, the essential mainspring, of psychoanalysis, one comes back – which is naturally the constant, daily-observed tendency of psychoanalysts – to all sorts of myths formed ages ago. How long ago remains to be defined, but they date more or less from the end of the eighteenth century. The myth of unity of the personality, the myth of synthesis, of superior and inferior functions, confusion about automatism, all these types of organization of the objective field constantly reveal cracks, tears and rents, negation of the facts, and misrecognition of the most immediate experience.

Make no mistake, though. I'm not going to fall into the myth of immediate experience that forms the basis of what people call existential psychology or even existential psychoanalysis. Immediate experience is no better placed to arrest or captivate us than in any other science. In no way is it the measure of the development that we must ultimately reach. Freud's teaching, which in this respect is in total agreement with what takes place in the rest of the scientific domain – however differently we have to conceive it from our own myth – brings resources into play that are beyond immediate experience and cannot be grasped in any tangible fashion. In psychoanalysis, as in physics, it's not the property of color as sensed and differentiated by direct experience that holds our attention. It's something which is behind this, and which conditions it.

17 Freudian experience is in no way preconceptual. It's not a pure experience, but one that is well and truly structured by something artificial, the analytic relation, as it's constituted by what the subject recounts to the doctor and by what the doctor does with it. It's by setting out from this initial mode of operation that everything gets worked out.

Throughout this reminder you must have already recognized the three orders that I'm forever harping on as so necessary to understanding anything at all about analytic experience – that is, the symbolic, the imaginary, and the real.

You saw the symbolic appear just now when I alluded, and from two different directions, to what is beyond all understanding, which all understanding is inserted into, and which exercises such an obviously disruptive influence over human and interhuman relationships.

You have also seen the imaginary indicated in the reference I made to

[7] On hearing someone praise Buffon's monumental work, *L'histoire naturelle,* Voltaire is said to have exclaimed, "Not so natural as all that!"

animal ethology, that is to the captivating or ensnaring forms that constitute the rails upon which animal behavior is conducted towards it natural aims. M. Piéron, who for us doesn't have an odor of sanctity, called one of his books *Sensation, the Guide to Life*.[8] It's a very pretty title, but I don't know that he applies himself to sensation as much as he says, and the book's contents certainly don't confirm this. What is correct in his approach is that the imaginary is surely the guide to life for the whole animal domain. While the image equally plays a capital role in our own domain, this role is completely taken up and caught up within, remolded and reanimated by, the symbolic order. The image is always more or less integrated into this order, which, I remind you, is defined in man by its property of organized structure.

What difference is there between what belongs to the imaginary or real orders and what belongs to the symbolic order? In the imaginary or real orders we always have more and less, a threshold, a margin, continuity. In the symbolic order every element has value through being opposed to another.

Take an example from the domain that we are beginning to explore.

One of our psychotics tells us how foreign the world is which he entered some time ago. Everything has become a sign for him. Not only is he spied upon, observed, watched over, not only do people speak to, point, look, and wink at him, but all this – you will see the ambiguity straightaway – invades the field of real, inanimate, nonhuman objects. Let us look at this a bit more closely. If he encounters a red car in the street – a car is not a natural object – it's not for nothing, he will say, that it went past at that very moment.

Let us inquire into this delusional intuition. The car has a meaning, but 18
the subject is very often incapable of saying what it is. Is it favorable? Is it threatening? Surely there is some reason for the car's being there. Of this, the most undifferentiated phenomenon there is, we can form three completely different conceptions.

We can consider the thing from the angle of an aberration of perception. Don't think we are currently so far removed from this. Not so long ago this was the level at which the question was raised concerning what a madman's rudimentary experience was. He might just be color blind and see red as green and *vice versa*. Perhaps he can't distinguish colors.

Again, we can consider the encounter with the red car along the lines of what happens when the robin redbreast, encountering its mate, displays the breast that gives it its name. It has been demonstrated that its dress corresponds to the guarding of the limit of its territory and that the encounter alone occasions a certain form of behavior towards its adversary. Here the red has an imaginary function which, precisely in the order of relations of understanding, can be translated into the fact that for the subject this red

[8] Henri Piéron, *The Sensations: Their Functions, Processes and Mechanisms*.

will have made him see red and seemed to him to bear within it the expressive and immediate character of hostility or anger.

Finally, we can understand the red car within the symbolic order, namely in the way one understands the color red in a game of cards, that is, as opposed to black, as being a part of an already organized language.

There you have the three registers distinguished from one another, and also distinguished from one another are the three planes on which our so-called understanding of the elementary phenomenon can be undertaken.

2

The novelty of what Freud introduced in investigating paranoia is even more dazzling than it is anywhere else – perhaps because it's more localized and breaks more with contemporary discoveries on psychosis. Here we see Freud proceed from the very first with an audacity that has the character of an absolute beginning.

To be sure, the *Traumdeutung* [*The Interpretation of Dreams*] is a creation, also. Despite its being said that interest had already been taken in the meaning of dreams, this had absolutely nothing to do with the pioneering work
19 that is performed before our eyes. This doesn't finish just with the formula that the dream tells you something, for the only thing that interests Freud is the elaboration through which the dream says this something – it says it in the same way as one speaks. No one had ever seen that before. People had been able to notice that dreams have a meaning, that something could be read in them, but not that dreams talk.

But let's allow that Freud's approach to the dream may have been prepared for by the artless practices that preceded his own attempt. By contrast there has never been anything comparable to the manner in which he proceeds with Schreber. What does he do? He takes the book of a paranoiac which, at the time he is writing his own work, he blithely recommends that one read – *do not fail to read him before reading me* – and gives it a Champollion-like decipherment. He deciphers it in the way hieroglyphics are deciphered.

Of all the literary productions of the type that plead a cause, of all the communications of those who, having gone beyond the limits, have spoken of the psychotic's alien experience, Schreber's work is certainly one of the most remarkable. Here we have an exceptional encounter between the genius of Freud and a unique book.

I said *genius*. Yes, there is a true stroke of genius on Freud's part that owes nothing to any intuitive insight – it's the genius of the linguist who sees the same sign appear several times in a text, begins from the idea that this must mean something, and manages to stand all the signs of this language right side up again. The prodigious identification that Freud makes between the birds of the sky and maidens is a part of this phenomenon – it's a remarkable hypothesis, which enables the entire chain of the text to be reconstituted, the famous *fundamental language* that Schreber talks about. More clearly than anywhere else, analytic interpretation is here demonstrated to be symbolic, in the structured sense of the term.

This translation is remarkable indeed. But, be careful, it leaves the fields of the psychoses and the neuroses both on the same level. If the application of the analytic method yielded no more than a symbolic-order reading, it would show itself incapable of explaining the distinction between the two fields. It's therefore outside this dimension that the problems forming the object of our research this year arise.

Since discourse, the lunatic's printed discourse, is at issue, it's therefore manifest that we are in the symbolic order. Now, what is the actual material of this discourse? At what level does the sense translated by Freud unfold? From what are the naming elements of this discourse borrowed? Generally 20
speaking the raw material is his own body.

In man the relation to one's own body characterizes, in the final analysis, the restricted, but really irreducible, field of the imaginary. If there is anything in man that corresponds to the imaginary function as it operates in animals, it's everything that, in a fundamental manner but one that is always barely graspable, relates him to the general form of his body at a point called an erogenous zone. Only analytic experience has been able to seize this relationship, always at the limit of the symbolic, at its mainspring.

This is what the symbolic analysis of the Schreber case demonstrates for us. It's only by entering through the symbolic that we can successfully make any inroads into the case.

3

The questions that arise touch upon exactly all the categories effective in our field of operation.

It's classically said that in psychosis the unconscious is at the surface, conscious. This is even why articulating it doesn't seem to have much effect. Within this perspective, quite instructive in itself, we can observe first of all that it's not purely and simply, as Freud always emphasized, from the negative trait of being an *Unbewusst*, a nonconscious, that the unconscious derives its efficacity. Translating Freud, we say – the unconscious is a language. Its being articulated doesn't imply its recognition, though. The proof of this is that everything proceeds as if Freud were translating a foreign language, even carving it up and reassembling it. The subject is, with respect to his own language, quite simply in the same position as Freud. If it's ever possible for someone to speak in a language that he is totally ignorant of, we can say that the psychotic subject is ignorant of the language he speaks.

Is this a satisfactory metaphor? Certainly not. The question is not so much why this unconscious, which is articulated at ground level, remains excluded for the subject, not adopted by him – but why it appears in the real.

I hope that there are enough of you who remember the commentary that M. Jean Hyppolite made for us here on *Die Verneinung,*[9] and I regret his absence this morning, which prevents me from being certain I'm not distorting the terms he uncovered in it.

21 What emerged clearly from his analysis of this striking text is that in what is unconscious not only is everything repressed, that is, misrecognized by the subject after having been verbalized, but that behind the process of verbalization there must be admitted a primordial *Bejahung,* an admission in the sense of the symbolic, which can itself be wanting. This point is borne out by other texts, and especially by a passage that is as explicit as can be where Freud admits a phenomenon of exclusion for which the term *Verwerfung* appears valid and from which *Verneinung,* produced at a much later stage, is distinguished. It can happen that a subject refuses access to his symbolic world to something that he has nevertheless experienced, which in this case is nothing other than the threat of castration. The subject's entire subsequent development shows that he wants to know nothing about it, Freud literally says, *in the sense of the repressed.*[10]

What comes under the effect of repression returns, for repression and the return of the repressed are just the two sides of the same coin. The repressed is always there, expressed in a perfectly articulate manner in symptoms and a host of other phenomena. By contrast, what falls under the effect of *Verwerfung* has a completely different destiny.

It's not pointless in this respect for me to remind you of the comparison I made last year between certain symbolic order phenomena and what happens in those machines, in the modern sense of the word, that do not quite talk yet but any day now will. One feeds figures into them and waits for them to give what would perhaps take us 100,000 years to calculate. But we can only introduce things into the circuit if we respect the machine's own rhythm –

[9] See "Introduction and Reply to Jean Hyppolite's Presentation of Freud's *Verneinung,*" Sem I:52–66; and "A Spoken Commentary on Freud's *Verneinung* by Jean Hyppolite," app. to Sem I:289–97.

[10] "When I speak of his having rejected it, the first meaning of the phrase is that he would have nothing to do with it, in the sense of having repressed it. This really involved no judgement upon the question of its existence, but it was the same as if it did not exist." "From the History of an Infantile Neurosis," SE 17:84. The German text reads, "Wenn ich gesagt habe, dass er von ihr nichts wissen wollte im Sinne der Verdrängung. Damit war eigentlich kein Urteil über ihre Existenz gefällt, aber es war so gut, als ob sie nicht existierte." GW 12:117.

otherwise they won't go in and can't enter the circuit. We can re-use the same image. Only it also happens that whatever is refused in the symbolic order, in the sense of *Verwerfung*, reappears in the real.

Freud's text is free of ambiguity on this point. It concerns the Wolf Man, as you know, who gives evidence of psychotic tendencies and qualities, as is demonstrated by the brief paranoia he enters between the end of Freud's treatment and when he is taken under observation again. Well, the fact that he has rejected all means of access to castration, which is nevertheless apparent in his conduct, all access to the register of the symbolic function, the fact that any assumption of castration by an *I* has become impossible for him, has the closest of links with his having had a brief hallucination in childhood, of which he recounts extremely precise details.

The scene is as follows. While playing with his knife he cut his finger, 22
which was left hanging on by only a small piece of skin. The subject recounted this episode in a style traced from lived experience. All temporal reference points seem to have disappeared. Then he sat on a bench, beside his nurse, who was precisely the confidant of his early experiences, and he didn't dare mention it to her. How significant is that suspension of all possible speech! – and precisely with the person he used to recount everything to, and especially things of that order! There is an abyss here, a temporal submersion, a rupture in experience, following which it turns out that he has nothing at all wrong with him, it's all over, let's drop the subject. The relation that Freud establishes between this phenomenon and this very special *knowing nothing of the thing, even in the sense of the repressed* expressed in this text translates as this – what is refused in the symbolic order re-emerges in the real.

There is a close relation between, on the one hand, negation and the reappearance in the purely intellectual order of what has not been integrated by the subject and, on the other, *Verwerfung* and hallucination, that is, the reappearance in the real of what the subject has refused. Here we have a range, a series, of relations.

What is involved in a hallucinatory phenomenon? This phenomenon has its own source in what we shall provisionally call the subject's history in the symbolic. I don't know whether I shall retain this combination of terms, because all history is by definition symbolic, but let's keep to this formula for the moment. The essential distinction is this – the origin of the neurotic repressed is not situated at the same level of history in the symbolic as that of the repressed involved in psychosis, even if there exists the closest of relations between their contents. This distinction alone provides a key that allows the problem to be raised in a much simpler fashion than up till now.

The same thing goes for the diagram from last year concerning verbal hallucination:

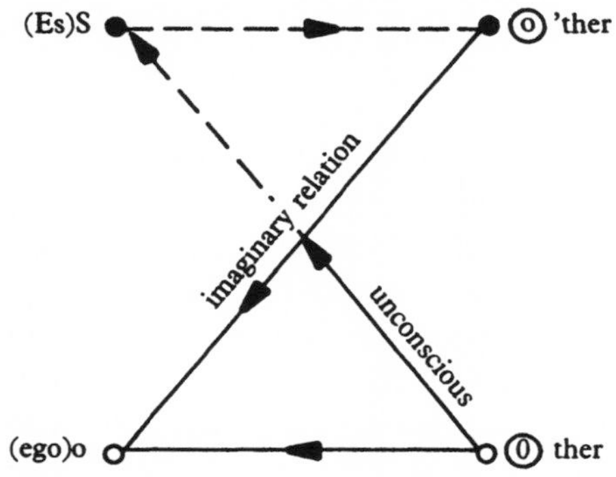

23 Our schema, I remind you, represents the interruption of full speech between the subject and the Other and its detour through the two egos, *o* and *o'*, and their imaginary relations. Here it indicates triplicity in the subject, which overlaps the fact that it's the subject's ego that normally speaks to another, and of the subject, the subject S in the third person. Aristotle pointed out that one must not say that man thinks, but that he thinks with his soul. Similarly, I say that the subject speaks *to himself with* his ego.

However, in the normal subject, speaking to oneself with one's ego can never be made fully explicit. One's relationship to the ego is fundamentally ambiguous, one's assumption of the ego always revocable. In the psychotic subject on the other hand certain elementary phenomena, and in particular hallucinations, which are their most characteristic form, show us the subject completely identified either with his ego, with which he speaks, or with the ego assumed entirely along instrumental lines. It's he who speaks of him, the subject, the S, in the two equivocal senses of the term, the initial S and the German *Es*.[11] This is what presents itself in the phenomenon of verbal hallucination. The moment the hallucination appears in the real, that is, accompanied by the sense of reality, which is the elementary phenomenon's basic feature, the subject literally speaks with his ego, and it's as if a third party, his lining, were speaking and commenting on his activity.

This is where our attempt to situate the diverse forms of psychosis in relation to the three registers of the symbolic, the imaginary, and the real will lead this year. It will enable us to get to the ultimate source of the function to give to the ego in the cure. The question of the object relation lies on the horizon.

The current handling of the object relation in the context of an analytic relation conceived as dual is founded on a misrecognition of the autonomy of

[11] "*Das Es*" is Freud's term for the id.

the symbolic order. This automatically introduces a confusion between the imaginary and real levels. But it doesn't eliminate the symbolic relation however, since we continue talking and, indeed, do nothing else. But it results from this misrecognition that what in the subject calls for recognition on the appropriate level of authentic symbolic exchange – which is not so easy to attain since it's always interfered with – is replaced by a recognition of the imaginary, of fantasy. Thus to authenticate everything of the order of the imaginary in the subject is properly speaking to make analysis the anteroom of madness, and we can only admire the fact that this doesn't lead to a deeper alienation – no doubt this indicates sufficiently that to be mad some predisposition, if not some precondition, is necessary.

In Vienna a charming young man to whom I was trying to explain a few 24
minor details asked me whether or not I believed that the psychoses were organic, so I said to him that the question was totally out of date, that for a very long time I had been making no distinction between psychology and physiology, and that, surely, *nobody goes mad through wanting to,* as I had stuck up on the wall of my medical quarters in those former, slightly archaic times.[12] It remains true though that we must attribute the well-known cases of fairly rapid onset of more or less persistent and sometimes lasting delusion to a certain way of handling the analytic relation, which consists in authenticating the imaginary, in substituting recognition on the imaginary level for recognition on the symbolic level.

The fact that an analysis can, right from its first stages, trigger a psychosis is well known, but no one has ever explained why. It's obviously a function of the subject's disposition, but also of an imprudent handling of the object relation.

I believe that today I have done nothing but put before you the interest there is in what we are going to study.

We shall find it useful to investigate paranoia. However thankless and arid this may be for us, it involves purifying, elaborating, and applying Freudian notions, and therefore also involves our training in analysis. I hope I have made you feel how it is that this conceptual elaboration can have the most direct effect on the ways we shall think, or be careful not to think, what our daily experience is and must be.

16 November 1955

[12] Lacan had recently been to Vienna, where, on 7 November 1955, he gave a lecture to the Neuro-Psychiatric Clinic of Vienna. This lecture later appeared in expanded form as "The Freudian Thing, or the Meaning of the Return to Freud in Psychoanalysis" in E, 401–36/114–45. See below, app. to chap. 5, 71.

25

II

The meaning of delusion

CRITIQUE OF KRAEPELIN
DIALECTICAL INERTIA
SÉGLAS AND PSYCHOMOTOR HALLUCINATION
PRESIDENT SCHREBER

The more one studies the history of the notion of paranoia, the more significant it seems and the more one appreciates the lesson that can be drawn from the progress, or lack of progress – whichever you like – that characterizes the psychiatric movement.

1

No notion is in the end more paradoxical. If I took care last time to put madness in the foreground, it was because it's quite possible to say that with the word *paranoia* authors have displayed all the ambiguity present in the use of the old term *madness*, which is the fundamental, common term.

The term doesn't date from yesterday, nor even from the birth of psychiatry. Without giving way to a facile deployment of erudition, I shall simply remind you that reference to madness has always been part of the so-called language of conventional wisdom. In this respect, the celebrated *Praise of Folly*[1] retains all its value for having identified it with normal human behavior – although this latter expression was not in use at that time. What was then said in the language of philosophers, between philosophers, eventually ended up being taken seriously and literally – a turning point that took place with Pascal, who formulated, with grave and meditative emphasis, that there is undoubtedly a necessary madness, that it would be another form of madness not to be mad with the madness of everybody.[2]

26 These reminders aren't useless, when you look at the paradoxes implicit in the premises of the theorists. It might be said that until Freud madness had been reduced to a number of modes of behavior, of patterns,[3] while others

[1] Desiderius Erasmus, *Praise of Folly and Other Writings*.

[2] "Les hommes sont si nécessairement fous que ce serait être fou par un autre tour de folie de n'être pas fou." "Men are so necessarily mad that not to be mad would be another form of madness." *Pensées*, section 6, no. 414.

[3] In English in the original.

thought of judging everybody's behavior in this way. In the end the difference, pattern for pattern, isn't obvious. The emphasis has never been fully placed where it would enable an image to be formed of what normal, or even understandable, conduct is and how properly paranoid conduct may be distinguished from it.

Let us remain at the level of definitions. The dissection of paranoia was incontestably much more extensive during the whole nineteenth century than it has been since the end of the last century, that is around 1899, at the time of the fourth or fifth edition of *Kraepelin*.[4] For a very long time Kraepelin remained attached to the vague notion that on the whole the man of experience knows, by a sort of sense, how to recognize natural signs. The true medical gift is to be able to perceive the signs that correctly dissect reality. It was only in 1899 that he introduced a finer subdivision. He brings the old paranoias back within the framework of *dementia praecox* by creating the paranoid sector and he puts forward quite an interesting definition of paranoia, distinguishing it from other modes of paranoid delusions with which it had until then been confused.

Paranoia is distinguished from the others because it is characterized by the gradual development of internal causes and according to a progressive evolution of a stable delusional system that is impossible to disturb and establishes itself with total preservation of clarity and order in thought, will, and action.[5]

This definition, coming as it does from the hand of an eminent clinician, is remarkable in that point by point it contradicts all clinical material. There isn't a word of truth in it.

Its development isn't gradual, there are always surges and phases. It seems to me, but I'm not absolutely sure of this, that it was I who introduced the notion of fertile moment. This fertile moment is always visible at the beginning of a paranoia. There is always a break in what Kraepelin goes on to call the progressive evolution of a delusion dependent on internal causes. It's obvious that the evolution of a paranoia can't be limited to internal causes. To be convinced of this one only has to go to the chapter "Aetiology" of his textbook and also read the contemporary authors, Sérieux and Capgras, whose work dates from five years later.[6] When one looks for the triggering causes of a paranoia, one always observes, with the required question mark, an emotional element in the subject's life, a life crisis that in fact does involve his

[4] The fifth edition of Emil Kraepelin's textbook, *Psychiatrie: Ein Lehrbuch für Studirende und Aerzte* appeared in 1896 and the sixth in 1899. A translation of the seventh (1903–04) edition, *Clinical Psychiatry,* was published in 1907.

[5] "Paranoia is a chronic progressive psychosis occurring mostly in early adult life, characterized by the gradual development of a stable progressive system of delusions, without marked mental deterioration, clouding of consciousness, or disorder of thought, will, or conduct." *Clinical Psychiatry,* 423.

[6] *Clinical Psychiatry,* 423–24; Paul Sérieux and J. Capgras, *Les folies raisonnantes: le délire d'interprétation.*

27 external relationships, and it would be astonishing were one not led to do this with respect to a delusion that is essentially characterized as a delusion of reference [*délire de relation*] – the term isn't Kretschmer's but Wernicke's.[7]

I read – . . . *progressive evolution of a stable delusional system that is impossible to disturb* . . . Nothing could be more false – the delusional system varies, whether it has been disturbed or not. As a matter of fact this question seems secondary to me. The variation comes from interpsychology, from external interventions, from the preservation or disruption of a certain orderliness in the world around the patient. He is very far indeed from not taking this into account and seeks, over the course of his delusion's evolution, to incorporate these elements into the composition of his delusion.

. . . *which establishes itself with total preservation of clarity and order in thought, will, and action*. Sure. But it's a question of knowing what clarity and order are. While something meriting these names can be discovered in the account the subject gives of his delusion, it still needs to be stated what this means, and this will by its very nature call into question the notions concerned. As for thought, will, and action, we are here to attempt to define them in terms of a number of specific forms of behavior, one of which is madness, rather than treat them as acquired notions at the outset. To us it seems that academic psychology has to be recast before it's capable of yielding concepts rigorous enough to be exchanged, at least at the level of our experience.

What is the ambiguity that surrounds the notion of paranoia due to? To many things, and perhaps to an inadequate clinical subdivision. I think that the psychiatrists among you have enough knowledge of the different clinical types to know for example that an interpretation delusion [*délire d'interprétation*] isn't at all the same thing as a litigious delusion [*délire de revendication*]. Equally there is every reason to distinguish between paranoid psychoses and passional psychoses, a difference that has been admirably emphasized by the work of my master, de Clérambault, whose function, role, personality, and doctrine I began pointing out to you last time.[8] It's precisely at the level of psychological distinctions that his work is the most significant. Does this mean that the clinical types have to be distributed more widely, that we have in some way to break them up? I do not believe so. The problem that arises for us bears on the framework of paranoia as a whole.

A century of clinical work has always just drifted around the problem. Every time psychiatry has made a bit of progress, advanced slightly, it has

[7] Ernst Kretschmer (1888–1964), professor of psychiatry at the University of Marburg. Carl Wernicke (1848–1905), psychiatrist and neurologist, noted for his work on aphasia.

[8] See de Clérambault, "Les délires passionnels; érotomanie, revendication, jalousie," where the author distinguishes between interpretation delusions, which are based on the paranoid character, and passional delusions, which comprise delusions of demands, delusions of jealousy, and erotomaniacal delusions.

also lost the ground it has won through its very manner of conceptualizing what is immediately accessible to observation. Nowhere is the contradiction 28
between observation and theorization more apparent. It can almost be said that there is no more apparent and visible discourse of madness than the psychiatrist's – and precisely on the subject of paranoia.

There is something here that, it seems to me, goes straight to the heart of the problem. If you read for example the work I wrote on paranoid psychosis, you will see that I emphasize what I call, borrowing the term from my master de Clérambault, the elementary phenomena and that I try to show how radically different these phenomena are in relation to what can be drawn from what he calls ideational deduction, that is, from what is understandable by everybody.[9]

Ever since that period I have strongly emphasized that the elementary phenomena are no more elementary than what underlies the entire construction of a delusion. They are as elementary as a leaf is in relation to the plant, in which a certain detail can be seen of the way in which the veins overlap and insert into one another – there is something common to the whole plant that is reproduced in certain of the forms that make it up. Similarly, analogous structures can be found at the level of the composition, motivation, and thematization of a delusion and at the level of the elementary phenomenon. In other words, it's always the same structuring force, as it were, at work in a delusion, whether it's the whole or one of its parts that is under consideration.

What is important isn't that the elementary phenomenon should be an initial nucleus, a parasitic point as de Clérambault used to say, inside the personality, around which the subject supposedly constructs something, a fibrous reaction destined to envelop and enclose it in a cyst, and at the same time to integrate it, that is to explain it, as is often said. A delusion isn't deduced. It reproduces its same constitutive force. It, too, is an elementary phenomenon. This means that here the notion of element is to be taken in no other way than as structure, differentiated structure, irreducible to anything other than itself.

The source of this structure has been so profoundly misrecognized that the whole discourse on paranoia I was talking about before bears the mark of that misrecognition. You can test this while reading Freud, or almost any author – you will find pages, sometimes entire chapters, on paranoia. Take them out of their context, read them out loud, and you will see the most wonderful descriptions of the behavior of everyone. It was touch and go whether what I read out loud before from Kraepelin's definition of paranoia defined normal 29
behavior. You will find this paradox time and again, and even among analyst

[9] See *Psychose paranoïaque*, 207–17.

authors, precisely when they put themselves on the level of what a while ago I called the pattern – a term whose domination of analytic theory is recent, but which has nonetheless been there potentially for a very long time.

To prepare for today's meeting I was re-reading an already old article, from 1908, in which Abraham describes the behavior of a case of dementia praecox and his so-called lack of affectivity, starting with his relationship to objects.[10] There he was for months on end, heaping up, stone by stone, the crude rocks that for him were affected with the greatest good. Now, because he has stacked them up on a plank, the plank breaks, there's a great din in the room, everything is swept out, and the character who seemed to attach such importance to these rocks doesn't pay the slightest bit of attention to what is going on, doesn't raise the slightest protest before the general evacuation of the objects of his desires. He simply starts again, accumulating others. And that is dementia praecox.

It is tempting to make a fable of this little apologue, one that would show that this is what we all do all the time. I should go even further – to accumulate a stack of things without value, to have to consider them lost at a moment's notice and start again is a good sign. Indeed, if the subject were to remain attached to what he loses, not being able to bear being deprived of it, it could be said that here you have a case of the overvaluation of objects.

These supposedly conclusive cases are so completely ambiguous that one wonders how it's possible to maintain the illusion for one second, unless through a sort of eclipse of the critical sense that seems to seize all readers as soon as they open a technical work, specially where our experience and profession are concerned.

It's surprising that the remark I made last time, that the understandable is an ever-fleeting and elusive term, is never assessed as being a lesson of prime importance, as an obligatory formulation at the threshold of the clinical. Begin by thinking you don't understand. Start from the idea of a fundamental misunderstanding. This is an initial attitude, failing which there is really no reason why you should not understand anything and everything. One author presents certain behavior as indicating a lack of affectivity in a certain context; for another it will be the contrary. Starting one's work again after having acknowledged its loss may be understood in completely opposite senses. Appeal is constantly made to notions that are thought to be commonly accepted, while they are not commonly accepted at all.

This is the point I wanted to get to – the difficulty of addressing the prob-
30 lem of paranoia arises precisely because it's situated on the plane of understanding.

[10] Karl Abraham, "The Psycho-Sexual Differences between Hysteria and Dementia Praecox."

The irreducible elementary phenomenon here is at the level of interpretation.

2

Let's return to the example we took last time.

We have, then, a subject for whom the world has begun to take on a meaning. What does this mean? For some time he has been prey to strange phenomena that consist in his noticing things going on in the street. But what things? If you question him you will see that some points remain mysterious to him while he will express himself about others. In other words, he symbolizes what is happening in terms of meaning. Very often he doesn't know, if you look closely, whether things are favorable or unfavorable towards him, but he looks for what is revealed by the way his counterparts act, or by some observed feature in the world, in this world which is never purely and simply inhuman since it's man-made. In discussing the red car I was attempting, with respect to this, to show you the different import the color red can have, according as its perceptive, imaginary, or symbolic value is considered. In normal behavior, too, features that have until then been neutral can take on value.

What is the subject ultimately saying, specially at a certain period of his delusion? That there is meaning. What meaning he doesn't know, but it comes to the foreground, it asserts itself, and for him it's perfectly understandable. And it's precisely because it's situated at the level of understanding as an incomprehensible phenomenon, as it were, that paranoia is so difficult for us to grasp and, also, of such great interest.

What has made it possible here to speak of reasonable madness, of the preservation of clarity, order, and will, is the feeling that, however far into the phenomenon we go, we remain in the realm of the understandable. Even when what one understands can't even be articulated, named, or inserted by the subject into a context that makes it clear, it's already situated at the level of understanding. It's a question of things that in themselves already make themselves understood. And by virtue of this fact we ourselves feel that we are within reach of understanding. This is where the illusion starts to emerge 31
– since it's a question of understanding, we understand. Well, no, precisely not.

Someone once pointed this out, but he didn't go beyond this basic remark. It was Charles Blondel, who in his book on the troubled conscience observed that psychopathologies characteristically deceive the understanding.[11] It's a valuable work, even though Blondel has obstinately refused to understand

[11] Charles Blondel, *The Troubled Conscience and the Insane Mind.*

anything of the subsequent development of ideas. This is nevertheless an appropriate point at which to take the problem up again – it's always understandable.

You will observe in the training we give to our students that this is always a good place to stop them. It's always at the point where they have understood, where they have rushed in to fill the case in with understanding, that they have missed the interpretation that it's appropriate to make or not to make. This is generally naively expressed in the expression – *This is what the subject meant*. How do you know? What is certain is that he didn't say it. And in most cases, on hearing what he did say, it appears that at the very least a question mark could have been raised which alone would have been sufficient for the valid interpretation, or at least for the beginnings of it.

Let me now give you an idea of the point on which this discourse is converging. Whether some moment in the subject's perception, in his delusional deduction, in his explanation of himself, or in his dialogue with you is more or less understandable isn't what is important. At some of these places something may occur that appears to be characterized by the fact that there is indeed a completely understandable kernel, if you really want to hold to this. Whether there is or not, is of absolutely no interest at all. What, on the contrary, is altogether striking is that it's inaccessible, inert, and stagnant with respect to any dialectic.

Take elementary interpretation. To be sure, this comprises an element of meaning, but it's a repetitive one, it proceeds by reiteration. Sometimes the subject does elaborate on this element, but what is certain is that it will remain, at least for a while, being constantly repeated with the one interrogative sign that is always involved, without any answer, any attempt to integrate it into a dialogue, ever being made. The phenomenon is closed to all dialectical composition.

Take what is known as passional psychosis, which seems so much closer to what is called normal. If in this case the prevalence of litigiousness is stressed, it's because the subject can't come to terms with a certain loss or injury and because his entire life appears to be centred around compensation for the injury suffered and the claim it entails. Litigation moves into the
32 foreground so much that sometimes it seems completely to dominate his interest in what is at stake. Here also the dialectic comes to a halt, centered of course in a totally different way from the preceding case.

I pointed out to you last time what the phenomenon of interpretation hinges on – it's linked to the relation between the ego and the other, inasmuch as analytic theory defines the ego as always being relative. In passional psychosis what is known as the understandable kernel, which is in fact a kernel of dialectical inertia, is situated obviously much closer to the I, the subject. In short, it's precisely because there has always been a radical misrecognition of the dialectical dimension in the phenomenology of pathological experience that the clinical has gone astray. This misrecognition, it may be said, characterizes a class of mind. It seems that from the entry into the field of human clinical observation a century and a half ago when, with the beginnings of psychiatry, this field as such was formed, from the moment we became concerned with man, we have radically misrecognized that dimension which everywhere else nevertheless seems to be alive, accepted, handled with ease in the sense of the human sciences, namely, that of the autonomy as such of the dialectical dimension.

Authors point to the integrity of the paranoid subject's faculties. Will and action, as Mr. Kraepelin was saying just before, seem to us to be homogeneous in him with what we expect from normal beings. There is no deficiency anywhere, no fault; there are no functional disorders. One forgets that the dialectical changeability of actions, desires, and values is characteristic of human behavior and that it makes them liable to change not only from one moment to the next but constantly and even that it makes them pass over to strictly opposite values as a function of a change of direction in the dialogue. This absolutely fundamental truth is present in the most popular of fables that show what was loss and disadvantage at one instant becoming happiness bestowed by the gods a moment later. The ever-present possibility of bringing desire, attachment, or even the most enduring meaning of human activity back into question, the constant possibility of a sign's being reversed as a function of the dialectical totality of the individual's position, is such a common experience that it's stupefying to see this dimension forgotten as soon as one's fellow whom one wants to objectify is concerned.

It's never completely forgotten, though. We find a trace of it whenever the observer allows himself to be guided by his feeling for what is going on. The term *interpretation* lends itself to all sorts of ambiguities in the context of this reasonable madness into which it's inserted. Authors speak of combinatory 33
paranoia – how fertile this term could have been had they been aware of what they were saying, that the secret effectively resides in the way the phenomena are combined.

The question that has been advocated frequently enough here to be of full value, that of *Who speaks?*, must dominate the whole subject of paranoia.

I already pointed this out to you last time when I reminded you that verbal hallucination plays a central role in paranoia. You know how long it took to perceive what is nevertheless sometimes quite visible, which is that the subject himself utters what he says he hears – it took M. Séglas and his book *Leçons cliniques*.[12] By a sort of brilliant stroke at the beginning of his career

[12] Jules Séglas, *Leçons cliniques sur les maladies mentales et nerveuses (Salpêtrière, 1887–1894).*

he pointed out that there were people having verbal hallucinations who could be observed, by quite obvious signs in some cases and by looking slightly more closely in others, to be uttering the words they accused their voices of having spoken to them, whether or not they were aware of it, or did not want to know. It constituted a small revolution to observe that the source of auditory hallucination was not external.

This is because, or so it was thought, the source is internal, and what is more tempting than to think that this corresponds to the tingling of a zone itself called sensory? It remains to be known whether this can be applied to the domain of language. Are there verbal psychical hallucinations properly so-called? Are they not always more or less psychomotor hallucinations? Can the phenomenon of speech, in both its pathological forms and its normal form, be dissociated from the fact, which is nonetheless perceptible, that when the subject speaks he hears himself? One of the essential dimensions of the phenomenon of speech is that the other isn't the only person who hears you. The phenomenon of speech can't be schematized by the image that serves a number of what are called communication theories – sender, receiver, and something that takes place in between. It seems to have been forgotten that among many other things in human speech the sender is always a receiver at the same time, that one hears the sound of one's own words. It's possible not to pay attention to it, but it's certain that one hears it.

Such a simple remark dominates the entire question of what is known as verbal psychomotor hallucination, and it's perhaps because it's too self-evident that in the analysis of these phenomena it has moved into the background. Of course the little Séglasian revolution is far from having brought
34 us a solution to the enigma. Séglas remained with the phenomenal exploration of hallucination, and he had to retract what was too absolute in his initial theory. He restored their place to certain hallucinations that are untheorizable in this register, and he threw some new clinical light and contributed a subtlety of description, neither of which can be ignored – I advise you to have a look at him.

If many of these episodes in the history of psychiatry are instructive, it's perhaps more by virtue of the errors they bring into focus than by the positive contributions that supposedly result from them. But it's not possible simply to devote oneself to negative experiences of the field concerned and construct solely on the basis of errors. Errors are in any case so abundant as to be almost inexhaustible. We shall just have to take a few shortcuts to try to get to the heart of the matter.

We shall do this by following Freud's advice and, with him, enter into the analysis of the Schreber case.

3

After a short illness between 1884 and 1885, a mental illness consisting of a hypochondriacal delusion, Schreber, who then occupied quite an important place in the German judiciary, left Professor Flechsig's Psychiatric Clinic completely cured, it would seem, with no apparent aftereffects.

For the next eight years or so he led an apparently normal life and he himself points out that the only shadow over his domestic happiness was the regret at not having had children. At the end of these eight years he was named Presiding Judge to the Court of Appeal in the city of Leipzig. Having received the announcement of this extremely important promotion before the vacation period, he took up office in October. He was, it seems, as so often happens in many mental crises, a bit overwhelmed by his functions. At fifty-one he was young to be presiding over a court of appeal of this importance and the promotion unhinged him slightly. He found himself among men far more experienced, more accustomed to dealing with such difficult matters, and for a month he overworked, as he himself says, and began to become disturbed again – insomnia, flight of ideas, the appearance of more and more disturbing themes in his thoughts, which led him to further consultations.

And once again he was confined. First in the same Psychiatric Clinic, Professor Flechsig's, then, after a short stay in the mental home of Dr. Pierson
in Dresden, in the Sonnenstein Asylum, where he was to remain until 1901. 35
It was there that his delusion went through an entire series of phases of which he gives us an account that is, it seems, extremely trustworthy and extraordinarily composed, written during the last months of his confinement. The book was to be published immediately upon his release. Therefore, at the time he claimed the right to leave he hid from no one that he would make his experience known to all humanity, with the view of informing everybody of the most important revelations for them that his experience contained.

This book, published in 1903, is the one Freud picked up in 1909. He spoke of it on his holidays with Ferenczi and it was in December 1910 that he wrote his "Psycho-Analytic Notes upon an Autobiographical Account of a Case of Paranoia."[13]

We shall quite simply open Schreber's book, *Memoirs of My Nervous Illness*. The letter preceding the body of the work, which is addressed to *Professor Flechsig, private consultant,* clearly shows the medium by which a delusional's critique of the terms he holds to most can be established. This, at least for those of you who have no experience of these cases, is of a value

[13] James Strachey, who says the book seems to have attracted Freud's attention in 1910, suggests it was September of the same year, while on vacation with Ferenczi, that Freud discussed the whole question of paranoia; see SE 12:3.

that deserves to be highlighted. You will observe that Dr. Flechsig occupies a central place in the construction of the delusion.

Lacan reads the letter, pp. vii–xii.

You will appreciate the courteous tone, the clarity and order. The first chapter is taken up with a whole theory concerning, at least in appearance, God and immortality. The terms at the centre of Schreber's delusion consist in an admission of the prime function of nerves.

Lacan reads the first paragraph, pp. 6–7.

Everything is there. These rays, which exceed the bounds of recognized human individuality, which are unlimited, form the explanatory network, but which he also experiences, on which our patient spins his entire delusion like a web.

The essential point stems from the relation between the nerves, principally between the subject's nerves and the divine nerves, which comprises an entire series of vicissitudes, among which there is the *Nervenanhang*, or nerve-contact, a form of attraction apt to put the subject in a state of dependence upon several characters, on whose intentions he decides in different ways over the course of his delusion. Initially these intentions are far from benevolent, if
36 only because of their catastrophic effects upon him, but are found over the course of the delusion to be transformed, integrated, into a real progressiveness, like the one you see dominating the personality of Dr. Flechsig at the beginning of the delusion and, at the end, the structure of God. There is examination and even progress characteristic of the divine rays, which are the foundation of souls. This is not to be confused with the identity of the said souls – Schreber strongly emphasizes that the immortality of these souls must not be reduced to the level of the person. The preservation of the ego's identity doesn't seem to him to require justification. All this is said with an air of likelihood that doesn't render the theory unacceptable.

On the other hand, an entire metabolic imagery is developed with extreme precision regarding the nerves, according to which the impressions registered by the nerves subsequently become the primary material which, reincorporated into the rays, nourishes divine action and may well be taken up again, reworked, and utilized in later creations.

The details of these functions matter enormously and we shall come back to them. But already it appears to be characteristic of these rays that they talk – they are obliged to, they have to speak. The nerves' soul intermingles with a certain *fundamental language* defined by the subject – I shall show you with what subtlety when I read out the appropriate passages. It's akin to a highly vigorous German, with an extremely developed use of euphemism, that includes using the ambivalent power of words – next time I shall give you a condensed reading to greater effect.

It's quite exciting to recognize a striking likeness here to Freud's famous article on the double meaning of primitive words.[14] You recall that Freud thought he had found an analogy between the language of the unconscious, which admits no contradiction, and primitive words that are characterized by their ability to designate the two poles of a property or quality, good and bad, young and old, long and short, etc. A lecture by M. Benveniste last year presented you with a convincing critique of that from the point of view of linguistics,[15] but it remains no less true that Freud's remark carries weight in our experience with neurotics, and if there were anything that guarantees its value it would be the emphasis that in passing Schreber confers on it.

This delusion, whose richness you will see, presents surprising analogies – not only through its content, the image's symbolism, but also through its construction, its very structure – with certain schemas that we can ourselves be called upon to draw out of our own experience. You may, in this theory of divine nerves that talk and may be integrated by the subject while remaining radically separate from him, vaguely see something that isn't totally different from what I teach about the way one has to describe the functioning 37
of the unconscious. The Schreber case objectifies certain structures supposed correct in theory – with the possibility of overturning that stems from this, which is in any case a question that arises concerning all species of emotional construction in these sensitive domains that we are habitually exploring. This remark was made by Freud himself, who in some ways authenticates the homogeneity I'm claiming. At the end of his analysis of the Schreber case he notes that he has never yet seen anything that so much resembles his own libido theory, with its disinvestments,[16] separation reactions, influence at a distance, as Schreber's theory of divine rays, which doesn't bother him, since the drift of his whole exposition is to reveal a surprising approximation between Schreber's delusion and structures of both interindividual exchange and intrapsychical economy.[17]

So, as you see, we are dealing with an advanced case of madness. His delusional introduction gives you an idea of the polished nature of Schreber's lucubrations. And yet, owing to this exemplary case and to the intervention

[14] "The Antithetical Meaning of Primary Words," SE 11:155–61.

[15] See Emile Benveniste, "Remarks on the Function of Language in Freudian Theory."

[16] "*Désinvestissements*," "withdrawal of cathexes" in SE.

[17] SE 12:78–79.

of such a penetrating mind as Freud's, we find ourselves for the first time in a position to grasp structural notions which it's possible to extrapolate to all cases – this vivid and at the same time illuminating novelty allows a classification of paranoia to be recast on completely new foundations. We also find in the very text of the delusion a truth that isn't hidden, as it is in the neuroses, but made well and truly explicit and virtually theorized. The delusion presents it – one can't even say from the moment one has the key to it, but as soon as one takes it for what it is, a double, perfectly legible, of what is explored by theoretical investigation.

This is where the exemplary character of the field of the psychoses, for which I have recommended that you reserve the greatest extension and the greatest suppleness, is located, and this is what justifies our giving special attention to it this year.

23 November 1955

III 39

The Other and psychosis

HOMOSEXUALITY AND PARANOIA

THE WORD AND THE REFRAIN

AUTOMATISM AND ENDOSCOPY

PARANOID KNOWLEDGE

GRAMMAR OF THE UNCONSCIOUS

The life of a psychoanalyst – as I was reminded by my analysands [*analysés*] several times on the one day – isn't rosy.

The comparison that can be made between the analyst and a rubbish dump is justified. All day long in fact he has to endure utterances that, surely, are of doubtful value to himself and even more so to the subject who communicates them to him. This is a feeling that the psychoanalyst, if he is a real one, has not only been accustomed to overcoming for a long time, but, to be honest, it's one that he purely and simply abolishes within himself in the exercise of his practice.

I must on the other hand say that this feeling comes alive again with all its force when one is led to go over the sum total of works that make up what is called the analytic literature. There is no more disconcerting an exercise for scientific attention than to be made aware over a short space of time of the points of view that authors have elaborated on the same subjects. And nobody seems to perceive the flagrant and permanent contradictions that are brought into play whenever basic concepts arise.

1

You know that psychoanalysis explains the case of President Schreber, and paranoia in general, by portraying the subject's unconscious drive as nothing
other than a homosexual tendency.[1] Drawing attention to all the facts grouped 40
around such a notion was surely fundamentally new, and it profoundly changed our outlook on the pathogenesis of paranoia. But as for knowing what this homosexuality is, at which point of subjective economy it acts, how it occa-

[1] *"Tendance"* has a meaning in both psychology and psychoanalysis. In psychoanalysis it has been used for *"Trieb,"* drive, though in more narrowly psychoanalytic contexts Lacan uses the term *"pulsion."*

sions the psychosis – I believe I can testify that, in this sense, all the outlines we have contain the most imprecise, even the most contradictory approaches.

People speak of defense against the supposed irruption – and why this irruption at this point? – of the homosexual tendency. But this is far from having been proved, if one is to give a meaning that is in any way precise to the term *defense* – which one is very careful not to do, so as to be able to continue cogitating in the dark. It's nevertheless clear that there is a constitutive ambiguity here and that the defense maintains a far from univocal relation with the cause that provokes it. It's thought either that the defense helps maintain a certain equilibrium or else that it provokes the illness.

We are also assured that the initial determinants of Schreber's psychosis are to be sought in the moment of onset of the different phases of his illness. You know that around 1886 he had his first crisis, whose co-ordinates people try to show us by means of his *Memoirs* – at that time he had nominated for the Reichstag, we are told.[2] Between this crisis and the second, which covers a period of eight years, Magistrate Schreber was normal, with the exception that his hope of paternity was unfulfilled. At the end of this period he happened to accede, in a way that up to a point was premature and certainly at an age at which it could not have been foreseen, to a very high function, that of Presiding Judge of the Leipzig Court of Appeal. This function, which was in the nature of an eminent distinction, conferred authority on him, so it's said, that elevated him to responsibility that, though not quite total, was at least greater and heavier than any he could have hoped for, which gives the impression that there was a relation between his promotion and the onset of the crisis.

In other words, in the former case one appeals to the fact that Schreber was unable to satisfy his ambition, and in the other that it was fulfilled from the outside, in a manner that is virtually consecrated as being undeserved. These two events are given the same value as trigger. It's carefully noted that the President had no children, so as to assign a prime role to the notion of paternity. But at the same time it's claimed that because he finally accedes to the position of father, the fear of castration thus comes to life in him again, with a corresponding homosexual craving. This is what is supposed to be
41 directly at issue in the onset of the crisis and to entail all the distortions, pathological deformations, and mirages that progressively evolve into a delusion.

Surely the fact that the masculine characters in the medical entourage are present from the outset, that they are named one after the other and successively come to the centre of President Schreber's extreme paranoid persecu-

[2] The onset of this first crisis occurred in October 1884, that of the second in November 1893.

tion, is enough to show their importance. This is, in a word, a transference – which is undoubtedly not to be taken in quite the sense that we usually mean, but it's something of that order, bound up in a special way with those in whose care he had been. Undoubtedly this is an adequate explanation of the choice of characters, but before we become too satisfied with this overall arrangement it needs to be observed that, in providing its motivation, the proof by the contrary is neglected. People fail to realize that both fear of the struggle and premature success are given the value of a sign with the same positive sense in each case. If by chance President Schreber had, between his two crises, become a father, this would be emphasized and much would be made of the fact that this paternal function would have been unbearable for him. In short, the notion of conflict is always played upon in an ambiguous manner – the source of conflict and, what is much less easy to see, the absence of conflict are placed on the same level. The conflict leaves an empty place, one might say, and it's in the empty place of the conflict that a reaction, a construction, a bringing into play of subjectivity, appears.

This suggestion is only designed to show you that the same ambiguity as the one our last lesson was about is at work, the ambiguity of the very meaning of a delusion, and which here is concerned with what is normally called the content and which I would prefer to call the psychotic statement [*dire*].

You think you are dealing with someone who is communicating with you because he speaks the same language as you. And then, what he is saying is so understandable that you get the feeling, particularly if you are a psychoanalyst, that here is someone who has penetrated, in a more profound way than is given to the common lot of mortals, into the very mechanism of the system of the unconscious. Somewhere in the second chapter Schreber expresses it in passing – *Enlightenment rarely given to mortals has been given to me.*[3]

My discourse today is about this ambiguity whereby the very system of the delusional is supposed to provide us with the elements of its own understanding.

2 42

Those of you who attend my case presentations are aware that last time I presented quite a clear case of psychosis and will recall the amount of time I put into drawing from her the sign, the stigma, that proved we were indeed dealing with a delusional and not simply with a person of difficult character who quarrels with those around her.

The examination went well beyond the hour that it usually takes for it to appear clearly that, at the limits of this language that there was no way of making her go beyond, there was another one. This is the language, which

[3] See Mem, 167.

has a particular and often extraordinary savor, of the delusional. It's a language in which certain words take on a special emphasis, a density that sometimes manifests itself in the very form of the signifier, giving it this frankly neologistic character that is so striking in the creations of paranoia. From out of the mouth of our patient of the other day there finally emerged the word *galopiner*,[4] which gave us the signature to everything that had been said up to that point.

This was something quite different from the frustration of her dignity, of her independence, of her daily affairs, of which the patient was the victim. This term *frustration* has belonged to the vocabulary of decent people for some time now – who doesn't go on all day long about the frustrations they have experienced or will experience or that others about them experience? She was obviously in another world, in a world in which this term *galopiner*, and doubtless many others that she hid from us, constitute essential reference points.

Let me pause here for a moment so you can appreciate how necessary are the categories of the linguistic theory that last year I was trying to make you feel comfortable with. You recall that in linguistics there is the signifier and the signified and that the signifier is to be taken in the sense of the material of language. The trap, the hole one must not fall into, is the belief that signifieds are objects, things. The signified is something quite different – it's the meaning, and I explained to you by means of Saint Augustine, who is as much of a linguist as Monsieur Benveniste, that it always refers to meaning, that is, to another meaning. The system of language, at whatever point you take hold of it, never results in an index finger directly indicating a point of reality; it's the whole of reality that is covered by the entire network of lan-
43 guage. You can never say that this is what is being designated, for even were you to succeed you would never know what I am designating in this table – for example, the color, the thickness, the table as object, or whatever else it might be.[5]

Let us pause at this quite simple little phenomenon of *galopiner* that came from the mouth of the patient the other day. Schreber himself constantly underlines the oddness of certain terms in his discourse. When he speaks to us for example of the *Nervenanhang*, nerve contact, he makes it quite clear that this word was spoken to him by the tested souls or the divine rays. These are key words, and he himself notes that he would never have found the formula for them, for the original words, the full words, which are very dif-

[4] As it happens, "*galopiner*" is not a neologism. Zola, e.g., employs the word, which derives from "*galopin*," street-urchin; see *Trésor de la langue française*, s.v. "*galopiner*."

[5] See the discussion in chaps. 20 and 21, Sem I:247–72.

ferent from the words he uses to communicate his experience. He himself makes no mistake about this, there are different levels here.[6]

At the level of the signifier, in its material aspect, the delusion is characterized precisely by that special form of discordance with common language known as a neologism. At the level of meaning, it's characterized by the following, which will appear to you only if you set out with the idea that a meaning always refers to another meaning, that is, precisely, that the meaning of these words can't be exhausted by reference to another meaning.

This can be seen in Schreber's text as well as in the presence of a patient. The meaning of these words that pull you up has the property of referring essentially to meaning *as such*. It's a meaning that essentially refers to nothing but itself, that remains irreducible. The patient himself emphasizes that the word carries weight within itself. Before being reducible to another meaning it signifies within itself something ineffable, it's a meaning that refers above all to meaning as such.

We can see this at the two poles of all the concrete manifestations of which these patients are the centre. However far the endophasia that covers the entire phenomena to which they are subject is taken, there are two poles where this characteristic is taken to its highest point, as Schreber's text stresses, two types of phenomena where the neologism is displayed – the intuition and the formula.

The delusional intuition is a full phenomenon that has an overflowing, inundating character for the subject. It reveals a new perspective to him, one whose stamp of originality, whose characteristic savor, he emphasizes, as Schreber does in speaking of the fundamental language to which his experience introduced him. There, the word – with its full emphasis, as when one says *the word for, the solution to, an enigma* – is the soul of the situation.

At the opposite pole there is the form that meaning takes when it no longer
refers to anything at all. This is the formula that is repeated, reiterated,
drummed in with a stereotyped insistence. It's what we might call, in con- 44
trast to the word, the refrain.

These two forms, the fullest and the emptiest, bring the meaning to a halt, it's like lead in the net [*plomb dans le filet*], in the network, of the subject's discourse – a structural characteristic in which, once we approach it clinically, we recognize the mark of delusion.

This is how this language we can let ourselves be taken in by in our first initial contact with the subject, sometimes even the most delusional subject, brings us to the point of going beyond his conception and positing the term *discourse*. For, to be sure, these patients speak to us in the same language as

[6] See, e.g., 30 n. 19.

ourselves. Without this component, we would be in total ignorance. It's therefore the economy of discourse, the relationship between meaning and meaning, the relationship between their discourse and the common organization of discourse, that allows us to ascertain that delusion is involved.

I once tried to outline an analysis of psychotic discourse in an article published in the *Annales médico-psychologiques* in the thirties.[7] It concerned a case of schizophasia where effectively one can, at every level of discourse, semanteme as well as taxeme, pick out the structure of what is, perhaps not without reason, but no doubt without full awareness of the term's significance, known as schizophrenic disintegration.

I've been talking about language. You must in this respect touch upon the inadequacy, the undesirable tendency that is betrayed in the expression – *One has to speak the patient's language*. No doubt those who say such things must be forgiven, like all those who don't know what they are saying. Evoking so summarily what is at issue is the sign of hasty thoughts, of repentance. One absolves oneself, pays one's debts – except that one only displays condescension and reveals at what distance one maintains the object in question, namely the patient. Since he, too, is present, well then, let's speak his language, the language of simpletons and idiots. To mark this distance, to make language a pure and simple instrument, a way of making oneself understood by those who understand nothing, is completely to elude what is at issue – the reality of speech.

Let's leave analysts to one side for the moment. On whom is the psychiatric discussion of delusion, whether it seeks to be phenomenological, psychogenetic, or organogenetic, centered? What do the extraordinarily penetrating analyses of a de Clérambault signify, for instance? Some people think that it is a matter of discovering whether or not delusion is an organic phenomenon. This, it seems, is supposed to be discernible in its very phenomenology. This is all very well, but let's look at the thing a bit more closely.

45 Does the patient speak? If we did not distinguish language and speech, it's true, he speaks, but he speaks like those sophisticated dolls that open and close their eyes, drink liquid, etc. When a de Clérambault analyzes the elementary phenomena, he looks for their signature in their mechanical, serpiginous structure, and God only knows what neologisms. But even on that analysis personality is never defined but is always assumed, since everything rests on the ideogenic character of a primary comprehensibility, on the link between affections and their linguistic expression. This is supposed to be self-evident, this is where the demonstration starts from. We are told this – the automatic character of what takes place is demonstrable phenomenologically,

[7] See Jacques Lacan, J. Lévy-Valensi, and Pierre Migault, "Ecrits 'inspirés': Schizographie."

and this proves that the disorder isn't psychogenetic. But it's in relation to a psychogenetic reference itself that the phenomenon is defined as automatic. It's assumed that there is a subject who understands by himself and who observes himself. Otherwise, how would the other phenomena be grasped as foreign?

Notice that this isn't the classical problem that has brought all philosophy since Leibniz to a standstill, that is, at least since consciousness has been emphasized as the foundation of certainty – must a thought, to be a thought, necessarily think of itself thinking? Must all thought necessarily perceive that it's thinking of what it is thinking? This is so far from being straightforward that it immediately leads into an endless play of mirrors – if it's the nature of thought to think of itself thinking, there will be a third thought that will think of itself thinking thought, and so on. This small problem, which has never been resolved, suffices on its own to demonstrate the insufficiency of the subject's foundation in the phenomenon of thought as transparent to itself. But this isn't at all what is at issue here.

Once we allow that the subject has knowledge as such of the parasitic phenomenon as such, that is, as subjectively unmotivated, as written into the structure of the mechanism, into the disturbance of the supposed neurological pathways, we cannot avoid the idea that the subject has an endoscopy of what is actually going on within his own mechanisms. This is a necessity imposed on any theory that makes intraorganic phenomena the center of what happens in the subject. Freud attacks this problem more subtly than other authors, but he is equally obliged to admit that the subject is somewhere, at a privileged point where he is able to have an endoscopy of what is going on inside himself.

This idea doesn't surprise anybody when it's a question of more or less delusional endoscopies that the subject has of what is happening inside his stomach or his lungs, but it's a more difficult matter when intracerebral phenomena are concerned. The authors are forced to admit, though usually with- 46
out being aware of it, that the subject has some endoscopy of what goes on inside the system of nerve fibers.

Take a subject who is the object of a thought-echo. Let's agree with Clérambault that this is the effect of a delay produced by a chronaxic deterioration – one of the two intracerebral messages, one of the two telegrams, as it were, is impeded and arrives after the other, thus as its echo. For this delay to be registered, there must be some privileged reference point at which this can occur, from which the subject notes a possible discordance between one system and another. However the organogenetic or automatizing theory is constructed, there is no escaping the consequence that some such privileged point exists. In a word, one is more of a psychogeneticist than ever.

What is this privileged point if it's not the soul? – except that one is even more idolatry than those who confer the crudest reality on the soul by locating it in a fiber or a system, in what President Schreber designates as the unique fiber attached to the personality. It's what is habitually called the function of synthesis, the nature of a synthesis being to have its point of convergence somewhere – even if ideal, this point exists.

So whether we are organogeneticists or psychogeneticists, we shall always be forced to assume the existence of a unifying entity somewhere. Does that entity suffice to explain the level of psychotic phenomena? The sterility of these sorts of hypotheses is astounding. If psychoanalysis has revealed anything significant, clarifying, illuminating, fruitful, rich, dynamic, it's through disturbing the minuscule psychiatric constructions pursued over the decades with the help of purely functional notions of which the ego, which camouflaged them, necessarily formed the essential hub.

But as for what psychoanalysis has contributed that is new, how do we approach it without again falling into the same rut from a different direction, through multiplying egos, themselves variously camouflaged? The only approach consistent with the Freudian discovery is to raise the issue within the same register in which the phenomenon appears to us, that is, in the register of speech. It's the register of speech that creates all the richness of the phenomenology of psychosis, it's here that we see all its aspects, decompositions, refractions. Verbal hallucination, which is fundamental to it, is precisely one of speech's most problematic phenomena.

47 Is there no way of dwelling on the phenomenon of speech as such? Simply by taking it into consideration, don't we see a primary structure emerge, an essential and obvious structure that enables us to make distinctions that are not mythical, that is, that do not assume that the subject is somewhere?

3

What is speech? Does the subject speak or does he not? *Speech* – let's dwell on this fact for a moment.

What distinguishes speech [*une parole*] from a registering of language? To speak is first of all to speak to others. I have on many occasions brought to the foreground of my teaching this characteristic which at first sight appears simple – speaking to others.

The notion of what a message is has, for some time, been in the foreground of the preoccupations of science. For us, the structure of speech, as I have said to you whenever we have had to use this term in its strict sense here, is that the subject receives his message from the other in an inverted form. Full speech, essential, committed speech, is based on this structure. We have two exemplary forms of this.

The first is *fides,* speech that gives itself, the *You are my woman* or the *You are my master*, which means – *You are what is still within my speech, and this I can only affirm by speaking in your place. This comes from you to find the certainty of what I pledge.*[8] *This speech is speech that commits you*. The unity of speech insofar as it founds the position of the two subjects is made apparent here.

If this doesn't seem obvious to you, confirmation by its contrary is, as usual, so much more obvious.

The sign by which the subject-to-subject relation is recognized, and which distinguishes it from the subject-to-object relationship, is the feint, the reverse of *fides*. You are in the presence of a subject insofar as what he says and does – they're the same thing – can be supposed to have been said and done to deceive you, with all the dialectic that that comprises, up to and including that he should tell the truth so that you believe the contrary. You know the Jewish joke, recounted by Freud, about the character who says – *I am going to Cracow*. And the other replies – *Why are you telling me you are going to Cracow? You are telling me that to make me believe that you are going somewhere else.*[9] What the subject tells me is always fundamentally related to a possible feint, in which he sends me, and I receive, the message in an inverted form.

There you have both sides of the structure, foundational speech and lying 48
speech which is deceptive as such.

We have generalized the notion of communication. In the present state of affairs, it's touch and go whether the entire theory of what goes on in living beings will be revised as a function of communication. Read anything by Mr. Norbert Wiener; its implications are huge. Among his many paradoxes he presents this strange myth of transmitting a man by telegraph from Paris to New York by sending exhaustive information on everything that constitutes his individuality. Since there is no limit to the transmission of information, the point-by-point resynthesis, the automatic recreation of his entire true identity at a distant place, is conceivable. Such things are curiously deceptive, and everyone wonders at them. They are a subjective mirage which collapses as soon as one points out that it would be no greater a miracle to telegraph over two centimeters. And we do nothing less when we move ourselves through the same distance. This extraordinary confusion is sufficient indication that the notion of communication has to be treated cautiously.

For my part, within the generalized notion of communication, I state what speech as speaking to the other is. It's making the other speak as such.

We shall, if you like, write that other with a big O.

And why with a big O? No doubt for a delusional reason, as is the case whenever one is obliged to provide signs that are supplementary to what language offers. That delusional reason is the following. *You are my woman*

[8] *"Cela vient de toi pour y trouver la certitude de ce que j'engage."*

[9] *Jokes and Their Relation to the Unconscious*, SE 8:115.

– after all, what do you know about it? *You are my master* – in point of fact, are you so sure? Precisely what constitutes the foundational value of this speech is that what is aimed at in the message, as well as what is apparent in the feint, is that the other is there as absolute Other. Absolute, that is to say that he is recognized but that he isn't known. Similarly, what constitutes the feint is that ultimately you do not know whether it's a feint or not. It's essentially this unknown in the otherness of the Other that characterizes the speech relation at the level at which speech is spoken to the other.

I am going to keep you at the level of structural description for a while, because it's only here that the problems can be raised. Is this all that distinguishes speech? Perhaps, but surely it has other characteristics – it doesn't speak only *to* the other, it speaks *of* the other as an object. And this is what is involved when a subject speaks to you of himself.

49 Take the paranoiac of the other day, the one who used the term *galopiner*. While she talks to you, you know that she is a subject by virtue of the fact that she tries to take you in. This is what you are expressing in saying that you are simply dealing with what you clinically call a partial delusion. It's precisely to the extent that it took me an hour and a half the other day to make her produce her *galopiner,* to the extent that during all that time she held me at bay and showed herself to be of sane mind, that she maintains herself at the limit of what can be clinically perceived as a delusion. What you call, in your jargon, the sane part of the personality derives from the fact that she speaks of the other, is capable of making fun of him. It's by virtue of this that she exists as a subject.

Now, there is another level. She is talking about herself, and she happens to say a little bit more than she would have liked to. This is where we perceive that she is deluding. Here she is talking about what is our common object – the other, with a small *o*. It is indeed still she who is talking, but there is another structure here, which moreover doesn't reveal itself entirely. It's not quite as if she were talking to me about nothing in particular, she is talking to me about something which to her is very interesting, vital, she is talking about something to which she nevertheless continues to be committed – in short, she bears witness.

Let us try to probe a bit the notion of bearing witness. Is bearing witness purely and simply communication, too? Surely not. It's clear however that everything we attach value to as communication is of the order of bearing witness.

Disinterested communication is ultimately only failed testimony, that is, something upon which everybody is agreed. Everyone knows that this is the ideal of the transmission of knowledge. The entire system of thought of the scientific community is based on the possibility of a communication that concludes with an experiment that everybody can agree on. The very institution of the experiment is a function of testimony.

Here we are dealing with another sort of otherness. I can't repeat all I once said about what I have called paranoid knowledge, since I shall also have to take it up again constantly over this year's discourse, but I am going to give you some idea of it.

What I designated thus in my first communication to the group Evolution psychiatrique, which at the time was quite remarkably original, was aimed at the paranoid affinities between all knowledge of objects as such. All human knowledge stems from the dialectic of jealousy, which is a primordial manifestation of communication. It's a matter of an observable generic notion, behavioristically observable. What takes place between two young children 50
involves this fundamental transitivism expressed by the fact that one child who has beaten another can say – *The other beat me*. It's not that he is lying – he *is* the other, literally.

This is the basis of the distinction between the human world and the animal world. Human objects are characterized by their neutrality and indefinite proliferation. They are not dependent on the preparation of any instinctual coaptation of the subject, in the way that there is coaptation, housing, of one chemical valency by another. What makes the human world a world covered with objects derives from the fact that the object of human interest is the object of the other's desire.

How is this possible? It's possible because the human ego is the other and because in the beginning the subject is closer to the form of the other than to the emergence of his own tendency. He is originally an inchoate collection of desires – there you have the true sense of the expression *fragmented body* – and the initial synthesis of the *ego* is essentially an *alter ego*, it is alienated. The desiring human subject is constructed around a center which is the other insofar as he gives the subject his unity, and the first encounter with the object is with the object as object of the other's desire.

This defines, within the speech relationship, something that originates somewhere else – this is exactly the distinction between the imaginary and the real. A primitive otherness is included in the object, insofar as primitively it's the object of rivalry and competition. It's of interest only as the object of the other's desire.

The said paranoid knowledge is knowledge founded on the rivalry of jealousy, over the course of the primary identification I have tried to define by means of the mirror stage. This rivalrous and competitive ground for the foundation of the object is precisely what is overcome in speech insofar as this involves a third party. Speech is always a pact, an agreement, people get on with one another, they agree – this is yours, this is mine, this is this, that is that. But the aggressive character of primitive competition leaves its mark on every type of discourse about the small other, about the Other as third party, about the object. It's not for nothing that in Latin testimony is called *testis* and that one testifies on one's balls. In everything of the order of testimony there is always some commitment by the subject, and a virtual struggle in which the organism is always latent.

This dialectic always carries the possibility that I may be called upon to annul the other, for one simple reason. The beginning of this dialectic being my alienation in the other, there is a moment at which I can be put into the position of being annulled myself because the other doesn't agree. The dialec-
51 tic of the unconscious always implies struggle, the impossibility of coexistence with the other, as one of its possibilities.

The master-slave dialectic reappears here. The *Phenomenology of Mind* probably doesn't exhaust the whole question, but surely its psychological and psychogenetic value can't be misrecognized. It's in a fundamental rivalry, in a primary and essential struggle to the death, that the constitution of the human world as such takes place. Except that at the end one is present when the stakes reappear.

The master has taken the slave's enjoyment from him, he has stolen the object of desire as object of the slave's desire, but at the same time he has lost his own humanity. It was in no way the object of enjoyment that was at issue, but rivalry as such. To whom does he owe his humanity? Solely to the slave's recognition. However, since he doesn't recognize the slave, that recognition literally has no value. As is habitual in the concrete development of things, the one who has triumphed and conquered the enjoyment becomes a complete idiot, incapable of doing anything other than enjoying, while he who has been deprived of it keeps his humanity intact. The slave recognizes the master, and thus he has the possibility of being recognized by him. Over the centuries he will engage in the struggle to be effectively recognized.

This distinction between the Other with a big O, that is, the Other in so far as it's not known, and the other with a small *o*, that is, the other who is me, the source of all knowledge, is fundamental. It's in this gap, it's in the angle opened up between these two relations, that the entire dialectic of delusion has to be situated. The question is this – firstly, is the subject talking to you? – secondly, what is he talking about?

4

I am not going to answer the first question. Is it true speech? – at the outset we can't know. On the other hand, what does he talk to you about? About himself no doubt, but first about one object that isn't like any of the others, about an object that is situated in the prolongation of the dual dialectic – he speaks to you about something that has spoken to him.

The very basis of the paranoid structure is the fact that the subject has understood something that he formulates, that something has taken the form of speech and speaks to him. No one, of course, is in any doubt that this is a 52
fantasized being, not even he, for he is always in a position to admit the totally ambiguous character of the source of the utterances that have been addressed to him. The paranoiac bears witness to you concerning the structure of this being that speaks to the subject.

You must already be able to tell the difference in level between alienation as the general form of the imaginary and alienation in psychosis. It's not simply a matter of identification, and of scenery swinging over onto the side of the little other. From the moment the subject speaks, the Other, with a big O, is there. Without this there would be no problem of psychosis. Psychotics would be speaking machines.

It's precisely insofar as he speaks to you that you take his testimony into account. The question is this. What is the structure of this being that speaks to him, and that everybody agrees is fantasmatic? It's precisely the S in the sense in which the analyst understands it, but an S with a question mark. What part in the subject talks? Analysis says it's the unconscious. Naturally, for this question to make sense you have to have already admitted that the unconscious is something that speaks within the subject, beyond the subject, and even when the subject doesn't know it, and that says more about him than he believes. Analysis says that in the psychoses this is what speaks. Is this enough? Absolutely not, for the whole question is how it [*ça*] speaks and what the structure of paranoid discourse is. Freud gave us an altogether gripping dialectic on this point.

It's based on the utterance [*énoncé*] of a fundamental tendency that might eventually be recognized in a neurosis, namely – *I love him* and *You love me*. There are three ways of negating this, says Freud.[10] He doesn't beat about the bush, he doesn't tell us why the unconscious of psychotics is such a good grammarian and such a bad philologist – from the philologist's viewpoint all this is in fact extremely suspect. Don't think that this works like a high-school grammar book – there are, depending on the language, many ways of saying *I love him*. Freud doesn't stop there, he says there are three ways, and three types of delusion, and it works.

The first way to negate it is to say – *It's not I who love him, it's she,* my conjoint, my double. The second is to say – *It's not him that I love, it's her*. At this level the defense isn't adequate for the paranoid subject, the disguise

[10] "Case of Paranoia," SE 12:63–65. Freud in fact mentions four kinds of contradiction. The fourth is: "I do not love him at all – I do not love anyone."

is inadequate, he isn't safe, projection has to enter into play. The third possibility – *I do not love him, I hate him*. Here inversion is also inadequate, this at least is what Freud tells us, and the mechanism of projection must also intervene, namely – *He hates me*. And there we have the delusion of persecution.

53 The high degree of synthesis that this construction contributes is illuminating for us, but you see the questions that remain open. Projection has to intervene as a supplementary mechanism whenever there is no effacement of the *I*. This isn't totally unacceptable, though we would like more information about it. Furthermore, it's clear that the *not,* the negation taken in its most categorical form, definitely doesn't have, when applied to these different terms, the same value. But on the whole this construction comes close to something, it works, and it situates things at their true level by tackling them from this angle of, I would say, principal logomachy.

Perhaps what I have said to you this morning will give you some indication that we can rephrase the question differently. *I love him* – is this a message, an utterance, a testimony, the brute recognition of a fact in its neutralized state?

Take things in terms of a message. In the first case, *It's she that loves him,* the subject gets another to carry his message. This alienation surely places us on the level of the little other – the *ego* speaks through the intermediary of the *alter ego,* which has meanwhile changed sex. We shall restrict ourselves to observing the inverted alienation. In delusions of jealousy, this identification with the other with a reversal of the sign of sexualization is in the foreground.

On the other hand, by analyzing the structure this way, you see that it isn't, in any case, a question of projection in the sense in which it can be integrated into a mechanism of neurosis. This projection consists in effect of imputing one's own infidelities to the other – when one is jealous of one's wife, it's because one has a few little peccadilloes of one's own to reproach oneself with. The same mechanism can't be invoked in the delusion of jealousy, probably psychotic, such as it's presented either in Freud's case or in the register into which I myself have just tried to insert it, where it's the person you are identified with through an inverted alienation, namely your own wife, that you make the messenger of your feelings concerning, not even another man, but, as the clinic shows, a more or less indefinite number of men. The properly paranoid delusion of jealousy is repeatable indefinitely, it re-emerges at every turning point of experience and may implicate fairly well any subject who appears on the horizon, and even ones that don't.

Now, *It's not him that I love, it's her*. This is another type of alienation, no longer inverted, but diverted. The other addressed in erotomania is very special, since the subject doesn't have any concrete relations with him, so much

so that it has been possible to speak in terms of a mystical bond or platonic love. He is very often a distant object with whom the subject is happy to 54
communicate in writing, without even knowing whether what's written will get to its destination. The least that can be said is that there is diverted alienation of the message. The accompanying depersonalization of the other is apparent in that heroic perseverance through every trial, as the erotomaniacs will themselves say. The erotomaniacal delusion is addressed to such a neutralized other that he is inflated to the very dimensions of the world, since the universal interest attached to the adventure, as de Clérambault used to say, is an essential part of it.

In the third case we are dealing with something much closer to negation. It's a converted alienation, in that love has become hatred. The profound deterioration of the entire system of the other, its reduction ratio, the extensive nature of interpretations about the world, shows you here the properly imaginary disturbance at its maximum extension.

The relations with the Other in delusions now call for investigation. Our terms will help us to reply all the better, through making us distinguish between the subject, he who talks, and the other with whom he is caught in the imaginary relation, the center of gravity of his individual ego, and in which there is no speech. These terms will enable us to characterize psychosis and neurosis in a new way.

30 November 1955

55

IV

"I've just been to the butcher's"

WHAT RETURNS IN THE REAL
PUPPETS OF DELUSION
R. S. I. IN LANGUAGE
THE EROTIZATION OF THE SIGNIFIER

In two articles respectively entitled "The Loss of Reality in Neurosis and Psychosis" and "Neurosis and Psychosis"[1] Freud provides us with interesting information on the question of what distinguishes neurosis from psychosis. I shall try to emphasize what distinguishes them from one another with respect to the disturbances they create in the subject's relations with reality.

It is also an opportunity to recall, in a precise and structured way, what is meant by repression in neurosis.

1

Freud stresses the extent to which the subject's relations with reality are not the same in neurosis and psychosis. In particular, the clinical characteristic of the psychotic is distinguished by this profoundly perverted relation to reality known as a delusion. For this great difference in organization, or disorganization, there must be, Freud tells us, a deep-seated structural reason. How are we to spell out this difference?

When we speak of neurosis, we ascribe a certain role to flight, to avoidance, in which conflict with reality plays a part. Attempts have been made to designate the function of reality in the onset of neurosis by the notion of traumatism, which is an etiological notion. This is one thing, but another is the moment in a neurosis when a certain rupture with reality occurs in the
56 subject. What is the reality involved? Freud stresses from the outset that the reality sacrificed in neurosis is a part of *psychical* reality.

We are already entering here upon a very important distinction – reality is not synonymous with external reality. When he triggers his neurosis the subject elides, scotomizes as it has since been said, a part of his psychical reality,

[1] SE 19:183–87 and 149–53.

or, in another language, a part of his *id*.[2] This part is forgotten but continues to make itself heard. How? In a manner that all my teaching emphasizes – in a symbolic manner.

In the first article I mentioned Freud evokes a storehouse that the subject sets aside in reality and in which he preserves resources to be used in constructing the external world – this is where psychosis will borrow its material from. Neurosis, Freud says, is something quite different, for the subject attempts to make the reality that he at one time elided re-emerge by lending it a particular meaning, a secret meaning, which we call symbolic.[3] But Freud does not emphasize this properly. Overall the impressionistic manner in which the term *symbolic* is used has until now never been made precise in a way that is really consistent with what is at stake.

I point out, in passing, that I don't always have the opportunity to provide the textual references that a number of you would like, because they mustn't interrupt my discourse. Nevertheless I do give you, it seems to me, quotations where necessary.

Many passages in Freud's work show that he felt the need for a complete articulation of the symbolic order, for this is what was at stake for him in neurosis, to which he opposes psychosis, where at some time there has been a hole, a rupture, a rent, a gap, with respect to external reality. In neurosis, inasmuch as reality is not fully rearticulated symbolically into the external world, it is in a second phase that a partial flight from reality, an incapacity to confront this secretly preserved part of reality, occurs in the subject. In psychosis, on the contrary, reality itself initially contains a hole that the world of fantasy will subsequently fill.

Can we be satisfied with so simple a definition, so summary an opposition between neurosis and psychosis? Surely not, and Freud himself indicates, subsequent to his reading of Schreber's text, that it's not enough just to see how symptoms are made. It is also necessary to discover the mechanism of their formation. Let's start with the idea that a hole, a fault, a point of rupture, in the structure of the external world finds itself patched over by psychotic fantasy. How is this to be explained? We have at our disposal the 57
mechanism of projection.

I shall start with that today, insisting upon it in particular because a number of you working on the Freudian texts I've already commented on have said that, in returning to a passage whose importance I've pointed out, you are still hesitant over the meaning to give to a fragment, even though it's very clear, concerning the episodic hallucination in which the paranoid potential-

[2] The concept of scotomization was introduced in France by Edouard Pichon and systematically elaborated by René Laforgue. See René Laforgue, "Verdrängung und Skotomisation," and *Relativité de la réalité*.

[3] See SE 19:187.

ities of the Wolf Man appear. While what I was stressing when I said that *what has been rejected from the symbolic reappears in the real* was grasped very well, a discussion arose over the way I translate *the patient does not want to know anything about it in the sense of repression.*[4] However, to act on the repressed through the mechanism of repression is to know something about it, for repression and the return of the repressed are one and the same thing, expressed elsewhere than in the subject's conscious language. The difficulty for some was their failure to grasp that what is involved is of the order of knowledge [*un savoir*].

I shall quote you another passage, taken from the Schreber case. While Freud is explaining to us the mechanism of projection as such, which is supposed to explain the reappearance of fantasy in reality, he pauses to observe that we cannot speak here purely and simply of projection. This is all too self-evident if one thinks of the way this mechanism functions, for example, in the delusion of so-called projective jealousy, which consists in imputing to one's spouse infidelities of which one imaginatively feels guilty oneself. The delusion of persecution is quite different and manifests itself through interpretive intuitions in the real. Here are the terms in which Freud expresses himself – *It is incorrect to say that the internally suppressed sensation – Verdrängung* is a symbolization, and *Unterdrückung* simply indicates that something has fallen underneath – *is once again projected outwards* – this is the repressed and the return of the repressed – *But instead we must say that what is rejected* – you perhaps recall the note of insistence that usage has given this word – *returns from without.*[5]

There you have a text to add to the ones that I've already quoted in the same vein, and which are pivotal. To be precise, the text *Die Verneinung* that M. Hyppolite gave us a commentary on has enabled us to articulate with precision that there is a moment that is, one might say, the point of origin of symbolization. Let it be clearly understood that this point of origin is not a point in development but answers to the requirement that symbolization has to have a beginning. Now, at any point in development something may occur
58 that is the contrary of *Bejahung* – a *Verneinung* that is in some way primitive, to which *Verneinung* in its clinical consequences is a sequel. The distinction between the two mechanisms, *Verneinung* and *Bejahung*, is absolutely essential.

We should be better off to abandon this term *projection*. What we are concerned with here has nothing to do with the psychological projection that makes us – when for example it concerns those about whom we have nothing

[4] See above, p. 12, n.10.

[5] "It was incorrect to say that the perception which was suppressed internally is projected outwards; the truth is rather, as we now see, that what was abolished internally returns from without." SE 12:71.

but extremely mixed feelings – always greet everything they do with at least a certain amount of confusion as to their intentions. Projection in psychosis is not that at all; it's the mechanism that makes what has got caught up in the *Verwerfung* – that is, what has been placed outside the general symbolization structuring the subject – return from without.

What is this three-card trick we are all prey to, this strange juggler's game between the symbolic, the imaginary, and the real? Since we don't know the juggler we can ask the question. I am putting it on this year's agenda. It will enable us to define what is called the relation to reality and at the same time to articulate what the goal of analysis is, without falling into the constant confusions made in analytic theory on this subject. What are we talking about when we talk about adaptation to reality? Nobody knows what reality is, until it has been defined, which is not altogether simple.

To introduce the problem I shall begin from a thoroughly up-to-the-minute element. No one can say that this seminar is merely a commentary of texts, in the sense in which it would involve a pure and simple exegesis – these things are alive for us in our daily practice, in our supervisions, in the way we conduct our interpretation, in the way we deal with resistances.

So I shall borrow an example from my case presentation of last Friday.

2

Those of you who attend my presentations will recall that I was dealing with two people and one single delusion, what is known as a *délire à deux*.

It wasn't very easy for me to draw out either daughter or mother. I've reason to think that the daughter had been examined and presented before I became involved with her and that she had seen the role that patients play in a teaching ward a good dozen times. It does not matter whether or not one is delusional, one gets fed up fairly quickly with these sorts of exercises, and 59
she wasn't particularly well disposed.

It was nevertheless possible to bring out certain things, and in particular the following. Paranoid delusion, since she is paranoid, is far from presupposing a character base of pride, mistrust, irritability, psychological rigidity, as people say. At least, alongside the chain of interpretations, difficult to grasp, of which she felt she was the victim, this young girl had, on the contrary, the feeling that a person as good and kind as herself who, into the bargain, was surrounded by the many trials she had undergone, could only benefit from benevolence, from a general sympathy – and indeed the head of her ward, in making his report on her, spoke of her only as a charming woman loved by all.

In a word, after having had all the difficulty in the world tackling the subject, I approached the center of what was manifestly present there. Of course, her basic concern was to prove to me that no element was subject to reticence, while at the same time not allowing the doctor any room for the wrong interpretation, of which she was certain in advance. All the same she confided to me that one day, as she was leaving her home, she had a run-in in the hallway with an ill-mannered sort of chap, which came as no surprise to her, since this shameful married man was the steady lover of one of her neighbors, someone of loose morals.

On passing her – she could not hide this from me, it still weighed upon her chest – he had said a dirty word to her, a dirty word that she was disinclined to repeat to me because, as she put it, it devalued her. Nevertheless, a certain gentleness that I had put into approaching her meant that after five minutes of chat we were on good terms with one another, and on that subject she confessed to me with a conceding laugh that she was not completely innocent in this matter for she herself had said something in passing. This something, which she confessed to me more easily than what she had heard, was this – *I've just been to the butcher's.*

Naturally, I'm like everybody else, I make the same mistakes as you, I do everything I tell you that you mustn't do. I'm no less in the wrong – even when it works. A true opinion remains no less an opinion from the point of view of science, as Spinoza shows. If you understand, so much the better, keep it to yourself. The important thing is not to understand, but to attain the true. But if you attain it by chance, even if you understand, you don't understand. Naturally, I understand – which proves that we all have a little
60 something in common with delusionals. I have within myself, as you have within yourselves, what there is that is delusional in the normal man.

I've just been to the butcher's – if I am told that there is something there to understand I may well declare that there is a reference to pig. I didn't say *Pig*, I said *Pork*.[6]

She agreed entirely. That was what she wanted me to understand. It was perhaps also what she wanted the other to understand. Except that this is precisely what one must not do. What one has to be interested in is the point of knowing why she wanted the other to understand this, precisely, and why she didn't say it to him clearly, but by allusion. If I understand I continue, I don't dwell on it, since I've already understood. This brings out what it is to enter into the patient's game – it is to collaborate in his resistance. The patient's resistance is always your own, and when a resistance succeeds it is because you are in it up to your neck, because you understand. You understand, you are wrong. What it is, precisely, that has to be understood is why there is

[6] That is, in the interview with the woman, he said *Pork* and not *Pig*. The *charcutier*, here translated as butcher, specializes in pork products.

something there given to be understood. Why did she say, *I've just been to the butcher's* and not *Pig?*

I limited my commentary, because of insufficient time, to pointing out to you that it contained a gem, and showed you the similarity with the discovery that consisted in observing one day that certain patients who complain of auditory hallucinations were manifestly making movements of the throat, of the lips; in other words, they were articulating them themselves. Here, it's not the same, it's similar, and it's even more interesting because it's not the same.

I said – *I've just been to the butcher's,* and then she blurts it out to us, what did *he* say? He said – *Sow!* This is the final word – *thread, needle, my soul, my life,* things happen thus in our existence.

Let's pause here a moment. *There he is, all pleased with himself,* you are saying to yourselves. *This is what he teaches us – in speech the subject receives his message in an inverted form.* Disabuse yourselves, this isn't true. The message in question is not identical with speech, far from it, at least not in the sense in which I describe it to you as the form of mediation where the subject receives his message from the other in an inverted form.

First, who is this character? We have already said he is a married man, the lover of a girl who is herself the friend of our patient and heavily implicated in the desire of which our patient is the victim – she is not its center but, I would say, its main character. Our subject's relations with this couple are ambiguous. They are no doubt persecutory and hostile characters, but they 61
are not grasped in such a terribly litigious style, which surprised those present at the interview. What characterizes this subject's relations with the outside is rather her perplexity – how was it possible, through malicious gossip, no doubt through taking legal action, to get them into hospital? The universal interest bestowed on them has a tendency to be repeated. From this there arise these beginnings of erotomaniacal elements that we observed in the presentation. They aren't properly speaking erotomaniacs, but they're inhabited by the feeling that one is interested in them.

Sow, what is that? It is effectively her message, but is it not rather her message to herself?

At the beginning of everything that was said, there was the intrusion of the said neighbor into the relationship of these isolated women, who had remained closely bound to one another in their existence, who were unable to separate when the younger married, who suddenly fled the dramatic situation that seems to have been created in the marital relations of the latter by the threats of her husband who, according to the medical certificates, wanted nothing less than to slice her up. We get the feeling here that the insult in question – the term *insult* is quite essential here and has always been stressed in the clinical phenomenology of paranoia – agrees with the process of defense, the pathway of expulsion, to which the two patients felt compelled to proceed in relation to the neighbor who was considered primordially invading. She would always come and knock at their door while they were at their toilet or just as they were dining or reading. Above all, it was a matter of distancing this person who was essentially taken to be intrusive. Things only started to become problematic when this expulsion, this refusal, this rejection, took full effect, I mean when they actually threw her out.

Is this to be located at the level of projection, as a defense mechanism? The entire intimate life of these patients has unfolded outside the masculine element, they have always made the latter into an outsider with whom they have never been in harmony, for them the world is essentially feminine. Is the relation they maintain with persons of their own sex of the projection type, in their supposed necessity to remain themselves, closed in on themselves, as a couple? Is it connected with that homosexual fixation, in the widest sense of the term, that is at the base, as Freud says, of social relations? This would explain how in the isolation of this feminine world in which these two women live they find themselves in a position, not to receive their message from the
62 other, but to speak it to the other. Is insult the mode of defense that is in some way reflected back into their relationship – a relationship which, it's understandable how, was extended to all others as such, whoever they may be, from the moment it was established? This is conceivable and already suggests that it's a matter of the subject's own message, and not of the message received in inverted form.

Should we stop there? Certainly not. This analysis may enable us to understand how the patient feels surrounded by feelings of hostility. But that is not the point. The important thing is that *Sow!* has been heard really, in the real.

Who is speaking? Since there is a hallucination it's reality that is speaking. This follows from our premises if we accept that reality is made up of sensations and perceptions. There is no ambiguity over this; she didn't say *I had the feeling that he answered me – "Sow!"* She said – *I said, "I've just been to the butcher's," and he said "Sow!" to me.*

Either we are satisfied with saying to ourselves – *There you are, she's hallucinating,* or we try – this may seem to be a senseless enterprise but hasn't the role of psychoanalysts so far been to give themselves over to meaningless enterprises? – to go a little bit further.

And first of all, is it the reality of objects that is at issue? Who normally speaks in reality, for us? Is it reality, exactly, when someone speaks to us? The point of the remarks I made to you last time on the other and the Other, the other with a small o and the Other with a big O, was to get you to notice that when the Other with a big O speaks it is not purely and simply the reality in front of you, namely the individual who is holding forth. The Other is beyond that reality.

In true speech the Other is that before which you make yourself recognized. But you can make yourself recognized by it only because it is recognized first. It has to be recognized for you to be able to make yourself recognized. This supplementary dimension – the reciprocity – is necessary for there to be any value in this speech of which I've given you some typical examples – *You are my master* or *You are my woman,* or, equally, mendacious speech which, although the contrary, equally presupposes recognition by an absolute Other, aimed at beyond all you can know, for whom recognition is to be valued only because it is beyond the known. It is through recognizing it that you institute it, and not as a pure and simple element of reality, a pawn, a puppet, but as an irreducible absolute, on whose existence as subject the very value of the speech in which you get yourself recognized depends. 63
Something gets born there.

In saying to someone, *You are my woman,* you are implicitly saying to her, *I am your man,* but you are saying to her first, *You are my woman,* that is, you are establishing her in the position of being recognized by you, by means of which she will be able to recognize you. This speech is therefore always beyond language. And such a commitment, like any other utterance, even a lie, conditions all the discourse that follows, and here, what I understand by *discourse* includes acts, steps, the contortions of puppets, yourselves included, caught up in the game. Beginning with an utterance a game is instituted, entirely comparable to what happens in *Alice in Wonderland* when the servants and other characters of the Queen's court start playing cards by dressing themselves up in the cards and themselves becoming the King of Hearts, the Queen of Spades, and the Jack of Diamonds. An utterance commits you to maintaining it through your discourse, or to repudiating it, or to objecting to it, or to conforming to it, to refuting it, but, even more, to complying with many things that are within the rules of the game. And even should the Queen change the rules from one moment to the next, this changes nothing essential – once you have entered the play of symbols, you are always forced to act according to a rule.

In other words, whenever a puppet talks it's not the puppet that talks, but it's someone behind it. The question is what is the function of the character one encounters on this occasion. What we can say is that for the subject it's clearly something real that is speaking. Our patient is not saying that there is someone else behind him who is speaking. She receives her own speech from him, but not inverted, her own speech is in the other who is herself, the little other, her reflection in the mirror, her counterpart. *Sow!* gives tit for tat, and one no longer knows whether the tit or the tat comes first.

That the utterance is expressed in the real means that it is expressed in the puppet. The Other at issue in this situation is not beyond the partner, it is beyond the subject herself – this is the structure of the allusion, it indicates itself in a beyond of what it says.

Let us try to orientate ourselves by means of this game of four implied by what I said last time.[7]

The small *o* is the gentleman she encounters in the corridor and there is no big O. It's small *o′* who says, *I've just been to the butcher's*. And who is *I've just been to the butcher's* said of? Of S. Small *o* said *Sow!* to her. The person who is speaking to us, and who spoke *qua* delusional, *o′*, undoubtedly receives
64 somewhere her own message in an inverted form from the small other, and what she says affects the beyond which she herself is as subject and which, by definition, simply because she is a human subject, she can only speak of by allusion.

There are only two ways one can talk about this S, about this subject that we radically are. These are – either truly to address oneself to the Other, the big Other, and to receive from it the message that concerns you in an inverted form – or to indicate its direction, its existence, in the form of an allusion. The reason that the woman is strictly a paranoiac is that for her the cycle contains an exclusion of the big Other. The circuit closes on the two small others who are the puppet opposite her, which speaks, and in which her own message resonates, and herself who, as an ego, is always an other and speaks by allusion.

This is the important thing. She speaks by allusion so well that she doesn't know what she is saying. What does she say? She says – *I've just been to the butcher's*. Now, who has just been to the butcher's? A quartered pig. She does not know that she is saying this, but she says it nevertheless. That other to whom she is speaking, she says to him about herself – *I, the sow, have just been to the butcher's, I am already disjointed, a fragmented body,* membra disjecta, *delusional, and my world is fragmenting, like me*. That's what she's saying. That way of expressing it, however understandable it might appear to us, is nevertheless, to put it mildly, a tiny bit amusing.

There is another thing which concerns temporality. It is clear from the patient's words that we do not know who spoke first. To all appearances it was not our patient, or at least it was not necessarily her. We will never know since we are not going to time dereal [*déréel*] utterances, but if what I've just sketched out is correct, if the response is the allocution – that is, what the patient actually said – then the *I've just been to the butcher's* presupposes the response, *Sow!*

In true speech, on the contrary, the allocution is the response. What responds to speech is in effect the consecration of the Other as *my woman* or as *my*

[7] See above, p. 14.

master, and so here it's the response that presupposes the allocution. In delusional speech the Other is truly excluded, there is no truth behind, there is so little truth that the subject places none there himself, and in the face of this phenomenon, this ultimately raw phenomenon, his attitude is one of perplexity. It will be a long time before he attempts to restore an order, which we shall call a delusional order, around this. He does not restore it, as is thought, through deduction and construction, but in a way that we shall later see is not unrelated to the primitive phenomenon itself.

The Other being truly excluded, what concerns the subject is actually said 65
by the little other, by shadows of others, or, as Schreber will express himself to designate all human beings he encounters, by *fabricated,* or *improvised* men. The small other effectively presents an unreal character, tending towards the unreal.

The translation that I've just given you is not entirely correct, there are resonances in German that I've tried to render with the word *foutu,* fabricated.[8]

3

After having looked at speech, we shall now take a quick look at language, to which the triple division of the symbolic, the imaginary, and the real appropriately applies.

Certainly, the care Saussure took to eliminate considerations of motor articulation from his analysis of language clearly shows that he discerns its autonomy.[9] Concrete discourse is real language, and language speaks [*le langage, ça parle*]. The registers of the symbolic and the imaginary recur in the two other terms in which he expresses the structure of language, namely, the signified and the signifier.

The signifying material, such as I am always telling you it is, for example on this table, in these books, is the symbolic. If artificial languages are stupid it is because they are constructed on the basis of meaning. Someone recently reminded me of the forms of deduction that rule over Esperanto and which are such that once one knows *ox* one can deduce *cow, heifer, vealer,* and whatever else one wants to. And I asked him how one says, *Death to the bastards!*[10] – this must be deducible from *Long live the king!* This alone suffices to refute the existence of artificial languages, which attempt to model themselves on meaning, this as a rule being the reason why they are unused.

And then there is meaning, which always refers to meaning. Of course, the

[8] Mem, 4 n.1. The German word is "*hingemachte.*"

[9] See "The Object of Linguistics," Introduction, chap. 3, *Course in General Linguistics,* 7–17.

[10] "*Mort aux vaches!*", literally, "Death to the cows!"

signifier may be caught up therein as soon as you give it a meaning, as soon as you create another signifier as signifier, something in this function of meaning. This is why it's possible to speak of language. But the signifier-signified division will always reproduce itself. There's no doubt that meaning is by nature imaginary. Meaning is, like the imaginary, always in the end evanescent, for it is tightly bound to what interests you, that is, to that in which you are ensnared. You would know that hunger and love are the same
66 thing, you would be like any animal, truly motivated. But owing to the existence of the signifier your personal little meaning – which is also absolutely heart-breakingly generic, human all too human – leads you much further. Since there is this damned system of the signifier, such that you have not yet been able to understand either how it came to be there, how it came to exist, what purpose it serves, or where it is leading you, it is what leads you away.

When he speaks, the subject has the entire material of language at his disposal, and this is where concrete discourse begins to be formed. Firstly, there is a synchronic whole, which is language as a simultaneous system of structured groups of opposition, then there is what occurs diachronically, over time, and which is discourse. One cannot but give discourse a certain direction in time, a direction that is defined in a linear manner, M. de Saussure tells us.[11]

I leave the responsibility for that statement with him. Not that I believe it to be false – it is basically true that there is no discourse without a certain temporal order, and consequently without a certain concrete succession, even if it is a virtual one. If I read this page starting from the bottom reading up, backwards, the effect won't be the same as if I read it in the right direction, and in certain cases this may give rise to an extremely serious confusion. But it is not quite exact to say that it is a simple line, it is more probably a set of several lines, a stave. It is in this diachronism that discourse is set up.

The signifier as existing synchronically is sufficiently characterized in delusional talk by a modification I've already pointed out here, namely that certain elements become isolated, laden, take on a value, a particular force of inertia, become charged with meaning, with a meaning and nothing more. Schreber's book is overflowing with them.

Take a word such as *Nervenanhang,* for example, nerve-contact, a word of the fundamental language. Schreber discerns perfectly well which words have come to him through inspiration, precisely by way of the *Nervenanhang,* which have been repeated to him in their elective meaning which he does not always understand terribly well. *Seelenmord, soul murder,* for example, is another of these words, which is problematic for him, but which he knows has a particular sense. Nevertheless, he talks about all this in a discourse that is indeed our own, and his book, it must be said, is remarkably written, clear, and

[11] See "The Linear Nature of the Signifier," *Course,* 70.

natural. Moreover, he is as coherent as are many philosophical systems of our time, where we constantly see somebody suddenly get stung, at a detour on
the path, by a tarantula that makes him regard Bovaryism and duration as 67
the key to the world and reconstruct the entire world around this notion, without one's knowing why it is this one that he has gone and picked out. I do not see how Schreber's system is of any less value than those of philosophers whose general theme I've just profiled. And what Freud remarks at the end of his study is that this character has written some amazing things that resemble what I, Freud, have described.

This book, then, written in ordinary discourse, signals the words that for the subject have taken on such a particular weight. Let's call this erotization, and let's avoid explanations that are too simple. When the signifier finds itself charged thus, the subject is perfectly well aware of it. The moment Schreber employs the term *instance* to define the various forces articulated in the world he is implicated in – he also has his little instances – he says, *Instance, that is mine. The others didn't say it to me, it is my normal discourse.*[12]

What happens at the level of meaning? The insult is always a rupture in the system of language, just as words of love are. Whether or not *Sow!* is charged with obscure meaning, and probably it is, we already have here an indication of this dissociation. This meaning, like all meaning worthy of the name, refers to another meaning. It is indeed what here characterizes the allusion. In saying, *I've just been to the butcher's,* the patient points out to us that it refers to another meaning. Naturally, it is a bit oblique, she would prefer it was I who understand.

Beware those who say to you – *You understand.* It is always so as to send you somewhere else than where it is a question of going. That's what she's doing. *You understand perfectly well,* this means that she herself isn't very sure of the meaning, and that the latter refers not so much to a system of continuous and reconcilable meaning as to meaning as ineffable, to the meaning of her own reality, to her own personal fragmentation.

And then there is the real, the well and truly real articulation, the other's sleight of hand. Real speech, I mean speech that is expressed, appears at another point of the field, not just at any point, but at that of the other, the puppet, as an element of the external world.

The big S whose medium is speech, analysis warns us, is not what a vain people thinks it is.[13] There is the real person who is before you and who takes up space – there is this in the presence of human beings, they take up space, at a pinch you can get ten of you into your office, but not a hundred and fifty

[12] Mem, 29 n.19. *"Instance"* is the French translation of Freud's *"Instanz,"* which SE translates as agency.

[13] *Ce n'est pas ce qu'un vain peuple pense,* an allusion to Voltaire, *Nos prêtres ne sont point ce qu'un vain peuple pense; Notre crédulité fait toute leur science.*
Voltaire, *Oedipe* 4, 1.

– there is he whom you see, who manifestly captivates you and is capable of
68 making you jump up and hug him – an ill-considered act of the imaginary order. And then there is the Other whom we were talking about, who is the subject also, but not the reflection of what you see in front of you, and not simply what takes place insofar as you see yourself seeing yourself.

If what I am saying is not true, then Freud said nothing true, for this is what the unconscious means.

There are several possible othernesses, and we shall see how they manifest themselves in a complete delusion like Schreber's. First there are day and night, the sun and the moon, those things that always return to the same place, which Schreber calls the natural world order.[14] There is the otherness of the Other that corresponds to the S, that is, the big Other, the subject who is unknown to us, the Other who is symbolic by nature, the Other one addresses oneself to beyond what one sees. In between there are objects. And then, at the level of the S, there is something that is of the dimension of the imaginary, the ego and the body, whether fragmented or not, but more fragmented than not.

I shall leave you there for today. This analysis of structure begins what I shall speak to you about next time.

We shall try to understand, on the basis of this little picture, what is happening to Schreber, the delusional who has arrived at complete fulfillment and, ultimately, at a perfectly adapted delusion. What is characteristic of Schreber in fact is that he never stopped raving at full bore, but had adapted himself so well that the director of the psychiatric hospital said of him – *He is such a nice man.*

We are fortunate in having in him a man who communicates his entire delusional system to us, and at a time when it is full-blown. Before we start wondering how he entered psychosis and giving the history of the prepsychotic phase,[15] before we take things up in the sense of their genesis, as everyone always does, which is the source of inexplicable confusions, we shall convey them such as they are given to us in Freud's observation, who only ever had this book, who never saw the patient.

You will see how the different elements of a system are modified when constructed as a function of the coordinates of language. This approach is certainly legitimate, concerning as it does a case that is only given to us through a book, and it is what will enable us to reconstitute its dynamics in an effective way. But we shall start with its dialectics.

7 December 1955

[14] *"Weltordnung,"* translated as Order of the World in Mem.
[15] In English in the original.

THEMATICS AND STRUCTURE OF THE PSYCHOTIC PHENOMENON

V

On a god who does not deceive and one who does 71

PSYCHOSIS IS NOT A SIMPLE FACT OF LANGUAGE

THE DIALECT OF SYMPTOMS

IT REALLY MUST BE RATHER PLEASANT TO BE A WOMAN . . .

GOD AND SCIENCE

SCHREBER'S GOD

The other day at my case presentation we saw a serious case.

It was a clinical case that I had certainly not chosen myself, but it was one that in a way brought the unconscious out into the open, in the difficulty it had in passing into the analytic discourse. It brought it out into the open because, owing to the exceptional circumstances, everything that in another subject would have passed into repression was found in him to be supported by another language, this language of quite limited scope known as a dialect.

As it happens, the Corsican dialect had functioned for this subject in conditions that accentuated even further the function of particularization belonging to all dialects. He had in fact lived in Paris from childhood, an only child of parents extremely closed in upon their own laws, speaking exclusively the Corsican dialect. The perpetual quarreling of these two parental characters, an ambivalent manifestation of their extreme attachment to one another and of the fear of seeing a woman, a foreign object, appear, was carried out quite openly, plunging him directly into their conjugal intimacy. All this in the Corsican dialect. Nothing of what went on in the house was conceived in anything but the Corsican dialect. There were two worlds, that of the elite, of the Corsican dialect, and then that which went on outside. This separation was still present in the subject's life and he recounted to us the difference in his relations with the world between when he was with his mother and when he was out in the street.

What did this result in? This is a most conclusive case. It resulted in two things. The first, apparent when he was questioned, is the difficulty he had in calling to mind anything at all from this former register, that is, in express- 72
ing himself in his childhood dialect, the only one he ever spoke with his mother. When I asked him to say something in this dialect, to repeat to me words he might have exchanged with his father, for example – *I can't get it out,* he replied. Moreover, one could see a neurosis in him, the traces of behavior that enabled us to divine a mechanism that one may call – this is a

term I always use cautiously – regressive. In particular, his unusual way of exercising his genitality tended to get confused on the imaginary level with the regressive activity of his excremental functions. But everything that was of the order of what is usually repressed, all the contents that are commonly expressed through the intermediary of neurotic symptoms, was perfectly limpid here, and I had no trouble in getting him to express it in words. Since it was borne by the language of the others, he expressed it in words all that much more easily.

I used the comparison of the censorship of a newspaper that not only has an extremely small circulation but is published in a dialect that is only understood by a minimum number of people. The establishment of a common discourse, of a public discourse I would almost say, is an important factor in the specific functioning of the mechanism of repression. In itself repression stems from the impossibility of granting discourse to a certain past of the subject's speech which is linked, as Freud stressed, to the specific world of his infantile relations. It's precisely this past of speech that continues to function in the primitive language. Now, for this subject, this language is his Corsican dialect in which he was capable of saying the most extraordinary things, of flinging at his father for example – *If you don't go away, I shall punch you in the hurt*. These things, which could have just as easily been said by a neurotic, having had to construct his neurosis in a different manner, were out in the open here in the register of the other language which was not only dialectal but intrafamilial.

What is repression for a neurotic? It's a language, another language that he manufactures with his symptoms, that is, if he is a hysteric or an obsessional, with the imaginary dialectic of himself and the other. The neurotic symptom acts as a language that enables repression to be expressed. This is precisely what enables us to grasp the fact that repression and the return of the repressed are one and the same thing, the front and back of a single process.

These remarks are not irrelevant to our problem.

73

1

What is our method concerning President Schreber?

It's undeniable that he expressed himself in common discourse to explain to us what had happened and was continuing to happen to him at the time he wrote his work. This testimony bears witness to structural transformations that are undoubtedly to be regarded as real, but here the verbal dominates since it's through the intermediary of the subject's written testimony that we have proof of this.

Let's proceed methodically. By setting out from our knowledge of the importance of speech in the structuring of psychoneurotic symptoms we shall make progress in the analysis of this territory, psychosis. We are not saying that psychosis has the same etiology as neurosis. We are not even saying that it is, like neurosis, a pure and simple fact of language – far from it. We are simply remarking that psychosis is very rich with respect to what it can express in discourse. We have proof of this in the work that President Schreber bequeathed us and which Freud's almost fascinated attention has recommended to our attention. On the basis of this testimony, by means of an internal analysis, Freud has shown us how this world was structured. We shall proceed in the same way, setting out from the subject's discourse, which will enable us to approach the constituent mechanisms of psychosis.

Let it be clearly understood that we shall have to proceed methodically, step by step, not leaving out any detail on the pretext that a superficial analogy with a mechanism of neurosis is apparent. In short, we shall do nothing of what is so often done in the literature.

A certain Katan, for example, who has taken a special interest in the Schreber case, takes it for granted that the origin of his psychosis is to be located in his struggle against threatening masturbation provoked by his homosexual erotic investments upon the character who formed the prototype and at the same time the nucleus of his persecutory system, namely, Professor Flechsig.[1] This is supposed to have driven President Schreber so far as to undermine reality, that is to say, to reconstruct, after a short period of *twilight of the world,*[2] a new, unreal world, in which he didn't have to give in to this masturbation that was thought to be so threatening. Don't we all feel that a mechanism of this kind, while it's true that it enters into play in the neuroses at a certain point of their articulation, would here be having altogether dis- 74
proportionate results?

President Schreber gives a very clear account of the first phases of his psychosis. And when he testifies that between the first psychotic attack, a phase called, not without foundation, prepsychotic, and the progressive establishment of the psychotic phase, at the height of the stabilization of which he wrote his work, he had a fantasy which was expressed in these words, *that it really must be rather pleasant to be a woman succumbing to intercourse.*[3]

He emphasizes that this thought, which takes him by surprise, has the character of having been imagined, while adding that he greeted it with indig-

[1] See Maurits Katan, "Schreber's Delusion of the End of the World," "Schreber's Hallucinations about the 'Little Men,' " "Further Remarks about Schreber's Hallucinations," and "Schreber's Prepsychotic Phase."

[2] *"le créspuscule du monde," "Weltuntergang,"* translated as the end of the world in Mem.

[3] Mem, 36.

nation. There is a sort of moral conflict here. We find ourselves in the presence of a phenomenon whose name nobody ever uses anymore, so that nobody knows how to classify things anymore – it's a preconscious phenomenon. This is the preconscious order at which Freud intervenes in the dynamics of the dream, and to which he attaches so much importance in the *Traumdeutung*.

One gets the strong impression that this is coming from the ego. The emphasis placed by this *It really must be rather pleasant* . . . has the character of a seductive thought, which the ego is far from misrecognizing.

In a passage in the *Traumdeutung* dedicated to dreams of punishment Freud admits that at the same level at which unconscious desires intervene in a dream another mechanism than the one that relies on the conscious-unconscious opposition may be present – *The mechanism of dream formation,* says Freud, *would in general be greatly clarified if instead of the opposition between conscious and unconscious we were to speak of that between the ego and the repressed.*[4]

This was written at a time when the notion of the ego was not yet part of Freudian theory, but you still see nevertheless that it was already present in his thought. *I will only add that punishment-dreams are not in general subject to the condition that the day's residue shall be of a distressing kind. On the contrary, they occur most easily where the opposite is the case – where the day's residues are thoughts of a satisfying nature but the satisfaction which they express is a forbidden one. The only trace of these thoughts that appears in the manifest dream is their diametric opposite. . . . The essential characteristic of punishment-dreams would thus be that in their case the dream-constructing wish is not an unconscious wish derived from the repressed (from the system* Ucs.)*, but a punitive one reacting against it and belonging to the ego, though at the same time an unconscious (that is to say, preconscious) one.*[5]

Anyone who is following the path I am gradually leading you down, by drawing your attention to a mechanism that is distinct from *Verneinung* and that can be constantly seen emerging in Freud's discourse, will find here, once again, the need to distinguish between something that has been symbolized and something that hasn't.

75 What relation is there between the emergence in the ego – and, let me emphasize, free from conflict – of the thought that *it must be rather pleasant to be a woman succumbing to intercourse,* and the conception which the delusion, achieving a degree of completion, will blossom into, namely that the man must be the permanent woman of God? There is reason, undoubtedly, to compare the two terms – the initial appearance of this thought that crossed Schreber's mind, who was apparently sane at the time, and the delusion's

[4] SE 6:558.
[5] SE 6:558. The passage was added to *The Interpretation of Dreams* in 1919.

final state which, before an all-powerful personality with whom he has permanent erotic relations, situates him as a completely feminized being, a woman – this is what he says. The initial thought legitimately appears to us to give a glimpse of the final theme. Nevertheless, we must not neglect the stages, the crises, that have made him pass from such a fleeting thought to such firmly delusional conduct and discourse.

We should not assume that the mechanisms in question are homogeneous with the mechanisms we are usually dealing with in the neuroses, and especially not with that of repression. Of course, to appreciate this one has to begin by understanding what repression means, that is, that it's structured like a linguistic phenomenon.

The question arises whether we have before us a properly psychotic mechanism, one that would be imaginary and that would extend from the first hint of identification with and capture by the feminine image, to the blossoming of a world system in which the subject is completely absorbed in his imagination by a feminine identification.

What I am saying, which is almost too artificial, clearly indicates to you in what direction we have to seek a resolution of our question. We shall lack the means to do it unless we can uncover its traces in the one element we do possess, namely the document itself, the subject's discourse. This is why I introduced you last time to what will orient our investigation, namely the structure of this discourse itself.

2

I began by distinguishing the three spheres of speech as such. You may recall that within the phenomenon of speech we can integrate the three planes of the symbolic, represented by the signifier, the imaginary, represented by meaning, and the real, which is discourse that has actually taken place in a 76
diachronic dimension.

The subject has at his disposal a whole lot of signifying material which is his language, whether maternal or not, and he uses it to circulate meanings in the real. To be more or less captivated, captured, by a meaning is not the same thing as to express that meaning in a discourse designed to communicate it and reconcile it with other variously received meanings. In this term *received* lies the driving force of what makes discourse a common discourse, a commonly admitted discourse.

The notion of discourse is fundamental. Even for what we call objectivity, the world objectified by science, discourse is essential, for the world of science – one always loses sight of this – is above all communicable, it's embodied in scientific reports. Even if you were to succeed in carrying out the most amazing experiments, if no one is able to repeat them on the basis of the report you give of them, they will have been to no avail. This is the criterion by which one ascertains that something has not been scientifically received.

When I drew up this triple-entry chart for you, I located the different relations in which we can analyze a delusional's discourse. This diagram is not the diagram of the world. It's the basic condition of any relationship. Vertically, there is the register of the subject, speech, and the order of otherness as such, the Other. The hub of the function of speech is the subjectivity of the Other, that is to say, the fact that the Other is essentially he who is capable, like the subject, of convincing and lying. When I told you that in the Other there must be a sector of entirely real objects, it was understood that this introduction of reality is always a function of speech. For it to be possible to relate anything at all in relation to the subject and the Other to a foundation in the real, somewhere there must be something nondeceptive. The dialectical correlate of the basic structure which makes of the speech of subject to subject speech that may deceive is that there is also something that does not deceive.

This function, you will notice, is fulfilled in various ways according to the cultural region in which the constant function of speech comes to function. You would be wrong to think that the same elements, qualified in the same way, have always fulfilled that function.

Take Aristotle. Everything he says is perfectly communicable, and never-
77 theless the position of the nondeceptive element is essentially different for him and for us. Where is this element for us?

Well, whatever minds satisfied with appearances – which is often the case with free-thinkers, and even the most positivist among you, indeed the most liberated from any religious idea – might think, the simple fact that you live at this precise moment in the evolution of human thought does not exonerate you from what was openly and rigorously formulated in Descartes's meditation about God as incapable of deceiving us.[6]

This is so true that so lucid a personality as Einstein, when it was a matter of handling that symbolic order that was his, recalled it – *God*, he said, *is clever, but he is honest*.[7] The notion that the real, as difficult as it may be to penetrate, is unable to play tricks on us and will not take us in on purpose, is, though no one really dwells on this, essential to the constitution of the world of science.

Having said this, I admit that the reference to a nondeceiving god, the one accepted principle, is based on results obtained by science. We have in fact never observed anything that would show us a deceiving demon at the heart

[6] See Descartes's Fourth Meditation, "Truth and Falsity," in *Meditations on First Philosophy*.

[7] This is perhaps an allusion to Einstein's remark, *"Rafiniert ist der Herrgott aber boshaft ist er nicht,"* "The good Lord may be tricky but he isn't mean."

of nature. But that does not prevent its being a necessary article of faith for the first steps of science and the constitution of experimental science. It need hardly be said that matter does not cheat, that it has no intention of crushing our experiments or blowing up our machines. This sometimes happens, but only when we have made a mistake. It's out of the question that it, matter, should deceive us. This step is not at all obvious. Nothing less than the Judaeo-Christian tradition was required for it to be taken with such assurance.

The reason that the emergence of science, as we have constituted it with the tenacity, obstinacy, and daring characteristic of its development, took place within this tradition is that it proposed a unique principle at the foundation, not only of the universe, but of the law. It's not simply the universe that was created *ex nihilo,* but also the law – this is where the entire debate between a certain rationalism and a certain voluntarism is played out, one that bothered and still bothers the theologians. Does the criterion of good and evil depend on what could be called God's whim?

It's the radicality of Judaeo-Christian thought on this point that made possible this decisive step, for which the expression *act of faith* is not out of place, which consists in supposing that there is something absolutely nondeceptive. That this step should be reduced to this act is an essential point. Just think what would happen, at the current pace of things, if we were to perceive that there is not only a proton, a meson, etc., but also an element we had not reckoned with, one member too many in atomic mechanics, a character who 78
lies. We wouldn't be laughing then.

For Aristotle, things are completely different. What assured him, in nature, of the truthfulness of the Other as real were those things that always return to the same place, namely the celestial spheres. The notion of celestial spheres as what is incorruptible in the world, as being of another, divine, essence, for a long time inhabited Christian thought itself, the medieval Christian tradition, which inherited classical thought. It's not just a question of a Scholastic heritage, for the notion is, it might be said, natural to man, and it's we who are in an unusual position in no longer being preoccupied with what goes on in the celestial sphere. Until a quite recent period what occurred in the heavens was mentally present as an essential reference in every culture, including those whose astronomy indicates the advanced state of their observations and reflections. Our culture is an exception, since it consented, very recently, to follow the Judaeo-Christian position strictly. Until then it had been impossible to pry the thought of the philosophers, like that of the theologians and therefore that of the physicists, away from the idea of the superior essence of the celestial spheres. Measurement is the materialized proof of this – but it's we who say this – in itself, measurement is the proof of what does not deceive.

Our culture is really the only one that has this characteristic – common to us all here, I think, with the exception of some who may have some curiosity for astronomy – this characteristic trait that we never think of the regular return of the stars, or of the planets, or of eclipses, either. For us, this has no importance, we know that these things take place all by themselves. There is a world of difference between what is called, to use a word I don't like, the *mentality* of people like us – for whom the guarantee of everything that occurs in nature is one simple principle, namely, that nature is incapable of deceiving us, that somewhere there is something that guarantees the truth of reality, which Descartes affirms in the form of his own nondeceptive god – and on the other hand the normal, natural position, the more common position, that which appears in the minds of the very great majority of cultures, which consists in locating the guarantee of reality in the heavens, however one represents them to oneself.

The account I have just sketched out is not unrelated to our subject, for here we are, all of a sudden, in the thick of the first chapter of President Schreber's *Memoirs*, which treats the system of the stars as the essential, rather unexpected, item in his struggle against masturbation.

79 **3**

What follows is interspersed with readings from Memoirs of My Nervous Illness, *chap. 1, pp. 6–12.*

According to this theory, each nerve of intellect represents the total mental individuality of a human being and has, as it were, the sum total of memories inscribed upon it. We have here a highly elaborate theory whose position it would not be difficult to encounter, even if it were only as a stage of the discussion, in standard scientific works. Through an unexceptional mechanism of the imagination, we touch on the connection between the notion of souls and that of the permanence of impressions. The basis for the concept of the soul in the demand for the preservation of imaginary impressions is quite apparent here. I would almost say that we have here the basis, I'm not saying the proof, of the belief in the immortality of souls. There is something irrepressible when the subject considers himself – he is incapable of not conceiving not only that he exists but, moreover, that there is an impression that conveys its eternity. Up to this point our delusional is no more deluded than an extremely large sector of humanity, without our saying that he is co-extensive with it.

The reading continues.

We are not far from the Spinozian universe, insofar as it is founded on the co-existence of the attribute of thought and the attribute of extension. A very interesting dimension for situating the imaginary quality of certain stages of philosophical thought.

The reading continues.

We shall see later why Schreber took the notion of God as his starting point. This point is certainly connected with his final discourse, the one in which he systematizes his delusion in order to communicate it to us. You already see him in the grips of this dilemma – who is going to draw more rays to himself, him or this God with whom he maintains his perpetual erotic relationship? Will Schreber win the love of God and thereby place his existence in danger, or will God possess Schreber and then leave him in the lurch? I am describing the problem for you in a humorous manner, but there 80
is nothing funny about it since it's the delusional text of a sick man.

There is a divergence in his experience between God who is for him the lining [*l'envers*] of the world – and if this one isn't quite the one I was talking about just before, who was linked to a certain conception of an equivalence between God and extension, he is nevertheless all the same the guarantee that extension is not an illusion – and on the other hand this God with whom, in the crudest of experiences, he has relations as if with a living organism, this living God, as he puts it.

While the contradiction between these two terms does become apparent to him, you can well imagine that it does not happen at the level of formal logic. Our patient hasn't got to this stage yet – any more than the rest of us have, moreover. The famous contradictions of formal logic have no more reason to be operant in him than in us, who make the most heterogeneous, or even the most discordant, systems exist simultaneously in our minds, in a simultaneity in which that logic seems completely forgotten, apart from those moments when we are provoked into discussion about, and then become very sensitive to, formal logic – just refer to your own personal experience. There is no logical contradiction, there is a lived, living contradiction, seriously considered and vividly experienced by the subject, between the almost Spinozian God whose shadow, whose imaginary outline, he supports and the God with whom he has this erotic relationship about which he is constantly testifying to him.

The by no means metaphysical question arises of what is really going on in the lived experience of the psychotic. We are not yet in a position to give an answer and perhaps at no time will the question ever have any meaning for us. Our job is to situate structurally the discourse that testifies to the subject's erotic relations with the living God who, through these divine rays and through an entire procession of forms and emanations, also speaks to him, expressing himself in that language, destructured from the point of view of common language, but also restructured on more fundamental relations, which he calls the *fundamental language*.

The reading continues.

Here we come across the emergence, which is striking in relation to the rest of the discourse, of the most ancient of beliefs – God is the master of the sun and the rain.

81 *The reading continues.*

We can't fail to note the link between the imaginary relation and the divine rays. And I'm under the impression that there is a literary reference in Freud when, on the subject of repression, he insists upon the fact that there is a double polarity – something is undoubtedly suppressed, repelled, but it's also attracted by what has previously been repressed.[8] In passing, we can't fail to recognize the striking similarity between these dynamics and the sentiment Schreber expressed in stating his experience.

A while ago I pointed out to you how divergent he feels the two demands by the divine presence to be, one that justifies his maintaining the scenery of the external world around himself – you will see how well founded that expression is – and one made by God whom he experiences as the partner of this oscillation of the living force that will become the dimension in which he suffers and palpitates. This gap is resolved for him in these terms– *Perhaps the full truth lies (by way of a fourth dimension) in the form of a humanly inconceivable diagonal between these two lines of thought.*[9]

He gets himself out of trouble, as is normal in the language of that form of communication too unequal to its object which is known as metaphysics when one has absolutely no idea how to reconcile two terms, freedom and transcendent necessity, for instance. One makes do with saying that somewhere there is a fourth dimension and a diagonal, or one pulls both ends of the chain at once. That dialectic, perfectly obvious in all use of discourse, can't escape you.

[8] See "Case of Paranoia," SE 12:67 and "Repression," SE 14:148. The reference is perhaps to Goethe's poem, "The Fisherman," "Partly she dragged him down, partly he sank." The passage is quoted by Schreber; see Mem, 11 n.5.

[9] Mem, 8.

The reading continues.

Ultimately God only has a complete, authentic relationship with corpses. God doesn't understand anything of living beings, his omnipresence grasps things only from the outside, never from the inside. Here we have propositions that don't appear to be self-evident or demanded by the coherence of the system, such as we ourselves might conceive it in advance.

I shall come back to this point next time, with greater emphasis. But you can already see that the psychotic relation, at its highest degree of development, entails the introduction of the fundamental dialectic of deception into a dimension that is, as it were, transversal in comparison with that of an authentic relationship. The subject can speak to the Other insofar as with 82
him it's a question of faith or feint, but here this permanent exercise of deception, which tends to subvert any order whatever, whether mythical or not, in thought itself, unfolds as a passive phenomenon, as an experience lived through by the subject, in an imaginary dimension that is suffered, which is a fundamental characteristic of the imaginary. This means that the world – as you will see emerge in the subject's discourse – is transformed into what we call a fantasmagoria, but which for him has the utmost certainty in his lived experience. This is the game of deception that he maintains, not with another like himself, but with this primary being, the very guarantor of the real.

Schreber himself remarks perfectly well that his prior categories had far from prepared him for this vivid experience of an infinite God – previously these questions had had no kind of existence for him and, even better than being an atheist, he had been indifferent.

One can say that in this delusion God is essentially the opposite term in relation to the subject's megalomania, but God as he is caught at his own game. Schreber's delusion will in fact reveal that God, through having wanted to harness his forces and turn him into detritus, excrement, carrion, the object of all the exercises of destruction that he has allowed his intermediary mode to bring about, has been caught at his own game. Ultimately God's greatest danger is to love Schreber, that transversally transversed zone, too much.

We shall have to structure the relationship between what guarantees the real in the other, that is, the presence and existence of the stable world of God, and Schreber the subject qua organic reality and fragmented body. We shall see, provided we borrow a number of references from analytic literature, that a major part of his fantasies, of his hallucinations, of his miraculous or marvelous construction, consists of elements in which all sorts of bodily equivalents are clearly recognizable. We shall see, for example, what the hallucination of the little men represents organically. But the pivot of these phenomena is the law, which here lies entirely within the imaginary dimension. I say it's transversal because it's diagonally opposed to the relation of subject to subject, the axis of effective speech.

We shall continue this analysis, which has only just begun, next time.

14 December 1955

Appendix 83

The following session: The discourse of the desk

I realized that last time you had a bit of difficulty, owing to the difference in potential between my discourse and the reading of President Schreber's nevertheless absorbing writings. This technical difficulty has made me think of relying less on a running commentary on the text in future. I had thought that we could read it from beginning to end and on the way pick out those elements of structure, of organization, where I would like you to make progress. The experience has shown that I shall have to organize things differently. First of all I shall make a choice.

This question of method, combined with the fact that I had not fully decided to give today's seminar, and the fact that only my great affection for you leads me to do so, added to which is the tradition that on the eve of vacations in establishments of secondary education, which is about your level, one gives a small reading, has led me to decide to read you something recent and unpublished, by me, and which is in line with our subject.

This is a paper I gave, or am supposed to have given, at Dr. Hoff's Psychiatric Clinic in Vienna on the theme, *The meaning of a return to Freud in psychoanalysis,* for them to learn about the Parisian movement and the style, if not the general orientation, of our teaching.

I gave this paper under conditions of improvisation that were the same as here, or even rather more so. The discourse I give here I prepare. There, the subject appeared sufficiently general for me to rely on my ability to adapt to the audience, in such a way that I am going to deliver a written reconstitution, as faithful as possible to the spirit of improvisation and the modulations of this discourse. I was led to elaborate certain passages a little and to add certain considerations that I went on to make in a smaller session that took place afterwards, where I found myself with a second, smaller circle of the analyst technicians who had attended the first lecture. I addressed them on a technical question, that of the meaning of interpretation in general. This was nonetheless a subject of some astonishment on their part, at least at first sight, which proves that there is always room for trying to establish a dialogue.

84 I am going to try, as far as possible, to read this in the spoken tone my text endeavors to reproduce, and which, I hope, will hold your attention better than the reading did last time.

Let me tell you, even if it's only so as to provoke your curiosity, that I had quite a curious adventure in the middle of this discourse – which, since the material is lacking, we won't be able to reproduce here, except in the somewhat simulated fashion in which it is inscribed in the text.

Over there I had a sort of desk in front of me, of better quality than this one, and it was probably at a moment when at least my interest, if not the audience's, was flagging a bit, for the contact is not always as good as I feel it is here with you, the said desk came to my aid, and in a fairly extraordinary way if we compare it with the words we heard recently from one of my old friends at the Sorbonne, who recounted some astonishing things to us last Saturday, namely the metamorphosis of the lacemaker into rhinoceros horns and finally into cauliflowers. Well! this desk began to speak. And I had all the trouble in the world getting the floor back from it.

This element will perhaps introduce a slight imbalance into the composition of my discourse.

Lacan reads the article, published in E, 401-36/114-45 as "The Freudian Thing, Or the Meaning of the Return to Freud in Psychoanalysis."

21 December 1955

VI 85

The psychotic phenomenon and its mechanism

CERTAINTY AND REALITY

SCHREBER IS NO POET

THE NOTION OF DEFENSE

VERDICHTUNG, VERDRÄNGUNG,

VERNEINUNG, AND *VERWERFUNG*

It is always a good thing not to let one's horizons close in. This is why today I should like to remind you not only of my general design regarding the Schreber case, but also of the basic purpose of these seminars. Whenever one pursues a certain course step by step for a while, one always ends up with a wall in front of one's nose. But still, if I lead you off into difficult places, perhaps we are a bit more demanding than others. I also think I need to remind you how this course is mapped out.

The plan of this seminar would need to be expressed in various ways that all confirm one another and that all come down to the same thing. First I should tell you that I am here to remind you that our experience should be taken seriously and that being a psychoanalyst does not exempt you from being intelligent and sensitive. The fact that you have been given a number of keys is no excuse for you to use them not to think anymore and to endeavor, as is the general inclination of human beings, to leave everything as it is. There are certain ways of using categories such as the unconscious, the drive, the pre-oedipal relation, and defense that consist in drawing none of the authentic consequences that they imply and considering that this is an affair that concerns others but does not go to the heart of your own relations with the world. It has to be said that though you may be psychoanalysts, this in no way obliges you, unless you give yourselves a bit of a shake, to bear in mind that the world is not quite like everyone imagines it to be, but is caught up in mechanisms you are supposed to be familiar with.

Now, there is no question, either – make no mistake – of my doing the 86
metaphysics of the Freudian discovery and drawing out its consequences for what may be called being, in the widest sense of the term. This is not my intention. This would not be useless, but I think that it can be left to others and that what we are doing here will indicate how it might be approached. Don't get the idea that you are forbidden to stretch your wings a bit in this direction – you will lose nothing in inquiring into the metaphysics of the

human condition as it is revealed to us by the Freudian discovery. But still, this is not the main point, for you receive this metaphysics on your head. One can have confidence in things as they are already structured – they are there and you are implicated in them.

It's not for nothing that the Freudian discovery was made in our time, and it's not for nothing that, through a series of extremely muddled accidents, you personally find yourselves its depositaries. The metaphysics in question can be inscribed entirely within man's relation to the symbolic. You are immersed in it to a degree that extends far beyond your experience as technicians and, as I sometimes point out to you, we find traces of it and its presence in all sorts of disciplines and inquiries bordering on psychoanalysis.

You are technicians, but technicians of things that exist within this discovery. Since this technique develops through speech, the world that in your experience you have to move about in is incurved in this perspective. Let us try at least to structure it correctly.

This is the requirement that my little square meets,[1] which goes from the subject to the other and, in a way, here, from the symbolic towards the real, subject, ego, body, and in the contrary sense towards the big Other of intersubjectivity, the Other that you do not apprehend as long as it is a subject, that is, as long as it can lie, the Other that on the contrary one always finds in its place, the Other of the heavenly bodies, or, if you will, the stable system of the world, of the object, and, between the two, speech, with its three stages of the signifier, meaning, and discourse.

This is not a world system, but a system of reference for our own experience – this is how it is structured, and we can situate within it the various phenomenal manifestations with which we have to deal. We shall not understand a thing unless we take this structure seriously.

Of course, this business of taking things seriously itself goes to the heart of the matter. What characterizes a normal subject is precisely that he never
87 takes seriously certain realities that he recognizes exist. You are surrounded by all sorts of realities about which you are in no doubt, some of which are particularly threatening, but you don't take them fully seriously, for you think, along with Paul Claudel's subtitle, that *the worst is not always certain*,[2] and maintain yourselves in an average, basic – in the sense of relating to the base – state of blissful uncertainty, which makes possible for you a sufficiently relaxed existence. Surely, certainty is the rarest of things for the normal subject. If he questions himself about this matter, he will be aware that certainty emerges in strict correlation to an action he undertakes.

I shall not pursue this any further, as we are not here to give the psychol-

[1] See above, chap. 1, p. 14.
[2] Paul Claudel, *Le soulier de satin, ou, le pire n'est pas toujours sûr*.

ogy and phenomenology of those closest to us. We have to attain it, as usual, by means of a detour, via those furthest from us. Today this is Schreber the madman.

1

If we keep our distance, we shall see that Schreber, in common with other madmen, possesses a feature that you will also find in the most readily observable data – this is why I do case presentations for you. Psychologists, because they don't really keep company with the insane, raise the false problem of why they think their hallucinations are real. Since it is readily seen that nevertheless this doesn't hang together, one therefore exhausts oneself in deliberating on how the belief came about. One should first specify what the belief is, since in point of fact the madman doesn't believe in the reality of his hallucinations.

There are thousands of examples of this, but I shall not go into them today because I want to stay with the text of Schreber the madman. But still, it is within the reach even of people who are not psychiatrists. Chance recently brought me to open Maurice Merleau-Ponty's *Phenomenology of Perception* at page 334 on the theme of the thing and the natural world. I refer you to it. You will find some excellent remarks on this subject – for example, that nothing is easier to obtain from the subject than the admission that what he can hear nobody else has heard. He says – *Yes, all right, so I was the only one who heard it, then.*

Reality is not the issue. The subject admits, by means of all the verbally expressed explanatory detours at his disposal, that these phenomena are of another order than the real. He is well aware that their reality is uncertain. 88
He even admits their unreality up to a certain point. But, contrary to the normal subject for whom reality is always in the right place, he is certain of something, which is that what is at issue – ranging from hallucination to interpretation – regards him.

Reality isn't at issue for him, certainty is. Even when he expresses himself along the lines of saying that what he experiences is not of the order of reality, this does not affect his certainty that it concerns him. The certainty is radical. The very nature of what he is certain of can quite easily remain completely ambiguous, covering the entire range from malevolence to benevolence. But it means something unshakable for him.

This constitutes what is called, whether rightly or wrongly, the elementary phenomenon or, as a more developed phenomenon, delusional belief.

You can obtain an example of this by leafing through the admirable summary Freud gave of Schreber's book when he analyzed it. Through Freud you can make contact with it and see its importance.

A central phenomenon in Schreber's delusion, we may even say an initial phenomenon in the conception he formed of the transformation of the world that constitutes his delusion, is what he calls *Seelenmord,* soul murder. Now, he himself presents this as being totally enigmatic.

To be sure, chapter 3 of the *Memoirs,* in which he gave reasons for his neuropathy and developed the notion of soul murder, was censored. Still, we know that it contained remarks concerning his family, which would probably have thrown light both on his initial delusion in relation to his father and brother, or to someone else close to him, and on what are commonly called the significant transferential elements. But that censorship is not as regrettable as all that, ultimately. Sometimes too many details prevent the basic formal features from being seen. What is essential is not that, because of the censorship, we should have lost the occasion to understand such and such an affective experience concerning those close to him, but that he, the subject, failed to understand it and yet was able to formulate it.

He characterizes it as a decisive moment in this new dimension that he has attained and described for us in his account of the various relational modes, the prospect of which has gradually unfolded for him. He is certain that soul murder is at the root of something, but it retains the character of an enigma, nevertheless. What on earth could it be to murder a soul? Moreover, it's not as if each and every one of us knows how to differentiate the soul from every-
89 thing that is connected to it, but this delusional does, with a degree of certainty that is an essential feature of his testimony.

We must pause at these things and not overlook their distinctive character if we want to understand what is really going on and not simply, with the aid of certain key words or of this opposition between reality and certainty, rid ourselves of the phenomenon of madness.

I must accustom you to finding this delusional certainty wherever it exists. You will then notice for example the extent to which the phenomenon of jealousy is different according to whether it presents itself in a normal or in a delusional subject. There is no need to recall at length what is humorous or even comical in the normal form of jealousy, which, one could say, spontaneously rejects certainty, whatever the reality is. There is the famous story of the jealous husband who pursues his wife to the door of the very bedroom in which she has locked herself with someone else. This contrasts sufficiently with the fact that the delusional exempts himself from any real references. This ought to make you mistrustful of using normal mechanisms such as projection to explain the genesis of a delusional jealousy. Yet it is common to see this extrapolation made. It is enough to read Freud's text on President Schreber to perceive that, though he does not have the time to explore the whole breadth of the question, he shows all the dangers there are in independently bringing projection, the relation between ego and ego, that is, between ego and other, to bear where paranoia is concerned. Despite this warning's being written black on white, the term *projection* is used without rhyme or reason to explain delusions and their genesis.

I would go even further – the delusional, as he climbs the scale of delusions, becomes increasingly sure of things that he regards as more and more unreal. This is what distinguishes paranoia from dementia praecox. The delusional articulates them with an abundance, a richness, that is precisely one of the most essential clinical features which, while one of the most massive, must nevertheless not be neglected. Moreover, the discursive products characteristic of the register of paranoia usually blossom into literary productions, in the sense in which *literary* simply means sheets of paper covered with writing. Notice that this fact militates in favor of maintaining a certain unity between those delusions that have been perhaps prematurely isolated as paranoid and the formations known as paraphrenic in classical nosology.

It is, however, important to notice what the madman – including our President Schreber who gives us such a gripping work in its completed, enclosed, 90
full, and finished form – lacks at this point, however much of a writer he might be.

The world he describes for us matches the conception to which he has raised himself after the period of the unexplained symptom of the profound, cruel, and painful disturbance of his existence. According to this conception which, moreover, gives him a certain mastery over his psychosis, he is the female correspondent of God. Henceforth, everything becomes understandable, everything works out, and I would even go so far as to say everything works out for everybody since he plays the role of intermediary between a humanity threatened to the very depths of its existence and this divine power with whom he has such special ties. Everything works out in the *Versöhnung*, the reconciliation, that positions him as the woman of God. His relationship with God, as he conveys it to us, is rich and complex, and yet we cannot fail to be struck by the fact that the text includes no indication of the slightest presence, the slightest fervor, the slightest real communication, that would give us the idea that there really is a relationship here between two beings.

Without resorting to a comparison with a great mystic, which would be out of place in relation to a text like this, open nevertheless St. John of the Cross at any page you like, if this test appeals to you. He, too, in the experience of the ascent of the soul, presents himself in an attitude of receiving and offering and even speaks of the soul's nuptials with the divine presence. Yet the tone of the two approaches has absolutely nothing in common. I would say that even in the briefest testimony of an authentic religious experience you can see a world of difference. Let us say that the lengthy discourse in which Schreber testifies to what he has finally resolved to acknowledge as the solution of his problem nowhere gives us the feeling of an original experience in which the subject is himself included – his testimony can be said to be truly objectified.

What are these testimonies of delusionals about? Don't say that the madman is someone who does without the other's recognition. Clearly, Schreber wrote this enormous work so that nobody would be unaware of what he experienced and, even, so that when the opportunity arose learned scientists would verify the presence in his body of the feminine nerves that had gradually penetrated him, in order to objectify his own unique relationship with the divine reality. This certainly looks like an effort to be recognized. Since it concerns a published discourse, this raises a question mark as to what the need for recognition might possibly mean to this character of the madman,
91 so isolated by his experience. At first sight what seems distinctive about a madman is the fact that he has no need for recognition. But his self-sufficiency in his own world, the auto-comprehensibility that seems characteristic of it, is not devoid of contradiction.

We could summarize the position we are in with respect to his discourse on first encountering it by saying that while he may be a writer, he is no poet. Schreber doesn't introduce us to a new dimension of experience. There is poetry whenever writing introduces us to a world other than our own and also makes it become our own, making present a being, a certain fundamental relationship. The poetry makes us unable to doubt the authenticity of St. John of the Cross's experience, or Proust's, or Gérard de Nerval's. Poetry is the creation of a subject adopting a new order of symbolic relations to the world. There is nothing like any of this in Schreber's *Memoirs*.

So what, in the final analysis, are we going to say about the delusional? Is he on his own? This isn't the feeling we get, either, since he is inhabited by all sorts of existences, improbable ones, certainly, but whose meaningful character is in no doubt. This is an initial datum, whose articulation becomes more and more elaborate as his delusion advances. He is raped, manipulated, transformed, spoken in every possible way, and, I should say, chattered. You can read in detail what he says about what he calls the birds of the sky and their chirping. This is clearly what is at issue – he is the seat of an entire aviary of phenomena – and this is the fact that inspired this enormous communication of his, this book of some five hundred pages, which is the result of a lengthy activity of construction that for him was the solution to his internal adventure.

In the beginning, and at a later moment as well, there is doubt over what the meaning refers to, but there is never any doubt for him that it does refer to something. With a subject like Schreber, things go so far that the whole world ends up caught up in this delusion of meaning, in such a way that it can be said that, far from his being alone, there is almost nothing in his surroundings that in some sense isn't him.

On the other hand, everything he brings into being in these meanings is in a certain sense void of him. He phrases it in a thousand different ways, and especially for example when he remarks that God, his imaginary interlocutor, understands nothing about what goes on within, nothing at all about living beings, and that he never has anything to do with anything but shadows or cadavers. Moreover, his whole world has been transformed into a fantasmagoria of shadows of *fleeting-improvised-men*.

2

92

To understand how such a process of construction might occur in a subject, we have, in the light of analytic perspectives, several avenues open to us.

The simplest are the ones we are already familiar with. A category in the foreground today is that of defense, which was introduced into analysis very early on. Delusion is regarded as one of the subject's defenses. Neuroses are explained in the same manner, moreover.

You know how much I insist upon the incomplete and perilous character of this reference, which lends itself to all sorts of hasty and harmful interventions. You also know how difficult it is to rid oneself of it. This concept is so insistent, so tempting, precisely because it touches something objectifiable. The subject defends, well then! we will help him to understand that he does nothing but defend, we will show him what he is defending against. As soon as you enter into that approach you find yourself confronted by numerous dangers – in the first instance, the danger of missing the level at which your intervention must be brought to bear. In point of fact, you must always rigorously differentiate the order within which the defense appears.

Suppose that this defense was obviously within the symbolic order and that you could elucidate it along the lines of an utterance in the complete sense, that is, one that in the subject involves both signifier and signified. If the subject presents you with both the signifier and the signified, then you may intervene by showing him the union of this signifier and this signified. But only if both are present in his discourse. If you do not have them both, if you have the feeling that the subject is defending against something that you yourself see and that he doesn't, if, that is, you clearly see that the subject is aberrant with respect to reality, then the notion of defense is insufficient to enable you to place the subject before reality.

You may recall what I once said about Kris's nice paper on the character haunted by the idea that he was a plagiarist and the accrued guilt.[3] It was in

[3] Ernst Kris, "Ego Psychology and Interpretation in Psychoanalytic Therapy." Lacan elaborated on these remarks about Kris's case in "Réponse au commentaire de Jean Hyppolite sur la *Verneinung* de Freud," E, 393-99. The case is discussed again in "The Direction of the Treatment and the Principle of its Power," E, 598-602 / 238-40. Finally, the same article was mentioned in "The Function and Field of Speech

the name of defense that Kris considered his intervention to be a stroke of genius. For some time now we have been getting nothing but this notion of defense and, as the ego has to struggle on three fronts, that is, against the *id*, the superego, and the external world, one believes one is authorized to inter-
93 vene on any one of these levels. When the subject alludes to the work of one of his colleagues whom he claims he has plagiarized yet again, one takes the liberty of reading the work and, observing that there is nothing there that merits being considered an original idea for the subject to plagiarize, makes this known to him. One considers such an intervention to be part of the analysis. We are fortunately both honest and blind enough to give as proof that our interpretation is well-founded the fact that the subject brings this nice little story along to the next session – on leaving the session he had gone into a restaurant and treated himself to his favorite dish, fresh brains.

One is delighted; there is a response. But what does it mean? It means that the subject has himself understood absolutely nothing of the matter, that he understands nothing of what he brings us, either, so that one fails to see very well where the progress that has been brought about is situated. Kris has pressed the right button. It is not enough to press the right button. The subject quite simply acts out.

I treat acting out as equivalent to a hallucinatory phenomenon of the delusional type that occurs when you symbolize prematurely, when you address something in the order of reality and not within the symbolic register. For an analyst, addressing the question of plagiarism in the symbolic register must first be centered on the idea that plagiarism doesn't exist. There is no symbolic property. This is precisely the question – if the symbolic belongs to everybody, why have things in the symbolic order taken on this emphasis, this weight, for the subject?

This is where the analyst has to wait for the subject to provide him with something before bringing his interpretation to bear. As we are dealing with a grand neurotic who has resisted a certainly non-negligible analytic effort – before going to Kris he had already had an analysis – the likelihood is that the plagiarism is fantasmatic. On the other hand, if you bring the intervention to bear at the level of reality, that is, if you return to the most elementary psychotherapy, what does the subject do? He responds in the clearest of manners at a deeper level of reality. He testifies that something emerges from reality that is obstinate, something that imposes itself upon him, and that nothing one says will in any way change the core of the problem. You show him that he isn't a plagiarist anymore. He shows you what is at stake by making you eat fresh brains. He renews his symptom, and at a point that has

and Language in Psychoanalysis" in relation to the difference between "need for love" and "demand for love," E, 296 / 83.

no more foundation or existence than the one at which he showed it at the outset. Is there something that he shows? I would go further—I would say that there is nothing at all that he shows, but that something shows itself.

Here we are at the heart of what I shall be trying to demonstrate on the subject of President Schreber this year. 94

3

President Schreber reveals to observation certain microscopic things in a dilated form. This is going to enable me to clarify for you what Freud clearly formulated on psychosis, without taking it too far, because in his day the problem had not attained the degree of acuteness or urgency for analytic practice that it has in ours. He says – a crucial sentence that I have already quoted many times – something that has been rejected from within reappears without. I shall come back to this.

I propose putting the problem in the following terms. Prior to all symbolization – this priority is not temporal but logical – there is, as the psychoses demonstrate, a stage at which it is possible for a portion of symbolization not to take place. This initial stage precedes the entire neurotic dialectic, which is due to the fact that neurosis is articulated speech, insofar as the repressed and the return of the repressed are one and the same thing. It can thus happen that something primordial regarding the subject's being does not enter into symbolization and is not repressed, but rejected.

This hasn't been demonstrated. Nor is it a hypothesis. It is a way of phrasing the problem. This first stage doesn't have to be situated anywhere genetically. I am not denying of course that what happens at the level of the first symbolic articulations, the essential appearance of the subject, raises questions for us, but do not allow yourselves to be fascinated by this genetic moment. The young child whom you see playing at making an object disappear and reappear, who is thereby working at apprehending the symbol, will, if you let yourselves be fascinated by him, mask the fact that the symbol is already there, that it is enormous and englobes him from all sides – that language exists, fills libraries to the point of overflowing, and surrounds, guides, and rouses all your actions – the fact that you are engaged, that it can require you to move at any moment and take you somewhere – all this you forget before the child being introduced into the symbolic dimension. So let us place ourselves at the level of the existence of the symbol as such, insofar as we are immersed in it.

In the subject's relationship to the symbol there is the possibility of a primitive *Verwerfung*, that is, that something is not symbolized and is going to appear in the real. 95

It is essential to introduce the category of the real, it is impossible to neglect it in Freud's texts. I give it this name so as to define a field different from the symbolic. From there alone is it possible to throw light on the psychotic phenomenon and its evolution.

At the level of this pure, primitive *Bejahung*, which may or may not take place, an initial dichotomy is established – what has been subject to *Bejahung*, to primitive symbolization, will have various destinies. What has come under the influence of the primitive *Verwerfung* will have another.

Today I am going to forge ahead and I will light my lamp so that you can see where I am headed. Do not take what I am expounding for you as an arbitrary construction, nor simply as the fruit of adherence to Freud's text, even if it is exactly what we read in this extraordinary text, *Die Verneinung*, that M. Hyppolite was kind enough two years ago to discuss for us.[4] If I say what I am saying now it is because it is the only way to introduce rigor, coherence, and rationality into what happens in psychosis, and namely in the psychosis in question here, President Schreber's. I shall subsequently show you the difficulties our entire understanding of the case raises and the need for this initial formulation.

In the beginning, then, there is either *Bejahung*, which is the affirmation of what is, or *Verwerfung*.

Obviously, it is not enough for the subject to have only selected a part of the text of what there is to say, while thrusting the rest aside, in the hope that at least with the part things will hang together. There are always things that don't hang together. This is an obvious fact, if we do not begin with the idea that inspires all classical, academic psychology, which is that human beings are, as they say, adapted beings, because they are living, and therefore it must all hang together. You are not a psychoanalyst if you accept this. To be a psychoanalyst is simply to open your eyes to the evident fact that nothing malfunctions more than human reality. If you believe that you have a well-adapted, reasonable ego, which knows its way around, how to recognize what is to be done and not to be done, and how to take reality into account, then there is nothing left to do but send you packing. Psychoanalysis, and this it shares with common experience, shows you that nothing is more stupid than human destiny, that is, that one is always being fooled. Even when one does do something successfully, it is precisely not what one wanted to do. There is nothing more disappointed than a gentleman who is supposed to have attained the pinnacle of his wishes. One only need speak with him for three minutes, frankly, as perhaps only the artifice of the psychoanalytic couch permits, to
96 know that in the end all that stuff is just the sort of thing he could not care less about and, furthermore, that he is particularly troubled by all sorts of things. Analysis is about becoming aware of this and taking it into account.

[4] See above, chap. 1, p. 12 n.9.

It is not by accident, because it couldn't be otherwise, that by a bizarre stroke of luck we go through life without meeting anyone but the unhappy. One says to oneself that there must be happy people somewhere. Well then! unless you get that out of your head, you have understood nothing about psychoanalysis. That is what I call taking things seriously. When I told you things had to be taken seriously, it was so that you would take precisely this point seriously, that you never take anything seriously.

So, within *Bejahung* all sorts of accidents occur. There is no indication that the primitive retrenchment has been done cleanly. Besides, there is a strong chance that in the long term we will know nothing about the motives for it, precisely because it is situated beyond all mechanisms of symbolization. And if someone does know something about this one day, then there is little chance that he will be an analyst. In any case, it is with what remains that the subject constructs himself a world and, above all, that he situates himself within it, that is, that he manages to be more or less what he has admitted that he was—a man when he finds himself to be of masculine sex, or, conversely, a woman.

If I put this in the foreground, it is because analysis strongly emphasizes that this is one of the essential problems. Never forget that nothing touching on the behavior of the human being as subject, or on anything in which he realizes himself, in which he quite simply is, can escape being bound by the laws of speech.

The Freudian discovery teaches us that all natural harmony in man is profoundly disconcerted. It is not just that bisexuality plays an essential role. This bisexuality is not surprising from the biological point of view, given that the means of access to regularization and normalization in man are more complex than and different from what we observe in mammals and in vertebrates in general. Symbolization, in other words the Law, plays an essential role here.

If Freud insisted on the Oedipus complex to the extent of constructing a sociology of totems and taboos, it is obviously because for him the Law is there *ab origine*. It is therefore out of the question to ask oneself the question of origins—the Law is there precisely from the beginning, it has always been there, and human sexuality must realize itself through it and by means of it. This fundamental law is simply a law of symbolization. This is what the Oedipus complex means.

So, within this, everything imaginable will occur under the three registers 97
of *Verdichtung*, *Verdrängung*, and *Verneinung*.

Verdichtung is simply the law of misunderstanding [*malentendu*], owing to which we survive or, even, owing to which we can, if we are a man, for example, completely satisfy our opposite tendencies by occupying a feminine position in a symbolic relation, while perfectly well remaining a man equipped with one's virility on both the imaginary and the real planes. This function which, with greater or lesser intensity, is a role of femininity, may thus find the means to satisfy itself in this essential receptivity that is one of the fundamental existing roles. This is not metaphorical – we do indeed receive something in receiving speech. Participating in speech relations may have several senses at once, and one of the meanings involved might be just that of obtaining satisfaction in the feminine position, as such essential to our being.

Verdrängung, repression, is not the law of misunderstanding, it is what happens when things don't hang together at the level of a symbolic chain. Each symbolic chain we are linked to comprises an internal coherence, which means that we can be forced at any given moment to render what we have received to someone else. Now, it sometimes happens that we are unable to do this on all levels at once – in other words, we find the law intolerable. Not that it is intolerable in itself, but the position we are in comprises a sacrifice that proves to be impossible at the level of meaning. So we repress some of our own acts, discourse, or behavior. But the chain nevertheless continues to run on beneath the surface, express its demands, and assert its claims – and this it does through the intermediary of the neurotic symptom. This is where repression is at the base of neurosis.

As for *Verneinung,* this belongs to the order of discourse and concerns what we are capable of bringing to the light of day in an articulated form. The so-called reality principle intervenes strictly at this level. We have gone over at different moments of our commentary the three or four places in his work where Freud expresses this most clearly. It concerns the attribution, not of the value of symbols, *Bejahung,* but of the value of existence. Freud gives, with a profundity a thousand times in advance of what was being said in his day, the following characteristic feature of this level, which he situates in his vocabulary as that of the judgment of existence – it always concerns the refinding of an object.

All human apprehension of reality is subject to this primordial condition –
98 the subject seeks the object of his desire, but nothing leads him to it. Reality, inasmuch as it is supported by desire, is initially hallucinated. The Freudian theory of the birth of the world of objects, of reality as it is expressed, for example, at the end of *Die Traumdeutung* and restated whenever essentially it is in question, implies that the subject remains suspended at the point of what makes his fundamental object the object of his essential satisfaction.[5]

This is the part of Freud's work, of Freudian thought, that is often returned to in all the developments that are currently taking place on pre-oedipal relations, which ultimately consist in saying that the subject always seeks to sat-

[5] See the last section of *The Interpretation of Dreams,* "The Unconscious and Consciousness—Reality," SE 7:610.

isfy the primitive maternal relation. In other words, whereas Freud introduced the dialectic of two inseparable principles that cannot be thought one without the other, the pleasure principle and the reality principle, one of them, the pleasure principle, is selected and emphasized through the claim that it dominates and englobes the reality principle.

But this reality principle is basically misrecognized. It expresses precisely this – the subject does not have to *find* the object of his desire, he is not led, channeled there, by the natural rails of a more or less pre-established instinctual and, moreover, more or less stumbling, adaptation, such as we see in the animal kingdom. He must on the contrary *refind* the object, whose emergence is fundamentally hallucinated. Of course, he never does refind it, and this is precisely what the reality principle consists in. The subject never refinds, Freud writes, anything but another object that answers more or less satisfactorily to the needs in question. He never finds anything but a distinct object since he must by definition refind something that he has on loan. This is the essential point that the introduction of the reality principle into the Freudian dialectic hinges on.

What has to be understood, because this is given in clinical experience, is that something else appears in the real than what the subject experiences and seeks, something other than what the subject is led towards by that apparatus of reflection, mastery, and research that is his ego, with all its fundamental alienations, something else that can appear either in the sporadic form of that hallucination that is emphasized in the case of the Wolf Man, or, in a much more extensive fashion, as what takes place in the case of President Schreber.

4 99

What is the psychotic phenomenon? It is the emergence in reality of an enormous meaning that has the appearance of being nothing at all—in so far as it cannot be tied to anything, since it has never entered into the system of symbolization—but under certain conditions it can threaten the entire edifice.

In the case of President Schreber there is obviously a meaning that concerns the subject, but it is rejected and merely sketches itself most indistinctly on his horizon and in his ethics, while its re-emergence occasions the psychotic invasion. You will see the extent to which what determines it is different from what determines the neurotic invasion – these are strictly opposite conditions. In President Schreber's case this rejected meaning is closely related to the primitive bisexuality I was speaking about just before. In no way has President Schreber ever integrated any type of feminine form – we shall try to see this in the text.

It is difficult to see how it could be purely and simply the suppression of a given tendency, the rejection or repression of some more or less transferential drive he would have felt toward Dr. Flechsig, that led President Schreber to construct his enormous delusion. There really must be something more proportionate to the result involved.

I point out to you in advance that this involves the feminine function in its essential symbolic meaning and that we can refind it only at the level of procreation. You will see why. We are not saying *emasculation* or *feminization* or *fantasy of pregnancy,* for this extends to procreation. Here we have what appears to him at a high point in his existence, and not at all at a moment of deficit, in the form of an irruption in the real of something that he has never known, a sudden emergence of a total strangeness that will progressively bring on a radical submersion of all his categories to the point of forcing him into a veritable reshaping of his world.

May we speak of a process of compensation, or even of cure, as some people would not hesitate to do, on the pretext that when his delusion stabilizes the subject presents a calmer state than at its appearance? Is he cured or
100 not? It is a question worth raising, but I think it can only be wrong to speak of a cure here.

What happens, then, when what is not symbolized reappears in the real? It wouldn't be useless here to bring forward the term *defense*. Clearly, what appears does so in the register of meaning, in the register of a meaning that comes from nowhere, and which refers to nothing, but is an essential meaning, one that concerns the subject. What intervenes whenever there is a conflict of orders, namely repression, is set in motion at this point. But why doesn't repression work here, that is, why isn't what happens when a neurosis is involved the end result?

Before we can know why, we must study the how. I shall focus on what creates the structural difference between neurosis and psychosis.

When a drive, let's say a feminine or pacifying one, appears in a subject for whom the drive has already been brought into play at different points of his previous symbolization, in his infantile neurosis for example, it manages to express itself in a certain number of symptoms. Thus what is repressed nevertheless expresses itself, repression and the return of the repressed being one and the same thing. The subject has the possibility, within repression, of getting by when something new happens. Compromises are made. This is what characterizes neurosis; it is both the most obvious thing in the world and the thing one doesn't want to see.

Verwerfung is not at the same level as *Verneinung*. When, at the beginning of a psychosis, the nonsymbolized reappears in the real, there are responses made from the side of the mechanism of *Verneinung,* but they prove inadequate.

What is the beginning of a psychosis? Does a psychosis, like a neurosis, have a prehistory? Is there, or is there not, an infantile psychosis? I am not saying that we shall answer this question, but at least we shall raise it.

It looks very much as if psychosis has no prehistory. However, it so happens that when, in exceptional circumstances that will have to be spelled out, something that has not been primitively symbolized appears in the external world the subject finds himself absolutely unequipped, incapable of making *Verneinung* succeed in respect of the event. What then occurs has the characteristic of being totally excluded from the symbolizing compromise of neurosis and, through a veritable chain reaction at the level of the imaginary, is translated into another register, that is, into the opposite diagonal of our little magic square.

For want of being able in any way to re-establish his pact with the other, for want of being able to make any symbolic mediation whatsoever between 101
what is new and himself, the subject moves into another mode of mediation, completely different from the former, and substitutes for symbolic mediation a profusion, an imaginary proliferation, into which the central signal of a possible mediation is introduced in a deformed and profoundly asymbolic fashion.

The signifier itself undergoes profound modifications that will give this particular quality to those intuitions that are most significant for the subject. President Schreber's fundamental language in fact indicates that the signifier is still required within this imaginary world.

The subject's relationship to the world is a mirror relation. The subject's world will essentially consist of the relationship with that being who is the other for him, namely God himself. Something of man's relation to woman is allegedly realized here. But on the contrary you will see, when we come to study this delusion in detail, that these two characters, that is, God, with all that he implies, the universe, the celestial sphere, and on the other hand Schreber himself, literally decomposed into a multitude of imaginary beings with their toing-and-froing and their various transfixions, are two strictly alternating structures. They develop in a way that is very interesting for us and that is permanently elided, veiled, domesticated in the life of a normal man—namely, the dialectic of the fragmented body in relation to the imaginary universe, which is subjacent to a normal structure.

The outstanding interest in studying Schreber's delusion is that it enables us to improve our grasp of the imaginary dialectic. If it is manifestly distinct from everything we can assume about an instinctual, natural relation, it is because of a generic structure we originally described, which is the mirror stage. This structure makes man's imaginary world something decomposed in advance. Here we find it in its advanced state, and that is a part of our interest in the analysis of delusions as such. As analysts have always emphasized, delusions show us the play of fantasies in a highly advanced state of duality. The two characters that the world is reduced to for President Schreber are constructed in relation to one another; they offer one another their inverted image.

The important thing is to see in what way this answers to the indirectly formulated demand to integrate what has emerged in the real, which for the subject represents something of himself that he has never symbolized. A requirement of the symbolic order, through being unable to be integrated into what has already been put into play in the dialectical movement on which
102 the subject has lived, brings about a serial disintegration, a removal of the woof from the tapestry, which is known as a delusion. A delusion is not necessarily unrelated to normal discourse and the subject is well able to convey it to us, to his own satisfaction, within a world in which communication is not entirely broken off.

Next time we shall continue our examination at the point where *Verwerfung* and *Verdrängung* intersect with *Verneinung*.

11 January 1956

VII 103

The imaginary dissolution

DORA AND HER QUADRILATERAL
EROS AND AGGRESSION IN THE MALE STICKLEBACK
WHAT IS CALLED THE FATHER
THE FRAGMENTATION OF IDENTITY

My intention was to penetrate today into the essence of madness, and I thought that was mad. I was reassured by the thought that what we are undertaking is not so isolated and hazardous.

The work isn't easy, however. Why not? Because by a singular piece of fate all human undertakings, particularly the difficult ones, always tend, by virtue of this mysterious thing called laziness, to lose ground. To assess this one only has to reread Freud's text on President Schreber without prejudice and with an eye and an understanding cleansed of all the noise that we hear around analytic concepts.

It is an absolutely extraordinary text, but it only puts us on the path to the enigma. The entire explanation he gives of the delusion links up with the notion of narcissism, which is certainly not elucidated for Freud, at least not at the time he writes on Schreber.

People today act as if narcissism were something that was self-explanatory – before extending to external objects, there is a stage at which the subject takes his own body as object. The term *narcissism* does, it is true, have a meaning in this dimension. Does this mean, though, that the term *narcissism* is used only in this sense? President Schreber's autobiography, in the way Freud used it to support this notion, shows us, however, that what was repugnant to the said President's narcissism was the adoption of a feminine position towards his father, which involved castration. Here is someone who is supposed to be better off obtaining satisfaction in a relation founded on a delusion of grandeur, since castration can no longer affect him once his part- 104
ner has become God.

In short, Freud's schema could be summed up thus, in line with the formulas for paranoia he gives in this same text – *I do not love him, I love God,* and reciprocally – *God loves me.*

I pointed out to you last time that this is perhaps not totally satisfactory, any more than Freud's formulas themselves are, as illuminating as they may be. The double reversal, *I do not love him, I hate him, he hates me,* undoubtedly gives us a clue to the mechanism of persecution. The problem is entirely one of this *he*. In effect, this *he* is multiplied, neutralized, emptied, or so it seems, of subjectivity. The persecutory phenomenon takes on the character of indefinitely repeated signs, and the persecutor, to the extent that he is its support, is no longer anything more than the shadow of the persecutory object.

This is no less true of the god in question in the blossoming of President Schreber's delusion. I pointed out to you in passing how far removed – it's so obvious that it's almost too silly to mention – Schreber's relationship with God is from anything that occurs in mystical experience. As detailed as it is, the description of this unique partner called God nevertheless leaves us perplexed as to his nature.

What Freud said to us about the withdrawal of libidinal interest from the external object goes right to the heart of the matter. But we still need to spell out what this might mean. At what level does this withdrawal occur? We very much get the impression that something has profoundly modified the object, but is it enough to attribute this to one of these displacements of libido that we see as central to the mechanisms of the neuroses? What are the levels, the registers, by which we can define these modifications to the character of the other that are always, we very much get the impression, central to the alienation of madness?

1

Here I shall take the liberty of going back a bit to try to get you to view in a new light certain aspects of phenomena with which you are already familiar. Take a case who is not psychotic, the almost inaugural case for the properly psychoanalytic experience developed by Freud, that of Dora.[1]

105 Dora is a hysteric, and as such she has unusual object relationships. You know the difficulty that the ambiguity surrounding the issue of who her love object really is contributes both to his observations and to the pursuit of the cure. Freud eventually realized his mistake and said that it was undoubtedly as a consequence of having misrecognized Dora's true love object that he caused the whole matter to fail and that the cure was prematurely broken off without allowing a sufficient resolution of what was at issue. You know that Freud was of the opinion that he had detected a relationship of conflict in her due to her finding it impossible to detach herself from her first love object, her father, and move towards a more normal object, namely, another man. Now, the object for Dora was none other than the woman known in this case as Frau K., who was precisely her father's mistress.

[1] "Fragment of an Analysis of a Case of Hysteria."

Let us start with the case. I shall comment on it afterwards. The history, as you know, is that of a minuet for four characters, Dora, her father, Herr K. and Frau K. Dora in fact uses Herr K. as her ego, in that it is by means of him that she is effectively able to support her relationship with Frau K. I ask you to accept this point and trust me, since I have written enough on this case in an intervention concerning the transference for you to refer to it easily.[2]

It's only Herr K.'s mediation that enables Dora to sustain a bearable relationship. While this mediating fourth person is essential for maintaining the situation, this is not because the object of her affection is of the same sex as herself, but because she has the most profoundly motivated relations of identification and rivalry with her father, further accentuated by the fact that the mother is a person completely obliterated in the parental couple. It is because the triangular relationship is supposed to have been particularly unbearable for her that the situation not only lasted but was effectively supported within the fourfold-group composition.

This is proved by what took place the day Herr K. pronounced that fateful sentence – *My wife is nothing to me.*[3] Everything then happened as if she had answered him – *So, what can you be to me, then?* She slapped his face there and then, whereas up until that moment she had maintained with him the ambiguous relationship necessary to preserve the four-person group. This disturbed the equilibrium of the situation.

Dora is only a little hysteric; she doesn't have many symptoms. You recall, I trust, my emphasizing this famous aphonia which occurred only at her moments of *tête à tête* with, of being confronted with, her love object, and which was definitely linked to a very special erotization of the oral function, 106
withdrawn from its usual employment as soon as Dora got too close to the object of her desire. This is no big deal, and this wouldn't have brought her to see Freud, or made those around her force her to see him. On the contrary, from the moment the fourth character withdrew and broke up the situation, a little syndrome of persecution, quite simply, appeared in Dora with respect to her father.

Until then the situation had been a bit improper, but without going beyond what we might call a Viennese operetta. As all the subsequent observations make clear, Dora behaved admirably in order to avoid any scenes and to ensure that her father had normal relations with the woman – in point of fact, the nature of these relations remains pretty much in the dark. Dora covered up the entire situation and she was on the whole reasonably comfortable with it. But when the situation broke up, she began making demands,

2 "Intervention on the Transference."
3 "You know I get nothing out of my wife." SE 7:98.

she declared that her father wanted to prostitute her and surrender her to Herr K. in exchange for maintaining his ambiguous relations with the latter's wife.

Am I about to say that Dora is a paranoiac? I have never said this, and I am fairly scrupulous when it comes to diagnosis in psychosis.

I made an effort here last Friday to see a female patient who obviously had behavioral problems, problems of conflict, with other people. I was brought in, in short, to declare that she was psychotic and not, as had at first appeared, an obsessional neurotic. I refused to diagnose her as psychotic for one decisive reason, which was that there were none of those disturbances that are our object of study this year, which are disorders at the level of language. We must insist upon the presence of these disorders before making a diagnosis of psychosis.

A claim against people who are supposedly acting against you is not enough for us to have a psychosis. It may well be an unjustified claim, contributing to a delusion of presumption, this doesn't make it a psychosis. This isn't unrelated to psychosis – there is a small delusion, one could describe it that way. That these phenomena are continuous is common knowledge – people have always known how to define the paranoiac as a touchy, intolerant, and distrustful gentleman, who is in a state of verbalized conflict with his surroundings. But for us to have a psychosis, there must be disturbances of language – this at least is the rule of thumb I suggest you adopt provisionally.

With respect to her father Dora experiences a significant, interpretative, or even hallucinatory phenomenon, but it does not add up to a delusion. This is nevertheless a phenomenon that is on the ineffable, intuitive road towards
107 imputing hostility and bad intentions to others – and concerning a situation the subject has, in a profoundly elective way, actually participated in.

What does this mean? This character's level of otherness becomes modified, and the situation deteriorates owing to the absence of one of the components of the quadrilateral that enabled it to be sustained. Here we can make use of the notion of distantiation, provided we know how to handle it prudently. People use it indiscriminately, but this is no reason to refuse to use it ourselves, provided we give it an application that is in better agreement with the facts.

This takes us to the heart of the problem of narcissism.

2

What notion of narcissism can we form on the basis of our work? We regard narcissism as the central imaginary relation of interhuman relationships. What crystallized analytic experience around this notion? Above all, its ambiguity. It is in fact an erotic relationship – all erotic identification, all seizing of the other in an image in a relationship of erotic captivation, occurs by way of the narcissistic relation – and it is also the basis of aggressive tension.

Ever since the notion of narcissism entered psychoanalytic theory, the aggressive component has been placed increasingly at the centre of technical preoccupations. But their elucidation has been rudimentary. We have to go further.

This is precisely where the mirror stage is useful. It brings to light the nature of this aggressive relation and what it signifies. If the aggressive relation enters into this formation called the ego, it's because it is constitutive of it, because the ego is already by itself an other, and because it sets itself up in a duality internal to the subject. The ego is this master the subject finds in an other, whose function of mastery he establishes in his own heart. In every relationship with the other, even an erotic one, there is some echo of this relation of exclusion, *it's either him or me*, because, on the imaginary plane, the human subject is so constituted that the other is always on the point of re-adopting the place of mastery in relation to him, because there is an ego in him that is always in part foreign to him, a master implanted in him over and above his set of tendencies, conduct, instincts, and drives. All I am doing here is putting into words, with a bit more rigor to bring out the paradox,
the fact that the drives and the ego are in conflict and that there is a choice 108
that has to be made. It adopts some, it doesn't adopt others, this is what is called the ego's function of synthesis – nobody knows why, given that on the contrary this synthesis never takes place and that one would do better to call it a function of mastery. And where is this master? Inside? Outside? He is always both inside and outside, which is why any purely imaginary equilibrium with the other always bears the mark of a fundamental instability.

Let me make a brief comparison with animal psychology.

We know that animals have a much less complicated life than ours. At least this is what we believe on the basis of what we see and there is enough evidence of this for man to have always used animals as a point of reference. Animals have relations with the other whenever they want to. For them there are two ways of wanting to – first, by eating it, second, by fucking it. This takes place according to what is called a natural rhythm which forms a cycle of instinctual behavior.

Now, it has been possible to bring out the importance of the fundamental role, in the triggering of these cycles, that images play in the relationship animals have with their counterparts. On seeing the silhouette of a predator to which they may be more or less sensitive, chickens and other poultry go berserk. The silhouette provokes reactions of flight, chirping, and cheeping. A slightly different silhouette will produce no reaction. The same goes for the triggering of sexual behavior. It's very easy to deceive both the male and the female stickleback. The dorsal aspect of the stickleback assumes a certain color in one of the partners at the time of parade, which triggers in the other the cycle of behavior finally culminating in their mating.

There is no reason for this borderline I was speaking about between eros and the aggressive relation in man not to exist in animals, and it is brought out clearly, and it is quite possible to make it manifest, even to externalize it, in the stickleback.

The stickleback is in fact territorial. This is particularly important when it comes to the period of parade, which requires a certain amount of space on the more or less grassy river-beds. An actual dance takes place, a sort of nuptial flight, in which the female is initially charmed, then gently induced to surrender herself and set up house in a sort of small tunnel that has been previously built for her. But there is something else again that is not all that well understood, which is that once all this has been accomplished, the male will still find time to dig a lot of little holes about the place.

109 I do not know if you recall the phenomenology of the hole in *Being and Nothingness,* but you know the importance that Sartre ascribes to it in the psychology of the human being, the bourgeois particularly, amusing himself at the sea-side. Sartre has observed here an essential phenomenon that is close to bordering on one of these artificial manifestations of negativity. Well then, I believe that the male stickleback is no slouch in this matter. He too digs his little holes and impregnates his surroundings with his very own negativity. With these holes one really gets the impression that he is appropriating a certain field within his surroundings and, in effect, there is no question of any other male entering the area thus marked without triggering fight reflexes.

Now, experimenters, full of curiosity, have tried to discover the extension of the said fight reaction, first by varying the distance of the rival's approach, then by replacing this character with a decoy. In both cases they observed that in fact the sinking of these holes, dug during the parade, or even beforehand, is an act essentially tied to the erotic behavior. Should the invader come closer than a certain distance from the area defined as territory, this produces the reaction of attack in the male. If the invader is a bit further off, it is not produced. There is thus a point, a borderline defined by a certain distance, at which the stickleback subject finds itself caught between attacking and not attacking. And what happens then? – this erotic manifestation of negativity, this activity of sexual behavior that consists in digging holes.

In other words, when the male stickleback does not know what to do at the level of his relation with his counterpart of the same sex, when he does not know whether or not to attack, he takes to doing something that he does when he's making love.[4] This displacement, which has not failed to strike ethologists, is in no way peculiar to the stickleback. It is a common occur-

[4] See Konrad Lorenz, *King Solomon's Ring,* 26–29.

rence for birds suddenly to cease fighting and for one bird to start madly glossing its wings, just as it would normally do when it is trying to please a female.

It is curious that although he has not participated in my seminars Konrad Lorenz thought it necessary to place a very pretty and enigmatic picture of a male stickleback before a mirror at the front of his book. What is it doing? It is lowering its nose, it's adopting an oblique stance, tail in the air, nose down, a position it only ever adopts when it's going to stick its nose in the sand to dig holes. In other words, it's not indifferent to its own image in the mirror, even if this image does not introduce the whole cycle of erotic behaviour the effect of which would be to produce in the stickleback that borderline reaction between eros and aggressiveness that is indicated by digging holes.

Animals are equally accessible to the enigma of a decoy. The decoy places 110
them in a clearly artificial and ambiguous situation which already contains a derangement and a displacement of behavior. We should not be astonished at this once we have grasped the importance for man of his own specular image.

This image is functionally essential for man, in that it provides him with the orthopedic complement of that native insufficiency, constitutive confusion or disharmony, that is linked to his prematurity at birth. He will never be completely unified precisely because this is brought about in an alienating way, in the form of a foreign image which institutes an original psychical function. The aggressive tension of this *either me or the other* is entirely integrated into every kind of imaginary functioning in man.

Let us try to picture what consequences follow from the imaginary character of human behavior. This question is itself imaginary, mythical, for the reason that human behavior is never purely and simply reduced to the imaginary relation. Let us imagine for a moment a human being, in a sort of Eden in reverse, entirely reduced to this capture that is both assimilating and dissimulating in his relations with his counterparts. What happens as a result?

By way of illustration, I have already had occasion to refer to the domain of these little animal-like machines that for some time we have been having fun creating. There's of course no resemblance at all, but they contain mechanisms which have been set up for the study of a number of types of behavior which are said to be comparable to types of animal behavior. This is true in one sense, and a part of this behaviour may be studied as something unpredictable, which is interesting because it coincides with conceptions we are able to form of a self-feeding mechanism.

Imagine a machine that has no mechanism for overall self-regulation, so that the organ designed to make the right leg walk was unable to coordinate with the one that makes the left leg walk unless a photo-electric receiver transmits the image of another machine functioning in a coordinated way.

Think of these little automobiles that you see at fairs going round at full tilt out in an open space, where the principal amusement is to bump into the others. If these dodg'em cars give so much pleasure, it is because bumping into one another must be something fundamental in the human being. What would happen if a certain number of little machines like those I describe were
111 put onto the track? Each one being unified and regulated by the sight of another, it is not mathematically impossible to imagine that we would end up with all the little machines accumulated in the center of the track, blocked in a conglomeration the size of which would only be limited by the external resistance of the panelwork. A collision, everything smashed to a pulp.

This is only a fable designed to show you that the ambiguity and the gap in the imaginary relation require something that maintains a relation, a function, and a distance. This is the very meaning of the Oedipus complex.

The Oedipus complex means that the imaginary, in itself an incestuous and conflictual relation, is doomed to conflict and ruin. In order for the human being to be able to establish the most natural of relations, that between male and female, a third party has to intervene, one that is the image of something successful, the model of some harmony. This does not go far enough – there has to be a law, a chain, a symbolic order, the intervention of the order of speech, that is, of the father. Not the natural father, but what is called the father. The order that prevents the collision and explosion of the situation as a whole is founded on the existence of this name of the father.

I emphasize this. The symbolic order has to be conceived as something superimposed, without which no animal life would be possible for this misshapen subject that man is. This, in any case, is how things are given to us today, and everything tends to suggest that it has always been like this. Indeed, whenever we find a skeleton we call it human if it has been placed in a grave. What reason can there be for placing this debris within a stone enclosure? For this to be possible a whole symbolic order must have already been instituted, which entails that the fact that a gentleman has been Mr. So-and-so in the social order requires that this be indicated on his headstone. The fact that he was called Mr. So-and-so extends beyond his living existence. This doesn't presuppose belief in the immortality of the soul, but simply that his name has nothing to do with his living existence, that it extends and perpetuates itself beyond it.

If you do not see that Freud's originality is to have brought this into relief, one wonders what you are doing in analysis. It is only after it has been clearly indicated that this is where the essential source is that a text like the one we are reading can become interesting.

To take what President Schreber presents in its structural phenomenology, you must first off have this schema in your head, which entails that the symbolic order subsists as such outside the subject, as distinct from, determin-

ing, his existence. Things bring one to a halt only when one considers them as possible. Otherwise one is happy to say, *This is how things are,* and one 112
does not even try to see that this is how things are.

3

The long and remarkable observation that makes up Schreber's *Memoirs* is no doubt exceptional, but it is certainly not unique. It is probably unique only because President Schreber was in a position to have his book published, although censored, and also because Freud became interested in it.

Now that you have got the function of symbolic articulation into your heads you will be more sensitive to this truly imaginary invasion of subjectivity that Schreber has us observe. There is an altogether striking predominance of the mirror relationship, a notable dissolution of the other qua identity. All the protagonists he talks about – when he does do this, for there is a long period during which he is unable to speak, and we shall return to the meaning of this period – divide into two categories which despite everything are on the same side of a certain border. There are those who are apparently alive and who are free to move about, his guards and his nurses, and who are the *fleeting-improvised-men – les ombres d'hommes bâclés à la six-quatre-deux*, as Pichon has put it, who is responsible for this translation – and then there are the more important protagonists, who invade Schreber's body, who are the souls, the majority of souls, and the longer this goes on, the more they are ultimately corpses.

The subject himself is only a second copy of his own identity. At a particular moment he has the revelation that the previous year his own death had occurred and that it was announced in the newspapers. Schreber remembers this former colleague as someone more gifted than he. He is an other. But he is nevertheless the same, who remembers the other. This fragmentation of identity brands all Schreber's relations with his counterparts on the imaginary level.[5] At other times he speaks of Flechsig, who is also dead and who has therefore ascended to where only souls exist, insofar as they are human, in a beyond where they are assimilated bit by bit into the grand divine unity, not without having gradually lost their individual characters. Before achieving this they still have to undergo a trial to free them from the impurity of their passions, from what is properly called their desire. There is literally a fragmentation of their identity, and the subject is undoubtedly shocked by this attack upon their personal identity, but this is how it is, *I can only bear witness,* he says, *to things that have been revealed to me*. And so we see, throughout 113
this entire history, a fragmented Flechsig, a superior Flechsig, the luminous

[5] See Mem, 73.

Flechsig, and an inferior part that ends up fragmented into between forty and sixty little souls.[6]

I shall pass over many things full of details that I would love you to take enough interest in for us to be able to follow them closely. Concerning his style, and its great strength of affirmation, typical of delusional discourse, we cannot but be struck by its convergence with the notion that the imaginary identity of the other has a profound relation to the possibility of fragmentation and segmentation. That the other is structurally multipliable and divisible is clearly manifested here in this delusion.

There is also the telescoping of these images inside one another. On the one hand one finds multiple identities of the one same character, on the other there are these little enigmatic identities, variously piercing and harmful inside him, that, for example, he calls little men. This fantasmatic has often struck the imagination of psychoanalysts, who have sought to discover whether they are children, or spermatozoa, or something else. Why couldn't they just be little men?

These identities, which in relation to his own identity have the value of an instance,[7] penetrate, inhabit, and divide Schreber himself. The notion he has of these images suggests to him that they are getting thinner and thinner, becoming reabsorbed in some way by Schreber's own resistance. They maintain themselves in their autonomy, which moreover means that they can continue to harm him, only through realizing the operation that he calls the tying-to-celestial-bodies,[8] a notion he would not have without the fundamental language.

This is not just the soil, these bodies are also the planetary bodies, the astral bodies. You can see this register which, in my little magic square of the other day, I was calling that of the heavenly bodies. I didn't invent it for the occasion; I have been speaking for a long time of the function of heavenly bodies in human reality. It is clearly not for nothing that always, and in all cultures, the names given to the constellations play an essential role in establishing a certain number of fundamental symbolic relationships, which become increasingly evident as we find ourselves in the presence of a more primitive culture, as we say.

A soul fragment thus ties itself on somewhere. Cassiopeia, *the brothers of Cassiopeia,* play a major role here.[9] In no way is this an idea pulled out of the air – it is the name of a student confederation from the time of Schreber's
114 studies. An attachment to such a fraternity, whose narcissistic, even homo-

[6] Mem, 111.

[7] Or agency, "*instance.*"

[8] "*attachement aux terres,*" "*Anbinden an Erden,*" Mem, 125. As the following paragraph makes clear, "*terre*" and "*Erde*" also have the meaning of soil or earth.

[9] Mem, 58.

sexual, character is brought out in the analysis, is moreover a characteristic mark of Schreber's imaginary antecedents.

It is suggestive to see how this network, which is symbolic by nature and maintains the image in a degree of stability in interhuman relationships, is necessary so that everything doesn't suddenly reduce to nothing, so that the entire veil of the imaginary relation does not suddenly draw back and disappear in the yawning blackness that Schreber was not so very far away from at the outset.

Psychoanalysts have caviled, employing all sorts of details, over what meaning, from the point of view of the subject's libidinal investments, the fact might have that at one stage it's Flechsig who dominates, at another it's a divine image, which is variously located in the realms of God, since God has his realms too – there is an anterior and a posterior realm. You can imagine how analysts have fiddled around with that. Of course, these phenomena are not incapable of being given a number of interpretations. But there is a register that outweighs them all, and that doesn't seem to have caught anyone's attention – as rich and amusing as this fantasmagoria is, as supple, also, in that we have located in it the various objects of the little analytic game, there are extremely nuanced auditory phenomena all throughout Schreber's delusion.

These range from low whispers to the voice of waters[10] when at night he encounters Ahriman. He subsequently corrects himself by the way – Ahriman wasn't the only one present, Ormuzd must have been there also, since the gods of good and evil are inseparable.[11] Thus he has a momentary encounter with Ahriman when he sees him with his mind's eye and not, as with some of his other visions, with a photographic clarity. He comes face to face with this God, who says the significant word to him, the one that puts all things in their place, the divine message *par excellence*. He says to Schreber, the only man remaining after the twilight of the world – *Wretch*.[12]

This translation is perhaps not exactly equivalent to the German word *Luder*. *Charogne* is the word the French translation uses, but the word is more informal in German than it is in French. In French it is rare to call your friends *charogne, carrion,* except at particularly exuberant moments. The German word does not just convey this element of annihilation, there are undercurrents that make it more akin to a word that would be more in the style of the feminization of the person, more frequently encountered in conversations between friends, that of being rotten, sweet rottenness [*douce pourriture*]. The

[10] *"la voix des eaux."* It's not clear what this means. Schreber speaks of a voice that "resounded in a mighty bass as if directly in front of my bedroom window." Mem, 136.

[11] Mem, 139 n.66.

[12] Mem, 136.

important thing is that this word which dominates his unique face-to-face encounter with God is not at all isolated. Insults are very frequent in the divine partner's relations with Schreber, as in an erotic relationship that one initially refuses to take part in and resists. This is the other face, the counterpart, of the imaginary world. The annihilating insult is a culminating point, it is one of the peaks of the speech act.

Around this peak all the mountain chains of the verbal field are laid out for you in a masterly perspective by Schreber. Everything that a linguist could imagine as decompositions of the function of language is encountered in what Schreber experiences, which he differentiates with a lightness of touch, in nuances that leave nothing to be desired as to their information.

When he speaks to us about things that belong to the fundamental language and bring order to the relationships he has with the one and only being that henceforth exists for him, he divides them into two categories. There is on the one hand what is *echt*, an almost untranslatable word, which means authentic, true, and which is always given to him in verbal forms worthy of our attention – there are several species of these, and they are very suggestive. There is on the other hand what is learned by rote, inculcated into a number of the peripheral, even fallen, elements of the divine power, and repeated with a total absence of sense, uniquely as a refrain. Added to this there is an extraordinary variety of modes of oratory flux which enable us to see in isolation the various dimensions in which the phenomenon of the sentence – I am not saying the phenomenon of meaning – unfolds.

Here we go to the heart of the function of the sentence in itself, insofar as it does not necessarily carry its meaning with it. I am thinking of this phenomenon of sentences that emerge in his asubjectivity as interrupted, leaving the sense in suspense. A sentence interrupted in the middle is auditivated.[13] The rest is implied meaning. The interruption evokes a fall which, while it may be indeterminate over a wide range, cannot be just any old one. Here the symbolic chain is emphasized in its dimension of continuity.

Here, both in the subject's relation to language and in the imaginary world, there is a danger, which he is constantly aware of, that all this fantasmagoria might be reduced to a unity which doesn't annihilate his existence, but God's, which is essentially language. Schreber states this explicitly – the rays must speak.[14] It is at all times necessary to produce diversionary phenomena so that God is not absorbed back into the central existence of the subject. This isn't self-evident but well illustrates the creator's relationship to what he cre-

[13] *"auditiver":* The meaning is unclear, but the context would suggest it means "to make audible."

[14] Mem, 130.

ates. The withdrawal of his function and his essence effectively allows the corresponding nothing that is his lining to appear.

Either speech is produced or it isn't. If it is, it is to a certain extent pro- 116
duced at the discretion of the subject. Hence the subject is here the creator, but he is also attached to the other, not as object, image, or shadow of an object, but to the other in his essential dimension which is always more or less passed over by us, to this other who is irreducible to anything other than the notion of another subject, that is, to the other qua *he*. What characterizes Schreber's world is that this *he* is lost, and only the *you* remains.

The notion of subject is correlative to the existence of someone of whom I think – *It's he who did that!* Not him, whom I see here, who of course has such an air of innocence, but him, the one who isn't here. This *he* is the guarantor of my being, without this *he* my being could not even be an *I*. The drama of the relationship with the *he* underlies the entire dissolution of Schreber's world, where we see the *he* reduced to a single partner, this God who is asexual and polysexual at one and the same time, englobing all that still exists in the world Schreber is confronted with.

To be sure, owing to this God there subsists someone able to speak true speech, but this speech has the property of always being enigmatic. This is characteristic of all speech in the fundamental language.

Moreover, this God also appears to be Schreber's shadow. He is tainted by an imaginary degradation of otherness, and as a result he is, like Schreber, stricken with a sort of feminization.

In any case, since we don't know Schreber the subject, we have to study him via the phenomenology of his language. It is therefore around the phenomenon of language, around the more or less hallucinated, parasitic, foreign, intuitive, and persecutory phenomena of language at issue in the case of Schreber, that we are going to shed light on a new dimension in the phenomenology of the psychoses.

18 January 1956

117

VIII

The symbolic sentence

THE NOTION OF DEFENSE
THE PATIENT'S TESTIMONY
THE SENSE OF REALITY
VERBAL PHENOMENA

We could, all the same, end up making a start on Schreber's text together, because the Schreber case for us is also Schreber's text.

This year I'm trying to gain a better conception of the economy of the case. You must have some sense of the shift that is slowly taking place in psychoanalytic conceptions. The other day I reminded you that Freud's explanation, briefly put, is that the patient enters an essentially narcissistic economy. This is a very rich idea, all the consequences of which should be drawn out, except nobody ever does, and one forgets what narcissism is at the point in his work Freud has got to when he writes the Schreber case. Consequently, nobody has a clear idea, either, how novel this explanation is, that is, of what other explanation it is to be situated in relation to.

I shall return to one of the authors who have spoken in the greatest detail about the question of the psychoses, namely, Katan. He emphasizes the notion of defense. But I don't want to proceed by means of commentaries on commentaries. We have to start with the book, as Freud recommends.

Since we are psychiatrists, or at least people who are in various ways familiar with psychiatry, it's quite natural that to get an idea of what is taking place in this case we should also read with the eyes of psychiatrists.

1

We must not forget the stages in the introduction of the notion of narcissism
118 in Freud's thought. The word *defense* is used today to refer to anything and everything, in the belief that one is repeating something with a long history in Freud's work. It's quite true that the notion of defense plays a role very early on and that from 1894–95 onwards Freud proposes the expression *neuropsychoses of defense*. But he uses this term in a quite specific sense.

When he speaks of *Abwehrhysterie*, he distinguishes it from two other types of hysteria, and this is the first attempt to carry out a properly psychoanalytic nosography. Look at the article I'm alluding to.[1] According to Breuer hysterias have to be thought of as a secondary production of hypnoid states, dependent on a certain fertile moment which corresponds to a disturbance of consciousness in the hypnoid state. Freud doesn't deny that there are hypnoid states, he simply says – *We are not interested in this, we don't take this to be a differential feature in our nosology.*[2]

One has to understand what one is doing when one classifies. You begin by counting the number of what appear to be the colored organs of a flower, which are called petals. It's always the same, a flower presents a certain number of units that can be counted – this is a very rudimentary botany. Later, you sometimes notice that the uninformed person's petals are not petals at all, but sepals, which don't have the same function. Likewise, in what concerns us, various registers – anatomical, genetic, embryological, physiological, functional – may enter into consideration and intersect with one another. For the classification to be significant it has to be a natural one. How are we to look for what is natural?

Thus Freud didn't reject hypnoid states, he said he would not take them into account because when he was initially working things out what was important to him in the register of analytic experience was something else, namely the memory of trauma. This is what the notion of *Abwehrhysterie* consists in.

The first time the notion of defense appears we are in the register of memory and its disturbances. The important thing is what may be called the patient's little story. Is he able to articulate it verbally or not? Anna O. – whose portrait on a postage stamp someone brought along for me, for she was the Queen of social workers – called this the *talking cure.*[3]

Die Abwehrhysterie is hysteria in which things are expressed in symptoms and the discourse has to be freed. There is therefore no trace of regression, or of the theory of instincts, and yet all of psychoanalysis is already present.

Freud distinguishes yet a third species of hysteria, characteristic of which 119
is that there is also something to recount, but which is recounted nowhere. Of course, at this stage of his theorizing, it would be astonishing indeed should he tell us where this might be, but it's already sketched out perfectly well.

Freud's work is full of these prefigurations [*pierres d'attente*], and it delights me. Whenever one takes up an article of Freud's, not only is it never what one expects, but it's never anything other than very simple and admirably clear. And yet, there is not one of them that is not nourished by these enig-

[1] "The Neuro-Psychoses of Defence"; see also "Further Remarks on the Neuro-Psychoses of Defence."

[2] See "Neuro-Psychoses of Defence," SE 3:46–47.

[3] In English in the original.

matic prefigurations. It can be said that he alone, in his own lifetime, brought out the original concepts necessary for attacking and organizing the new field he was discovering. He gives us each of these concepts accompanied by a world of questions. What's so good in Freud is that he doesn't hide these questions from us. Each of these texts is a problematic text, such that to read Freud is to open these questions up again.

We always have to come back to disturbances of memory to know what the point of departure for psychoanalysis was. Even if we assume that we have gone beyond this, we have to assess the road travelled, and it would be quite astonishing indeed should we be able to allow ourselves to misrecognize history. I don't have to follow in detail the road covered between this stage and that at which Freud introduced the regression of instincts. I have done enough in previous years for me now to say simply that it's through exploring disturbances of memory, through wanting to repair the void presented by the subject's history, and through tracking down what the events of his life have become, that we have ascertained that they will lodge themselves where one does not expect them to.

I spoke last time about displacements of behavior – one realizes that it can't simply be a matter of rediscovering the mnemic, chronological localization of events, of restoring a piece of lost time, but that things also take place on the topographical level. The distinction in regression between entirely different registers is implicit here. In other words, what is constantly being forgotten is that it's not the case that if one thing comes to the fore another loses its price, its value, within topographical regression. It's here that events acquire their fundamental behavioral meaning.

And this is when narcissism was discovered. Freud realized that there are modifications to the imaginary structure of the world and that they interfere with modifications to the symbolic structure – this is really how it has to be described, since remembering necessarily takes place within the symbolic order.

120 When Freud explains delusion by a narcissistic regression of libido, with this withdrawal from objects ending in a disobjectualization, this means, at the point he has attained, that the desire that is to be recognized in delusion is situated on a completely different level from the desire that has to make itself recognized in neurosis.

If one doesn't understand this, one will completely fail to see what differentiates psychosis from neurosis. Why should it be so difficult in psychosis to restore the subject's relation to reality, when the delusion is in principle entirely legible? This, at least, is what can be read in some passages in Freud, which you have to know how to emphasize in a less summary way than is usual. Delusions are indeed legible, but they are also transcribed into another register. In neurosis, one always remains inside the symbolic order, with this duality of signifier and signified that Freud translates as the neurotic compromise. Delusions occur in a completely different register. They are legible, but there is no way out. How does this come about? This is the economic problem that remains open at the time Freud completes the Schreber case.

I'm making some large claims. In the case of the neuroses the repressed reappears *in loco* where it was repressed, that is, in the very midst of symbols, insofar as man as agent and actor integrates himself into them and participates in them. The repressed reappears *in loco* beneath a mask. The repressed in psychosis, if we know how to read Freud, reappears in another place, *in altero*, in the imaginary, without a mask. This is quite clear, it's neither new nor heterodox, it just has to be appreciated that this is the main point. This is far from being a settled issue at the time Freud puts the last full stop to his Schreber study. On the contrary, this is where the difficulties begin to appear.

Others have tried to pick up where Freud left off. Read Katan for example, who tries to give us an analytic theory of schizophrenia in volume five of the collection, *Psychoanalysis of the Child*.[4] Read it and you will see very clearly the path that analytic theory has taken.

In Freud the question of the subject's center always remains open. In the analysis of paranoia, for example, he proceeds step by step to show the evolution of an essentially libidinal disturbance, a complex play of an aggregate of transferable, transmutable desires, which may regress, and the center of this entire dialectic is still problematic for us. Now, the turn that took place in analysis at around the time of Freud's death led to the rediscovery of this good old ever-lasting center, the ego at the controls, guiding defense. Psychosis is no longer interpreted on the basis of the complex economy of the dynamics of the drives, but on the basis of procedures used by the ego to escape from various requirements, to defend itself against the drives. The 121
ego again becomes not only the center but the cause of the disorder.

Henceforth the term *defense* makes no more sense than does talk of defending oneself against temptation, and the entire dynamics of the Schreber case are explained to us on the basis of the ego's efforts to escape from a so-called homosexual drive threatening its completeness. Castration no longer has any other symbolic meaning than that of a loss of physical integrity. We are solemnly told that the ego, which is not yet strong enough to establish points of attachment in the external milieu in order to exercise its defense against the drives in the id, finds another resource, that is, it foments this neo-production we call a hallucination, which is another way of acting and transforming its dual instincts – sublimation, in its own way, but with serious drawbacks.

The narrowing of perspective, the clinical inadequacies of this construction, are self-evident. That there exists an imaginary way of satisfying the

[4] "Structural Aspects of a Case of Schizophrenia."

thrust[5] of need is an explicit notion in Freudian theory, but it's only ever taken as one of the elements that occasion the phenomena. Freud never defined hallucinatory psychosis on the simple model of fantasy, like hunger which can be satisfied by a dream of satisfaction of hunger. A delusion in no way serves such an end. It is always pleasing to rediscover what one has previously pictured to oneself, and Freud even teaches us that this is the path that the creation of the world of human objects takes. We, too, always experience great satisfaction in rediscovering certain neurotic symbolic themes in psychosis. There is nothing illegitimate in this, but one really must recognize that it only covers a tiny bit of the picture.

For Schreber, as for homosexuals, it's possible to summarize the imaginary transformation of the homosexual thrust into a delusion that makes the subject the wife of God, the repository of good will and divine good manners. This summary is fairly convincing, and all sorts of refined modulations can be found to justify it in the text itself. Similarly, the distinction I drew last time between the realization of repressed desire on the symbolic level in neurosis and on the imaginary level in psychosis is already fairly satisfactory, but it doesn't satisfy us. Why not? Because this isn't all there is to psychosis, which isn't the development of an imaginary, fantasmatic relationship with the external world.

Today I would simply like to get you to see how massive the phenomenon is.

Does the entire delusion consist of the dialogue of this unique Schreber, who, with his enigmatic partner, the Schreberian God, is the starting point
122 for the regeneration of humanity through the birth of a new Schreberian generation? No, it doesn't. Not only is this not the whole delusion, but it's quite impossible to understand it entirely at this level. It's rather curious that in only retaining what is clear in the imaginary events, people happily accept such a partial explanation of a massive phenomenon like psychosis. If we wish to make any progress in understanding psychosis, we must develop a theory that justifies the bulk of these phenomena, several samples of which I shall give you this morning.

2

We shall begin at the end and attempt to understand by working backwards. If I adopt this course, it's not simply contrived for the presentation but also suits the matter at hand.

Here you have a subject who was ill from 1883 to 1884, who then had eight

[5] *"Poussée"* translates Freud's *"Drang,"* pressure, one of the four elements of the drive.

years respite and, at the end of the ninth year after the start of the first crisis, in October 1893, things in his pathology began again. He entered the same clinic directed by Dr. Flechsig in which he had been treated on the first occasion, and he remained there till mid June 1894.[6] His state was complex. The clinical aspect of it may be characterized as a hallucinatory confusion or even a hallucinatory stupor. Later on he was to give a no doubt distorted report of all that he had lived through. We speak of *confusion* to characterize his hazy recollection of certain episodes, but other elements, and specially his delusional relations with various people about him, remained sufficiently intact for him to be able to give valuable testimony about them. This is nevertheless the most obscure period of the psychosis. Take note that it's only via his delusion that we know anything about it, since we weren't there either and the medical certificates on this first period are not rich. Schreber certainly recalled it well enough at the time he started to give testimony to be able to draw distinctions here, and in particular to be able to pick out a displacement of the center of interest onto his personal relations with what he calls souls.

Souls aren't human beings, nor are they these shadows he has dealings with. They are dead human beings with whom he has special relations, connected with all sorts of feelings of bodily transformation, of being enclosed, 123
of intrusion, and of exchanges of bodies. This is a delusion in which an element of pain plays a very important role. I'm not speaking of hypochondria, which is in any case too vague a term in our vocabulary, I'm sketching the outline.

From the phenomenological point of view, and remaining cautious, we can admit that there is a state here that can be described as the twilight of the world. He is no longer amongst real beings – this *being no longer amongst* is typical, for he is amongst other much more burdensome elements. Suffering is the dominant strain in his relations with them, which involve the loss of his autonomy. This profound, intolerable disturbance of his existence motivates in him all sorts of behaviour of which he can only give us a hazy indication, but of which we get an indication by the way he is treated – he is placed under surveillance, at night he is placed in a cell, and he is deprived of all implements. At this moment he appears to be a patient in a very seriously acute state.

There is a moment of transformation, he tells us, around February–March 1894.[7] The so-called posterior realms of God take the place of the souls with which he has had dealings of the order of intrusions or somatic fragmentations. There is a metaphorical intuition here of what lies behind appearances.

6 See the chronology of events, which differs slightly from this, in SE 12:6–7.
7 Mem, 44 & chap. 7, 81ff.

These realms appear in two forms, Ormuzd and Ahriman. The pure rays also appear, behaving quite differently from the so-called tested souls, which are impure rays. Schreber refers to the profound perplexity he is left in by the effects of this apparent purity, which can only be attributed to a divine intention. They are constantly disturbed by elements arising from the tested souls, which play all sorts of tricks on the pure rays and place themselves between Schreber and their beneficial action. The tactics of the majority of these souls, motivated by very evil intentions indeed, are very precisely described – and notably those of the ringleader, Flechsig, who fragments his soul in order to redistribute the pieces in the hyperspace located between Schreber and the distant God in question.[8] *I am he who is distant,* we find this formula which has a Biblical echo in a footnote in which Schreber tells us what God has confided in him. God for Schreber isn't he who is, but he who is . . . a long way away.[9]

The pure rays speak, they are essentially speaking rays. There is an equivalence between the speaking rays, the nerves of God, plus all the particular forms they are capable of adopting, including their variously miracled forms, such as the scissors. This corresponds to a period during which what Schre-
124 ber calls the *Grundsprache* dominates, a sort of extremely vigorous High German with a tendency to express itself in euphemisms and antiphrases – a punishment for example is called a reward, and in fact punishment is a reward in its own way.[10] We shall have to return to the style of this fundamental language, so as to address again the problem of the opposite meaning of primitive words.

On this subject there remains a gross misunderstanding over what was said by Freud, who simply made the mistake of taking as his reference a linguist who was regarded as a bit advanced, but had put his finger on something correct, namely Abel. Last year M. Benveniste gave us a very valuable contribution on this, namely that it is out of the question that in a signifying system any word should designate two contradictory things at the same time. Words are made precisely for distinguishing between things. Where words exist, they are necessarily made from pairs of contraries, they are unable in themselves to join two extremes together. When we move on to meaning, it's a different matter. There is nothing astonishing in calling a deep well *altus* because, he says, from the mental starting point of Latin this starts from the bottom of the well. We only have to reflect that in German the Last Judgment is called *das Jüngste Gericht,* that is, *the youngest judgment,* which is not the image employed in France. And yet we do say, *votre petit dernier,* your little

[8] Mem, 111.
[9] Mem, 252 & n.101.
[10] Mem, 12–13.

last one, to refer to the youngest. But the Last Judgment rather suggests old age for us.

In 1894 Schreber was transported to Dr. Pierson's mental home in Coswig, where he stayed for a fortnight. This was a private mental home, and the description he gives of it shows it to be, if I may say, extremely amusing. You will recognize, from the patient's point of view, features that will not fail to delight those who have retained something of their sense of humor. It's not that it's bad, it's agreeable enough and has that aspect of the good public face of the private mental home with its character of profound neglect, about which we are spared nothing. Schreber didn't stay there long, and he was sent to the asylum in Pirna, the oldest, in the venerable sense of the word, in Germany.

Before his first illness he had been at Chemnitz, he was appointed to Leipzig, then in Dresden he was appointed President of the Court of Appeal just before his relapse. From Dresden he went to Leipzig for treatment. Coswig is located somewhere on the other side of the Elbe from Leipzig, but the place in which he spent ten years of his life is upstream on the Elbe.

When he was admitted at Pirna he was still very ill, and he only began writing his *Memoirs* in 1897–98. Given that he was in a public asylum, and that it's not unknown for decisions to be a bit slow there, from 1896 to 1898 125
he was still being placed at night in a so-called cell for dements, taking with him a pencil and some pieces of paper in a little tin-plate container, and he started to write down a few notes which he called his little studies.[11] There are in fact, over and above the work he has left us, fifty-odd small studies he refers to from time to time, which are notes he took at the time and used as his material. It's obvious that this text, which was not started before 1898 and not completed before 1903, when Schreber was released, since it includes his court case, bears witness in a more certain, more assured, manner to the terminal state of his illness. As for the rest, we don't even know when Schreber died, but only that he had a relapse in 1907 and that he was again admitted to a mental home – which is very important.[12]

We shall start at the date at which he wrote his *Memoirs*. What he is able to give evidence of at that date is already quite problematic enough to be of interest to us. Even if we don't resolve the problem of the economic function of what I called just now the phenomena of verbal alienation – let's provisionally call them verbal hallucinations – we are interested in what is distinctive about the analytic viewpoint in the analysis of a psychosis.

[11] Mem, 195–96.

[12] Schreber died April 14, 1911. See SE 12:6–7 and Franz Baumeyer, "The Schreber Case."

3

We are all disillusioned with the prevailing psychiatric point of view.

As far as a real understanding of the economy of the psychoses is concerned, we can now read a report on catatonia written around 1903 – carry out this experiment yourselves, naturally take a good study – not one step forward in the analysis of the phenomena has been made. If there is something that is distinctive about the analyst's point of view, is it to wonder, on the subject of a verbal hallucination, whether the subject hears a little bit, or a great deal, or whether it's very loud, or whether it explodes, or whether he really does hear it with his ear, or whether it comes from within, from the heart, or from the stomach?

These extremely interesting questions arise from the fact, fairly infantile in the final analysis, that we are flabbergasted that a subject should hear things that we don't. As if we don't, all of us, all of the time, have visions, as if we are never in the grip of phrases that just pop into our heads, sometimes
126 brilliant, illuminating phrases that orientate us. Obviously, we don't put them to the same use as the psychotic does.

These things take place in the verbal order, and the subject experiences them as being received by him. If, as we were taught to be at school, we are interested above all else in the question of whether it's a sensation, a perception, an apperception, or an interpretation, if in short we cleave to the elementary relation to reality in the scholarly academic register, by putting our faith in a clearly incomplete theory of knowledge, we shall lose all its value. Besides, contrary to a theory that moves from the level of sensation through that of perception to that of causation and the organization of the real, philosophy has for some time now, at least since Kant, been attempting in no uncertain terms to bring to our attention that there are different fields of reality and that the problems are expressed, organized, and raised in registers that are equally different. Consequently, the most interesting question perhaps isn't whether the speech is heard or not.

This still leaves us up in the air. What do our subjects give us three-quarters of the time? Nothing other than what we are getting them to do in suggesting to them that they reply to us. We introduce distinctions and categories which interest us, not them, into what they experience. The imposed, external character of the verbal hallucination needs to be taken into consideration on the basis of the way the patient reacts. It's not what he hears the best – as one says, in the sense in which one thinks that hearing is hearing with one's ears – that strikes him the most. Extremely vivid hallucinations remain hallucinations, recognized as such, while others that are on the contrary no less vivid endophasically are of the most decisive character for the subject and give him certainty.

The distinction I introduced at the beginning of our course between certainty and reality is what counts. It introduces us to differences which, to our mind, as analysts, are not superstructural but structural. It's a fact that this can be the case for us alone, because contrary to all other clinicians we know that speech is always there, whether articulated or not, present in an articulated state, already historicized, already caught in the network of symbolic couples and oppositions.

Some imagine that we have to totally restore the undifferentiated lived experience of the subject, the succession of images projected onto the screen of his lived experience, in order to grasp it *qua* duration, *à la* Bergson. What we apprehend clinically is never like this. The continuity in everything a subject has lived through since birth tends never to emerge and doesn't interest us in the slightest. What interests us are the decisive moments of symbolic 127
articulation, of history, but in the sense in which we say the History of France.

One day Mlle de Montpensier was at the barricades. She was there perhaps by chance, and perhaps this was of no importance from a certain point of view, but what is certain is that this is all that remains in History. She was there, and a meaning, whether true or not, has been given to her presence there.[13] Besides, the meaning is always a bit more true at the time, but it's what has become true in history that counts and operates. Either this comes about through a later reworking, or else it has already begun to be articulated at the time itself.

Well then, what we call the sense of reality [*le sentiment de réalité*] where the restoration of memories is concerned is something ambiguous, which consists essentially in the fact that a recollection – that is, a resurgence of an impression – is organized in historical continuity. Neither provides the mark of reality, both of them are required, a certain way of combining the two registers. I shall go even further – it's equally a certain mode of combining these two registers that gives the sense of unreality. Within this field whatever is a sense of reality is a sense of unreality. The sense of unreality is present only as a signal that being in reality is at issue and that one is a hair's breadth from some little thing that is still lacking. We could describe the sense of *déjà vu,* which has been such a problem for psychologists, as a homonym – it's always a symbolic key that half-opens the mainspring. *Déjà vu* occurs when a situation is lived through with a full symbolic meaning which reproduces a homologous symbolic situation that has been previously lived

[13] During the third war of the Fronde, on February 2, 1652, Mlle de Montpensier is reputed to have saved Condé's army from destruction by ordering the cannon of the Bastille to be fired against the royal troops. The importance of the Fronde in French history is to have shown the inability of the nobility and the Parlement to form a legitimate alternative to the king; it was the last serious threat to the monarchy till the Revolution of 1789.

through but forgotten, and which is lived through again without the subject's understanding it in all its detail. This is what gives the subject the impression that he has already seen the context, the scene, of the present moment. *Déjà vu* is a phenomenon extremely close to what analytic experience offers to us as the *déjà raconté,* the already recounted – except that it is its inverse. This is not situated in the order of the already recounted, but in that of the never recounted. But it's the same register.

If we admit the existence of the unconscious as Freud elaborates it, we have to suppose that this sentence, this symbolic construction, covers all human lived experience like a web, that it's always there, more or less latent, and that it's one of the necessary elements of human adaptation. The fact that this may happen without one's knowledge might have been described as outlandish for a long time, but for us this isn't so – the very idea of an unconscious thought, this great practical paradox that Freud gave, means nothing
128 else. When Freud formulated the term *unconscious thought,* adding *sit venia verbo* in his *Traumdeutung,* he was saying nothing other than that *thought* means the thing articulated in language.[14] At the level of the *Traumdeutung* there is no other interpretation of the term than this.

We could call this language internal, but this adjective already falsifies everything. This so-called internal monologue is entirely continuous with the external dialogue, and indeed this is why we can say that the unconscious is also the discourse of the Other. While there is indeed something of the order of continuity, it's not present at every instant. Here, too, one must begin to say what one means, move in the direction in which one is moving, and at the same time know how to correct it. There are properly symbolic laws of intervals, of suspension, and of resolution, there are suspensions and scansions that mark the structure of every calculation, the effect of which is that it's precisely not in a continuous manner that this internal sentence, let's say, gets registered. This structure, which is already attached to ordinary possibilities, is the very structure, or inertia, of language.

For man it is precisely a question of knowing how to get by in the face of this continuous modulation without becoming too preoccupied by it. This is why things work out in such a way that his consciousness shies away from it. However, to admit the existence of the unconscious is to say that even if consciousness shies away from it, the modulation I'm talking about, the sentence in all its complexity, continues regardless. There is no other sense than this to give to the Freudian unconscious. If this is not what it is, then it's a

[14] The expression does not appear in *The Interpretation of Dreams,* but in "Sexuality in the Aetiology of the Neuroses," SE 3:274, and in the Wolf Man case, "From the History of an Infantile Neurosis," SE 14:84.

six-legged, absolutely incomprehensible monster – incomprehensible in any case from the perspective of analysis.

Since we are looking for the functions of the ego as such, let me say that one of its tasks is precisely not to become poisoned by this sentence that always continues circulating and seeks only to re-emerge in a thousand more or less camouflaged and disturbing forms. In other words, the sentence of the Gospels, *They have ears so as not to hear*, is to be taken literally. It's a function of the ego that we do not have to perpetually listen to this articulation that organizes our actions like spoken actions. This isn't drawn from the analysis of psychosis, it's only making evident, once again, the postulates of the Freudian notion of the unconscious.

In these phenomena – let's provisionally call them teratological – of the psychoses, this is out in the open. I'm not making this the essential characteristic, any more than a while ago I was making the imaginary element the essential characteristic, but it's too often ignored that in cases of psychosis we see this sentence, this monologue, this internal discourse I was speaking to you about, reveal itself in the most highly articulated manner. We are the first to be able to grasp this because, to a certain extent, we are already prepared to hear it.

Henceforth, we have no reason to refuse to recognize his voices when the 129
subject testifies that they are something that forms a part of the very text of his lived experience.

4

Reading of the Memoirs, *pp. 308–12.*

This is what the subject tells us in a retrospective addition to his *Memoirs*. He metaphorically refers the slowing down of sentences over the years to the vast distance to which the rays of God have withdrawn. Not only is there a slowing down but also a delay, a suspension, an adjournment. It's highly significant for us that the very phenomenology under which the seamless web of the accompanying discourse presents itself changes and evolves over the years, and that the very full sense at the beginning subsequently empties itself of its sense. Moreover, the voices also make extremely curious commentaries, like this for instance – *All nonsense cancels itself out.*[15]

The structure of what happens is worth noting. Let me give you an example. He hears – *Lacking now is* . . . and then the sentence is interrupted, he hears nothing more. We only have his word for it, but for him this sentence has

[15] Mem, 312.

the implicit meaning of – *Lacking now is the leading thought.*[16] In an interrupted sentence, as such always subtly articulated grammatically, meaning is present in two ways – as anticipated on the one hand, since it's a question of its suspension, and as repeated on the other, since he invariably refers it to an impression of having already heard it.

When one enters into the analysis of language, it's important also to take some interest in the history of language. Language isn't as natural a thing as all that, and the expressions that appear to us to be self-evident can be ranked according to whether they are more or less grounded.

The voices that preoccupy Schreber with their continuous discourse are psychologists. A major part of what they recount concerns the *conception of souls,* the psychology of the human being. They contribute catalogues of registers of thought, the thoughts of all thoughts, of assertion, of reflection, of fear, they point them out, articulate them as such, and say which are regular. They also have their conception of *patterns,*[17] they are at the forefront of behaviorism. Just as on the other side of the Atlantic people are attempting
130 to explain the normal way to offer a bunch of flowers to a young girl, so too they have precise ideas on the manner in which man and woman should make advances to one another and, even, go to bed together. Schreber is nonplussed by it – *This is how it is,* he says, *though I have never seen it myself.* The text itself is reduced to rote learning or refrains that sometimes strike us as just a little embarrassing.

Concerning the interrupted sentence, *Lacking now is . . .,* I remember something that had struck me when I was reading M. Somaize, who around 1660–1670 wrote a *Dictionnaire des précieuses.*[18] To be sure, the *Précieuses* are ridiculous, but the so-called movement of the *Précieuses* is an element at least as important for the history of the language, of thought, of mores, as our dear surrealism which, as we know, doesn't amount to nothing – surely if a movement of people who handled symbols and signs in a strange way around 1920 had not occurred, we would not have the same style of poster. The movement of the *Précieuses* is much more important than one thinks from the point of view of language. Obviously, there is everything that this genius of a character called Molière recounted, but on this subject he has probably been made to say a bit more than he wanted to.[19] You have no idea how many locutions that seem perfectly natural to us today date from then. Somaize notes for example that it's the poet Saint-Amant who was the first to say *Le*

[16] Mem, 218.
[17] In English in the original.
[18] The two principal works of Baudeau de Somaize are his *Dictionnaire des précieuses* and *Grand dictionnaire historique des précieuses.*
[19] See *Les précieuses ridicules.*

mot me manque.[20] If today no one calls an armchair *les commodités de la conversation*, it's by pure chance – there are things that succeed and others that don't. These expressions that have passed into the language thus have originated in a form of conversation in salons where people were trying to introduce a more refined language.

The state of a language can be characterized as much by what is absent as by what is present. In the dialogue with the famous miracled birds you find funny things like this – they are told something like *breathlessness* and they hear *twilight*.[21] It's all pretty interesting – who among you has not heard *amnesty* and *armistice* commonly confused in language that is not especially uneducated? If I asked each of you in turn what you understand by *superstition*, for example, I'm sure that we would get a fair idea of the confusion that is possible in your minds on the subject of a word in current usage – after a while *superstructure* would end up appearing. Similarly, *epiphenomena* has a quite special meaning in medicine – Laënnec calls *epiphenomena* phenomena such as fever that are common to all illnesses.

The origin of the word *superstition* is given by Cicero in his *De natura deo-* 131
rum, which you would do well to read.[22] You can for example judge how far we are from, and also how close we are to, the problems that the classical authors raised about the nature of the gods. The *superstitiosi* were people who would pray and make sacrifices all day long so that their descendants would survive them. Superstition was the monopolizing of devotion by people in the pursuit of a goal that they regarded as essential. This tells us a great deal about the conception these people had of the notion, so important in all primitive cultures, of the continuity of one's line of descent. This reference could, perhaps, also give us the best hold on the true definition to give of *superstition*, which consists in extracting one part of the text of conduct at the expense of others. This tells us how it's related to everything that is compartmentalized, methodically displaced, in the mechanism of neurosis.

What is important is to understand what one is saying. And in order to understand what one is saying it's important to see its lining, its other side, its resonances, its significant superimpositions. Whatever they may be – and we can include every misconstrual – there is no element of chance. Whoever reflects upon the organism of language must know as much as possible and construct as complete a catalogue as possible, not only concerning a word but also a turn of phrase or a locution. Language entirely operates within ambiguity, and most of the time you know absolutely nothing about what you are

20 "The word escapes me," literally "I am missing the word."
21 "*Atemnot*" and "*Abendrot*," Mem, 210.
22 Cicero, *The Nature of the Gods*, 152–53.

saying. In your most ordinary conversations language has a purely fictional character, you give the other the feeling that you are always there, that is to say, that you are capable of producing the expected response, which bears no relation to anything whatsoever that is susceptible to being pursued any further. Nine-tenths of discourses that have effectively taken place are completely fictional in this respect.

This primordial fact is necessary to whoever wants to penetrate the economy of President Schreber and understand what this nonsense means that he himself locates within his relations with his imaginary interlocutors. This is why I invite you to make a closer examination of the evolution of the verbal phenomena in President Schreber's history, so as to be able later to link them to the libidinal displacements.

25 January 1956

IX 133

On nonsense and the structure of God

PRINCIPLES OF THE ANALYSIS OF DELUSION

DELUSIONAL INTERLOCUTION

BEING FORSAKEN

DIALOGUE AND VOLUPTUOUSNESS

GOD'S POLITICS

Regarding an expression Schreber uses, namely that voices tell him that they lack something, I remarked that such expressions don't appear out of the blue,[1] that they are born over the course of a language's history, and at a level of creation sufficiently elevated for this to have taken place within a circle interested in questions of language. These expressions appear to flow quite naturally from the given arrangement of signifiers, but their appearance at a given moment is historically verifiable.

I was saying, then, that *le mot me manque, the word escapes me,* an expression that seems so natural to us, is recorded in Somaize as having issued from the coteries of the *précieuses.* It was considered so remarkable at the time that he recorded its appearance, attributing it to Saint-Amant. I've collected nearly a hundred of these expressions – *C'est la plus naturelle des femmes,* She's the most natural of women; *Il est brouillé avec Untel,* He's fallen out with So-and-so; *Il a le sens droit,* He is a good judge; *Tour de visage,* The outline of the face; *Tour d'esprit,* Turn of mind, personal style; *Je me connais un peu en gens,* I'm quite a good judge of people; *Jouer à coup sûr,* To play with no chance of losing; *Il agit sans façons,* He acts without ceremony or in an offhand way; *Il m'a fait mille amitiés,* He was effusively friendly; *Cela est assez de mon goût,* That is quite to my taste; *Il n'entre dans aucun détail,* He doesn't go into details; *Il s'est embarqué en une mauvaise affaire,* He has embarked upon a bit of bad business; *Il pousse les gens à bout,* He drives people mad; *Sacrifier ses amis,* To sacrifice one's friends; *Cela est fort,* That is a bit much; *Faire des avances,* To make approaches or advances to someone; *Faire figure dans le monde,* To cut a figure in the world. These expressions, which seem quite natural to us and have become standard, are recorded in Somaize and also in Berry's rhetoric of 1663 as having been created in the circle of the *Précieuses.* This tells you to what extent one must avoid the illusion that language is

[1] See above, chap. 8, pp. 114–115.

modeled on a simple and direct apprehension of the real. They all presuppose a lengthy elaboration, the implications, the reductions, of the real, what we
134 might call metaphysical progress. That people act in a certain way with certain signifiers involves all sorts of presuppositions. *Le mot me manque,* for example, presupposes first of all that the word exists.

1

Today we shall take up our subject again according to the methodic principles we have laid down. To press on a little bit further into President Schreber's delusion we shall proceed by taking up his document again. Besides, we haven't got anything else.

I pointed out that the document was composed by Schreber at a period sufficiently late in his psychosis for him to be able to put his delusion into words. In this respect I have some reservations, legitimate ones, since something that we may suppose is more primitive, prior, originary, escapes us – the lived experience, the famous ineffable and incommunicable lived experience of psychosis in its primary or fertile period.

We are at liberty to be fascinated by this and to think that we have lost the best part. To deplore the fact that one has lost the best part is in general a way of neglecting what one has at hand, which is perhaps worth taking into consideration.

Why should a terminal state be any less instructive than an initial state? It's not certain that this terminal state represents a drop in value if we accept the principle that in unconscious matters the relation of the subject to the symbolic is fundamental.

This principle requires that we abandon the idea, implicit in many systems, that what the subject puts into words is an improper and always distorted enunciation of a lived experience that would be some irreducible reality. This is the hypothesis at the bottom of Blondel's *La Conscience morbide,* a good reference point I occasionally use with you. There is, according to Blondel, something so original and irreducible in the lived experience of the delusional subject that when he expresses himself he gives us something that can only be misleading. All we can do is renounce any idea of ever penetrating this impenetrable lived experience. The same psychological presupposition, implicit in what might be called the thought of our times, is indicated in the customary, and incorrect, use of the word *intellectualization*. There is, for an entire species of modern intellectual, something irreducible that intelligence is by definition bound to miss. Bergson did much to establish this dangerous prejudice.

135 One of two things has to be true. Either a delusion is in no way part of our own personal domain as analysts and has nothing to do with the unconscious,

or it's dependent upon the unconscious such as we – we've been through this together – have thought we could elaborate it over recent years.

The unconscious is fundamentally structured, woven, chained, meshed, by language. And not only does the signifier play as big a role there as the signified does, but it plays the fundamental role. In fact, what characterizes language is the system of signifiers as such. The complex play between signifier and signified raises questions that we are skirting since we aren't doing a course in linguistics here, but you have a good enough idea of it now to know that the relationship between signifier and signified is far from being, as they say in set theory, one-to-one.

The signified is not the things in their raw state, already there, given in an order open to meaning. Meaning is human discourse insofar as it always refers to another meaning. M. Saussure in his famous courses on linguistics produces a diagram with one flux that is the meaning and another that is the discourse, what we hear. This diagram illustrates that the cutting up of a sentence into its different elements already involves a certain degree of arbitrariness. These units called words undoubtedly exist, but when one looks at them closely they are not so unitary. This is of no concern here. Well then, M. de Saussure thinks that what enables the signifier to be cut up is a certain correlation between the signifier and the signified. Obviously, for it to be possible to cut the two of them up together there must be a pause.

This diagram is questionable. It's in fact clear that in the diachronic sense, across time, shifts occurs, and that at any given moment the evolving system of human meanings is being displaced and modifies the content of the signifiers, which adopt different usages. I hope I have made you feel this with the examples I gave you before. Underneath the same signifiers there have been over the course of time these shifts which prove that no one-to-one correspondence between the two systems can be established.

A system of signifiers, a language, has certain characteristics that specify the syllables, the usage of words, the locutions into which they are grouped, and this conditions what happens in the unconscious, down to its most original fabric. If the unconscious is as Freud depicts it, a pun can in itself be the linchpin that supports a symptom, a pun that doesn't exist in a related language. This is not to say that symptoms are always based on puns, but that they are always based on the existence of signifiers as such, on a complex 136
relationship of totality to totality, or more exactly of entire system to entire system, of universe of signifiers to universe of signifiers.

This is so clearly Freud's doctrine that there is no other meaning to give to his term *overdetermination*, or to his necessary requirement that for a symptom to occur there must be at least a duality, at least two conflicts at work, one current and one old. Without this fundamental duality of signifier and signified no psychoanalytic determinism is conceivable. The material linked to the old conflict is preserved in the unconscious as a potential signifier, as a virtual signifier, and then captured in the signified of the current conflict and used by it as language, that is, as a symptom.

Henceforth, when we explore delusions with the idea that they can be understood in the register of psychoanalysis, in the order of the Freudian discovery, according to the mode of thought that regarding symptoms it makes possible, you readily see that there is no reason to reject the explanation Schreber gives of his world system as being the effect of a purely verbal compromise, as a secondary elaboration of the terminal state, even if the testimony he provides is, undoubtedly, not always beyond criticism.

We are well aware that as he progresses the paranoiac retroactively rethinks his past and discovers, even in his very early years, the origin of the persecutions of which he has been the object. He can have the greatest difficulty in situating an event, and one clearly senses his tendency through a play of mirrors to project it into a past that itself becomes rather indeterminate – a past of eternal recurrence, as Schreber writes. But this isn't what is essential. A document as extensive as President Schreber's retains all its value provided we suppose a continuous and profound solidarity between the signifying elements from the beginning to the end of the delusion. In short, the final organization of the delusion enables us to grasp the primary elements that were at work – in any case it is legitimate to look for them.

It's in this respect that analysis of the delusion provides us with the subject's fundamental relationship to the register in which all the manifestations of the unconscious are organized and unfold. Perhaps it will even explain to us, if not the ultimate mechanism of psychosis, at least the subjective relationship to the symbolic order it contains. Perhaps we shall be able to understand how over the course of the evolution of the psychosis, from the time of its origin to its final stage, assuming that there is a final stage in psychosis, the subject is situated in relation to the whole symbolic, original order – an environment distinct from the real environment and from the imaginary
137 dimension, with which man is always involved, and which is constitutive of human reality.

We must not, under the pretext that the subject is deluded, proceed from the idea that his system is in conflict. There is no doubt that it is without application, that's one of the distinctive signs of delusion. In what is communicated within society it's absurd, as they say, and even extremely disturbing. A psychiatrist's first reaction to a subject who starts raving at him is to find it unpleasant. He's disturbed at hearing a gentleman make statements that are both peremptory and contrary to what one is accustomed to regarding as the normal order of causality, and his first concern in the interview is to get the little pegs back into the little holes, as Péguy would say in his late works when speaking of the experience he had taken upon himself, about these people who, when the great catastrophe declares itself, want to retain the same relationship with things as beforehand. *Proceed in an orderly manner, Sir!* they say to the patient, and the chapters are already done.

Like all discourse a delusion is to be judged first of all as a field of meaning that has organized a certain signifier, so that the first rules of a good interview, and of a good investigation of the psychoses, might be to let him speak for as long as possible. One forms an opinion afterwards. I'm not suggesting that in an observation it should always be like this, and clinicians have on the whole approached things fairly well. But the notion of an elementary phenomenon, the distinctions between hallucinations, between disorders of attention, perception, and the various levels within the order of faculties, have certainly contributed to obscuring our relationship to the delusional.

As for Schreber, he was free to speak for the good reason that no one ever said anything to him, and he had all the time in the world to write his big book for us.

2

We saw last time that Schreber introduces distinctions into his concert of voices in that they are the work of these various entities he calls the realms of God.

This plurality of agents of discourse alone raises a serious problem, since the subject nevertheless doesn't think of it as being autonomous. There are some quite beautiful bits in this text that describe these voices and give us a sense of their relationship with the divine essence. We shouldn't allow our- 138
selves to slide from there into saying that they emanate from it, because then we would be making the construction. We must follow the subject's own language, and he doesn't mention emanation.

In the copy I had in my possession there were traces in the margin of annotations by a person who must have considered himself very erudite, because he had written down a number of explanations opposite Schreber's term *emanation*. This person had no doubt heard of Plotinus, but this is one of those cases of hasty understanding one has to guard against. I don't think anything like a Plotinian emanation is involved here.[2]

In the passage I read out,[3] the noise the discourse makes – the subject insists upon this – is spoken so softly that he calls it whispering. But this discourse is always present, uninterrupted. The subject can, as he says, drown it out with his actions and his own words, but it's always ready to recommence at the same noise level.

[2] In Plotinus's theory as expounded in *The Enneads* Intelligence "emanates" from the One, and Soul "emanates" from Intelligence.

[3] Mem, 308–12.

As a working hypothesis, as they say these days, we can accept that it's not impossible that this discourse is verbalized by the subject. This is accepting a lot, perhaps too much, but let's leave that to one side for the moment. In any case, this discourse is related to what we suppose is the continuous discourse which memorizes each subject's conduct for him at every moment and is a sort of understudy to his life. Not only are we obliged to accept this hypothesis because of what we have just been taking to be the structure and fabric of the unconscious, but it's what immediate experience allows us to grasp.

Someone recounted to me, not very long ago, that they had had the following experience. The threat of being about to be run over by a car had suddenly surprised this person who, as everything indicates, possessed the necessary movements for getting out of the way. The phrase *brain damage* leapt into his head, uttered mentally, as it were. No one can say that this verbalization is an operation that forms part of the chain of reflexes for avoiding a shock that might lead to the said brain damage. On the contrary it's slightly removed from the situation, quite apart from the fact that it presupposes all sorts of determinants in the subject that make brain damage something particularly significant for him. Here you can see this latent discourse appear which is always ready to emerge and which intervenes at a level of its own, to a different score from the music of the subject's total conduct.

This discourse which is presented to the subject Schreber at the period of the illness he's describing has a dominant characteristic of *Unsinn*. But this *Unsinn* is not entirely simple. The subject who is writing and confiding in us
139 depicts himself as undergoing this discourse, but the subject who speaks – and the two are not unrelated, otherwise we wouldn't be characterizing him as mad – says some things very clearly, such as what I've already quoted to you, *Aller Unsinn hebt sich auf! All nonsense is annulled, rises, is transposed!*[4] This is what President Schreber tells us he has heard in the register of the allocution made to him by his permanent interlocutor.

This *Aufheben* is a very rich word indeed. It's the sign of implication, of a search, of a recourse proper to this *Unsinn*, which is far from being, as Kant says in his analysis of negative magnitudes,[5] a pure and simple absence, a privation of sense. This *Unsinn* is very positive and organized, it consists of interlocking contradictions, and, of course, the entire sense of our subject's delusion is located here, which makes his novel so enthralling. This *Unsinn* is what is an obstacle, is composite, continues, and is articulated in the delu-

[4] "All nonsense cancels itself out." Mem, 182–83 & 312.

[5] Immanuel Kant, "*Versuch, den Begriff der negativen Größen in die Weltweisheit einzuführen.*"

sion. Negation here is not a privation, and we shall see what it has value in relation to.

What is the connection in this discourse between the subject who speaks in these voices and the subject who reports these things to us as meaningful? This is extremely complex.

I began this demonstration last time by insisting on the significant nature of the suspension of sense produced by the fact that the voices never complete their sentences.

There is here a specific procedure by which meaning is evoked, which undoubtedly reserves for us the possibility of conceiving this meaning as a structure, the one I stressed with respect to that patient who, when she heard someone say, *Sow!* to her, whispered between her teeth, *I've just been to the butcher's* – namely the allusive voice, the subject's indirect aim. We have already managed to get a bit of an idea here of a structure that is very close to the schema we give for the relationships between the subject who speaks concretely, who sustains the discourse, and the unconscious subject who is literally present, in this hallucinatory discourse. He's present, alluded to – one can't say in a beyond, since the Other is lacking in delusion – but on this side, in a sort of internal beyond.

It would not be impossible to pursue this demonstration further. But this would be to introduce schemas too quickly, perhaps, which, if we want to proceed rigorously, might appear preconceived in relation to the data. In the content of a delusion there are sufficient data that are of easier access so that we can proceed differently and take our time.

As a matter of fact, taking one's time is a part of that attitude of good faith which I maintain is necessary if we are to make any progress on the structure of delusion. Bracketing it at the outset as psychiatric is the source of the state 140
of incomprehension in which people have always remained until now. It's assumed at the outset to be an abnormal phenomenon that is involved and, as such, one is condemned not to understand it. One defends oneself against it, one defends oneself thus against its seduction, so tangible in President Schreber, who naively asks the psychiatrist, *Aren't you sometimes afraid of going mad?* But the fact is that this is absolutely true. One of the better masters I have known had a good sense of where listening to these characters who rave on at you all day with such odd things might lead him.

Don't we analysts know that the normal subject is essentially someone who is placed in the position of not taking the greater part of his internal discourse seriously? Observe the number of things in normal subjects, including yourselves, that it's truly your fundamental occupation not to take seriously. The principal difference between you and the insane is perhaps nothing other than this. And this is why for many, even without their acknowledging it, the insane embody what we would be led to if we began to take things seriously.

So let us, without too great a fear, take our subject seriously, our President Schreber, and since we are unable at the outset to penetrate into either the aim, articulations, or ends of this singular *Unsinn*, let's try to use certain questions to explore as much of it as we can, where we aren't rudderless.

3

First, is there an interlocutor?

Yes, there is, and he's fundamentally unique. This *Einheit* [oneness] is very amusing when you think about, if we think of this text on "Logos" by Heidegger I have translated, which is going to be published in the first issue of our new journal, *La Psychanalyse*, and which identifies the logos with Heraclitus's *En* [One].[6] And in fact we shall see that Schreber's delusion is in its own way a mode of relationship between the subject and language as a whole.

What Schreber expresses shows us both the unity he feels there is in him who maintains this continuous discourse before which he feels himself to be alienated, and a plurality in the modes and in the secondary agents that he attributes to the various parts. But the unity is very fundamental, dominating, and he calls it God. We are at home here. If he says it's God, the man has his reasons. Why deny him the use of a term whose universal importance
141 we are aware of? For some this has even been one of the proofs of his existence. We well know how difficult it is to grasp what the precise content of this is for the majority of our contemporaries, so why should we more especially withhold belief from a delusional when he speaks of God?

What's striking is that Schreber is a disciple of the *Aufklärung*, he's even one of its last representatives, he spent his childhood in a family where religion was not an issue. He lists his reading – all this is valid proof for him of the seriousness of what he experiences.[7] After all, he doesn't enter into a discussion of whether he has made a mistake or not. He says, *This is how it is. It's a fact of which I have the most direct proofs, this can only be God, if the word is to have any meaning. I had never taken this word seriously before, and at the moment at which I experienced these things, I experienced God. The experience is not the guarantee of God, it's God who is the guarantee of my experience. I am speaking to you of God. I must have got it from somewhere, and as I didn't get if from the baggage of my childhood prejudices, my experience is true.*[8] He's very

[6] "Logos (Heraclitus Fragment B 50)."
[7] Mem, 63–64 & n.36.
[8] See Mem, 78–80.

clever here. Not only is he on the whole a good witness, but he commits no theological mistakes. Moreover, he's well informed, I would even say he's a good classical psychiatrist.

In his text one finds a quotation from the sixth edition of Kraepelin that he has plucked out by his own devices, which causes him to laugh at what Kraepelin marks as being a strange thing, that the delusional's experience carries a great capacity to convince.

Beware, says Schreber, *this isn't right at all. Here it's obvious that I am not the delusional the doctors say I am, because I am quite capable of reducing things not only to what people say, but even to common sense. Thus I happen to hear the noise of a train or chain-steamer, which makes a great deal of noise, and the things I think register themselves in the regular intervals between these monotonous noises, just as one modulates the thoughts that churn over inside one's head upon these noises that we are familiar with from being in a railway carriage. But I can discriminate things very well, and the voices I hear are something different again – you fail to give sufficient weight and meaning to this.*[9]

This Schreberian analysis provides us with an opportunity to criticize from within certain genetic theories about interpretation or hallucination. And there are many other examples in the text.

What is this God, then, who has revealed himself to him? First, he is presence. And his mode of presence is the speaking mode.

First, a remark. I don't need to go very far to find testimony that will show 142
the importance of the providential function for the idea subjects have of the Divinity. I'm not saying that this is the best way of approaching the thing from the theological point of view, but nevertheless, opening half by chance a book that attempts to speak of the gods of Epicurus, I read these very nicely written lines – *Ever since people have believed in gods, they have been convinced that they control human affairs, that these two aspects of faith are connected. Faith . . . is born of the many-times repeated observation that the majority of our actions do not achieve their aim, there necessarily remains a margin between our best conceived plans and their accomplishment, and thus we remain in uncertainty, the mother of hope and fear.*[10]

The text is by Father Festugière, a very fine author and extremely knowledgeable about Ancient Greece. Doubtless the slightly apologetic style of this introduction dedicated to the persistence of belief in gods is a bit distorted by its subject matter, that is, by the fact that Epicurianism was constructed around the issue of the presence of the gods in human affairs, since one can't but be astonished by the partiality of reducing the divine hypothesis to a

[9] See Mem, 309 & n.113; cf. Mem, 236–37.
[10] André Festugière, *Epicurus and his Gods,* 51.

providential function, that is, to the requirement that we be recompensed for our good intentions – when they're nice good things happen to them. But anyway, it's significant.

All the more so because there is no trace of it in Schreber, whose delusion is in large part theological and whose partner is divine. To be sure, noting an absence is less decisive than noting a presence, and the fact that something isn't there is always, in the analysis of phenomena, subject to caution. If we had more details on President Schreber's delusion, perhaps this would be contradicted. On the other hand, taking note of an absence is extraordinarily important for localizing a structure. I therefore point out to you that, whether theologically valid or not, the notion of providence, of an agency that rewards, so essential to the functioning of the unconscious, and which protrudes into consciousness, leaves no trace in Schreber. And consequently, let's say, to be brief, that it isn't certain that this divine erotomania is to be immediately inscribed in the register of the superego.

So, here is this God, then. We already know it's he who is always talking, who is forever talking without saying anything. This is so much so that Schreber dedicates many pages to considering what it might mean, that there is this God who talks without saying anything and who nevertheless never stops talking.

143 This troublesome function can't for one second be separated from the mode of presence that is God's. But Schreber's relationships with him are far from being limited to this, and I would now like to emphasize the fundamental and ambiguous relation Schreber has with his God, and which is situated in the same dimension as the one in which he is there, chattering away incessantly.

In a way, this relation is present from the beginning, even before God has unveiled himself, at a time when the delusion is borne by characters like Flechsig, and initially by Flechsig himself, his first therapist. The German expression that, following Freud, I shall emphasize expresses for the subject his essential mode of relationship with his fundamental interlocutor. It establishes a continuity between the initial and the final interlocutors of the delusion, in which we can recognize that there is something in common between Flechsig, the tested souls, the realms of God with their various meanings, posterior and anterior, upper and lower, and, finally, the ultimate god to whom everything appears to be reduced at the end, when Schreber has placed himself in a position of megalomania. Whether it be at the beginning of the delusion, when, as Freud emphasizes, his imminent rape, a threat to his virility, is at issue, or whether it be at the end, when an effusion of voluptuousness is established in which God is supposed to find even greater satisfaction than our subject, it's a matter of this, the greatest of atrocities, that he's going *to be forsaken*.

The translation of this *liegen lassen, laisser en plan,* is not too bad, because it has connotations of feminine sentiments. In German it's much less emphatic and it's also much broader, it's *to let lie*. Throughout the entire Schreberian delusion the threat of this *being forsaken* returns like a musical theme, like the unbroken thread one finds running through a literary or historical theme.

Right at the outset this forms part of the sinister intentions of the persecuting violators and has to be avoided at all cost. One cannot escape the impression that the subject's global relationship with the whole of the phenomena to which he is prey consists in this essentially ambivalent relation – whatever the painful, weighty, troublesome, unbearable, character of these phenomena, maintaining his relationship with them constitutes a necessity the rupture of which would have been absolutely intolerable to him. When this rupture is realized, that is, whenever he loses contact with God – whom he has relations with on two levels, an auditory one and another, more mysterious one, that of his presence, which is linked to what he calls the blessedness of the partners, and his partner's blessedness even more than his own – whenever the relationship is interrupted, whenever the withdrawal of the divine presence occurs, all sorts of variously intolerable internal phenomena 144
of tearing apart, of pain, break out.

This character with whom Schreber is involved in a twofold relation, a dialogue and an erotic relationship which are distinct and yet never disjoined, is also characterized by the fact that he has absolutely no understanding of anything that is specifically human. This feature is often quite touching in Schreber's hands. Of the questions that God asks him so as to incite him to give the response implied by the questioning itself, which Schreber never allows himself to give, he says – *These really are stupid traps that I am offered*. Schreber even elaborates all sorts of quite agreeably rationalized remarks about the dimensions of certainty, and offers an explanation. How can one successfully conceive of a God such that he understands absolutely nothing about human needs? How can one be so stupid as to believe, for example, that if I cease for an instant to think of anything, I will have become a complete idiot, have even fallen into nothingness? Yet this is what God does, taking advantage of this to withdraw. Whenever this occurs, I apply myself to some intelligent occupation and manifest my presence. For God, despite his thousand-fold experiences, to be capable of believing this, he really must be ineducable.

Schreber elaborates on this point in ways that are far from being stupid. He hypothesizes and argues in ways that wouldn't be out of place in a properly theological discussion. God being perfect and imperfectible, the very notion of progress through acquired experience is altogether unthinkable. Schreber does find this argument a bit sophistical nevertheless, since this irreducible perfection is completely cut off from things human. Contrary to the god who probes loins and hearts, Schreber's god knows things only on their surface, he sees only what he sees.[11] As to what is inside he doesn't understand a thing, but since everything is written down somewhere, on little cards, by what is called the writing-down system, he will ultimately, at the end of this totalization, nevertheless be totally informed.

Moreover, Schreber explains very well how it stands to reason that God cannot have access to things as contingent and childish as the existence of steam engines and locomotives. But all this having been recorded in the form of discourse by the souls ascending towards blessedness, God collects it together and thereby still has some idea of what happens on Earth in terms of minor inventions, from the game of diabolo to the atomic bomb. This is a very nice system, and one gets the impression that it was discovered through an extraordinarily innocent development, through the working out of significant consequences, in a harmonious and continuous unfolding through its various
145 phases, whose motor is the subject's disturbed relationship to something that affects the total functioning of language, the symbolic order, and discourse.

I can't discuss all the richness there is here. There is for example a discussion, which is extraordinarily brilliant, of God's relationship to games of chance.[12] Can God foresee what number will get drawn in a lottery? It's not a silly question, and it would be good if the people here who have a strong belief in God asked themselves the same question. The order of omniscience that is presupposed by being able to guess which little piece of paper gets drawn from a huge ball presents considerable difficulties. From the point of view of the real, the only difference between the pieces of paper in this balanced mass is a symbolic difference. It therefore has to be supposed that God enters the discourse. It's an extension of the theory of the symbolic, the imaginary, and the real.

There is one thing that this implies, which is that God's intentions are unclear. There is nothing more fascinating than to see how the delusional voice that has emerged from an indisputably original experience involves in this subject a sort of burning of language that manifests itself in the respect with which he upholds omniscience and good intentions as being essential to the Divinity. But he can't fail to see, particularly at the beginning of his delusion when these painful phenomena come at him from all sorts of harmful characters, that God has despite everything allowed it all to happen. This God practices the absolutely inadmissible politics of half-measures, of half-tormenting, in respect of which Schreber lets slip the word *perfidie*.[13] In the end one has to suppose that there is a fundamental disturbance in the univer-

[11] See Mem, 20.
[12] Mem, 258.
[13] Mem, 226.

sal order. As the voices say – *Remember that all that is worldizing implies a self contradiction.*[14] There is beauty here that I don't need to highlight for you.

We shall stop for today on this analysis of the structure of the divine person.

The next move will consist in analyzing the relation between the entire fantasmagoria and the real itself. With the symbolic register, the imaginary register, and the real register, we shall break new ground which will enable us to uncover, I hope, the nature of what is at issue in the delusional interlocution.

1 February 1956.

[14] "Don't forget that the end of the world is a contradiction in itself." Mem, 183.

147

X

On the signifier in the real and the bellowing-miracle

PSYCHIATRY'S MAIN FACT
THE DISCOURSE OF FREEDOM
THE PEACE OF THE EVENING
SUBJECTIVE TOPOLOGY

Some thought I went a bit swiftly last time in mentioning President Schreber's reflections on divine omnipotence and omniscience and appearing to endorse their appropriateness.

I was simply observing that this man, for whom the entire experience of God is discourse, was wondering about what there is to be found at the junction of the symbol and the real, that is, about what introduces the symbolic opposition into the real. Perhaps I ought to have gone on to add how remarkable it is that this was precisely what caught the patient's attention – that within the register of his experience it seemed to him difficult to see how God could foresee what numbers would be drawn in a lottery.

This remark doesn't of course exclude the criticisms that such an objection might lead to for anyone who should find himself inclined to respond. Someone pointed out to me for example that numbers are distinguishable by their spatial coordinates and that, when the problem of the principle of individuation is raised, distinguishing between individuals is based on nothing different.

As far as I was concerned, I took notice of the subject's sensitivity, in his reasoning part, to the difference there is between language as symbolic and his own permanent internal dialogue – or more exactly this oscillation in which a discourse that the subject experiences as foreign and as revealing a presence to him itself asks the questions and itself gives the answers.

It was a belief in God for which he was totally unprepared that engendered in him the experience he conveys. It was for him a question of discerning
148 what order of reality could account for this presence extending over a part of the universe – not all of it, since the divine power has no knowledge of man. Nothing of his interior, of his feeling for life, of his life itself, is comprehensible to God, who only gathers it up once everything has been transformed into infinite note-taking.[1]

[1] I.e., the *writing-down-system*.

Now, a deeply reasoning character like Schreber, confronted by an experience which for him has all the characteristics of a reality and in which he can discern the full weight of the undeniable presence of a god of language, pauses, to evoke the limits of his power, before an example that concerns a human, artificial handling of language. It concerns a future contingent, in relation to which there is a real issue of human freedom and, by the same token, of what God can't foresee.

What is of interest to us is that Schreber distinguishes between two spheres of language use, which are extremely different for him. This distinction can only have value for us within the perspective that admits the radically primary nature of the symbolic opposition between plus and minus, insofar as these are distinguished by nothing other than their opposition, though they must have material support. They nevertheless evade all real coordinates apart from the law of their equiprobability.

As soon as we introduce a game of symbolic alternation, we must effectively assume that nothing differentiates the real efficiency of one element from that of another. It isn't the result of a law of experience but of an a priori law that we have to have equal chances of selecting a plus or a minus. The game will not be considered correct unless it meets the criterion that the likelihood of outcomes be equal. In this sphere we can say that, at least at the nosological level of apprehending the term, here the symbolic yields an a priori law and introduces a type of operation that lies outside anything we could arrive at by inference from facts in the real.

1

We must constantly ask ourselves why we're so attached to the question of delusion.

To understand why, one need only recall the formula that is sometimes used, carelessly, regarding the way analysis works, namely that our leverage point is the healthy part of the ego. Is there no clearer example of the contrast in existence between a healthy part and an insane part of the ego than the delusions classically referred to as partial? Is there no more striking example 149
of this than the work of this President Schreber who offers us such a sensitive, engaging, tolerant exposition of his conception of the world and experiences, and who doesn't exhibit any less assertively the inadmissible mode of his hallucinatory experiences? Now, who is not aware – this is I would say psychiatry's main fact – that no amount of leverage on the healthy part of the ego would enable us to gain an inch of ground over the manifestly insane part?

Psychiatry's main fact, by means of which the beginner is initiated into the very existence of madness as such, leads to the abandonment of all hope of a cure by such an approach. Moreover, this is how things had always been before the arrival of psychoanalysis, whatever more or less mysterious force had been appealed to – affectivity, imagination, coenaesthesia – to explain this resistance to reducing through reason a delusion that nevertheless presents itself as fully articulated and in appearance accessible to the laws of coherent discourse. Psychoanalysis, on the other hand, gives a curious endorsement to the psychotic's delusion because it legitimates it in the same sphere as the one in which analytic experience normally operates and because it rediscovers in his discourse what it usually discovers as the discourse of the unconscious. But it still doesn't contribute any success to the experience. This discourse, which has emerged in the ego, shows itself – as articulated as it may be, and it could even be said to be in large part inverted, bracketed by *Verneinung* – to be irreducible, unmanageable, incurable.

In short, it could be said that the psychotic is a martyr of the unconscious, giving this term *martyr* its meaning, which is to be a witness. It's an open testimony. The neurotic is also a witness to the existence of the unconscious, he gives a closed testimony that has to be deciphered. The psychotic, in the sense in which he is in a first approximation an open witness, seems arrested, immobilized, in a position that leaves him incapable of authentically restoring the sense of what he witnesses and sharing it in the discourse of others.

I shall try to get you to sense the difference there is between open and closed discourse on the basis of a homology, and you will see that in the normal world of discourse there is a certain dissymmetry that already adumbrates the dissymmetry at issue in the opposition between neurosis and psychosis.

We live in a society in which slavery isn't recognized. It's nevertheless clear to any sociologist or philosopher that it has in no way been abolished. This
150 has even become the object of some fairly well-known claims. It's also clear that while bondage hasn't been abolished, one might say it has been generalized. The relationship of those known as the exploiters, in relation to the economy as a whole, is no less a relationship of bondage than that of the average man. Thus the master-slave duality is generalized within each participant in our society.

The deep-seated bondage of consciousness in this unhappy state of affairs is to be attributed to the discourse that provoked this profound social transformation. We can call this discourse the message of brotherhood. It concerns something new which didn't just appear in the world with Christianity, since Stoicism, for instance, had already laid the ground for it. In short, behind this generalized bondage there is a secret discourse, a message of liberation, which in a way subsists in a state of repression.

Does the same thing hold for what we can call the patent discourse of freedom? No, it doesn't. Some time ago an imbalance was observed between the pure and simple fact of revolt and the capacity of social action to transform. I would even say that the entire modern revolution was founded on this distinction and on the notion that the discourse of freedom was, by definition, not only ineffectual but also profoundly alienated from its aim and object, that everything probative that is linked to it is properly speaking the enemy of all progress towards freedom, to the extent that freedom can have a tendency to animate any continual movement in society. Nonetheless, this discourse of freedom is articulated deep within us all as representing a certain right of the individual to autonomy.

A certain mental breathing space seems indispensable to modern man, one in which his independence not only of any master but also of any god is affirmed, a space for his irreducible autonomy as individual, as individual existence. Here there is indeed something that merits a point-by-point comparison with a delusional discourse. It's one itself. It plays a part in the modern individual's presence in the world and in his relations with his counterparts. Surely, if I asked you to put this autonomy into words, to calculate the exact share of indefeasible freedom in the current state of affairs, and even should you answer, *the rights of man,* or *the right to happiness,* or a thousand other things, we wouldn't get very far before realizing that for each of us this is an intimate, personal discourse which is a long way from coinciding with the discourse of one's neighbor on any point whatsoever. In a word, the existence of a permanent discourse of freedom in the modern individual seems to me indisputable.

Now, how can this discourse be matched up not only with the other's 151
discourse but with his conduct as well, assuming that he tends to base it on this discourse at all? There is a truly discouraging problem here. And the facts show that there is invariably not just a coming to terms with what everyone effectively contributes, but actually resigned abandonment to reality. In the same way, our delusional Schreber, after having believed himself the sole survivor of the twilight of the world, resigns himself to acknowledging the permanent existence of external reality. He can barely explain why this reality is there, but he has to recognize that the real is indeed still there, that nothing has perceptibly altered. This for him is the strangest thing of all, since there is here an order of certainty inferior to what his delusional experience gives him, but he resigns himself to it.

To be sure, we ourselves place much less confidence in the discourse of freedom, but as soon as it's a matter of acting, in the name of freedom in particular, our attitude towards what in reality we have to endure, or towards the impossibility of our acting together to further this freedom, has entirely the character of resigned abandonment, of a renunciation of what is nevertheless an essential part of our internal discourse, namely that we have not only certain indefeasible rights but that these rights are founded on certain primary freedoms, which can be demanded for any human being in our culture.

There is something ridiculous in the effort of psychologists to reduce thought to an incipient action, or to an elided or represented action, and to seek its origins in what would put man permanently at the level of the experience of an elementary real, of a real of objects that would be his own. It's far too obvious that for each of us thought is a thing of little value which we could call vain mental rumination – but why belittle it?

We are constantly raising problems closely related to these notions of internal freedom and of the manifestation of something enclosed within oneself. This point of view comes to a dead end very quickly, given that every type of living reality immersed in the spirit of the modern world's cultural arena is essentially going round in circles. This is why one always comes back to the restricted, hesitant character of one's personal actions, and one only begins to think the problem is confused when one actually takes things in hand *qua* thinker, which is not everyone's fate. We all remain at the level of an insoluble contradiction between a discourse that is at a certain level always necessary and a reality to which, both in principle and in a way proved by experience, we fail to adjust.

152 Moreover, don't we see that analytic experience is deeply bound up with this discursive double of the subject, his discordant and ridiculous ego? The ego of every modern man?

Isn't it clear that analytic experience began with the fact that ultimately nobody feels at ease in the current state of interhuman relations in our culture? Nobody who has had to face even the smallest request for advice, however elementary, that encroaches on principles feels he is being honest. It's not simply because we are too ignorant of the subjects' lives that we are unable to tell them whether they would do better to marry or not in such and such circumstances and will, if we're honest, tend to be reticent – it's because the very meaning of marriage is for each of us a question that remains open, and open in such a way that, as to its application in a particular case, we don't feel ourselves to be in a position to give the answer when called upon to become directors of conscience. This attitude, the pertinence of which can be experienced by anyone who doesn't abandon himself for the sake of becoming a somebody and who doesn't set himself up as a moralist or as omniscient, is also the first condition to be demanded of what can be called a psychotherapist – psychotherapeutics will have taught him the risks of taking such perilous initiatives.

Analysis began precisely by refusing to take sides within the sphere of common discourse, with its profound rifts as to the essence of mores and the status of the individual in our society, precisely by avoiding this sphere. It limits itself to a different discourse, one that is inscribed in the very suffering of the being we have before us and is already articulated in something – his symptoms and his structure – that escapes him, in so far as obsessional neurosis, for instance, doesn't simply consist of symptoms but is also a structure.

Psychoanalysis never places itself at the level of the discourse of freedom, even though this discourse may always be present, constant within each of us, with our contradictions and dissonances, this discourse that is personal and yet common, and always, whether imperceptibly or not, delusional. Psychoanalysis is otherwise directed at the effect of discourse within the subject.

Henceforth, isn't the experience of a case like Schreber – or of any other patient who could give us as extensive an account of discursive structure – of such a nature as to enable us to get a bit closer to the problem of what the ego really signifies? The ego isn't reducible to a function of synthesis. It's indissolubly linked to this sort of mortmain, of a necessary and unbearable enigmatic element, that is partially constituted by the discourse of the real man we are dealing with in our experience, this foreign discourse within 153
everyone's heart in so far as one thinks of oneself as an autonomous individual.

2

Schreber's discourse has a different structure, to be sure. Schreber notes at the beginning of one of his chapters, very amusingly – *They say I'm paranoid.* As it happens, people at that time were still sufficiently bound to Kraepelin's first classification to describe him as paranoid, whereas his symptoms went much further than this. But in calling him paraphrenic Freud went further still, since paraphrenia was the name he suggested for *dementia praecox*, Bleuler's schizophrenia.[2]

Coming back to Schreber, *They say I'm paranoid, and they say that paranoiacs are people who refer everything to themselves. In this case they're mistaken, it's not I who refer everything to myself, it's he who refers everything to me, it's this God who speaks non-stop inside me, through his various agents and extensions. It's he who has the unfortunate habit, whatever I experience, of immediately pointing out to me that something is meant for me, or even that something comes from me. I can't play an aria from* The Magic Flute – Schreber is a musician – *without having him who speaks immediately attribute the corresponding feelings to me, but I don't have them myself.*[3] You can also see President Schreber become highly indignant at the fact that the voice should intervene to tell him that what he is in the process of saying concerns him. Of course, we are in a play of mirages, but this is no ordinary mirage, this Other considered as radically foreign, as errant, who intervenes so as to cause a convergence to the second degree upon the subject, an intentionalization of the external world, which the subject himself, insofar as he asserts himself as *I*, vigorously repels.

[2] Freud mentions Schreber's *paraphrenic traits*, but retains the diagnosis of paranoia. See SE 12:78.

[3] See Mem, 262–63.

We talk about hallucinations. Do we absolutely have the right to do so? They are not presented to us as such when we hear them recounted. According to the commonly received notion, which treats them as a false perception, we're dealing with something that emerges in the external world and forces itself on one as a perception, a disorder, a rupture in the text of the real. In other words, the hallucination is located in the real. The prior question is whether a verbal hallucination doesn't require a certain preliminary analysis that questions the very legitimacy of this definition.

Here I have to take the same path I've already somewhat bored you with,
154 by reminding you of the very foundations of the order of discourse and by rejecting its status as superstructure, its relationship of pure and simple reference to reality, its having the character of signs, and the equivalence that is supposed to exist between naming and the world of objects. Let's try to re-examine the question from an angle that is a bit closer to experience.

Nothing is as ambiguous as verbal hallucination. The classical analyses already give us some indication, at least for a portion of the cases, of the subject's role in their creation. This is what has been called the psychomotor verbal hallucination, and the observed adumbrations of utterances have been gleefully recorded because they offer the hope of a satisfactory rational explanation of the phenomenon of hallucination. If this problem warrants investigation, the starting point is the relationship between the mouth and the ear. This doesn't only exist between subjects, but also exists for each subject himself, who when he speaks hears himself. Having got this far, one thinks that one has already taken a step forward and gained insight into a whole lot of things. In fact, though, the remarkable sterility of the analysis of the problem of verbal hallucination is due to the inadequacy of this observation. That the subject hears what he says is precisely the point at which it's appropriate not to stop but to return to the experience of what is going on when he hears someone else.

What happens if you pay attention solely to the saying of what you hear, to the accent, or even to the regional expressions, to whatever is literal, in registering your interlocutor's discourse? You have to bring a little imagination to this, since it can perhaps never be carried out entirely, but it's very clear when a foreign language is involved – what you understand in a discourse is different from what is registered acoustically. It's even simpler if we think of deaf-mutes, who are able to receive a discourse through visual signs given by means of the fingers, according to the deaf-mute alphabet. If a deaf-mute is fascinated by the pretty hands of his interlocutor, he will fail to register the discourse the hands convey. I would add this – can it be said that properly speaking he sees what he registers, namely the sequence of signs, their opposition without which there is no sequence?

Even so, we can't stop there. As it happens, a deaf-mute, even as he registers the sequence put to him, may well understand nothing if addressed in a language he doesn't know. Like someone who hears a discourse in a foreign language, he will have seen the said sentence perfectly well, but it will be a dead sentence. The sentence becomes alive only when it conveys a meaning.

What does this mean? Even if we are quite convinced that the meaning always relates to something, that it has value only to the extent that it refers to another meaning, it's clear that the life of a sentence is very deeply bound up with the fact that the subject is listening in, that he intends this meaning for himself. What makes the sentence as understood different from the sentence as not understood, which doesn't prevent it from being heard, is precisely what the phenomenology of delusion highlights so well, namely the anticipation of meaning. 155

It's of the nature of meaning, insofar as it takes shape, continually to tend to close itself off for the listener. In other words the contribution of the listener of the discourse to the listener who is uttering it is constant and there is a link between listening and speaking which isn't external, in the sense in which one hears oneself speak, but which is located at the level of the language phenomenon itself. It's at the level at which the signifier conveys meaning, and not at the sensory level of the phenomenon, that listening and speaking are like front and back. To listen to words, to give them one's hearing, is already more or less to obey them. To obey is nothing else, it's to be on the look-out, in listening.

Let me sum this up. The sense is always moving towards something, towards another meaning, towards the closure of meaning. It always refers to something that is out ahead or that turns back upon itself, but there is a direction. Does this mean that we have no endpoint? I'm sure that this point still remains uncertain in your mind given the insistence with which I state that meaning always refers to meaning. You are wondering whether the aim of discourse, which is not simply to cover over or even conceal the world of things, but to find a foothold there from time to time, would not in the end be an irremediable failure.

Now, in no way can we consider that the fundamental endpoint is to point to a thing. There is an absolute non-equivalence between discourse and pointing. Whatever you take the ultimate element of discourse to be reduced to, you will never be able to replace it with your index finger – recall the quite correct remark by Saint Augustine. If I designate something by pointing to it, no one will ever know whether my finger is designating the object's color or its matter, or whether it's designating a stain or a crack, etc. You need words, discourse, to discern this. Discourse has an original property in comparison with pointing. But that's not where we shall find the fundamental reference of discourse. Are we looking for where it stops? Well then, it's always at the level of this problematical term called being.

156 I don't want to give an overly philosophical discourse here but want to show you for example what I mean when I tell you that discourse is essentially directed at something for which we have no other term than *being*.

I ask you, then, to think about this for a moment. You are at the close of a stormy and tiring day, you regard the darkness that is beginning to fall upon your surroundings, and something comes to mind, embodied in the expression, *the peace of the evening*.

I don't think anybody who has a normal affective life is unaware that this is something that exists and has a completely different value from the phenomenal apprehension of the close of the clamor of the day, of an attenuation of contours and passions. There is in *the peace of the evening* both a presence and a choice from everything that surrounds you.

What link is there between the expression *the peace of the evening* and what you experience? It's not absurd to ask oneself whether beings who didn't give this peace of the evening a distinct existence, who didn't formulate it verbally, could distinguish it from any of the other registers under which temporal reality may be apprehended. This might be a panic feeling, for example, over the presence of the world, an agitation that you observe at that moment in the behavior of your cat which appears to be searching left and right for the presence of a ghost, or this anxiety which, although unknown to us, we attribute to primitive peoples over the setting of the sun, when we think they are perhaps afraid that the sun will not return – which, moreover, isn't unthinkable. In short, a feeling of disquiet, of a quest. There's something here – isn't there? – that leaves intact the question of what the relationship is between this order of being, which has its existence equivalent to all sorts of other existences in our lived experience, and which is called *the peace of the evening*, and its verbal expression.

We can now observe that something quite different happens according to whether we, who have called up this peace of the evening ourselves, have formulated this expression before uttering it, or whether it takes us by surprise or interrupts us, calming the movement of agitation that dwelled within us. It's precisely when we are not listening for it, when it's outside our field and suddenly hits us from behind, that it assumes its full value, surprised as we are by this more or less endophasic, more or less inspired, expression that comes to us like a murmur from without, a manifestation of discourse insofar as it barely belongs to us, which comes as an echo of what it is that is all of a sudden significant for us in this presence, an utterance such that we don't know whether it comes from without or from within – *the peace of the evening*.

Without going to the heart of the issue of the relationship between the
157 signifier, *qua* signifier of language, and something that without it would never be named, it's noticeable that the less we express it, the less we speak, the more it speaks to us. The more foreign we are to what is at issue in this being,

the more it has a tendency to present itself to us, accompanied by this pacifying expression that presents itself as indeterminate, lying on the border between the field of our motor autonomy and this something that is said to us from outside, this something through which the world borders on speaking to us.

What does this being, or not, of language, this *the peace of the evening,* mean? To the extent that we're not expecting it, or wishing for it, or haven't even thought about it for a long time, it's essentially as a signifier that it presents itself to us. No experimentalist construction can justify its existence, there is a datum here, a certain way to take this time of the evening as a signifier, and we can be open to it or closed to it. And it's precisely insofar as we have been closed to it that we receive it through this peculiar echo phenomenon, or at least the start of it, which consists in the appearance, at the limit of the phenomenon's grip on us of what will most commonly be expressed for us by these words, *the peace of the evening.* We have now come to the limit at which discourse, if it opens onto anything beyond meaning, opens onto the signifier in the real. We shall never know, in the perfect ambiguity in which it dwells, what it owes to this marriage with discourse.

You can see how the more this signifier takes us by surprise, that is, in principle escapes us, the more it's already presented to us with a more or less appropriate fringe of discourse phenomena. Well then, the issue for us – this is the working hypothesis I propose – is to look for what there is at the center of President Schreber's experience, what he senses without knowing it at the edge of the field of his experience, at the fringe, carried away as he is in the froth created by this signifier he fails to perceive as one but which, at its limit, organizes all these phenomena.

3

I said last time that the continuity of this perpetual discourse is not only felt by the subject as a test of his capacities for discourse, but also as a challenge and a requirement in the absence of which he suddenly feels he is at the mercy of a rupture with the sole presence in the world that still exists at the time of his delusion, that of this absolute Other, this interlocutor who has 158
emptied the universe of any authentic presence. Where does the ineffable voluptuousness – a fundamental feature of the subject's life – which is attached to this discourse, stem from?

In this particularly true-to-life observation, and with an infrangible attachment to the truth, Schreber notes what happens when this discourse upon which he is painfully dependent ceases. Different phenomena from those of the continuous internal discourse arise – things slow down, there are interruptions, discontinuities, which the subject is forced to complement.

The withdrawal of the ambiguous and double god in question, who habitually presents himself in his so-called lower form, is accompanied by sensations that are very painful for the subject, but above all by four connotations of a linguistic order.[4]

In the first place, there is what he calls the bellowing-miracle. He is unable to contain a prolonged shout, which grips him so brutally that, as he himself notes, if at that instant he had had anything in his mouth it would have forced him to spit it out. He has to restrain himself if this is not to occur in public, and he is a long way from always being able to do so – quite a striking phenomenon if we see in this shouting the mouth's motor participation in speech reduced to its most extreme aspect. If there is anything by means of which speech comes to be combined with an absolutely a-signifying vocal function, and which nevertheless contains all possible signifiers, it must surely be what it is that makes us shiver in a dog's baying at the moon.

Secondly, there is the call for help, supposedly heard coming from the divine nerves that have become separated from God but that trail a sort of comet's tail behind them. In the first period, at the time of the tying-to-celestial-bodies, Schreber could not enter into effusive communion with the divine rays without having one or more tested souls leap into his mouth. But following a certain stabilization of his imaginary world, this no longer occurred. In contrast, anxiety-making phenomena recur when some of these animated entities that he is living in the midst of are, on God's withdrawal, left trailing and call out for help.

This phenomenon of the call for help is different from the bellowing. The bellowing is a pure signifier only, whereas the call for aid has a meaning, however elementary.

This isn't all. Thirdly, there are all sorts of noises from without, whatever they might be – something that happens in the corridor of the mental home, or a noise outside, a bark or a neigh which, he says, has been miracled, done expressly for him. It's always something that has a human meaning.

159 Between the vanishing meaning of the bellowing and the emission obtained from the call for help – which is not even his according to him, since it surprises him from without – we can observe a whole range of phenomena that are characterized by the outbreak of meaning. Schreber is well aware that these are real noises that he is accustomed to hearing in his surroundings, nevertheless he is convinced that they do not occur by chance just at that moment, but for his sake, on their return to abandonment in the external world, and in a way that corresponds to the intermediate periods of absorption in the delusional world.

[4] See Mem, 205–6. The fourth phenomenon, not discussed here by Lacan, consists of blasts of wind that coincide with pauses in Schreber's thinking.

The other miracles, for which he constructs an entire theory of divine creation, consist in the call of a number of living beings which in general are singing birds – as distinct from the speaking birds that form part of the divine entourage – that he sees in the garden. There are also known species of insects – the subject had an entomologist great grandfather – created quite intentionally for him by the omnipotence of divine speech. Thus between these two poles, the bellowing-miracle and the call for help, a transition occurs in which can be seen traces of the passage of the subject absorbed in an undeniably erotized link. The connotations are there – this is a male-female relationship.

The fundamental phenomenon of Schreber's delusion stabilized into an *Unsinnig,* nonsensical, field of erotized meanings. With time the subject managed to neutralize to its utmost the task he set himself, which consisted in completing the interrupted sentences. Any other way of responding, by questioning them or by insulting them, would not have been playing the game. It is necessary, he says, for me to be linked to the activity of God himself who speaks to me in his fundamental language, however absurd or humiliating the character of his questioning. Well then, whenever the subject leaves this enigmatic field, whenever a state occurs whose arrival one would think he must be wishing for as a respite, an illumination occurs on the fringe of the external world and goes through him with all the component elements of language in a dissociated form. On the one hand there is vocal activity in its most elementary form, even accompanied by a sort of feeling of disarray linked in the subject to a certain sense of shame. On the other hand there is a meaning that has the connotation of being a call for help, correlated at that moment with his abandonment and, subsequently, with this something which on our analysis ultimately appears much more hallucinatory than these language phenomena that on the whole remain entirely mysterious. Furthermore, he never calls them anything but internal speech.

Schreber describes the peculiar trajectory of the rays that precede the 160
induction of the divine words – transformed into threads of which he has a certain visual, or at least spatial, apprehension, they come towards him from the horizon, spin around inside his head, and finally stab into him from behind. All this leads us to think that this phenomenon, which is a prelude to the coming into play of the divine discourse as such, unfolds in what could be called a trans-space linked to the structure of the signifier and of meaning, a spatialization prior to any possible dualization of the phenomenon of language.

What happens when this phenomenon ceases is different. Reality becomes the support of other phenomena, those that are classically reduced to belief. If the term *hallucination* must be attributed to a transformation of reality, this is the only level at which we have the right to maintain it, if we are to preserve any coherence for our language. What indicates a hallucination is this unusual sense the subject has at the border between the sense of reality and the sense of unreality, a sense of proximate birth, of novelty – and not just of any novelty but of novelty over its use breaking through into the external world. This is not of the same order as what appears with respect to meaning or meaningfulness. It is a created reality, one that manifests itself well and truly within reality as something new. Hallucination, as the invention of reality, here constitutes the support for what the subject is experiencing.

I think today I've got you to grasp the schema I have tried to present, with all the problems it comprises.

We are inquiring into the sense to give the term *hallucination*. In order to be able to classify hallucinations in the appropriate way, it's best to observe them in the reciprocal contrasts, the complementary oppositions, that the subject himself points out. As a matter of fact, these oppositions form part of the one same subjective organization and, having been given by the subject, they have greater value than if they were provided by the observer. Moreover, one has to follow their progress over time.

I have tried to give you an idea of how in Schreber there is something that is always liable to surprise him, that never unveils itself, but is located in the order of his relations with language, of these language phenomena that the subject remains attached to by a very special compulsion and that constitute the center in which the resolution of his delusion finally results.

There is a subjective topology here based entirely upon the fact, given to us by analysis, that there may be an unconscious signifier. We need to know
161 how this unconscious signifier is situated in psychosis. It appears to be external to the subject, but it's another exteriority than the one that is evoked when hallucination and delusion are presented to us as a disturbance of reality, since the subject remains attached to it through an erotic fixation. Here we have to conceive of space speaking as such, so that the subject can't do without it without a dramatic transition in which hallucinatory phenomena appear, that is, in which reality itself is presented as affected and also as signifying.

This topographical notion tends in the same direction as the question already raised about the difference between *Verwerfung* and *Verdrängung* as to their subjective localization. What I've tried to get you to understand today constitutes a first approach to this opposition.

8 February 1956

XI 163

On the rejection of a primordial signifier

A TWIN THAT IS BIG WITH DELUSION

DAY AND NIGHT

VERWERFUNG

LETTER 52

We've been approaching the problem of the psychoses via the question of Freudian structures. This approach is a modest one, and it isn't actually going in the direction in which our investigations are pointing, namely that of the economy of the psychoses, which we are investigating through an analysis of the structure.

The structure appears in what can be called the phenomenon, in the strict sense of the term. It would be surprising if nothing of the structure were to appear in the way that, for example, the delusion presented itself. But our confidence in the analysis of the phenomenon is quite distinct from that of the phenomenological point of view, which strives to discover what it contains of reality in itself. From the point of view that guides us we don't have this a priori confidence in the phenomenon, for the simple reason that our way of proceeding is scientific and that it's the starting point of modern science not to trust the phenomena and to look for something more subsistent behind them that explains them.

One must not retreat from this word. If some time ago psychiatry took a backward step that consisted in distrusting explanation so as to extol understanding, it was because the explanatory path had led to dead ends. But we ourselves have evidence of the explanatory efficacity of analytic investigation, and it's on the assumption that here, too, an appropriate analysis of the phenomenon will lead us to the structure and the economy that we shall make advances in the domain of the psychoses.

It is not for the simple pleasures of the nosographer that we're grappling with the distinction between the neuroses and the psychoses. This distinction
is only too evident. It's by comparing the two that relationships, symmetries, 164
and contrasts will appear that will enable us to erect an admissible structure for psychosis.

Our starting point is this – the unconscious is present but not functioning. Contrary to what has been thought, the fact that it's present doesn't imply a solution but, on the contrary, a very special inertia. Furthermore, psychoanalysis doesn't consist in making thought conscious or in making the ego's defenses less paradoxical, so as to obtain what is rashly called its strengthening. This rejection of the two paths psychoanalysis took, first at its emergence and then in its present, deviated state, is almost self-evident when one explores the psychoses.

In the forthcoming journal of our Society, in its first number on language and speech, you will find this statement in the foreword – *If psychoanalysis inhabits language, in its discourse it cannot misrecognize it with impunity*. This is the whole sense of what I have been teaching you for a number of years, and this is where we are with respect to the psychoses. The emphasis on, the importance given to, language phenomena in psychosis is for us the most fruitful lesson of all.

1

The question of the *ego* is obviously primordial in the psychoses since the *ego* in its function of relating to the external world is what breaks down. It's therefore not free of paradox to want to give it the power to handle the relationship with reality and transform it for the aims of what is defined as defense.

Defense, in the cursory form in which it's currently understood, is said to be at the origin of paranoia. The *ego*, which is gaining in strength in the modern conception of analysis, in effect having the power to bring the external world into play in various ways, is in the case of psychosis said to cause a signal, intended as a warning, to appear in the external world in the form of a hallucination. Here we rediscover this archaic idea that a pressure [*poussée*] emerges which is perceived by the *ego* as dangerous.

165 I should like to remind you here of the sense of what I say regarding the *ego* and to phrase it in another way.

Whatever the appropriate role to attribute to it in psychical economy is, the ego is never alone. It always implies a strange twin, the ideal ego, which I spoke of in my seminar two years ago.[1] The most apparent phenomenology of psychosis tells us that this ideal ego speaks. It's a fantasm [*fantaisie*], but unlike the fantasm, or fantasy [*fantasme*], that we highlight in the phenomena of neurosis it's a fantasm that speaks, or more exactly, it's a spoken fantasm. This is where this character who echoes the subject's thoughts, who intervenes, spies upon him, names his actions in the sequence in which they occur, and commands them is not adequately explained by the theory of the imaginary and the specular ego.

I tried last time to show you that the ego, whatever we make of its function,

[1] See, e.g., "Ego-Ideal and Ideal Ego," chap. 11, Sem I:129–42.

and I shall go no further than to give it the function of a discourse of reality, always implies as a correlate a discourse that has nothing to do with reality. With the impertinence that, as everyone knows, is characteristic of me I designated this the discourse of freedom, essential to modern man insofar as he is structured by a certain conception of his own autonomy. I pointed out its fundamentally biased and incomplete [*partiel et partial*], inexpressible, fragmentary, differentiated, and profoundly delusional nature. I set out from this general parallel to point out to you what, in relation to the ego, is apt, in the subject fallen prey to psychosis, to proliferate into a delusion. I'm not saying it's the same thing. I'm saying it's in the same place.

There is, then, no *ego* without this twin that is, let's say, big with delusion. Our patient, who provides us with valuable images from time to time, says at one stage that he is *a leprous corpse leading another leprous corpse along behind him.*[2] A nice image indeed of the ego, since there is in the ego something that is fundamentally dead and always lined with this twin discourse. The question we are asking ourselves is this – how does it happen that this double, which only ever makes the ego half of the subject, becomes a speaking double? Who is speaking?

Is it the other whose function of reflection in the dialectic of narcissism I have expounded, the other of the imaginary part of the master-slave dialectic which we have sought in the transitivism of children, in the games of prestige in which the integration of the *socius* is put into effect, the other whom the captivating action of the total image in the counterpart encapsulates so well? Is it really this reflected other, this imaginary other, this other that for us is every counterpart in so far as he gives us our own image, captivates us by an 166
appearance, and provides the projection of our totality – is it he who is speaking?

The question is worth raising. One implicitly resolves it each time one mentions the mechanism of projection.

Projection doesn't always have the same sense, but for our part we restrict it to this imaginary transitivism by means of which when a child hits his counterpart he can say without lying – *He hit me,* because for him it's exactly the same thing. This defines an imaginary order of relations that is constantly found in all sorts of mechanisms. In this sense there is a type of jealousy by projection, one that projects onto the other the subject's unfaithful tendencies, or the accusations of unfaithfulness that he himself has to bear.

It's a rudimentary observation that delusional projection has nothing in common with this. One may well say that it, too, is a mechanism of projection in the sense that something whose source is within the subject appears without, but it's certainly not the same as the one I have just presented to

[2] Mem, 92.

you as the transitivism of evil intentions, which is much closer to so-called common or normal jealousy. One need only examine the phenomena to see this, and the distinction is fully drawn in Freud's own writings on jealousy. The mechanisms at work in psychosis are not limited to the imaginary register.

Where shall we look for them, given that they escape libidinal investment? Is it sufficient to appeal to libidinal reinvestment of the body? This mechanism, commonly held to be that of narcissism, is explicitly invoked by Freud himself to explain the phenomenon of psychosis. Briefly put, in order to mobilize the delusional relationship, it's supposed to be a matter of nothing other than enabling him, as one so quickly says, to become an object again.

From one angle this coincides with a number of the phenomena involved, but it doesn't exhaust the problem. Each and every one of us knows, provided he's a psychiatrist, that in a fully developed paranoiac there is no question of mobilizing this investment, while in schizophrenics the properly psychotic disturbance is as a rule much more extensive than in the paranoiac.

Wouldn't this be because in the imaginary order there is no way of giving a precise meaning to the term *narcissism?* Alienation is constitutive of the imaginary order. Alienation is the imaginary as such. Nothing is to be expected from the way psychosis is explored at the level of the imaginary, since the
167 imaginary mechanism is what gives psychotic alienation its form but not its dynamics.

This is the point we always get to together, and if we don't get there unarmed, if we don't give in, it's precisely because in our exploration of analytic technique, and then of beyond the pleasure principle with the structural definition of the *ego* that it implies, we have the idea that beyond the little other of the imaginary we have to admit the existence of another Other.

It's not only because we give it a capital letter that we are satisfied with it, but because we locate it as the necessary correlate of speech.

2

These premises alone cast doubt on a theory of analytic treatment that with ever-increasing insistence is reduced to a relation of two. It's henceforth captivated in the relationship between the subject's ego and the ideal ego, between the ego and the other, an other whose qualities may no doubt vary, but who will always be – experience proves it – the one unique other of the imaginary relation.

As for the supposed object relation that is to be rehabilitated, the subject is reduced to a curious experience that could be called the Kleinian substructure of the imaginary, namely, the oral complex. Of course, in a subject who isn't inclined towards alienation of his own accord this can only persist on the basis of a misunderstanding constituted by a sort of imaginary incorporation or devouring which, given that the analytic relation is a relation of speech, can only be an incorporation of the analyst's discourse. On this deviant conception analysis can't be anything other than the incorporation of the suggested, even supposed, discourse of the analyst – that is, the exact contrary of analysis.

I'm lighting my lantern and I shall therefore tell you my thesis. I'm going to tell it to you the wrong way round – that is, by situating it on this genetic level that seems to be so necessary for you to feel at ease. I shall tell you afterwards that this isn't it, but still, let's begin by saying that if this were it then it would be as I'm about to say it is.

It's a question of a thesis involving the entire psychical economy, which is important for an understanding of the confused debates still going on over
the Kleinian fantasmatic, for the refutation of certain objections made against 168
it, and also for better situating what it can truly or fruitfully contribute to an understanding of the precocity of the repressions it implies. As a matter of fact, contrary to what Freud says, that there is no repression properly so-called before the decline of the Oedipus complex, the Kleinian theory on the other hand entails the claim that repression exists right from the earliest pre-oedipal stages.

My thesis may equally throw light on a contradiction concerning autoerotism that appears insoluble in Freud himself. On the one hand he talks about the primitive object of the first mother-child relation. On the other he formulates the notion of primordial autoerotism, that is to say, of a stage, however short we suppose it to be, in which there is no external world for the child.[3]

The question is that of the human being's primordial access to his reality insofar as we assume that there is a reality correlative to him – an assumption always implied at the outset of this theme, but which we also know that we shall have in part to abandon, because there would be no question about this reality were it itself not constantly being called into question. Is there anything in man that has this both enveloping and coapted character which causes us to invent the notion of *Umwelt* for animals?

I point out to you in passing that we make use of this hypothesis concerning animals to the extent that an animal is for us an object and that there are conditions that are in fact strictly indispensable to its existence. We're happy to investigate how an animal functions so as always to be in harmony with these primordial conditions, and this is what we call an instinct, an instinc-

[3] See *Three Essays on the Theory of Sexuality*, SE 7:181–84 & 222.

tual cycle or instinctual behavior – if there are things that aren't in there, one has to assume that we can't see them, and since we can't see them we're happy, and in fact why shouldn't we be?

It's very clear that this is inadequate where man is concerned. The open and proliferating nature of his world prevents us from making it into his biological correlate. This is where I try, because it seems coherent and useful for me to do so, to differentiate for you between the three orders of the symbolic, the imaginary, and the real. It's abundantly clear that everything that our analytic experience shows us can be satisfactorily classified into these three orders of relationships, the question being at what moment each of these relationships is established.

My thesis, and perhaps it will give the answer to the enigma that for some of you my purple passage of last time on the peace of the evening seems to have consisted in, is as follows – reality is *at the outset* marked by symbolic nihilation [*néantisation*].

169 Although all of last year's work prepared us for it, I'm nevertheless going to illustrate it once again, even if only so as to come back to this peace of the evening that got such a mixed reception.

This is not a detour that, as Plato says, is discordant or lacking in analytic tone. I don't think I'm being at all innovative. If you read Freud's text on President Schreber you will see that, as a clinical argument for understanding the said President, he explores the function that Nietzsche's saga in his *Zarathustra*, called *Before the dawn*, played for another patient of his.[4] If you refer to this moment – it was precisely so as not to read it out to you that I indulged in this invocation of the peace of the evening – you will see the same thing represented I wanted to bring to your attention a week ago, which I'm going to put to you again now in speaking to you about daytime.

The day is a being distinct from all the objects it contains and manifests, it's probably even more weighty and more present than any of them, and it's impossible to think of it, even in the most primitive human experience, as the simple return of an experience.

It suffices to mention the prevalence of a rhythm of sleep in the first few months of human life for us to have all sorts of reasons to believe that it isn't due to any empirical apprehension that at a given moment – this is how I illustrate the initial symbolic nihilations – the human being detaches itself from the day. The human being is not, as everything leads us to think is the case for the animal, simply immersed in a phenomenon such as that of the alternation of day and night. The human being poses the day as such, and the day thereby becomes presence of the day – against a background that is not a background of concrete nighttime, but of possible absence of daytime,

[4] SE 12:54–55.

where the night dwells, and *vice versa* moreover. Very early on, day and night are signifying codes, not experiences. They are connotations, and the empirical and concrete day only comes forth as an imaginary correlative, originally, very early on.

That's my supposition, and seeing that I speak from the genetic point of view, I don't otherwise have to justify it in experience. It's structurally necessary to admit a primitive stage in which the world of signifiers as such appears.

Since this level leaves you somewhat confused, I will put things to you dogmatically, which I detest doing – you know my style is dialectical.

Before a child can learn to articulate language, we have to assume that signifiers, which are already of the symbolic order, have appeared. When I speak of a primitive appearance of the signifier, this is something that already 170
implies language. All this does is link up with the emergence of this being that is nowhere, the day. The day *qua* day is not a phenomenon, the day *qua* day implies symbolic connotation, the fundamental alternation of the vocal connoting presence and absence, on which Freud hinges his whole notion of beyond the pleasure principle.

It's exactly this field of symbolic articulation that I'm currently aiming at in my discourse, and it's here that *Verwerfung* occurs.

I'm delighted by the fact that some of you are bothered by this subject of *Verwerfung*. After all, Freud doesn't mention it very often, and I have gone and dug it out of the two or three crannies where the tip of an ear is showing, and even sometimes those where nothing at all is showing, but where the comprehension of the text demands that one assume it is there.

On the subject of *Verwerfung,* Freud says that *the subject did not want to know anything about castration, even in the sense of repression.*[5] As a matter of fact, in the sense of repression one still knows something about the very thing one doesn't want, in some sense, to know anything about, and the whole of analysis consists in showing us that one knows it very well indeed. If there are things the patient wants to know nothing about, even in the sense of repression, another mechanism is implied. And as the word *Verwerfung* appears in direct connection with this sentence as well as several pages before, I grab it. I set no great store by the term, I set store by what it means, and this is what I believe Freud meant.

It has been objected to me, most pertinently I must say, that the closer one gets to the text the less one manages to understand it. This is indeed why a text has to be brought to life by what follows and by what precedes. It's always by means of what follows that a text has to be understood.

Those who make the most objections to me suggest, incidentally, that I

[5] See above, chap. 1, 12 & n.10.

look in some of Freud's other texts at something that might not be *Verwerfung* but, for instance, *Verleugnung* – it's strange to see the proliferation of this *Ver* in Freud. I have never given you any purely semantic lesson on Freud's vocabulary, but I assure you that I could serve up a good dozen of them straightaway. I would begin by talking about the banking connotations of all these terms, *conversion, displacement,*[6] etc., and this would take us a long way, right into the major implications of this direct approach Freud had to the phenomena of neurosis. But we can't spend forever on these different approaches. Trust me a bit concerning this work on the sense. I have chosen *Verwerfung* to make myself understood because it's the fruit of long reflection, my work leads me to it. At least for a while, take my honey such as I offer it to you and try to put it to some use.

171 This *Verwerfung* is implicated in the text *Die Verneinung,* which M. Jean Hyppolite presented here two years ago, and this is why I have chosen to publish his presentation in the first number of the review *La Psychanalyse.*[7] There you will be able to see, with text in hand, whether or not we were right, Hyppolite and I, to set off down the path of *Verneinung.*

Freud's text, undeniably brilliant, is far from being satisfactory. It mixes everything up. This has nothing to do with a *Verdrängung.*

What is at issue when I speak of *Verwerfung?* At issue is the rejection of a primordial signifier into the outer shadows, a signifier that will henceforth be missing at this level. Here you have the fundamental mechanism that I posit as being at the basis of paranoia. It's a matter of a primordial process of exclusion of an original within, which is not a bodily within but that of an initial body of signifiers.

It's inside this primordial body that Freud posits the constitution of a world of reality, which is already punctuated, already structured, in terms of signifiers. Freud then describes the entire operation by which representation and these already constituted objects are brought together. The subject's initial apprehension of reality is the judgment of existence, which consists in saying – *This is not my dream or my hallucination or my representation but an object.*

It's a matter of testing the external by the internal – it's Freud saying this, not me–, a matter of the constitution of the subject's reality in a refinding of the object. The object is refound in a quest, and moreover the object one refinds is never the same. This constitution of reality, essential to the explanation of all mechanisms of repetition is registered on the basis of an initial bipartition, one that curiously coincides with certain primitive myths that evoke something primordially crippled that has been introduced into the sub-

[6] I. e., "*Konversion*" and "*Verschiebung.*"
[7] See above, chap. 1, p. 12 n.9.

ject's access to human reality. Here you have what is presupposed by this unusual priority that in *Die Verneinung* Freud attributes to what he explains analogically as a judgment of attribution, as distinct from a judgment of existence. There is in Freud's dialectic an initial division into the good and the bad that can only be understood if we interpret it as the rejection of a primordial signifier.

What does *primordial signifier* mean? It's clear that it quite precisely means nothing.

What I'm explaining to you here has all the characteristics of the myth that I was tempted to mention on that occasion and that M. Marcel Griaule recounted to you last year – namely, the division into four of the primeval placenta. The first was the fox who, tearing out his portion of the placenta, introduced an imbalance from which there stemmed the cycle that would
involve the division of the fields, the bonds of kinship, etc.[8] What I'm 172
recounting to you is also a myth, for I in no way believe that there is anywhere at all a moment, a stage, at which the subject first acquires the primitive signifier, that subsequently the play of meanings is introduced, and that after that, signifier and signified having linked arms, we then enter the domain of discourse.

All the same, there is a representation here that is so indispensable that I feel comfortable about giving it to you, so as to satisfy your demands, but also because Freud himself tends in this direction – we shall have to wait and see how.

3

In his Letter 52 to Fliess, Freud returns to the circuit of the psychical apparatus.[9]

You are, I hope, familiar with the Fliess correspondence, which has been delivered to us by certain testamentary or testimonial hands with a series of cuts and expurgations that, whatever their justification, the reader cannot fail to feel is scandalous. Nothing can justify the cutting of a text at the point at which the remainder, even if it were regarded as outdated and weaker, might enlighten us on Freud's thought.

The psychical apparatus that preoccupies Freud isn't the psychical apparatus as conceived by a professor behind a table and in front of a blackboard, who modestly gives you a model which, all things considered, looks like it

[8] This is no doubt the lecture Griaule gave on 15 March 1955 to the Société Française de Psychanalyse entitled "Symbolization of the World and the Conditions of Communication in the Sudanese." See Sem II:161.

[9] Letter of 6 December 1896, Freud-Fliess, 207–15; Letter 52, Origins, 173–81.

might work – whether it works well or poorly, it doesn't much matter, what is important is to have said something that seems in some simple way to resemble what is known as reality. For Freud, it's a matter of the psychical apparatus of his patients, not of the ideal individual, and it's this that introduces him to this really astounding productiveness that we see here, even more than anywhere else, in this famous Letter 52. What he is seeking to explain is not just any old psychical state, but that from which he set out, because it alone is accessible and proves to be fruitful in the experience of the treatment – the phenomena of memory. The schema of the psychical apparatus in Freud is invented to explain phenomena of memory, that is, what isn't going well.

You must not think that the general theories of memory that have been proposed are particularly satisfactory. Because you're psychoanalysts you're not excused from reading the works of psychologists, some have done some
173 sensible things, have discovered some remarkable discrepancies in valuable experiments – you will see their difficulty, the twists and turns they perform, in trying to explain the phenomenon of reminiscence.[10] However, Freudian experience shows that the memory which interests psychoanalysis is quite distinct from what psychologists speak of when they display its mechanism to us in an animate being in an experiment.

I shall illustrate what I mean.

The octopus. It's the most beautiful animal there is. It has played a fundamental role in Mediterranean civilizations. Nowadays it's very easy to catch. You put it into a little jar, insert electrodes, and watch. The octopus extends its limbs and, suddenly, it retracts them. And one observes that it's very soon wary of our electrodes. So we dissect it and we discover, in what serves as its head, a large nerve, large not only in size but also in the diameter of the neurons, visible under the microscope. This is what serves as its memory, that is, if you sever it in the live octopus, the apprehension of experience works much less well, a deterioration is produced in the registrations of memory, which is why it's thought this is the seat of its memory. And nowadays people tell themselves that perhaps the octopus's memory functions like a little machine, in that it's something that goes round in circles.

I'm not in the process here of distinguishing man from the animal, since what I teach you is that in man, too, memory is something that goes round in circles. However, it's made up of messages, it's a succession of little signs of plus or minus, which file in one after the other and go round and round like the little electric lights on the Place de l'Opéra that go on and off.

This is what human memory is. However, the primary process, the plea-

[10] In psychology *"réminiscence"* has the meaning of an image that comes to mind without being recognized as a memory.

sure principle, means that the psychoanalytic memory Freud talks about is, contrary to that of the octopus, something completely inaccessible to experience. What else would it mean to say that desires in the unconscious are never extinguished, because those that do become extinguished are by definition never spoken of again? There are some that are never extinguished and continue to circulate in memory. In the name of the pleasure principle, they cause the human being to recommence the same painful experiences, in cases in which things are connected to one another in memory in such a way as to persist in the unconscious. What I'm saying here is only the simple expression of what you already know in principle, but which of course is what you know as if you didn't know it. I'm not only trying to make you know it, but 174
also to get you to recognize that you know it.

Freudian memory is not located along a sort of continuum from reaction to reality considered as a source of excitation. It's striking that we have to go to all this trouble whereas this is all Freud ever speaks of – disorder, restriction, registration – this is not only the vocabulary of this letter, this is the very thing at issue. *What is essentially new in my theory,* says Freud, *is the claim that memory is not simple, it's registered in various ways.*[11]

So what are these different registers? It's here above all that this letter brings grist to my mill, which I regret, because you're going to jump on it and you're going to say to yourselves – *Yes, it's like this in this letter, but in the next one it's not like this.* It's in all the letters. It's the very soul of the development of Freud's thought. Otherwise a mass of things would be inexplicable. He would have become Jungian, for example.

So what are these registers? You're going to see something appear that you've never seen before, because until now there have been for you the unconscious, the preconscious, and the conscious. It's been known for a long time that the phenomenon of consciousness and the phenomenon of memory exclude one another. Freud stated it not only in this letter, but also in the system of the psychical apparatus he gives at the end of *The Interpretation of Dreams.*[12] It's for him a truth that absolutely cannot be called experimental, it's a necessity that imposes itself on him from the point of view of handling the system as a whole, and at the same time one feels that there is here an initial signifying a priori in his thought.

At the beginning of the circuit of psychical apprehension there is perception. This perception implies consciousness. This must be something like what he shows us in his famous metaphor of the magic writing pad.[13]

The magic writing pad is made of a sort of bluish-grey substance on which

[11] Freud-Fliess, 207; Origins, 173.
[12] See SE 5:536ff.
[13] See "A Note upon the 'Mystic Writing-Pad.' "

there sits a strip of transparent paper. You write on the strip of paper and when you lift it up there is nothing there anymore, it remains blank. On the other hand, everything you have written down reappears on the surface of the slightly adhesive substance, which enables what you write to be recorded by virtue of the fact that the tip of your pencil makes the paper adhere to this surface which, becoming darkened slightly, becomes momentarily visible. There you have, as you know, the basic metaphor by which Freud explains what he understands by the workings of perception in connection with memory.

What memory? The memory he is interested in. There are two zones in
175 this memory, that of the unconscious and that of the preconscious, and after the preconscious one sees a complete consciousness emerge which cannot but be articulated.

The requirements of his own conception of things are manifest in the fact that between the essentially ephemeral *Wahrnehmungen* [perceptions], which disappear as soon as they appear, and the constitution of the system of consciousness and, even at this stage, of the *ego* – he calls it the *official ego,* and *official* in German means the same as *officiel* in French, in the dictionary it's not even translated – there are the *Niederschriften* [registrations], of which there are three. Here we witness Freud's development of an initial apprehension of what memory might be in its analytic functioning.

Freud gives a number of chronological divisions – that there are systems formed for example between birth and one and a half, then between one and a half and four years of age, then between four and eight, etc. But despite his saying this, we aren't required to believe, any more than we did before, that these registers are constituted successively.

Why distinguish them from one another and how do they become apparent? They become apparent in the defense system, which consists in the fact that things that don't give us pleasure don't reappear in any of the registers. Thus here we are in the official economy, and this is where we don't recall what doesn't give us pleasure. This is absolutely normal. Call it defense, but it isn't pathological for all that. It's even what one has to do – if we forget things that are disagreeable to us we can only come out ahead. A notion of defense that doesn't start from this falsifies the entire question. What gives defense its pathological character is the fact that, around the famous affective regression, topographical regression takes place. A pathological defense, when produced in an uncontrolled fashion, provokes unjustifiable reverberations, because what goes for one system doesn't go for another. The disturbance stems from this confusion between mechanisms, and it's from this point on that we speak of a system of pathological defense.

To understand it properly we shall begin with the best known phenomenon, from which Freud always started, the one that explains the existence of the system *Unbewusstsein*.

The mechanism of topographical regression here is perfectly clear at the level of finished discourse, which is that of the official *ego*. Here one finds agreements and coherences between discourse, signifier, and signified superimposed upon one another, forming the intentions, the plaints, the obscurity, the confusion, in which we live and due to which, whenever we spell something out, we always have this feeling of discordance, of never being com- 176
pletely up to what we want to say. This is the reality of discourse. We are nevertheless well aware that the signified is sufficiently captured by our discourse for everyday purposes. It's when we want to do a bit better, to get to the truth, that we are in total disarray, and rightly so. It is, moreover, why most of the time we give up the game.

There is indeed a relationship between meaning and the signifier, it is what the structure of discourse supplies. Discourse, which is what you hear when you listen to me, and it does exist – the proof is that sometimes you don't understand it –, is a signifying temporal chain. But at the level of neurosis, which brought about the discovery of the realm of the Freudian unconscious *qua* register of memory, our good fellow, instead of using words, uses everything at his disposal – he empties his pockets, he turns his trousers inside out, he puts his functions, his inhibitions inside, he gets completely inside himself, with the signifier, it's he who becomes the signifier. His real, or his imaginary, enters into the discourse.

If this isn't what a neurosis is, if this isn't what Freud taught, then I give up.

In the problematic field of the phenomena of *Verneinung*, phenomena occur that must originate in a fall in level, in the passage from one register to another, and that curiously manifest themselves with the characteristic of the negated and the disavowed – it's as if they are not existent. This is a very early property of language, since the symbol is as such the connotation of presence and absence.

This doesn't exhaust the question of the function of negation within language. There is an illusion of privation that stems from the ordinary usage of *negation*. Moreover, all languages possess a whole range of negations, each worthy of separate study – negation in French, negation in Chinese, etc.

What's important is this. What appears to be a simplification in discourse harbors dynamics which escape us, are secret. There is an illusion in thinking that a *Verneinung* is observable simply in the fact that apropos of a dream the subject stresses, *It's not my father*. Everyone's familiar with this, the subject is noticeably affected by the interpretation and ends up saying that it's his father, and as we're happy with this, we don't go any further. The subject

says to you – *I don't want to tell you something that is unpleasant.* Here it's quite different. He says it nicely, but through dynamics whose immediacy is perceptible, he is in effect engaged in saying something unpleasant. It's because
177 we experience this that we are alert to the mystery that this illusion of privation can represent. Think of what Kant calls a negative value in its function, not only of privation, but of subtraction, in its true positivity.

The question of *Verneinung* remains entirely unresolved. What's important is to notice that Freud was only able to understand it by relating it to something more primitive. He expressly acknowledges in his Letter 52 that the primordial *Verneinung* comprises an initial putting into signs, *Wahrnehmungszeichen*. He admits the existence of this field I am calling that of the primordial signifier. Everything he subsequently says in this letter about the dynamics of the three great neuropsychoses that he applies himself to – hysteria, obsessional neurosis, paranoia – presupposes the existence of this primordial stage, which is the chosen locus of what for you I am calling *Verwerfung*.

In order to understand this, consider something that Freud is constantly pointing out, namely that one has to assume a prior, and at least partial, organization of language in order for memory and historicization to work. The memory phenomena that Freud is interested in are always language phenomena. In other words, one already has to have the signifying material to make anything signify at all. In *The Wolf Man* the primitive impression of the famous primoraial scene has remained over the years, serving no purpose, though already signifying, before having its word to say in the subject's history. The signifier is thus primitively given, but it remains nothing as long as the subject doesn't cause it to enter into his history, which becomes important between the ages of one and a half and four and a half. Sexual desire is effectively what man uses to historicize himself, insofar as it's at this level that the law is introduced for the first time.

You now see the general economy of what Freud gives us with his simple schema in this little letter. This is confirmed by a hundred other texts. One of you, whom I have praised for having contradicted what is being developed here, pointed out to me that the end of the text on "Fetishism" refers quite directly to what I'm now explaining to you. There Freud makes an essential revision to the distinction he had drawn between neurosis and psychosis, saying that in the psychoses reality is reworked, that a part of reality is suppressed, and that reality is never truly scotomized.[14] Ultimately, and you will see this from the context, it's to a deficiency, to a hole in the symbolic, that he is referring, even if in the German text it's the term *reality* that is used.

178 Haven't you seen what the primordial phenomenon is when I present concrete cases to you of people who have recently plunged into psychosis? I

[14] SE 21:155–56.

showed you a person who thought he had been receiving advances from a character who had become his friend and the essential point of attachment in his existence. This character withdrew, and then there he was in a state of perplexity linked to a correlate of certainty, which is how the approach to the prohibited field announces itself, access to which on its own constitutes the onset of psychosis.

How does one enter psychosis? How is the subject led, not into alienating himself in the little other, but into becoming this something which, from within the field in which nothing can be said, appeals to all the rest, to the field of everything that can be said? Isn't this something that evokes what you see displayed in the case of President Schreber – namely, these fringe phenomena at the level of reality which have become significant for the subject?

Psychotics love their delusion like they love themselves.[15] Having said this, Freud, who hadn't yet written his article on narcissism, added that the entire mystery lies here. This is true. What is the relationship between the subject and the signifier that is distinctive of the very phenomena of psychosis? How come the subject falls entirely into this problematic?

These are the issues that we are raising this year and I hope we are able to make some headway with them before the long vacation.

15 February 1956

[15] "Thus they love *their delusion as they love themselves*. That is the secret." "Draft H," Freud-Fliess, 111; Origins, 113.

ON THE SIGNIFIER AND THE SIGNIFIED

XII 181

The hysteric's question

ON THE PREVERBAL WORLD
PRECONSCIOUS AND UNCONSCIOUS
SIGN, TRACE, SIGNIFIER
A TRAUMATIC HYSTERIA

We've got to the point where the analysis of Schreber's text has led us to emphasize the importance of language phenomena in the economy of psychosis. It is in this sense that one may speak of Freudian structures of the psychoses.

1

What function do these language phenomena have in the psychoses?

It would be surprising if psychoanalysis didn't offer us a new way of treating the economy of language in the psychoses, a way that differs through and through from the traditional approach, which refers to classical psychological theories. Our own point of reference is different – it is our schema of analytic communication.

Between S and O, the fundamental speech that analysis must uncover, we have the interference of the imaginary circuit, which resists its passage. The imaginary poles of the subject, *o* and *o'*, coincide with the said specular relation, that of the mirror stage. The subject, in the corporeity and multiplicity of his organism, in his natural fragmentation, which is in *o'*, refers to this imaginary unity that is the ego, *o*, where he knows himself and misrecognizes himself [*se connaît et se méconnaît*], and which is what he speaks about – he doesn't know to whom, since he doesn't know who speaks in him either.

I used to say schematically, in the archaic period of these seminars, that
the subject begins by talking about himself, he doesn't talk to you – then, he 182
talks to you but he doesn't talk about himself – when he talks about himself, who will have noticeably changed in the interval, to you, we will have got to the end of the analysis.

If one wants to position the analyst within this schema of the subject's speech, one can say that he is somewhere in O. At least he should be. If he enters into the coupling of the resistance, which is just what he is taught not to do, then he speaks from *o′* and he will see himself in the subject. This occurs in the most natural of ways if he has not been analyzed – which does happen occasionally, and I'd even say that in a certain way the analyst is never fully an analyst, for the simple reason that he is a man, and that he, too, partakes of the imaginary mechanisms that are obstacles to the passage of speech. He must not identify with the subject, he must be dead enough not to be caught up in the imaginary relation, within which he is always solicited to intervene, and allow the progressive migration of the subject's image towards the S, the thing to be revealed, the thing that has no name, that can only find its name to the extent that the circuit from S to O has been completed directly. What the subject has to say through his false discourse will find a passage all the more easily when the economy of the imaginary relation has been progressively pared down.

I'm moving quickly, since I'm not here today to go over the whole theory of analytic dialogue for you. I simply want to indicate to you that the *word* – to be understood with the emphasis that this comprises, the solution to an enigma, a problematic function – is located in the Other, through the intermediary of which all full speech is realized, this *you are* in which the subject locates himself and recognizes himself.

Well then, through analyzing the structure of Schreber's delusion at the time it became stabilized into a system that links the subject's ego to this imaginary other, this strange god who understands nothing, who doesn't reply, who deceives the subject, we have been able to recognize that in psychosis the Other, where being is realized through the avowal of speech, is excluded.

The phenomena in question in verbal hallucination exhibit in their very structure the subject's relationship of internal echo to his own discourse. They ultimately become increasingly meaningless, as Schreber puts it, emptied of sense, purely verbal, learned by rote, pointless refrains. What, then, is this special relationship to speech? What does the subject lack for him to be able to get to the point where it is necessary for him to construct this entire imaginary world, for him to undergo within himself this automatism of the function of discourse? Not only does discourse invade him, not only is it a parasite in him, but he is dependent on its presence.

183 I've shown you *in vivo* in a case presentation that the subject is only able in psychosis to reconstitute himself in what I've called the imaginary allusion. This is precisely the point we have come to. The subject's constitution in imaginary allusion is the problem on which we need to make progress.

Until now people have been satisfied with this. The imaginary allusion has seemed to be very significant. People have rediscovered all the material, all the elements, of the unconscious in it. They seem never to have wondered what was significant from the economic point of view about the fact that by itself this allusion has no power to resolve anything. They were aware of this nevertheless, but as a mystery, and over time they strove to efface the radical differences between this structure and the structure of the neuroses.

I was asked the same questions in Strasbourg as in Vienna. People who seemed fairly open to certain views I was putting forward ended up saying to me – *How do you work with psychotics?* – as if stressing the ABC of technique wasn't enough, with an audience as unprepared as that one was. I replied – *The question is still somewhat in progress. We have to try to locate some reference points before we can discuss technique, let alone any psychotherapeutic recipes.* They persisted – *Nevertheless, one can't just do nothing for them. – No, certainly not. Before we discuss this, let's wait until certain things have been made clear.*

To take a further step forward here, we must, as is often the case, take a step back and return to the fascinating character offered by language phenomena in psychosis – as it happens, this is liable to reinforce what just now I called a misunderstanding.

I hear it said that I hold that everything the subject communicates he expresses in words and thus that I deny the existence, to which people are much attached, of the preverbal.

This extreme position doesn't fail to produce, in those who dwell on this, fairly lively recantations, which manifest themselves in two attitudes – *the hand on the heart,* related to what we shall call the authentic attestation through a displacement upwards, and *the bowing of the head,* supposed to be weighed in the balance, which I reputedly unload too much at the wishes of my interpellator.

2

People sometimes also say to me – *Fortunately you're not alone in the Société
de psychanalyse. There's also a woman of genius, Françoise Dolto, who shows us 184
the essential function of the image of the body and throws light on the way the subject leans on it in his relations with the world. We are delighted to rediscover a substantial relation here, which the language relation is undoubtedly tacked onto, but it is infinitely more concrete.*

I'm not at all criticizing what Françoise Dolto teaches. She makes excellent use of her technique and her extraordinary apprehension of the subject's imaginary sensibility. She speaks of all this and she also teaches those who listen to her to speak of it. But making this remark doesn't resolve the question.

I'm not surprised that something of a misunderstanding remains to be dispelled, even in people who think they're following me. Don't think I'm expressing any disappointment here. That would be to be in disagreement with myself, since I teach you that misunderstanding is the very basis of interhuman discourse.

But that is not the only reason that I'm not surprised that my discourse may have created a certain margin of misunderstanding. This is because in addition, if one is to be consistent in practice with one's own ideas, if all valid discourse has to be judged precisely according to its own principles, I would say that it is with a deliberate, if not entirely deliberated, intention that I pursue this discourse in such a way as to offer you the opportunity to not quite understand. This margin enables you yourselves to say that you think you follow me, that is, that you remain in a problematic position, which always leaves the door open to a progressive rectification.

In other words, if I were to try to make myself very easily understood, so that you were completely certain that you followed, then according to my premises concerning interhuman discourse the misunderstanding would be irremediable. On the contrary, given the way I think that I have to approach problems, you always have the possibility of what is said being open to revision, in a way that is made all the easier by the fact that it will fall back upon me entirely if you haven't been following sooner – you can hold me responsible.

It is on this basis that today I shall take the liberty of going back over an essential point.

I'm not saying that what is communicated in the analytic relation passes through the subject's discourse. I am therefore absolutely not required to distinguish, in the very phenomenon of analytic communication, between the domains of verbal and preverbal communication. That this pre- or even
185 extraverbal communication is always present in analysis is not in doubt, but it is a question of seeing what it is that constitutes the properly analytic field.

What constitutes the analytic field is identical with what constitutes the analytic phenomenon, namely the symptom – and also a very large number of other phenomena that are called normal or subnormal, the sense of which wasn't elucidated before analysis, and that extend well beyond discourse and speech, since they involve things that happen to the subject in his daily life, like slips, memory disturbances, dreams, and the phenomenon of jokes, whose value to the Freudian discovery is essential because it enables the perfect coherence in Freud's work between the analytic phenomenon and language to be isolated.

Let's start by saying what the analytic phenomenon is not.

Analysis has thrown an immense amount of light on the preverbal. In analytic doctrine this is linked essentially to the preconscious. It is the sum of internal and external impressions, of information the subject receives from the world he lives in, of the natural relations he has with it – assuming that there are any relations in man that are entirely natural – some are, however perverted they may be. Everything of the order of this preverbal thus partakes of what we can call an intraworldly *Gestalt*, within which the subject is the infantile doll that he once was, he is an excremental object, a sewer, a leech. Analysis has called upon us to explore this imaginary world, which partakes of a sort of barbaric poetry – though it is in no way the first to make it felt, certain poetic works have been.

Here we're in the innumerable shimmering of the great affective meaning. The words to express it come to the subject in great abundance, they are at his disposal, as accessible and as inexhaustible in their combinations as the nature to which they are a response. This is the world of the child, in which you feel at ease, all the more because you are familiar with his fantasies – high is equivalent to low, the back is equivalent to the front, etc. Universal equivalence is the law of this world, and it is even this that leaves us sufficiently uncertain whether any structure in it can be pinned down.

This discourse of affective meaning attains the sources of confabulation straight away. On the other hand the discourse of passional demands, for instance, is poor by comparison and is already drivel. This is because of the impact of reason. The preverbal support of the imaginary relation therefore quite naturally expresses itself in discourse here. We find ourselves here in a familiar domain, one that has always been explored by empirical deduction as much as by a priori categorial deduction. The source and storehouse of this preconscious of what we call imaginary is not unfamiliar, it has already 186
been successfully explored in the philosophical tradition, and it may be said that Kant's schema-ideas are situated on the border of this domain – this at least is where they might find their most brilliant credentials.

The classical theory of the image and the imagination is obviously surprisingly inadequate. This is ultimately an unfathomable domain. While we've made remarkable progress into its phenomenology, we are a long way from having mastered it. While analysis has enabled the issue of the image's formative value – which tends to be confused with the problem of the origins or even of the essence of life – to be brought to light, it's unquestionably from biologists and ethologists that we must expect any progress. While the analytic inventory enables certain essential characteristics of the economy of the imaginary function to be displayed, the question is not thereby exhausted.

Therefore, I have never said of this preconscious world, which is always ready to emerge into the daylight of consciousness, and which is at the subject's disposal unless there are orders to the contrary, that in itself it has the structure of language. I'm saying, because it is obvious, that it is recorded there and that it is recast there. But it retains its own pathways, its characteristic ways of communication. And this is not the level at which analysis has made its essential discovery.

It is highly surprising to observe that an exclusive preponderance of the world of imaginary relations is responsible for the emphasis in analysis on the object relation, which has elided what is properly speaking the field of analytic discoveries. One can follow the increasing predominance of this perspective by reading what the analyst Kris has been producing in recent times. With respect to the economy of progress in an analysis, he emphasizes what he calls – since he has read Freud – the preconscious mental processes and the fruitful nature of ego regression, which amounts to placing the means of access to the unconscious entirely on the level of the imaginary. If we follow Freud it is on the contrary clear that no exploration of the preconscious, however profound or exhaustive it is, will ever lead to an unconscious phenomenon as such. The excessive prevalence of ego psychology in the new American school introduces an illusion similar to that of the mathematician – we can assume he is ideal – who having got a vague idea of the existence of negative magnitudes sets about indefinitely dividing a positive number by two in the hope of finally crossing over the zero line and entering the dreamt-of domain.

The error is all the more gross because there is nothing Freud places greater insistence upon than the radical difference between the unconscious and the preconscious. But one imagines that however much of a barrier there is, it's
187 like putting up a partition in a grain store – the rats get through in the end. The fundamental image that currently seems to regulate analytic practice is that there must be something connecting neurosis and psychosis, the preconscious and the unconscious. It is a matter of pushing, of nibbling away, and one will succeed in perforating the partition wall.

This idea leads authors who are even a little bit coherent to make altogether surprising theoretical additions, like the notion of a sphere that is, as they say, conflict-free – an extraordinary notion – that is not regressive but transgressive. The likes of this had never been heard before, even in the most neo-spiritualist psychology of faculties of the soul. No one had ever thought of making the will an agency located in a conflict-free empire. It's clear what leads them to it. For them the ego is the prevailing framework of phenomena, everything goes through the ego, ego regression is the sole means of access to the unconscious. Where, therefore, are we to locate the mediating element that is indispensable for understanding the action of analytic treatment, if it is not located in this type of ego that is really ideal, in the worst sense of the word, which is the conflict-free sphere, which thus becomes the mythical locus of the most incredible reaction entifications?

In comparison with the preconscious we have just been describing, what is the unconscious?

If I say that everything that belongs to analytic communication has the structure of language, this precisely does not mean that the unconscious is expressed in discourse. The *Traumdeutung, The Psychopathology of Everyday Life,* and *Jokes* make this transparent – nothing in Freud's detours is explicable unless it is because the analytic phenomenon as such, whatever it may be, isn't a language in the sense in which this would mean that it's a discourse – I've never said it was a discourse – but is structured like a language. This is the sense in which it may be called a phenomenal variety, and the most revealing one, of man's relations to the domain of language. Every analytic phenomenon, every phenomenon that comes from the analytic field, from the analytic discovery, from what we are dealing with in symptoms and neurosis, is structured like a language.

This means it's a phenomenon that always presents the essential duality of signifier and signified. This means that here the signifier has its own coherence and nature which distinguish it from every other species of sign. We are going to follow its trail in the imaginary preconscious domain.

Let's begin with the biological sign. In the very structure, in the morphology, of animals there is something that has this captivating value due to which its receiver, who sees the red of the robin redbreast for instance, and who is 188
made for receiving it, undertakes a series of actions or henceforth unitary behavior that links the bearer of this sign to its perceiver. Here you have what gives us a precise idea of what may be called natural meaning. Without otherwise seeking how this might take place in man, it is clear that by means of a series of transitions we can manage to purify, neutralize, the natural sign.

Then there is the trace, the footprint in the sand, the sign about which Robinson Crusoe makes no mistake. Here sign and object separate. The trace, in its negative aspect, draws the natural sign to a limit at which it becomes evanescent. The distinction between sign and object is quite clear here, since the trace is precisely what the object leaves behind once it has gone off somewhere else. Objectively there is no need for any subject to recognize a sign for it to be there – a trace exists even if there is nobody to look at it.

When have we passed over into the order of the signifier? The signifier may extend over many of the elements within the domain of the sign. But the signifier is a sign that doesn't refer to any object, not even to one in the form of a trace, even though the trace nevertheless heralds the signifier's essential feature. It, too, is the sign of an absence. But insofar as it forms part of language, the signifier is a sign which refers to another sign, which is as such structured to signify the absence of another sign, in other words, to be opposed to it in a couple.

I spoke about day and night. Day and night are in no way something that can be defined by experience. All experience is able to indicate is a series of modulations and transformations, even a pulsation, an alternation, of light and dark, with all its transitions. Language begins at the opposition – day and night. And once the day is there as a signifier, it lends itself to all the vicissitudes of an arrangement whereby it will come to signify things of great diversity.

This characteristic of the signifier essentially marks everything of the order of the unconscious. Freud's opus, with its huge philological framework at work deep in the heart of the phenomena, is absolutely unthinkable unless we place the signifier's dominance in analytic phenomena at centre stage.

This reminder should take us a step further.

189

3

I spoke to you of the Other of speech as being where the subject recognizes himself and gets himself recognized. This, and not the disturbance of some oral, anal or even genital relation, is the determining factor in a neurosis. We are only too well aware how much trouble the handling of the homosexual relation gives us, since we bring out its permanence in subjects who are diverse at the level of instinctual relations. The issue here is a question that arises for the subject at the level of the signifier, of the *to be or not to be,*[1] at the level of his being.

I want to illustrate this for you with an example, an old observation of traumatic hysteria—no trace of hallucinatory elements.

The reason I have chosen this one is that it brings into play, in the foreground, this fantasy of pregnancy and procreation which dominates the history of President Schreber, since this is where his delusion ends up, that a new humanity, Schreberian in spirit, has to be re-engendered by him.

It concerns an observation we owe to Joseph Eisler, a psychologist of the Budapest School, made at the end of the First World War, which recounts the story of a chap who was a tram conductor during the Hungarian revolution.[2]

He is thirty-three years of age, a Hungarian protestant – austerity, stability, peasant tradition. He left his family to move to the city at the end of his adolescence. His working life was marked by changes that were not without meaning – he started out as a baker, then he worked in a chemical laboratory, and finally he became a tram conductor. He used to ring the bell and punch the tickets, but he had also been a driver.

One day, alighting from his tram, he stumbled, fell, and was dragged a short distance. He had some swelling and his left side hurt. He was taken to hospital where they found that there was nothing wrong with him. He was given a few stitches in the scalp to close the wound. Everything was fine. He left after a thorough examination. They took a lot of x-rays, and they were quite certain that there was nothing wrong with him. He had been putting on a bit of a show.

And then, gradually, he fell victim to crises characterized by an increase

[1] In English in the original.
[2] Michael Josef Eisler, "*Analyse eines Zwangssymptoms.*"

in pain in his lower rib, a pain that spread out from this point and drove the subject into a state of increasing discomfort. He would stretch out, lie down on his left side, use a pillow to block it. And things stayed that way, getting worse as time went on. The crises would last several days, returning at reg- 190
ular intervals. They kept getting worse, reaching the point of actually causing the subject to lose consciousness.

Once again he was given a thorough examination. They found absolutely nothing. They suspected a traumatic hysteria and sent him to our author, who analyzes him.

This man belongs to the first generation of analysts, he sees the phenomena with a lot of freshness, investigates them from beginning to end. Nevertheless, this observation dates from 1921 and already belongs to this type of systematization that began to affect – correlatively, it would seem – observation and practice and that would produce this turning point from which the reversal that stressed the analysis of resistance emerged. Eisler is already extremely impressed by the new *ego* psychology. On the other hand, he knows the early things very well, Freud's early analyses of the anal character, he recalls the idea that the economic elements of the libido can play a decisive role in the formation of the ego. And one feels that he is deeply interested in his subject's ego, in his style of conduct, in the things that indicate regressive elements in him, insofar as they are inscribed not only in the symptoms but also in the structure.

His record of the subject's curious behavior is very pertinent. At the end of the first session the subject abruptly sits down on the couch and starts looking at him with eyes like lottery balls, mouth agape, as if he has discovered an unexpected and enigmatic monster. On other occasions the subject gives some fairly surprising expressions to the transference. On one occasion in particular he stands up abruptly and falls down again the other way round, but with his nose against the couch, offering his dangling legs to the analyst in a manner whose general meaning does not escape him.

This subject is adapted well enough. His relations with his friends are those of a militant unionist, he is something of a leader, and he is very interested in what binds him to them socially. He enjoys undeniable prestige there. Our author also particularly notes the way in which his being self-taught functions, his papers are all in order. You can see that Eisler is trying to find the features of an anal character, and not without some success. But the interpretation he finally gives the subject of his homosexualizing tendencies doesn't affect him either way – nothing changes. There is the same dead end that Freud encountered with the Wolf Man some years before, not all of the clues to which are given in this case study, because at the time the object of his research was something else.

Let's take a closer look at this study. The onset of the neurosis in its symp- 191 tomatic aspect, which made the analyst's intervention necessary, undoubtedly presupposes a trauma which must have aroused something. In the subject's childhood we find traumas by the bucketful. When he was very small, starting to crawl about the place, his mother had stood on his thumb. Eisler doesn't fail to point out that at this moment something decisive must have occurred, since according to the family tradition he is supposed to have started to suck his thumb after this incident. You see? – castration – regression. One can find others. However, there is one small difficulty, which is that it is noticed when the material is being produced that what was decisive in the decompensation of the neurosis wasn't the accident but the radiographic examinations.

The analyst doesn't see all the implications of what he gives us, and whatever preconceived idea he has tends in the opposite direction. It is at the time of the examinations which subject him to mysterious instruments that the subject's crises are triggered. And these crises, their sense, their regularity, their style, very obviously appear linked to a fantasy of pregnancy.

The manifestation of the subject's symptoms is dominated by those relational elements that in an imaginary way colour his relations with objects. One can recognize in them an anal relation, or a homosexual relation, or this or that, but these very elements are caught up in the question that arises – *Am I or am I not someone capable of procreating?* This question is obviously located at the level of the Other, insofar as integration into sexuality is tied to symbolic recognition.

If the recognition of the subject's sexual position is not tied to the symbolic apparatus, then nothing remains for analysis, Freudianism, but to disappear – it means absolutely nothing. The subject finds his place in a preformed symbolic apparatus that institutes the law in sexuality. And this law no longer allows the subject to realize his sexuality except on the symbolic plane. This is what the Oedipus complex means, and if analysis didn't know this, it would have discovered absolutely nothing.

What is at issue for our subject is the question – *What am I?*, or *Am I?*, a relation of being, a fundamental signifier. It is to the extent that this question was aroused as symbolic, and not reactivated as imaginary, that the decompensation of his neurosis was triggered and his symptoms became organized. Whatever their qualities, their nature, the material from which they are borrowed, his symptoms have the value of being a formulation, a reformulation, or even an insistence, of this question.

This key is not sufficient on its own. It is confirmed by elements of his past life which retain all their significance for the subject. One day he managed,
192 while hiding, to observe a woman from the neighborhood of his parents who was uttering these endless groans. He came upon her writhing about, her legs in the air. He knew what was going on, especially as she was unable to

give birth and the doctor had to intervene and carry the infant off in a bag, in pieces, which was all that could be removed.

Moreover, the feminized character of the subject's discourse is so immediately noticeable that when our analyst acquaints the subject with its major elements, he obtains from him this remark which the doctor who examined him had made to his wife – *I fail to see what's wrong with him. It seems that if he were a woman I should understand him much better*. He perceived the significant aspect, but he didn't perceive – for the simple reason that he didn't have the analytic apparatus, which is only conceivable in the register of the structurations of language – that all this is only material, favorable material admittedly, that the subject uses for expressing his question. Any other could have been used just as easily, in order to express what is beyond any relation, current or not current, a *Who am I? a man or a woman?* and *Am I capable of procreating?*

Once one holds this clue, the subject's entire life is reorganized from its point of view. One mentions his anal preoccupations, for example. But what does the interest he brings to his excrement revolve around? Around the question of whether in his excrement there may be fruit seeds still capable of growing if they're buried in the ground.

The subject has one great ambition, which is to be involved in raising chickens and, more particularly, in the marketing of eggs. He is interested in all sorts of botanical questions, all centered on germination. One may even say that a whole series of accidents that happened to him during his job as tram conductor is tied to the dismembering of the child he witnessed. This is not the ultimate origin of the subject's question, but it is a particularly expressive one.

Let's finish where we began, with the last accident. He fell from the tram which for him had become a significant machine, he fell down, he delivered himself. The sole theme of a pregnancy fantasy dominates, but in what way? As a signifier – the context makes this clear – of the question of his integration into the virile function, into the function of the father. It may be noted that he contrived to marry a woman who already had a child and with whom he could only ever have inadequate relations.

The problematic nature of his symbolic identification underlies any possible understanding of the observation. Everything that's said, expressed, gestured, manifested, assumes its sense only as a function of a response that 193
has to be formulated concerning this fundamentally symbolic relation – *Am I a man or am I a woman?*

When I set things out for you like this, you can't fail to compare it with what I emphasized in the case of Dora. Where does she end up in fact, if not confronted by a fundamental question on the subject of her sex? Not on what sex she is, but *What is it to be a woman?* Dora's two dreams are absolutely transparent in this respect – one speaks of nothing else, *What is it to be a woman?* and specifically, *What is a feminine organ?* Notice that here we find ourselves before something odd – the woman wonders about what it is to be a woman, just as the male subject wonders about what it is to be a woman.

We shall take things up from there next time. We shall highlight the dissymmetries that Freud always stressed in the Oedipus complex, which confirm the distinction between the symbolic and the imaginary that I have taken up today.

For the woman, the realization of her sex is not accomplished in the Oedipus complex in a way symmetrical to that of the man's, not by identification with the mother, but on the contrary by identification with the paternal object, which assigns her an extra detour. Freud always stuck by this conception, whatever people, women particularly, have since tried to do to re-establish the symmetry. But the disadvantage the woman finds herself in with respect to access to her own sexual identity, with respect to her sexualization as a woman, is turned to her advantage in hysteria owing to her imaginary identification with the father, who is perfectly accessible to her, particularly by virtue of his position in the composition of the Oedipus complex.

For the man, on the other hand, the path is more complex.

14 March 1956

XIII 195

The hysteric's question (II): *What is a woman?*

DORA AND THE FEMININE ORGAN

THE SIGNIFYING DISYMMETRY

THE SYMBOLIC AND PROCREATION

FREUD AND THE SIGNIFIER

What was the meaning of my lecture last night on the training of analysts? It was that it is essential to carefully distinguish between symbolism properly so-called, that is, symbolism as structured in language, that in which we understand one another here, and natural symbolism. I have summed this up in the expression, *To read coffee grounds is not to read hieroglyphics.*

For the audience that it was, it was necessary to bring the difference between signifier and signified to life a bit. I gave examples, some of them humorous, I gave the schema, and I went on to some applications. I reminded them that analysts' practice makes them fascinated by highly seductive imaginary forms, by the imaginary meaning of the subjective world, whereas what one needs to know – this is what interested Freud – is what organizes this world and enables it to be displaced. I pointed out that the dynamics of phenomena in the analytic field are linked to the duality that results from the distinction between the signifier and the signified.

It's no accident that it was a Jungian who brought in the term *symbol.* At the heart of the Jungian myth the symbol is effectively thought of as a flower that rises up from the depths, a blossoming of what lies in the depths of man *qua* typical. The question is whether this is what a symbol is, or whether on the contrary it's something that envelops and forms what my interlocutor nicely called creation.

The second part of my lecture concerned the consequences in analysis of forgetting the signifier-signified structuration. And there I was only able to give an indication of the way in which the theory of the ego currently being promoted in New York circles completely changes the perspective from which 196
the analytic phenomena have to be approached, and that it is party to the same effacement. This effectively ends up placing the ego-to-ego relation in the foreground. And a simple inspection of Freud's articles between 1922 and 1924 shows that the ego is nothing like what it's currently made out to be in analytic usage.

1

If what is called strengthening the ego exists, it can only be the accentuation of the fantasy relation that is always correlative of the ego, especially in the case of the neurotic with a typical structure. As far as the latter is concerned, the strengthening of the ego moves in exactly the opposite direction from that of the dissolution, not only of symptoms, which are strictly speaking within their own meaningfulness but may when the occasion arises be mobilized, but also of the structure itself.

What is the sense of what Freud contributed with his new topography when he stressed the imaginary nature of the ego's function? It's precisely the structure of neurosis.

Freud relates the ego to the object's fantasmatic character. When he writes that the ego has the privilege of reality using, of reality testing, that it's the ego that indicates reality for the subject, the context leaves no doubt – the ego is here as an illusion, what Freud called the ego ideal. Its function, which is not that of objectivity but that of illusion, is fundamentally narcissistic, and it's on the basis of this function that the subject gives something its connotation of reality.

From this topography there arises what in typical neuroses is the place of the ego. The ego in its imaginary structuration is for the subject like one of its elements. In the same way that Aristotle declared that one must not say, *Man thinks,* nor, *The soul thinks,* but, *Man thinks with his soul,* we shall say that the neurotic asks his neurotic question, his secret and muzzled question, with his ego.

The Freudian topography of the ego shows us how a hysteric, or an obsessional, uses his or her ego in order to raise the question, that is, precisely in order not to raise it. The structure of a neurosis is essentially a question, and indeed this is why for a long time it was for us purely and simply a question. The neurotic is in a position of symmetry, he is the question that we ask ourselves, and it's indeed because it affects us just as much as him that we have the greatest repugnance to formulating it more precisely.

This is illustrated by the way in which I have always spoken to you about
197 hysteria, to which Freud has given illumination of the highest kind in the case of Dora.

Who is Dora? She is someone who is trapped in a very clear symptomatic state, with the qualification that Freud, by his own admission, makes a mistake over the object of Dora's desire in that he himself is too centered on the question of the object, that is, in that he doesn't bring out the fundamental subjective duality implicated in it. He asks himself what Dora desires, before asking himself who desires in Dora. And in the end Freud realizes that in this quartet – Dora, her father, Herr and Frau K. – Frau K. is the object that really interests Dora, in so far as she is identified with Herr K. The question of where Dora's ego is located is thus resolved – Herr K. is Dora's ego. The function filled by the specular image in the schema of the mirror stage, where the subject situates his sense so as to recognize himself, where for the first time he situates his ego, this external point of imaginary identification, is, for Dora, placed in Herr K. It is insofar as she is Herr K. that all her symptoms adopt their definitive sense.

Dora's aphonia occurs during Herr K.'s absences, which Freud explains quite nicely – she no longer needs to talk since he is no longer present, only writing remains. This leaves us a bit perplexed, nevertheless. If she has dried up, it's in fact because the mode of objectification hasn't been raised anywhere else. The aphonia arises because Dora is left directly in the presence of Frau K. Everything she has heard about Frau K.'s relations with her father revolves around fellatio, and here there is something infinitely more significant for understanding the appearance of the oral symptoms.

Dora's identification with Herr K. is what holds this situation together up until the neurotic decompensation. While she may complain about the situation, this is still part of the situation, for it is insofar as she is identified with Herr K. that she complains.

What is Dora saying through her neurosis? What is the woman-hysteric saying? Her question is this – *What is it to be a woman?*

This leads us further into the dialectic of the imaginary and the symbolic in the Oedipus complex.

What in fact characterizes the Freudian understanding of the phenomena is that it always shows the structural planes of the symptom, despite the outburst of enthusiasm by psychoanalysts for the imaginary phenomena stirred up in analytic experience.

Concerning the Oedipus complex there has been no shortage of well-meaning people to stress the analogies and symmetries along the paths that the boy and girl have to follow – and Freud himself pointed out many common fea- 198
tures. However, he never stopped insisting on the essential dissymmetry of Oedipus in the two sexes.

What is this dissymmetry due to? To the primary love relation with the mother, you will say, but Freud was a long way away from this point at the time he was beginning to put order into the facts that he was observing in experience. He mentions, among other things, the anatomical component, which means that for the woman the two sexes are identical. But is this the reason for the dissymmetry?

The detailed studies that Freud did on this subject are closely argued. I shall name some of them – "Some Psychical Consequences of the Anatomical Distinction between the Sexes," "Female Sexuality," "The Dissolution of the Oedipus Complex." What do they bring out, if it isn't that the reason for the dissymmetry is located essentially at the symbolic level, that it's due to the signifier?

I should say that strictly speaking there is no symbolization of woman's sex[1] as such. In any case, the symbolization isn't the same, it doesn't have the same source or the same mode of access as the symbolization of man's sex.[1] And this is because the imaginary only furnishes an absence where elsewhere there is a highly prevalent symbol.

It's the prevalence of the phallic *Gestalt* that in bringing about the oedipal complex forces the woman to take a detour via identification with the father and therefore for a while to follow the same paths as the boy. The woman's access to the oedipal complex, her imaginary identification, is accomplished via the father, exactly as in the boy's case, by virtue of the prevalence of the imaginary form of the phallus, but insofar as this form is itself taken as the symbolic element central to the Oedipus complex.

If for the girl as much as for the boy the castration complex assumes a pivotal value in bringing about the Oedipus complex, it does so precisely as a function of the father, because the phallus is a symbol to which there is no correspondent, no equivalent. It's a matter of a dissymmetry in the signifier. This signifying dissymmetry determines the paths down which the Oedipus complex will pass. The two paths make them both pass down the same trail – the trail of castration.

The experience of the Oedipus complex is evidence of the predominance of the signifier in the ways open to subjective realization, since the girl's assumption of her own situation is in no way unthinkable on the imaginary plane. All the ingredients are there for the girl to have direct experience of the feminine position, symmetrical to the realization of the masculine position. There would be no obstacle if this realization were to be brought about
199 in the order of lived experience, of *ego* sympathy, of sensations. And yet, experience shows a striking difference – one of the sexes is required to take the image of the other sex as the basis of its identification. That things are so can't be considered a pure quirk of nature. This fact can only be interpreted from the perspective in which it's the symbolic organization that regulates everything.

Where there is no symbolic material, there is an obstacle, a defect, in the way of bringing about the identification that is essential for the subject's sexuality to be realized. This defect comes from the fact that on one point the symbolic lacks the material – for it does require material. The female sex is characterized by an absence, a void, a hole, which means that it happens to be less desirable than is the male sex for what he has that is provocative, and that an essential dissymmetry appears. If all this could be grasped within the

[1] *"le sexe,"* which may also mean the genitals.

order of a dialectic of drives, we would not see why such a detour, such an anomaly, would be necessary.

This remark is nowhere near adequate for us concerning the matter at hand, namely the function of the ego in male and female hysterics. The question isn't simply linked to the material, to the trappings of the signifier, but to the subject's relationship with the signifier as a whole, with what the signifier is capable of answering to.

When I spoke about beings of language last night it was intended to have an impact upon my audience. Beings of language aren't organized beings, but there is no doubt that they are beings, that they stamp their form upon man. The comparison I made with fossils was therefore quite appropriate up to a point. It nevertheless remains true that they don't have any substantial existence in themselves.

2

Consider the paradox that results from certain functional interweavings between the two planes of the symbolic and the imaginary.

On the one hand, it seems that the symbolic is what yields us the entire world system. It's because man has words that he has knowledge of things. And the number of things he has knowledge of corresponds to the number of things he is able to name. This is not in doubt. On the other hand, there is no doubt either that the imaginary relation is linked to ethology, to animal psychology. The sexual relation implies capture by the other's image. In other words, one of these domains appears to be open to the neutrality of the order of human knowledge, the other seems to be the very domain of the erotiza- 200
tion of the object. This is what initially manifests itself to us.

Now, the bringing about of the sexual position in the human being is linked, Freud tells us – and experience tells us – to the trial of traversing a fundamentally symbolized relationship, that of the Oedipus complex, which includes a position that alienates the subject, that makes him desire an other's object and possess it through the proxy of an other. We therefore find ourselves here in a position structured within the very duality of the signifier and the signified. It is insofar as the function of man and woman is symbolized, it is insofar as it's literally uprooted from the domain of the imaginary and situated in the domain of the symbolic, that any normal, completed sexual position is realized. Genital realization is submitted to symbolization as an essential requirement – that the man be virilized, that the woman truly accept her feminine function.

Conversely, no less paradoxically, it's in the order of the imaginary that we find the relation of identification on the basis of which the object is realized as an object of competition. The domain of knowledge is fundamentally inserted into the primitive paranoid dialectic of identification with the counterpart. The initial opening of identification with the other, that is, with an object, starts from here. An object is isolated, neutralized, and as such particularly erotized. This is what makes an infinitely greater number of objects enter the field of human desire than enter animal experience.

In this interweaving of the imaginary and the symbolic lies the source of the essential function that the ego plays in the structuring of neurosis.

When Dora finds herself wondering, *What is a woman?*, she is attempting to symbolize the female organ as such. Her identification with the man, bearer of the penis, is for her on this occasion a means of approaching this definition that escapes her. She literally uses the penis as an imaginary instrument for apprehending what she hasn't succeeded in symbolizing.

There are many more women hysterics than men hysterics – this is a fact of clinical experience – because the path to the woman's symbolic realization is more complicated. Becoming a woman and wondering what a woman is are two essentially different things. I would go even further – it's because one doesn't become one that one wonders and, up to a point, to wonder is the contrary of becoming one. The metaphysics of the woman's position is the detour imposed on her subjective realization. Her position is essentially
201 problematic, and up to a certain point it's unassimilable. But once the woman is locked into hysteria it must also be said that her position presents an unusual stability by virtue of its structural simplicity – the simpler a structure is, the fewer the points of rupture it displays. When her question takes shape in the form of hysteria it's very easy for the woman to raise it by taking the shortest path, namely identification with the father.

In masculine hysteria the situation is certainly much more complex. To the extent that in man the oedipal realization is better structured, the hysteric's question has less chance of arising. But if it's raised, what is it? Here there is the same dissymmetry as in the Oedipus complex – hysterics, whether men or women, ask themselves the same question. The question of the male hysteric also concerns the feminine position.

The question of the subject whom I mentioned last time revolved around a fantasy of pregnancy. Is this sufficient to exhaust the question? It has long been known that fantasmatic anatomical fragmentation is a hysterical phenomenon. This fantasmatic anatomy has a structural character – neither paralysis nor anesthesia occurs according to the pathways and topography of the nerve branches. Nothing in neural anatomy corresponds to anything whatsoever that occurs in hysterical symptoms. It's always a question of an imaginary anatomy.

Can we now spell out the factor common to the feminine position and the masculine question in hysteria – a factor that is no doubt situated at the symbolic level, but perhaps isn't entirely reducible to it? It concerns a question of procreation. Paternity, like maternity, has a problematic essence – these are terms that are not situated purely and simply at the level of experience.

Recently I was discussing problems, raised long ago, about the *couvade* with one of my students and he reminded me of the light ethnographers have recently managed to throw on this problem. Facts of experience obtained from an investigation carried out on some Central American tribe, because this is where it appears clearly, effectively enable the resolution of certain questions that have arisen over the meaning of this phenomenon. It is now possible to see here that the function of the father and of what he contributes to the creation of the new individual is called into question. The *couvade* is located at the level of a question concerning masculine procreation.

In this vein perhaps it won't strike you as artificial if I elaborate in the following way.

The symbolic provides a form into which the subject is inserted at the level 202
of his being. It's on the basis of the signifier that the subject recognizes himself as being this or that. The chain of signifiers has a fundamental explanatory value, and the very notion of causality is nothing else.

There is nevertheless one thing that evades the symbolic tapestry, it's procreation in its essential root – that one being is born from another. In the symbolic order procreation is covered by the order instituted by this succession between beings. But nothing in the symbolic explains the fact of their individuation, the fact that beings come from beings. The entire symbolism declares that creatures don't engender creatures, that a creature is unthinkable without a fundamental creation. In the symbolic nothing explains creation.

Nor does anything explain why some beings must die for others to be born. There is an essential relationship between sexual reproduction and the appearance of death, the biologists say, and if this is true then it shows that they, too, mull over the same question. The question of what links two beings in the appearance of life only arises for a subject when he or she is in the symbolic, realized as a man or as a woman, but so long as an accident has prevented him or her from acceding to it. This may just as easily occur to anyone by virtue of his or her biographical accidents.

Freud raises these same issues in the background of *Beyond the Pleasure Principle*. Just as life reproduces itself, so it's forced to repeat the same cycle, rejoining the common aim of death. For Freud this reflects his experience. Each neurosis reproduces a particular cycle in the order of the signifier on the basis of the question that man's relationship to the signifier as such raises.

There is, in effect, something radically unassimilable to the signifier. It's quite simply the subject's singular existence. Why is he here? Where has he come from? What is he doing here? Why is he going to disappear? The signifier is incapable of providing him with the answer, for the good reason that it places him beyond death. The signifier already considers him dead, by nature it immortalizes him.

As such, the question of death is another mode of the neurotic creation of the question – its obsessional mode. I indicated this last night, and I'll leave it to one side today because we are dealing with the psychoses this year and not with the obsessional neuroses. The considerations about structure I'm proposing to you here are still a prelude to the problem raised by the psychotic. If I'm particularly interested in the question raised in hysteria, it's because at issue is the way in which it's distinct from the mechanism of psy-
203 chosis, especially that of President Schreber, where the question of procreation, of feminine procreation in particular, is also sketched out.

3

I would like to finish by pointing out to you those texts by Freud that justify what I said to you last night.

My own work is to understand what Freud did. Consequently, to interpret even what is implicit in Freud is legitimate in my eyes. I say this to tell you that I'm not backing away from my responsibilities in asking you to refer to what certain texts have powerfully expressed.

Refer to those years, around 1896, when as Freud himself tells us he was assembling his doctrine – he took a long time to state what he had to say. He stresses the time of latency, which always lasted three to four years, between the composition of his major works and their publication. The *Traumdeutung* was written three or four years prior to its publication. The same goes for *The Psychopathology of Everyday Life* and the Dora case.

One can observe that the twofold structuring of the signifier and signified doesn't appear after the event. As early as Letter 46, for example, Freud states that he is beginning to see the stages of the subject's development appear in his experience, how to construct them, and also to show its relationship to the existence of the unconscious and its mechanisms. One is struck by seeing him employ the term *Übersetzung* to designate a given stage of the subject's experiences, according as it's translated or not. *Translated* – what does that mean? It's a question of what happens at levels defined by the subject's age – from one to four years of age, then from four to eight years of age, then the prepubertal period, and finally the period of maturity.[2]

It's interesting to note the stress Freud places on the signifier. *Bedeutung*

[2] See letter of 30 May 1896, Freud-Fliess, 187–90; Letter 46, Origins, 163–67.

can't be translated as specifying the signifier in relation to the signified. Likewise, in Letter 52, I've already pointed out that he says this – *I am working on the assumption that our psychic mechanism has come into being by a process of stratification: the material present in the form of memory traces being subjected from time to time to a* rearrangement *in accordance with fresh circumstances – to a* retranscription. *Thus what is essentially new about my theory is the thesis that memory is present not once but several times over, that it is laid down in various kinds of indications.*[3]

I'm pointing out to you the kinship between what is said here and the schema I gave a commentary on for you the other day. Freud emphasizes that these different stages are characterized by the plurality of mnemic inscriptions. 204

There is *Wahrnehmung,* perception, first of all. This is a primordial, primary position which remains hypothetical since in a way none of it comes to light in the subject. Then there is *Bewusstsein,* consciousness.

Consciousness and memory as such are mutually exclusive. This is a point on which Freud never varied. It always seemed to him that pure memory, *qua* inscription and acquisition by the subject of a new means of reacting, should remain completely immanent to the mechanism and bring no apprehension of the subject by himself into play.

The *Wahrnehmung* stage is there to show that something simple must be presupposed at the origin of memory, conceived as consisting of a plurality of registers. The first registration of perceptions, which is also inaccessible to consciousness, is arranged according to associations by simultaneity. Here we have the original requirement of a primitive installation of simultaneity.

This is what I showed you last year in our probative exercises concerning symbols.[4] Things became interesting, you'll remember, when we established the structure of groups of three. Putting these groups of three together effectively establishes a relationship of simultaneity between them. Simultaneity is the birth of the signifier and, equally, its existence is a synchronic coexistence. Saussure emphasizes this point.

Unbewusstsein is of the order of conceptual memories. The notion of causal relation as such appears here for the first time. This is the moment at which the signifier, once constituted, is secondarily arranged according to something else, which is the appearance of the signified.

It's only subsequently that the *Vorbewusstsein,* the third mode of rearrangement, comes into play. It's from this preconscious that investments will become conscious, according to certain precise rules. This second thought conscious-

[3] Letter of 6 December 1896, Freud-Fliess, 207; Letter 52, Origins, 173.
[4] See Sem II:191–94.

ness is in all likelihood linked to the hallucinatory experience of word representations,[5] the emission of words. The most radical example of this is verbal hallucination, connected with the paranoid mechanism by which we auditivate word representations. The appearance of consciousness which is linked to this would otherwise always be without any link to memory.

In everything that follows, Freud shows that the phenomenon of *Verdrängung* consists in the loss of something of the order of a signifying expression
205 at the moment of passage from one stage of development to another. The signifier recorded at one of these stages doesn't cross over into the next, with the mode of retroactive regrouping required by any new phase of signifier-meaning organization that the subject enters.

This is where any explanation of the existence of repression has to begin. The notion of inscription in a signifier that dominates the registration is essential to the theory of memory insofar as it's at the basis of Freud's first investigation of the phenomenon of the unconscious.

21 March 1956

[5] I. e., "word presentations" in SE.

XIV 207

The signifier, as such, signifies nothing

THE NOTION OF STRUCTURE
SUBJECTIVITY IN THE REAL
HOW TO LOCATE THE BEGINNING OF A DELUSION
THE BETWEEN-I'S

Ad usum autem orationis, incredibile est, nisi diligenter attenderis, quanta opera machinata natura sit.

How many marvels there are concealed by the function of language, if you want to pay diligent attention to it! You know that this is what we are striving towards here. You won't be astonished, therefore, that I should offer you this sentence from Cicero as an epigraph, since it is on this theme that this term we are going to return to the study of the Freudian structures of the psychoses.

Effectively, it's a question of what Freud left behind concerning the structures of the psychoses, this being why we call them Freudian.

1

The notion of structure by itself deserves our attention. Given the manner in which we efficaciously apply it in analysis, it implies a number of coordinates, and the very notion of coordinate is part of it. A structure is in the first place a group of elements forming a covariant set.

I said a *set,* I didn't say a *totality.* As a matter of fact, the notion of structure is analytic. A structure is always established by referring something coherent to something else, which is complementary to it. But the notion of totality only comes into it if we are dealing with a closed relation with a correspondent, where the structures are interdependent. On the other hand it is possible to have an open relation, which we shall call a relation of supplementarity. 208
For those who have gone in for structural analyses the ideal has always appeared to be to find what links the two, the closed and the open, to discover circularity on the side of the open.

I think that you're well enough oriented to understand that the notion of structure is by itself already a manifestation of the signifier. The little I've just indicated about its dynamics, about what it implies, points you towards the notion of signifier. To be interested in structure is to be unable to neglect the signifier. In structural analysis, as in the analysis of the relationship between signifier and signified, we discover relations between groups founded on sets that, whether open or closed, essentially comprise reciprocal references. In the analysis of the relationship between signifier and signified we have learned to stress synchrony and diachrony, and this reappears in a structural analysis. In the end, if we observe them closely, the notion of structure and that of signifier appear inseparable. In fact, when we analyze a structure it's always at least ideally a question of the signifier. What satisfies us the most in a structural analysis is an uncovering, that is as radical as possible, of the signifier.

We situate ourselves in a field that is distinct from the field of the natural sciences and that, as you know, it isn't enough to call the field of the human sciences. Where are we to draw the dividing line? How closely do we have to approximate to the ideals of the sciences of nature such as they have developed for us – for instance, physics as we know it? To what extent are we unable to avoid differentiating ourselves from them? Well then, it's in relation to these definitions of the signifier and of structure that the appropriate boundary can be drawn.

In physics we have adopted the law that we proceed from the idea that in nature nobody uses the signifier to signify. This is what distinguishes our physics from mystical physics and even from the physics of antiquity, which had nothing mystical about it, but which didn't adopt this strict requirement. It has become a fundamental law for us, one required of every utterance within the order of the natural sciences, that there is nobody who uses the signifier.

The signifier is nevertheless there in nature, and if we weren't looking for the signifier, we shouldn't find anything there at all. To extract a natural law is to extract a meaningless formula. The less it signifies anything, the happier we are. This is why we're perfectly happy with the achievements of Einstei-
209 nian physics. You would be wrong to think that those little equations of Einstein's that express the relationship of inertial mass to a constant plus some exponents have the slightest meaning. They are pure signifiers. And this is why thanks to him we hold the world in the palm of our hand.

The idea that the signifier signifies something, that there is someone who uses this signifier to signify something, is called the *Signatura rerum*. This is the title of a work by Jakob Boehme.[1] It means that God is present in natural phenomena and speaks to us in his language.

You must nevertheless not think that our physics implies the elimination of all meaning. There is a meaning at the limit, but there is nobody to signify

[1] Jakob Boehme, *Signature of All Things*.

it. In physics the mere existence of a signifying system implies, at the very least, the meaning that there is an *Umwelt*. Physics implies the minimal conjunction of the two signifiers, *one* and *all* – that all things are one or that the one is all things.

You would be wrong to think that these signifiers belonging to science, however simple they are, are given or that any form of empiricism would enable one to abstract them. No empirical theory is able to account for the existence of even the first whole numbers. Despite Mr. Jung's best efforts to convince us of the contrary, history, observation, and ethnography show us that at a certain level of the signifier in a given culture, community, or tribe of people, it's an accomplishment to get access to the number five, for instance. One can clearly distinguish on the banks of the Orinoco between a tribe that has learned to signify the number four and not beyond, and one for which the number five opens up surprising possibilities, consistent moreover with the entire signifying system into which the tribe is inserted.

This isn't a joke. It's to be taken literally. The extraordinary effect the number three had when it arrived in a certain Amazon tribe has been recorded by people who knew what they were talking about. Uttering a series of whole numbers isn't self evident. It's altogether conceivable, and experience shows that this is so, that beyond a certain limit in this series things get mixed up and one no longer sees anything but a confused multitude. Experience also shows that since the number one necessarily implies its maximum effect, it's not the number one whose origin we are able, in acquiring the signifier, to understand clearly.

These considerations appear to contradict my remarks to you about the fact that any system of language includes, or covers, the totality of possible meanings. This isn't so, for that didn't mean that every system of language
exhausts the possibilities of the signifier, which is quite different. The proof 210
of this is the fact that, for example, the language of an Australian tribe may express a given number by a crescent moon.

These remarks may appear to you to be way off the mark. It's essential however to take them up again at the beginning of our topic for this year. Our starting point, the point we keep coming back to, since we shall always be at the starting point, is that every real signifier is, as such, a signifier that signifies nothing.

2

Experience proves it – the more the signifier signifies nothing, the more indestructible it is.

They go off in a foolish direction, those who make fun of what one may call the power of words, by demonstrating, which is always easy, the contradictions into which one falls with the play of a given concept, those who mock nominalism, as it's called, in a given philosophy.

It's of course easy to criticize what may be arbitrary or fleeting in the use of a notion like that of society, for instance. It's not so very long ago that this word was invented, and it's amusing to see what dead ends result in the real from the notion that the society is responsible for what happens to the individual – a notion the requirement for which was ultimately expressed in socialist constructions. There is in effect something radically arbitrary in the emergence of the notion of society – I'm not saying of the city. Recall that for our friend Cicero in the above work the nation is, as it were, only the goddess of the population – it presides over births. As a matter of fact the modern idea of the nation is not even on the horizon of classical thought, and it is not merely the fortunes of a word that demonstrate this to us.

None of these things is self-evident. One is free to conclude from this that doubt can be cast on the notion of society. But it's precisely insofar as we are able to cast doubt upon it that it's a signifier. It's also for this reason that it has entered our social reality like the prow of a ship, like a ploughshare.

When one speaks of the subjective, and even when here we call it into question, the illusion always remains in our minds that the subjective is the opposite of the objective, that it's on the side of the speaker, and finds itself, by virtue of this very fact, on the side of illusions – it either distorts or restricts the objective. The dimension elided until now in the understanding
211 of Freudianism is that the subjective isn't on the side of the speaker. It's something we encounter in the real.

The real in question is no doubt not to be taken in the sense in which we normally understand it, which implies objectivity, a confusion constantly being made in analytic writings. The subjective appears in the real insofar as it implies that we have opposite us a subject capable of using the signifier, the play of signifiers. And capable of using it like us – not to signify something but precisely to deceive us over what there is to signify. This is to use the fact that the signifier is something other than meaning in order to present a deceptive signifier. This is so essential that it is strictly speaking the first step of modern physics. The Cartesian discussion of the deceptive god is a step that is impossible to avoid for any foundation of physics in the sense in which we understand the term.

The subjective is for us that which distinguishes the field of science in which psychoanalysis is grounded from the entire field of physics. It's the instance of subjectivity as present in the real that is the essential source of the fact that we are saying something new when we single out, for example, these series of apparently natural phenomena that we call neuroses or psychoses.

Do the psychoses form a series of natural phenomena? Do they fall within a field of natural explanation? What I'm calling *natural* is the field of science in which there is no one who uses the signifier to signify.

Please remember these definitions, because I'm only giving them to you after having carefully decanted them.

I think they are suited, in particular, to contributing the greatest clarity on the subject of final causes. The idea of final cause is repugnant to science in its present form, but science constantly makes use of it in a camouflaged way, in the notion of a return to a state of equilibrium, for instance. If by *final cause* one simply understands a cause that acts in advance, which tends towards something out ahead, it's absolutely ineliminable from scientific thought, and there is just as much final cause in Einstein's equations as in Aristotle. The difference is precisely this – there is no one who uses this signifier to signify anything – unless it's this, which is that there is a universe.

I was reading in Mr. [. . .] how amazed he was at the existence of the element water – how well this shows the care that the Creator has taken with order and with our pleasure, for if water were not this element that is so wonderfully fluid, heavy, and solid, we wouldn't see little boats sailing so 212
beautifully on the sea. This is written and it would be a mistake to think that the author is an idiot. It's just that he was still a captive of the atmosphere of a time when nature was made for speaking. We overlook this because of a kind of purification that has taken place in our causal requirements. But this alleged naivety was natural for people for whom everything that presents itself with a signifying nature is made for signifying something.

People are currently engaging in a very curious operation, which consists in overcoming certain difficulties presented by certain frontier domains into which the question of the use of the signifier as such has to be introduced, precisely by means of the notion of communication which we've discussed on occasion. And the reason I've placed the article by Tomkins in this issue of the journal you've all become somewhat familiar with is to give you an example of the naive way the notion of communication can be used.[2] You will see that this can be taken a very long way, which people haven't failed to do.

There are people who will claim that the various orders of internal secretion inside an organism send one another messages in the form, for instance, of hormones that notify the ovaries that everything's going well, or on the contrary that there's a bit of a problem somewhere. Is this a legitimate use of the notions of communication and message? Why not, if a message is simply of the order of what takes place when we project a light beam, whether invis-

[2] Silvan S. Tomkins, "Consciousness and the Unconscious in a Model of the Human Being." Published as *"La conscience et l'inconscient représentés dans un modèle de l'être humain"* in *La Psychanalyse* no. 1 (1956), 275–86.

ible or not, onto a photoelectric cell? This can be taken a very long way. If, on sweeping the sky with the beam of a spotlight, we see something appear in the middle, it may be taken as the sky's response. This produces its own criticism. But this is still to take things too lightly.

When may one really speak of communication? You are going to tell me that it's obvious – there has to be a response. This is defensible, it's a question of definition. Shall we say that there is communication whenever a response is registered? But what's a response? There's only one way defining it, which is to say that it's when something returns to the starting point. This is the schema for feedback. Every return of something that, having been registered somewhere, thereby triggers an operation of regulation, constitutes a response. And this is where communication begins, with self-regulation.

But notwithstanding this, are we now at the level of the function of the signifier? I don't think so. In a thermoelectric machine supported by feedback the signifier is not employed. Why not? Isolating the signifier as such
213 requires something else which, like any dialectical distinction in the first instance presents itself in a paradoxical manner. There is appropriate use of the signifier whenever, at the level of the receiver, what is important is not the effect of the content of the message, nor the triggering in the organ of a given reaction due to the appearance of a hormone, but this – that at the message's point of arrival one makes a note of it.

Does this imply a subjectivity? Look at it very closely. It's not certain that it does. What is distinctive about the existence of the signifier as such, the signifier which I have just been trying one more time to give a precise formulation to, insofar as it's a correlated system of elements that derive their place synchronically and diachronically in relation to one another?

I'm at sea, the captain of a small ship. I see things moving about in the night, in a way that gives me cause to think that there may be a sign there. How shall I react? If I'm not yet a human being, I shall react with all sorts of displays, as they say – modeled, motor, and emotional. I satisfy the descriptions of psychologists, I understand something, in fact I do everything I'm telling you that you must know how not to do. If on the other hand I am a human being, I write in my log book – *At such and such a time, at such and such a degree of latitude and longitude, we noticed this and that.*

This is what is fundamental. I shelter my responsibility. What distinguishes the signifier is here. I make a note of the sign as such. It's the acknowledgment of receipt [*l'accusé de réception*] that is essential to communication insofar as it is not significant, but signifying. If you don't articulate this distinction clearly, you will keep falling back upon meanings that can only mask from you the original mainspring of the signifier insofar as it carries out its true function.

Let's keep the following in mind. Even when inside an organism, whether living or not, things are transmitted that are founded upon the effectiveness of all or nothing, even when, by virtue of the fact that, for example, a threshold exists, there is something which doesn't exist below a certain level and then all of a sudden has a certain effect – keep the example of the hormones in mind –, we still can't speak of communication if by communication we imply the originality of the order of the signifier. Indeed, it isn't as all or nothing that something is a signifier, it's to the extent that something constituting a whole, the sign, exists and signifies precisely nothing. This is where the order of the signifier, insofar as it differs from the order of meaning, begins.

If psychoanalysis teaches us anything, if psychoanalysis constitutes a novelty, it's precisely that the human being's development is in no way directly deducible from the construction of, from the interferences between, from the 214
composition of, meanings, that is, instincts. The human world, the world that we know and live in, in the midst of which we orientate ourselves, and without which we are absolutely unable to orientate ourselves, doesn't only imply the existence of meanings, but the order of the signifier as well.

If the Oedipus complex isn't the introduction of the signifier then I ask to be shown any conception of it whatever. The level of its elaboration is so essential to sexual normalization uniquely because it introduces the functioning of the signifier as such into the conquest of the said man or woman. It's not because the Oedipus complex is contemporary with the genital dimension or tendency that it's possible to imagine even for a single instant that it's essential to an actual human world, to a world that has its structure of human reality.

Think about it for a second – if there is something that is clearly unsuited to introducing articulation and differentiation into the world, it's the genital function. That which in its strict essence tends towards the most mysterious of effusions is that which is the most paradoxical in relation to any real structuring of the world. It's not the instinctual dimension that is operative in the stage to be passed through in the Oedipus complex. In this respect, it's on the contrary the so highly diverse material we are shown by the pregenital stages that enables us to imagine easily how, by analogy with meaning, the mode of matter, to call it by its name, is linked up to what man has in his immediate field. The bodily, excremental, pregenital, exchanges are quite adequate for structuring a world of objects, a world of complete human reality, that is, one in which there are subjectivities.

There's no other scientific definition of subjectivity than one that proceeds from the possibility of handling the signifier for purely signifying, not significant ends, that is, expressing no direct relation of the order of appetite.

Things are simple. But the subject still has to acquire, conquer, the order of the signifier, be given his place in a relationship of implication that attains his being, which results in the formation of what in our language we call the superego. One doesn't have to go very deeply into analytic literature to see that the use made of this concept is congenial to the definition of the signifier, which is that it signifies nothing and is therefore always capable of yielding various meanings. For us the superego raises the question of what is the order of entrance, of introduction, of present instance, of the signifier, which is indispensable to the functioning of a human organism that has to come to terms not only with a natural environment but with a signifying universe.

215 Here we return to the crossroads at which I left you last time on the subject of the neuroses. What do symptoms result from, if it's not from the human organism's being implicated in something that is structured like a language, whereby such and such an element of its functioning will come into play as a signifier? I went further on this topic last time, taking the example of hysteria. Hysteria is a question centered on a signifier that remains enigmatic as to its meaning. The question of death and the question of birth are as it happens the two ultimate questions that have precisely no solution in the signifier. This is what gives neurotics their existential value.

Now for the psychoses. What do they mean? What is the function of the subject's relationships to the signifier in the psychoses? We have already tried to spell this out on a number of occasions. The reason that we are always thus forced to investigate things in a roundabout way must lie in the question itself. We're obliged to acknowledge this for the moment. There is an obstacle here, a resistance, which will yield its meaning only to the extent that we have gone into things deeply enough to explain why things are like this.

3

Let's explore the problem again with the aim of taking a further step forward, as we've done on each occasion.

You remember the schema we arrived at. I pointed out to you that there must have been something there that had not materialized, at a certain moment, in the field of the signifier, that had been *verworfen,* thereby making the object of a *Verwerfung* reappear in the real. This mechanism is distinct from everything that in other ways we know from our experience, concerning the relationships between the imaginary, the symbolic, and the real.

Freud gave powerful expression, in the text on Schreber we're working on among others, to the radical distinction between passional conviction and delusional conviction. The former depends upon the projection of intentions. It is, for example, jealousy where I'm jealous of my own feelings in the other, where it's my own drives to be unfaithful that I impute to the other. As to the second, Freud formulates it thus, that what has been rejected from within
216 reappears without, or again, as one tries to say in an expanded form, that

what has been suppressed in the idea reappears in the real. But what does this mean, exactly?

In neurosis, too, we see this action of the drive and its consequences. Doesn't this formulation leave something to be desired, something confused, defective, even absurd? Every author confines himself to this formulation, and in putting it to you in this form I wasn't wanting to contribute anything original. I think I can find someone among you to help me look more closely at the works in which Katan has tried to grasp the mechanism of psychotic neoformation. You will observe what an extraordinary dead-end he arrives at, from which he escapes only at the price of contradictory formulations. This testifies to the conceptual difficulties one is committed to if one confuses, however slightly, the notion of reality with that of objectivity, or even with that of meaning, if one moves away from a reality distinct from the test of the real, from a reality in the sentiment of the real.

An entire phenomenological supposition, which extends well beyond the field of psychoanalysis and holds sway there only insofar as it equally holds sway elsewhere, is based on confusing the realm of meaningfulness with the realm of meaning. Proceeding from works that are extremely rigorous elaborations upon the function of the signifier, supposedly psychological phenomenology slides into the realm of meaning. This is its basic point of confusion. It's led towards it like a dog on a scent, and, like the dog, this will never lead it to any kind of scientific result.

You know the would-be opposition between *Erklären* and *Verstehen*. Here we must maintain that the only scientific structure is where there is *Erklären*. *Verstehen* opens onto all kinds of confusion. *Erklären* doesn't at all imply mechanical meaning or anything else of that order. The nature of *Erklären* lies in the recourse to the signifier as the sole foundation of all conceivable scientific structuration.

At the beginning of the Schreber case we find a period of disorder, of fertile moment. It presents a whole set of symptoms which, because it has generally been hidden away or, more exactly, because it has slipped through our fingers, has been unable to be elucidated analytically and is most of the time only reconstructed. Now, in reconstructing it we can discover, with very few exceptions, what appear to be the meanings and mechanisms we see at work in neurosis. There is nothing that more closely resembles a neurotic symptomatology than a prepsychotic symptomatology. Once the diagnosis has been made, we are told that one finds that the unconscious is displayed on the
outside, that everything belonging to the *id* has passed into the external world, 217
and that the meanings in play are so clear that we are precisely unable to intervene analytically.

This is the classical position, and it still has some value. The paradox it contains has escaped nobody, but all the reasons that have been advanced to explain it are of a tautological or contradictory character. They are superstructurations of totally absurd hypotheses. It suffices to take an interest in analytic literature as a symptom to realize this.

Where does it spring from? From the fact that the world of objects is in some way affected, captured, induced, by a meaning in relation with drives characteristic of the psychoses? Is the construction of an external world distinctive of the psychoses? However, if there is any way of equally defining neurosis, this is it. When do we decide that the subject has crossed over the limits, that he is delusional?

Take the prepsychotic period. Our President Schreber is living out something in the nature of perplexity. He gives us in living form this question that I was saying lies at the bottom of every form of neurosis. He is prey to strange forebodings – he indicates this to us after the event. He is abruptly invaded by this image which would seem to be the least likely to enter the mind of a man of his kind and his style, that it really must be rather pleasant to be a woman succumbing to intercourse. This is a period of confusion and panic. How are we to locate the border between this moment of confusion and the point at which his delusion ended with the construction that he was in actual fact a woman, and not just any woman, but the divine woman, or more exactly God's fiancée? Is there anything here that is sufficient for locating the onset of psychosis? Certainly not. Katan reports a case that he saw declare itself at a much earlier period than Schreber's, and about which he was able to form a direct idea, having come onto the scene at the turning point of the case.[3] It was the case of a youth at the age of puberty, whose whole prepsychotic period the author analyses very well, while conveying the idea that there was nothing in this subject of the order of accession to anything that would realize in him the virile type. Everything failed. And while he did try to conquer the typically virile attitude, it was by means of imitation, of a latching on, following the example of one of his friends. Like him and following him, he engaged in the first sexual maneuvers of puberty, namely masturbation, which he subsequently renounced under the injunction of the said friend, and he began to identify with him for a whole series of exercises that were called exercises of self-conquest. He behaved as if he were at the mercy of a severe father, which was the case with his friend. Like him, he became interested in a girl
218 who, as if by chance, was the same one his friend was interested in. And once this identification with his friend has gone quite a way, the young girl will readily fall into his arms.

Here we obviously find the *as if* mechanism that Mrs. Helene Deutsch has stressed as being a significant dimension in the symptomatology of the schi-

[3] See "Structural Aspects of a Case of Schizophrenia."

zophrenias.[4] It's a mechanism of imaginary compensation – you can verify the usefulness of the distinction between the three registers – for the absent Oedipus complex, which would have given him virility in the form, not of the paternal image, but of the signifier, *the name of the father*.

Once the psychosis has broken out, the subject will conduct himself in the same way as before, as an unconscious homosexual. No meaning emerges that is fundamentally different from the prepsychotic period. All his conduct in relation to the friend, who was the pivotal element in his attempt at structuration at the time of puberty, can be rediscovered in his delusion. When did he start to delude? When he said that his father was pursuing him to kill him, to rob him, to castrate him. All the contents implied in neurotic meanings are there. But the essential point, which isn't highlighted, is that the delusion began the moment the initiative came from the Other, with a capital O, when the initiative was founded on a subjective activity. *The Other wants* this, and above all he wants this to be known, he wants to signify it.

As soon as there is a delusion, we enter at full tilt upon the domain of intersubjectivity, where the whole problem is to know why it's fantasized. But in the name of fantasy, omnipresent in neurosis, attached as we are to its meaning, we forget its structure, namely that it's a question of signifiers, of signifiers as such, handled by a subject for signifying aims, signifying so purely that the meaning very often remains problematic. What we have encountered in this symptomatology always implies what I indicated to you last year in relation to the dream of Irma's injection – the inmixing[5] of subjects.

It's characteristic of the intersubjective dimension that you have a subject in the real capable of using the signifier as such, that is, to speak, not so as to inform you, but precisely so as to lure you. This possibility is what is distinctive about the existence of the signifier. But this isn't all. As soon as there is a subject and use of the signifier, use of the between-I [*l'entre-je*] is possible, that is to say, of the interposed subject. This inmixing of subjects is one of the most obvious elements in the dream of Irma's injection. Recall the three practitioners called in one by one by Freud, who wants to know what it is that's in Irma's throat. And these three farcical characters operate, 219
defend theses, talk only nonsense. They are the between-I's, who play an essential role here.

They are marginal to Freud's inquiry, whose major preoccupation at this

[4] See "Some Forms of Emotional Disturbance and their Relationship to Schizophrenia."

[5] *"immixtion;"* term used by Damourette and Pichon for the semantically different ways the subject's participation in an event or action can be described by a verb alone or by one of the verbs *"faire," "voir,"* or *"laisser"* plus an infinitive: e.g., *"opérer," "faire opérer," "voir opérer,"* and *"laisser opérer."* See *Essai de grammaire de la langue française* 5:791–817.

time is defense. In a letter to Fliess he says this – *I am right in the middle of what is outside nature.*[6] This is what defense is, in effect, insofar as it has an essential relationship to the signifier, not to the prevalence of meaning, but to idolatry of the signifier as such. This is merely a pointer.

Isn't it precisely the inmixing of subjects that appears in delusion? This is a characteristic that is so essential to any intersubjective relation that, it may be said, there is no language that doesn't include quite special grammatical expressions to indicate it.

I'll give you an example. It's all the difference there is between *The head of department who had this patient operated on by his resident* and *The head of department who was to operate on this patient had him operated on by his resident.*[7] You must be able to see that, although they lead to the same action, they mean two completely different things. It's this that is constantly involved in delusion. One *makes them do* this. This is where the problem lies, we are a long way from being able just simply to say that the *id* is quite abruptly present and reappears in the real.

At the heart of the psychoses there is a dead end, perplexity concerning the signifier. Everything takes place as if the subject were reacting to this by an attempt at restitution, at compensation. Fundamentally the crisis is undoubtedly unleashed by some question or other. Which is . . . ? I've got no idea. I suppose that the subject reacts to the signifier's absence by all the more emphatically affirming another one that as such is essentially enigmatic. I told you that the Other with a big O, qua bearer of the signifier, is excluded. The Other is thereby all the more powerfully affirmed between it and the subject, at the level of the little other, of the imaginary. This is where all the between-I phenomena that make up what is apparent in the symptomatology of psychosis take place – at the level of the other subject, of the one who holds the initiative in the delusion – in the case of Schreber, Professor Flechsig or God who is potentially so seductive that he places the world order in danger by virtue of the attraction.

It's at the level of the between-I, that is, of the little other, of the subject's double, who is both his ego and not his ego, that words appear that are a kind of running commentary on existence. We observe this phenomenon in mental automatism, but it's much more accentuated here, as there is a sort of teasing use of the signifier in the sentences that are begun then interrupted.
220 That level of the signifier which is that of the sentence comprises a middle, a beginning, and an end, and thus requires a conclusion. This is what enables

[6] This may be a reference to the remark, "All I was trying to do was to explain defense, but just try to explain something from the very core of nature!" Letter of August 16, 1895, Freud-Fliess, 136; Letter 27, Origins, 123.

[7] The two sentences are *Le médecin-chef qui a fait opérer ce malade par son interne* and *Le médecin-chef qui devait opérer ce malade, il l'a fait opérer par son interne.*

the play upon expectation, a slowing down that occurs at the imaginary level of the signifier, as if the solution to the enigma, for want of being able to be formulated in any really open manner other than through the primordial assertion of the other's initiative, is given by showing that it's a question of the signifier.

Just as the formula in bold letters that appears at the conclusion to the dream of Irma's injection shows the solution to what is at the end of Freud's desire – nothing more important in effect than a formula of organic chemistry – so we find, in the phenomenon of delusion, in the commentaries and in the buzzing of discourse in its pure form, the indication that it's a question of the signifier.

11 April 1956

221

XV

On primordial signifiers and the lack of one

A CROSSROADS
BASIC SIGNIFIERS
A NEW SIGNIFIER IN THE REAL
APPROACHES TO THE HOLE
IDENTIFICATORY COMPENSATION

The distinction I have been insisting upon this year between the signifier and the signified turns out to be particularly justified by examination of the psychoses. Today I would like to make you feel this.

1

What are we looking for, we analysts, when we investigate a mental disturbance, whether it's confirmed in a patent manner or is latent, whether it masks itself or reveals itself in symptoms or conduct? We are always looking for meaning. This is what makes us different. The psychoanalyst is credited with not letting himself be deceived over the true meaning. When he uncovers the significance that an object has acquired for the subject, the register of meaning is always involved, that of a meaning which he regards as concerning the subject in some way. This is where I want you to pause, for there is a crossroads here.

The interest, the desire, the craving, which captures the subject in a meaning leads to a search for its type, mold, preformation, in the register of instinctual relations in which this subject appears correlated to an object – hence the construction of the theory of instincts, the foundations on which the analytic discovery rests. Here we have a relational world or, I should almost say, maze which comprises so many bifurcations, communications,
222 turnings back, as to leave us satisfied – that is to say, ultimately, that we lose ourselves in them. This is a tangible fact in our daily handling of these meanings.

Take homosexual attachment as an example, which is an essential component of the Oedipal drama. We say that the meaning of the homosexual relation tends to emerge in the inverted Oedipus complex. In the case of neurosis we say most of the time that the subject defends against this attachment that is more or less latent in his conduct, but still tends to appear. We speak of defense – it has several modes. We look for its cause, which we define as the fear of castration. We are never short of an explanation, moreover – if this one won't do, we shall find another one.

But whether it be this one here or another one, isn't it apparent, as the slightest familiarity with analytic literature will show, that the question of the order of coherence at work is never raised?

Why should we allow that the homosexual orientation of libidinal investment involves causal coherence for the subject from the outset? In what way does being captured by the homosexual imago entail for the subject that he lose his penis? What is the order of causality that implies what is known as the primary process? Up to what point is a causal relation to be admitted here? What are the modes of causality that the subject fears in imaginary capture? Is it sufficient that we observe this imaginary relation – with all its implications, which are themselves constructed since it's a question of the imaginary – for it to be given in the subject, whereas we see it from the outside? I'm not saying that we are wrong to think that the fear of castration, with all its consequences, enters into play automatically in a male subject caught in the pacifying capture of the homosexual relation. I'm saying that we never question it. And there would no doubt be different answers according to different cases. The causal coherence here is constructed, through an unwarranted extrapolation from things of the imaginary onto the real. When it is the pleasure principle, resolution and return to an equilibrium, a requirement of desire, that is at issue, we quite naturally slide into bringing the reality principle – or something else – into play.

This enables us to return to our crossroads. Desire is at first sight understood as an essentially imaginary relation. Setting out from here, we set about cataloguing instincts, their equivalences and interconnections. Let's instead stop and ask ourselves whether these are merely biological laws that render a number of meanings instinctually interesting for the human subject. What part does that which depends on the signifier play in all this?

In fact, the signifier, with its own action and insistence, intervenes in all 223
of the human being's interests – however profound, primitive, elementary we suppose them to be.

I have spent days and lessons trying by all available means to give you a glimpse of what we might provisionally call the autonomy of the signifier, that is, the fact that it has its own laws. Undoubtedly, they are extremely difficult to isolate, since we always set the signifier to work among meanings.

This is to state the interest of linguistic considerations on the problem. It's impossible to study how this phenomenon called language, which is the most fundamental of interhuman relations, functions unless one draws this distinction between the signifier and the signified from the outset. And the step I ask you to take in this seminar is to follow me when I say to you that the sense of the analytic discovery isn't simply to have found meanings but to have gone much further than anyone has ever gone in reading them, namely right to the signifier. That this fact is neglected explains the dead ends, the confusions, the circles and tautologies, that analytic research encounters.

2

The mainspring of the analytic discovery isn't to be found in the so-called libidinal or instinctual meanings relative to a whole range of behavior. These exist, it's true. But in the human being those meanings that are the closest to need, meanings that are relative to the most purely biological insertion into a nutritive and captivating environment, primordial meanings, are, in their sequence and in their very foundation, subject to laws that are the laws of the signifier.

If I spoke to you about day and night, it was to make you feel that the day, the very notion of the day, the word *day,* the notion of the coming of the day, is something that is properly speaking ungraspable in any reality. The opposition between day and night is a signifying opposition, which goes infinitely beyond all the meanings it may ultimately cover, indeed beyond every kind of meaning. If I took day and night as examples, it's of course because our subject is man and woman. The signifier *man* and the signifier *woman* are something other than a passive attitude and an active attitude, an aggressive attitude and a yielding attitude, something other than forms of behavior. There is undoubtedly a hidden signifier here which, of course, can nowhere
224 be incarnated absolutely, but which is nevertheless the closest to being incarnated in the existence of the word *man* and the word *woman*.

If these registers of being are anywhere, in the final analysis it's in words. It isn't obligatory that they be verbalized words. It may be a sign on a wall, it may be, for the so-called primitive, a painting or a stone, but it's elsewhere than in types of conduct or patterns.[1]

This is not new. When we say that the Oedipus complex is essential for the human being to be able to accede to a humanized structure of the real, it can't mean anything else.

Everything that abounds in our literature, the fundamental principles on which we agree, imply it – in order for there to be reality, adequate access to reality, in order for the sense of reality to be a reliable guide, in order for reality not to be what it is in psychosis, the Oedipus complex has to have been lived through. Now, we are only able to express this complex, its triangular crystallization, its various modalities and consequences, its terminal

[1] In English in the original.

crisis, called a decline,[2] which is ratified by the subject's entry into a new dimension, insofar as the subject is at once himself and the other two partners. This is what is meant by the term *identification* that you are always using. Thus here we have intersubjectivity and dialectical organization. This would be unthinkable if the field we have localized under the name of the Oedipus complex didn't have a symbolic structure.

I don't believe that this analysis can be questioned. The fact that it isn't generally accepted alters nothing. It's enough that certain people take it to be certain for it to be raised, by this very fact alone, as an issue. Equilibrium, the right situation for the human subject in reality, depends, at one of its levels at the very least, on a purely symbolic experience, on an experience that implies the conquest of the symbolic relation as such.

On reflection, do we need psychoanalysis to tell us this? Aren't we astounded that philosophers didn't emphasize ages ago that human reality is irreducibly structured as signifying?

Day and night, man and woman, peace and war – I could enumerate more oppositions that don't emerge out of the real world but give it its framework, its axes, its structure, that organize it, that bring it about that there is in effect a reality for man, and that he can find his bearings therein. The notion of reality that we bring to bear in analysis presupposes this web, this mesh of signifiers. This isn't new. It's constantly being implied in analytic discourse, but is never isolated as such. This isn't necessarily a drawback, but it is one 225
in, for example, what has been written on the psychoses.

Concerning the psychoses, the same mechanisms of attraction, repulsion, conflict, and defense as in the neuroses have been invoked, whereas the results are phenomenologically and psychopathologically distinct from, if not opposed to, one another. One is content with the same effects of meaning. This is where the mistake is. Thus the need to pause over the existence of the structure of the signifier as such – in a word, such as it exists in psychosis.

I'll pick things up again from the beginning and I'll keep myself to the bare minimum – since we have distinguished between the signifier and the signified, we must allow for the possibility that psychosis not only depends on what appears at the level of meanings, of their proliferation, of their labyrinth, in which the subject is supposedly lost or, even, arrested at a fixation, but also that essentially it stems from something that is situated at the level of the subject's relations with the signifier.

The signifier is to be thought of initially as distinct from meaning. It's characterized by not in itself possessing a literal meaning [*signification propre*]. Try to imagine, then, what the appearance of a pure signifier might be like.

2 The French translation of "The Dissolution of the Oedipus Complex" is "*Le déclin du complexe d'Oedipe.*"

Of course, we can't imagine this, by definition. And yet, since we ask ourselves questions about origins, we must try to get closer to what this might represent.

Our experience makes us constantly feel that these basic signifiers without which the order of human meanings would be unable to establish itself exist. Isn't this what all mythologies explain to us, also? *Magical thought* is how modern scientific drivel puts this whenever it is confronted with something that goes beyond the little shrunken brains of those to whom it seems that the necessary condition for penetrating the cultural domain is that nothing should capture them in any desire that might humanize them. *Magical thought* – does this term strike you as sufficient for explaining why people who, in every likelihood, have had the same relationships to birth as we have should have interpreted day, night, earth, and sky as entities that combine and copulate in a family studded with murders, with incest, with extraordinary eclipses, with disappearances, metamorphoses, mutilations, with one or other of the terms? Do you believe that these people really take these things literally? This really is putting them at the mental level of the evolutionist of our day, who thinks he has explained it all.

I think that as far as the inadequacy of thought is concerned, we've got no reason to be envious of the ancients.

226 Isn't it on the contrary clear that these mythologies are aimed at installing man, at placing him upright, in the world – and that they tell him what the primordial signifiers are, how to conceive their relationships and their genealogy? There is no need here to inquire into Greek or Egyptian mythology, since M. Griaule came and explained African mythology to you.[3] This was about a placenta that had been cut into four, and one of the pieces, ripped out before the others, introduced into the four primitive elements the initial dissymmetry and the dialectic by which are explained not only the division of the fields but also the manner in which clothing is worn, what it is that clothing, weaving, such and such an art, etc., signify. This is the genealogy of signifiers insofar as it's essential if a human being is to find his bearings in them. They aren't just signposts, or external, stereotyped moulds, layered over forms of behavior, nor are they just *patterns*.[4] It makes possible for him free circulation in a world that henceforth has order in it. Modern man is perhaps less well off.

It's through these myths that the primitive finds his bearings in the order of meaningfulnesses. He possesses keys for all sorts of extraordinary situations. Should he be in breach of everything, signifiers still support him, which for example will tell him exactly the form of punishment entailed by the

[3] See above, chap. 11, p. 151 & n.8.
[4] In English in the original.

outburst that produced the disturbances. The rule imposes its fundamental rhythm upon him. As for us, we're reduced to very fearfully remaining conformist, we are afraid that we'll go a little bit mad as soon as we don't say exactly the same thing as everybody else. This is the situation of modern man.

Let's flesh out the signifier's presence in the real, insofar as this is possible. The emergence of a new signifier, with all the consequences, down to one's most personal conduct and thoughts, that this may entail, the appearance of a register such as that of a new religion, for example, isn't something that is easily manipulated – experience proves it. Meanings shift, common sentiments and socially conditioned relations change, but there are also all sorts of so-called revelatory phenomena that can appear in a sufficiently disturbing mode for the terms we use in the psychoses not to be entirely inappropriate for them. The appearance of a new structure in the relations between basic signifiers and the creation of a new term in the order of the signifier are devastating in character.

This is no concern of ours. We don't need to take any interest in the appearance of a signifier, since it's a phenomenon that we never encounter professionally. On the other hand, we do deal with subjects in whom we 227
apparently bring to light something, an irreducible kernel, that occurs at the level of the Oedipal relation. The further question I invite you to ask yourselves is this – can't one conceive of considering the consequences of the essential lack of a signifier in these immediately accessible subjects called psychotics?

Here again, I'm saying nothing new. I'm simply clearly articulating what is implied in our discourse when we speak of the Oedipus complex. A neurosis without Oedipus doesn't exist. This question has been raised, but there's no truth in it.[5] We readily acknowledge that in psychosis something hasn't functioned, is essentially incomplete, in the Oedipus complex. A certain analyst has had a paranoid-like case to study *in vivo,* homologous in certain respects to the case of President Schreber. He says a number of things that in the end come very close to what I've been telling you, except that obviously he gets confused because he's unable to formulate things as I'm suggesting they should be in saying that psychosis consists of a hole, a lack, at the level of the signifier.

This may strike you as vague, but it's adequate, even if we can't say straightaway what this signifier is. We shall nevertheless figure it out by approximation, beginning from the meanings connoted as we approach it. May one speak of approaching a hole? Why not? There is nothing more dangerous than approaching a void.

[5] See Charles Odier, *"Une névrose sans complexe d'Oedipe."*

3

There is another form of defense that a forbidden tendency or meaning will provoke. It's the defense that consists in not approaching the place where there is no answer to the question.

One is more at ease this way and, after all, this is the characteristic of normal people. *Don't ask us questions,* we've been taught, and this is why we're here. But as psychoanalysts it's nevertheless our business to try to enlighten these poor unfortunates who have asked themselves questions. We're certain that neurotics have asked themselves a question. Psychotics, it's not so sure. The answer has perhaps come to them before the question – this is a hypothesis. Or else, the question has asked itself of its own accord – this isn't inconceivable.

There is no question for a subject without another to whom he has addressed it. Someone was saying to me recently, in analysis – *In the final analysis, I have got nothing to ask of anyone*. It was a sad avowal. I pointed out to him
228 that if in any case he had anything to ask he would necessarily have to ask it of someone. This is the other side of the same question. If we implant this relation firmly in our heads, it won't appear extravagant if I say that it's also possible that the question asks itself first, that it's not the subject who has asked it. As I've shown you in my case presentations, what happens at the beginning of a psychosis is of this order.

Recall this little subject who, to us, appeared evidently very lucid. Given the way he had grown up and prospered in existence, in the midst of the anarchy, which was merely a bit more patent than in other cases, of his family situation, he had attached himself to a friend who had become his point of implantation in existence, and all of a sudden something happened, he wasn't able to explain what. It became very clear to us that this was bound up with the appearance of his partner's daughter, and we can add that he experienced this fact as incestuous, hence defense.

We haven't been very stringent about the rigor of our remarks ever since we learned from Freud that the principle of contradiction doesn't work in the unconscious – a suggestive and interesting formulation but, if one doesn't go any further than this, a bit brief – when something fails to work in one sense it's explained by its contrary. And this is why analysis explains things so admirably. This simple little chap had understood a lot less than we had. He was knocking against something, and he didn't have any keys, he spent three months in bed in order to find his bearings again. He was in a state of perplexity.

A minimum of the sensitivity that our trade gives us clearly demonstrates something that can always be seen in what is known as prepsychosis, namely the feeling that the subject has come to the edge of a hole. This is to be taken

literally. It's not a matter of understanding what is going on when we aren't present. It isn't a matter of phenomenology. It's a matter of understanding, not imagining, what happens for a subject when the question comes to him from where there is no signifier, when it's a hole, a lack, that makes itself felt as such.

I repeat, it's not a matter of phenomenology. It's not a matter of playing the madman – one does this enough ordinarily, in one's internal dialogue. It's a matter of determining what the consequences are of a situation that is determined thus.

Not every stool has four legs. There are some that stand upright on three. Here, though, there is no question of their lacking any, otherwise things go very badly indeed. Well then, let me tell you that the significant points of purchase that uphold the little world of the solitary little men in the modern 229
crowd are very few in number. It's possible that at the outset the stool doesn't have enough legs, but that up to a certain point it will nevertheless stand up, when the subject, at a certain crossroads of his biographical history, is confronted by this lack that has always existed. To designate it we've made do until now with the term *Verwerfung*.

This may lead to more than one conflict, but it isn't essentially a matter of conflicting constellations which in neurosis are explained by a significant decompensation. In psychosis it's the signifier that is in question, and as the signifier is never solitary, as it invariably forms something coherent – this is the very meaningfulness of the signifier – the lack of one signifier necessarily brings the subject to the point of calling the set of signifiers into question.

Here you have the fundamental key to the problems of the beginning of psychosis, the sequence of its stages, and its meaning.

In fact, the terms in which these questions are usually framed imply what I'm telling you. A Katan, for example, states that hallucination is a mode of defense like any other.[6] He's aware, however, that there are phenomena here which though very closely related are different – the certainty of meaning without content, which may simply be called interpretation, is, effectively, different from hallucination properly so-called. He explains the two by mechanisms designed to protect the subject according to another mode than the one in operation in the neuroses. In the neuroses it's meaning that temporarily disappears, is eclipsed, and goes and lodges itself somewhere else, whereas reality itself remains. Such defenses are inadequate in the case of psychosis, where what is to protect the subject appears in reality. The subject places outside what may stir up inside him the instinctual drive that he has to confront.

It's obvious that the term *reality* as it's used here is totally inadequate. Why

[6] See "Schreber's Hallucinations about the 'Little Men.' "

not have the courage to say that the mechanism being appealed to is the *id* – since it's considered to have the power to modify and disturb what one may call the truth of the thing?

According to this explanation it's a matter of the subject's protecting himself against homosexual temptations. Nobody has ever gone on to say – Schreber less so than anyone else – that all of a sudden he could no longer see people, that the very face of his male counterparts was, by the hand of eternal God, covered with a cloak. He could always see them perfectly well. One simply believes that he couldn't see them for what they really were for him, namely attractive love objects. At issue is, therefore, not what one vaguely calls real-
230 ity, as if this were the same thing as the reality of a wall we might bump into, but a meaningful reality, which doesn't present us simply with footholds and obstacles, but a truth that verifies itself and installs itself by itself as orienting this world and introducing beings, to call them by their name, into it.

Why not admit, then, that the *id* is capable of conjuring away the truth of the thing?

But we can also raise the question from the opposite direction, namely, *What happens when the truth of the thing is lacking, when there is nothing left to represent it in its truth, when for example the register of the father defaults?*

The father is not simply the generator. He's also the one who has rightful possession of the mother – and in peace, in principle. His function is central to the realization of the Oedipus complex and conditions the son's accession – which is also a function, correlative to the first – to the model of virility. What happens if a certain lack occurs in the formative function of the father?

The father may well have had a certain mode of relation such that the son does indeed adopt a feminine position, but it's not through fear of castration. We are all familiar with cases of these delinquent or psychotic sons who proliferate in the shadow of a paternal personality of exceptional character, one of these social monsters referred to as venerable. They are often characters strongly marked by a style of radiance and success, but in a unilateral manner, in the register of unbridled ambition or authoritarianism, sometimes of talent, of genius. They don't necessarily have to be a genius, have merit, or be mediocre or nasty, it's sufficient that this be unilateral and monstrous. It's certainly not by chance that a psychopathic personality subversion, in particular, is produced in such a situation.

Let's suppose that this situation entails for the subject the impossibility of assuming the realization of the signifier *father* at the symbolic level. What's he left with? He's left with the image the paternal function is reduced to. It's an image which isn't inscribed in any triangular dialectic, but whose function as model, as specular alienation, nevertheless gives the subject a fastening point and enables him to apprehend himself on the imaginary plane.

If the captivating image is without limits, if the character in question manifests himself simply in the order of strength and not in that of the pact, then a relation of rivalry, aggressiveness, fear, etc. appear. Insofar as the relationship remains on the imaginary, dual, and unlimited plane, it doesn't possess the meaning of reciprocal exclusion that is included in specular confrontation, but possesses instead the other function, that of imaginary capture. The 231
image, on its own, initially adopts the sexualized function, without any need of an intermediary, an identification with the mother, or with anything else. The subject then adopts this intimidated position that we can observe in the fish or lizard. The imaginary relation alone is installed on a plane that has nothing typical about it and is dehumanizing because it doesn't leave any place for the relation of reciprocal exclusion that enables the ego's image to be founded on the orbit given by the model of the more complete other.

The alienation here is radical, it isn't bound to a nihilating signified, as in a certain type of rivalrous relation with the father, but to a nihilation of the signifier. The subject will have to bear the weight of this real, primitive dispossession of the signifier and adopt compensation for it, at length, over the course of his life, through a series of purely conformist identifications with characters who will give him the feeling for what one has to do to be a man.

The situation may be sustained for a long time this way, psychotics can live compensated lives with apparently ordinary behavior considered to be normally virile, and then all of a sudden, mysteriously, God only knows why, become decompensated. What is it that suddenly renders insufficient the imaginary crutches which have enabled the subject to compensate for the absence of the signifier? How does the signifier as such again lay down its requirements? How does what is missing intervene and question?

Before trying to resolve these problems, I would like you to notice how the appearance of the question raised by a lack of a signifier manifests itself. It manifests itself through fringe phenomena in which the set of signifiers is brought into play. A great disturbance of the internal discourse, in the phenomenological sense of the term, comes about and the masked Other that is always in us appears lit up all of a sudden, revealing itself in its own function, for this function is the only one that henceforth maintains the subject at the level of discourse which threatens to fail him entirely and disappear. Such is the sense of the twilight of reality that characterizes the beginning of psychoses.

We shall try to advance a bit further next time.

18 April 1956.

233

XVI

Secretaries to the insane

A READING
SOUL MURDER
THE IMPLICATIONS OF THE SIGNIFIER
THE LITTLE MEN
THE THREE FUNCTIONS OF THE FATHER

That Schreber was *exceptionally gifted,* as he himself puts it, at observing phenomena of which he is the center and at searching for their truth, makes his testimony incomparably valuable.

Reading from the Memoirs

1

Let's pause for a moment. I began with this reading in order to give you an indication of what I intend doing today, namely, take you through a number of passages that I have chosen as the best I could from the four or five hundred-odd pages of Schreber's book.

We are apparently willingly going to become secretaries to the insane. This expression is generally used to reproach alienists for their impotence. Well then, not only shall we be his secretaries, but we shall take what he recounts literally – which till now has always been considered as the thing to avoid doing.

Wasn't it because they didn't go far enough in listening to the insane that the great observers who drew up the first classifications impoverished the material they were given – to such an extent that it appeared problematic and fragmentary to them?

234 On Friday I presented a case of chronic hallucinatory psychosis. Weren't you struck, those of you who were there, by how much more alive what one obtains is if, instead of trying at all cost to establish whether the hallucination is verbal or sensory or nonsensory, one simply listens to the subject? That patient the other day brought forth, invented, as though by a sort of imaginative reproduction, questions that one really felt had been previously implied by her own situation, without having been, strictly speaking, formulated by her. Of course, one can't stop there if one wants to understand it entirely,

for one has to know why things happen this way. But one has to begin by looking at things in a balanced way, and this is located at the level of the signifier-signified phenomenon.

This dimension is far from having been exhausted by psychology, or metapsychology, or traditional classical parapsychology, which make use of academic categories – hallucination, interpretation, sensation, perception. One does indeed feel that the problem doesn't arise at this level and that this is even a very bad beginning, one that leaves no hope of ever correctly raising the question of what delusion is, or of the level at which the displacement of the subject in relation to the sense phenomena occurs.

It can't be too often suggested to psychologists and doctors that they make use of what is nevertheless accessible to the experience of the common man. I propose an exercise for you. Reflect a bit on what reading is.

What is it that you call reading? What is the optimum moment for reading? When are you quite certain that you are reading? You will tell me that there is no room for doubt, and that one has a feeling of reading. There are many things that count against this. In dreams, for example, we are quite capable of having the feeling of reading something, whereas, obviously, we can't claim that there is any correspondence with a signifier. Consuming certain toxic substances may lead us to the same feeling. Doesn't this suggest the idea that we can't trust the apprehension of the thing by our feelings, and that the objectivity of the relation between the signifier and the signified has to be introduced? This is where the problem and its complications really begin.

There is for example the case of someone pretending to read. Long ago, when I was traveling in countries that had just gained their independence, I saw a gentleman, the attendant to a lord of the Atlas,[1] take a small document that was intended for him, and I noticed immediately that he didn't understand one word of it, for he was holding it upside down. But, with great seriousness, he uttered something – a story about not losing face before the 235
respectful circle. Was he reading or wasn't he? Undeniably he was reading the essential part, namely, that my credentials were sound.

The other extreme is when you already know what is in the text by heart. This happens more often than one thinks. Those texts of Freud's that are in common use in your psychological and medical training you can be said to know by heart already. You only read what you already know by heart. This is what makes it possible for what forms the basis of so-called scientific literature to be singularly relativized, at least in our domain. One often gets the impression that what orientates, fundamentally, the point of a discourse is perhaps nothing other than to stay exactly within the limits of what has already been said. It seems that the ultimate point of the discourse is to give a sign

[1] A mountain chain situated in northern Africa.

to its readers and to prove that the signatory is, if I can put it like this, a non-nobody, that he is capable of writing what everybody else writes.

Here one observes a flagrant lack of correspondence between the intellectual capacities of authors, which clearly range over very great limits indeed, and the remarkable uniformity of what they contribute to the discourse. The most ordinary scientific life presents us with this patent lack of correspondence. Why, then, stigmatize in advance, as null and void, what issues from a subject who is presumed to be in the order of the meaningless, but whose testimony is more unusual or, even, entirely original? However disturbed his relations with the external world may be, perhaps his testimony still remains valuable.

As a matter of fact, we notice, and not simply concerning a case as remarkable as President Schreber but concerning any one of these subjects, that if we know how to listen the delusion of the chronic hallucinatory psychoses reveals that the subject has a very specific relationship with respect to the entire system of language in its various orders. Only the patient is able to bear witness to this, and he bears witness most energetically.

We have no reason not to take down word for word what he says, under the pretext of something or other that is supposed to be ineffable, incommunicable, affective – you know, everything that is constructed around supposedly primitive phenomena. The subject effectively bears witness to a certain turning [*virage*] in the relationship to language, which may be called erotization or pacification. His way of falling under the phenomenon of discourse as a whole undoubtedly reveals to us, as soon as we give up looking for the lowest common denominator in mental life, a dimension that is constitutive of this phenomenon. This dimension is the distance between psychical lived experience and the half-external situation in which, in relation to all language
236 phenomena, not only the insane but all human subjects find themselves.

Methodologically we are therefore correct in accepting the testimony of the insane about their position with respect to language, and we should take it into account in the overall analysis of the subject's relationships to language. This is the major and enduring interest of the legacy that Schreber has left us in his *Memoirs*, an effectively memorable thing and one worthy of our meditation.

2

Schreber himself points out that something in him was at a certain moment profoundly disturbed. A fissure appeared in the order of his relations with the other, which he mysteriously calls *soul murder*.

This remains obscure, but our experience of analytic categories enables us to find our bearings here. It's a matter of something essentially related to the origins of the ego, to what for the subject is the ellipsis of his being, to this image in which he is reflected under the name of ego.

This problematic is inserted between the image of the ego and the image that is raised, elevated, in relation to the first, that of the big Other, the paternal imago, insofar as it founds the double perspective within the subject of the ego and the ego ideal – leaving the superego to one side on this occasion. We get the impression that it's insofar as he hasn't acquired or has lost this Other that he encounters the purely imaginary other, the fallen and meager other with whom he is not able to have any relations except relations of frustration – this other negates him, literally kills him. This other is that which is most radical in imaginary alienation.

Now, this capture by the double is correlative of the appearance of what can be called the permanent discourse that underlies the inscription of what takes place over the course of the subject's history and doubles all his acts. It isn't impossible, moreover, to see this discourse emerge in a normal subject.

I'll give you an example that almost lends itself to an extrapolation from lived experience, that of the solitary character on a desert island. Robinson Crusoe is effectively one of the themes of modern thought, appearing for the first time, to my knowledge, in Baltasar Gracián.[2] This is a psychological problem which is accessible, if not to the imagination, at least to experience
– what happens when the human subject lives all alone? What becomes of 237
the latent discourse? At the end of two or three years of solitude what becomes of the order of vocalization, *I'm going to sell some wood?*

You may also wonder what becomes of vocalization for a person who gets lost in the mountains – and it's undoubtedly not without reason that the phenomenon is clearer in the mountains, since these places are perhaps less humanized. That which takes place, namely the perceptible mobilization of the external world concerning a meaning liable to emerge from any quarter, may give us an idea of this aspect, constantly liable to crop up, of a half-insane discourse. The continuous existence of this discourse may be considered analogous to what is going on in the insane – the verbalization phenomena in Schreber only accentuate it, on the whole. The question now is this – why does the phenomenon appear in the delusional subject? in the margin of what does it appear? in order to signify what? what is it mobilized by?

I shall take another passage, equally chosen at random, because all this is so insistent in Schreber that confirmation of the phenomena I'm indicating can be found everywhere.

[2] See *El Criticón*.

Reading from the Memoirs, *308–10*

Following this you'll find some thoughts on the slowing down of the tempo. This is where we have to push our analysis further.

It's essential to the phenomena of meaning that the signifier be indivisible. One can't section a piece of signifier like one can section the tape of a tape-recorder. If you cut the tape of a tape-recorder the sentence breaks off, but the effect of the sentence doesn't come to a halt at the same point. The signifier contains all kinds of implications, and it's not because you are listeners or decipherers by profession that in certain cases you are able to complete the sentence. The unit of meaning is constantly showing the signifier functioning according to certain laws. The fact that within a delusion voices play upon this property can't be taken to be a matter of indifference, and we can't exclude the hypothesis that it is fundamentally motivated by a precisely more radical, more global, relationship to the phenomenon of the signifier.

On this basis we shall ask ourselves why it's effectively in the relationship to the signifier that the subject invests all his capacities for interest. To explore the problem at this level is not at all to alter the function of energetics. It is in no way to reject the notion of libido. It's only to ask what, in psychosis, the elective interest in the relationship to the signifier means.

238 Here is a brief note concerning the relationship between divine intelligence and human intelligence.

Reading from the Memoirs, *300–01*

However much it appears to have been worked over, the equivalence between nerves and presenced remarks is founded on the subject's primitive experience. The nerves are this verbiage and these refrains, this verbalized insistence that has become his universe. At the same time, on the other hand, the incidental presences in his surroundings are afflicted with unreality and become *fleeting-improvised-men*. The presences that count have become essentially verbal, and the sum of these verbal presences is for him identical with the divine presence, this sole and unique presence that is his correlative and his guarantor.

The notion that the divine intelligence is the sum of human intelligences is stated in formulas that are sufficiently rigorous and elegant for us to gain the impression that we have before us a small fragment of a philosophical system. If I had asked you who this was by, perhaps you may not have been far short of replying – *Spinoza*.

The question is what this testimony by the subject is worth. Well then, he is giving us his experience, which imposes itself as the very structure of reality for him.

The fifth chapter particularly concerns the so-called fundamental language which, as I've already taught you, is, on the subject's own testimony, made up of a species of particularly vigorous High German, crammed with archaic expressions drawn from the underlying etymologies of this language.

Reading of the Memoirs, *46–47*

We are getting closer. One gets the sense that the subject has certainly meditated longer on the nature of the emergence of speech than perhaps we ourselves have done so far. He is well aware that speech is located at another level than that at which the organs capable of materializing it are put into use. You will notice that he introduces the dream as something that belongs essentially to the world of language. It isn't beside the point to observe the surprising illogicality that this represents on the part of an insane person who isn't supposed to be aware of the highly significant character that since Freud we give to dreams. It's certain that Schreber had no inkling of this.

3 239

The note on pages 49–50 is phenomenologically very rich concerning the ambient meanings in the context of a German bourgeoisie of quite a lengthy tradition, for we can map out the history of the Schrebers as far back as the eighteenth century.[3] They have been part of the intellectual life of their country in a fairly brilliant way – I shall return to the personality of Schreber's father later. The themes that emerge in a second early stage of his delusion are obviously tied to this complex of cultural encirclement which sadly blossomed into the renowned party that was to throw all Europe into war. The encirclement by the Slavs, by the Jews, all this is already there in this worthy fellow who doesn't at all seem to have participated in any passionate political tendency, except, at the time of his studies, in these student societies he speaks of.

We shall come back to the existence of the souls who are the support of the sentences that constantly include the subject in their turmoil. They waste away with time, down to these famous *little men* that have greatly attracted the attention of analysts. Katan, in particular, devotes an article to these little men who have been the occasion for all sorts of more or less ingenious interpretations, such as assimilating them to spermatozoa that the subject, having rejected masturbation at a certain point, refuses to lose.[4] There is no need to reject such an interpretation but, even if we allow it, it doesn't exhaust the problem.

[3] This appears to refer to the body of the text rather than to the footnote.
[4] See Katan, "Schreber's Hallucinations about the 'Little Men.' "

The important thing is that it involves regressive characters who have returned to their original procreative cell. Katan seems to have forgotten some very early works by Silberer, who was the first to speak of dreams in which there occur certain images of spermatozoa or of the primitive female cell of the ovum.[5] At that time, which may be regarded as archaic, Silberer had nevertheless observed perfectly well that it is above all a question of grasping what the function played by these images was, whether they were fantasized or oneiric. It's moreover curious to see someone, in 1908, take into consideration the notion of what these images signify. According to him, their appearance has a meaning of mortality. It's a question of a return to origins. It's equivalent to a manifestation of the death instinct. We can see this clearly in the present case since the little men occur in the context of the twilight of the world, a properly constitutive phase of the delusion's development.

240 Be that as it may, on this occasion we're unable to avoid wondering whether a certain incompleteness in the realization of the paternal function isn't involved in Schreber's case. Every author has in fact attempted to explain the onset of Schreber's delusion with reference to the father. Not that Schreber was in conflict with his father at the time – he had disappeared a long time previously. Not that he was at a time of setback in acceding to paternal functions, since on the contrary he was entering a brilliant stage of his career and had been placed in a position of authority that seems to have solicited him to truly adopt a paternal position, to have offered him a support for idealizing and referring himself to this position. President Schreber's delusion would therefore depend more on the giddiness of success than on a sense of failure. This is what the understanding generated by authors of the mechanism determining the psychosis revolves around, at least on the psychical level.

For my part, I would make three responses on the subject of the function of the father.

Normally, the conquest of the Oedipal realization, the integration and introjection of the Oedipal image, is carried out – Freud says this unambiguously – by way of an aggressive relationship. In other words, it's by way of an imaginary conflict that symbolic integration takes place.

There is another way, different in nature. Ethnological experience shows us the importance, however residual it may be, of the phenomenon of *couvade* – imaginary realization here takes place by the symbolic putting into play of conduct. Isn't it something of this order that we have been able to locate in neurosis? The hysterical pregnancy that Eisler describes, which occurred fol-

[5] See Herbert Silberer, "Zur Frage der Spermatozoenträume," "Spermatozoenträume," and "Zum Thema: Spermatozoenträume."

lowing a traumatic breakdown of his equilibrium, isn't imaginary but symbolic.[6]

Isn't there a third way, which is in some sense embodied in delusions? These little men are forms of reabsorption, but they're also the representation of what will take place in the future. The world will be repeopled by Schreber men, men of a Schreberian spirit, small, fantasmatic beings – procreation after the deluge. Such is the prospect.

In sum, in the normal form the emphasis is placed upon the symbolic realization of the father by way of imaginary conflict – in the neurotic or paraneurotic form, upon the imaginary realization of the father by way of a symbolic exercise of conduct. And here, what do we see if not the real function of generation?

There's something here that nobody's interested in, neither neurotics nor primitives. I'm not saying that the latter don't know the real function played by the father in generation, simply that they're not interested in it. What
they're interested in is the begetting of the soul, the begetting of the mind by 241
the father, the father as either symbolic or imaginary. But, curiously, in delusion it's in fact the father's real function in generation that we see emerge in an imaginary form, at least if we accept the identification analysts make between the little men and spermatozoa. There's a movement of retreat here between the three functions that define the problematic of the paternal function.

We are now engaged in reading this text and in the task of actualizing it to the utmost in the dialectical register of signifier and signified.

To each and everyone of you here I shall say this – if you investigate, as is certainly legitimate, the question of being, don't be too arrogant about it. In the articulated phenomenal dialectic I've put to you, speech is indeed the central reference point.

25 April 1956

[6] See above, chap. 12, p. 168, n. 2.

243

XVII

Metaphor and metonymy (I): "His sheaf was neither miserly nor spiteful"[1]

THE TRUTH OF THE FATHER
THE INVASION BY THE SIGNIFIER
SYNTAX AND METAPHOR
WERNICKE'S APHASIA

Sie leben also den Wahn wie sich selbst. Das ist das Geheimnis. This sentence is taken from the correspondence with Fliess,[2] where the beginnings of the themes that will appear successively in Freud's work can be found with singular prominence.

Would we have Freud's style if we didn't have these letters? Yes, we still would, but they teach us that this style, which is nothing other than the expression of what orientates and animates his research, never deviated. Even in 1939, when he wrote *Moses and Monotheism,* one feels that his passionate questioning hasn't waned and that it's still with the same almost desperate tenacity that he strives to explain how it is that man, in the very position of his being, should be so dependent upon these things for which he is obviously not cut out. This is said and named – it's a question of the truth.

I reread *Moses and Monotheism* with the intention of preparing for the paper I have been asked to give in two weeks time on the person of Freud.[3] It seems to me that in this work we find confirmation yet again of what I'm here trying to make you feel, namely that analysis is absolutely inseparable from a fundamental question about the way truth enters into the life of man. The dimension of truth is mysterious, inexplicable, nothing decisively enables the necessity of it to be grasped, since man accommodates himself to non-truth perfectly well. I shall try to show you that this is indeed the question that is troubling Freud to the end in *Moses and Monotheism*.

In this little book one senses a gesture of renunciation and a hidden face.
244 Having accepted death, he continues. The renewed questioning over the person of Moses, over his hypothetical fear, has no other motive than to answer this question – by what path does the dimension of truth enter in a living

[1] *"Sa gerbe n'était point avare, ni haineuse,"* Victor Hugo, *Booz endormi*.

[2] "Thus they love *their delusion as they love themselves*. That is the secret." "Draft H," Freud-Fliess, 111; Origins, 113. See above, chap. 11, p. 157.

[3] See below, chap. 19.

way into life, into the economy of man? Freud's answer is that it's mediated by the ultimate meaning of the idea of the father.

The father belongs to a reality that is sacred in itself, more spiritual than any other, since ultimately nothing in lived reality strictly speaking points to his function, his presence, his dominance. How does the truth of the father, how does this truth that Freud himself calls spiritual,[4] come to be placed in the foreground? The thing is thinkable only by means of this ahistorical drama, inscribed in the very flesh of men at the origin of all history – the death, the murder of the father. A myth, obviously, a very mysterious myth, one impossible to avoid in the coherence of Freud's thought. There is something veiled here.

All the work we did last year meets at this point – one can't deny the inevitability of Freud's intuition. Ethnographic criticisms are beside the point. It's a question of an essential dramatization through which an internal movement going beyond the human being enters into life – the symbol of the father.

The nature of the symbol remains to be clarified. We have come close to its essence by locating its genesis at the same point as that of the death instinct. We are expressing one and the same thing. We are moving towards a point of convergence – what does the signifier essentially signify in its signifying role? What is the original and initiatory function, in human life, of the existence of the symbol qua pure signifier?

This question takes us back to our study of the psychoses.

1

The sentence I have written on the blackboard is typical of Freud's style and I give it to you so that we may continue to hear its resonances.

In this letter Freud speaks of the different types of defence. The word has been so overused in our usage that we cannot help but wonder – who is defending himself? What is being defended? What is one defending oneself against? In psychoanalysis defence is directed against a mirage, a nothingness, a void, and not against anything that exists and carries weight in life. This latter enigma is veiled by the phenomenon itself even as we apprehend it. This letter shows us for the first time, in an especially clear way, the 245
various mechanisms of the neuroses and the psychoses.

Nevertheless, when he comes to psychosis it's as if Freud has been struck by a more profound enigma. He says – *As for those suffering from paranoia, delusions, psychosis, they love their delusion as they love themselves.*

[4] See "The Advance in Intellectuality," section C, pt. 2, essay 3, *Moses and Monotheism*, SE 23:111–15. Freud's *"geistigkeit,"* "intellectuality" in SE, is translated by Lacan as *"spiritualité."*

There is an echo here, which should be given full weight, of what is said in the commandment, *Love thy neighbor as thyself.*

A sense of mystery is never absent from Freud's thought. It's its beginning, middle, and end. I believe that if we allow it to vanish, we lose what's essential to the very procedure upon which every analysis has to be founded. If we lose the mystery for one single moment we get lost in a new type of mirage.

Freud had the profound impression that something in the psychotic's relationship to his delusion goes beyond the workings of the signified and meanings, the workings of what we would later call *id* drives. There is an affection here, an attachment, an essential bringing to presence, the mystery of which remains almost total for us, which is that the delusional, the psychotic, clings to his delusion as to something which is himself.

With this resonance in our ears we shall once again raise the question raised last time concerning the economic function that the relationship to language assumes in the form and development of psychosis.

Let us start by taking as our data the sentences that Schreber tells us he hears coming from those intermediate beings, diverse in their nature – the forecourts of Heaven, the deceased souls or the blessed souls, these shadows, these ambiguous forms of beings dispossessed of existence and carriers of voices.

The full part of the sentence, which contains the kernel-words, as the linguists say, which give the sentence its sense, is not experienced as hallucinatory. On the contrary, the voice stops, forcing the subject to utter the meaning in question in the sentence.

Now it's time . . . that he was subdued![5] Here it's the implied expression that carries the significant weight. Our subject signifies to us that he is not hallucinating. He is placed in the overhang [*porte à faux*], in what remains empty after the grammatical or syntactic part of the sentence, consisting of auxiliaries, connectives, conjunctions, or adverbs, which is suddenly verbalized, as coming from without, as a sentence by the other. It's a sentence by this subject, who is both empty and full, whom I have named the inter-I of delusion.

246 *Now that is going too far according to the conception of the souls.* The entire function of this conception of the souls resides in what, according to Schreber, is put into words by somewhat higher agencies than the subjects that convey the refrains, learned by rote, made up of words he considers empty. It alludes to functional notions that decompose his various thoughts. A psychology does indeed have a place within his delusion, a dogmatic psychology

[5] I.e., "He must be done now." Mem, 311 n.114; see also Mem, 217–18.

that is expounded to him by the voices that interpellate him, by explaining to him how his thoughts are formed.

In particular, that which is implied has assumed a hallucinatory form and is not expressed out loud in the hallucination. This is the *principal thought.* The subject's delusional lived experience presents its own essence in the phenomenon. It indicates that the hallucinatory phenomenon lived through, whether elementary or not, lacks the principal thought. *We rays lack thought,* that is, that which signifies something.

With respect to what we might call the chain of the delusion, the subject seems to be both agent and patient. He undergoes rather than organizes the delusion. To be sure, as a finished product this delusion can up to a point be described as reasoning madness, in the sense that in certain respects its articulation is logical, though from a secondary point of view. That madness should achieve a synthesis of this nature is no less a problem than its very existence. It takes place over the course of a genesis that starts from elements perhaps immanent to [*gros de*] this construction, but which in their original form present themselves as closed or even enigmatic.

First there were several months of prepsychotic incubation in which the subject was in a state of profound confusion. This is the period in which the phenomena of the twilight of the world occur, which are characteristic of the beginning of a delusional period. Towards the middle of March 1894 he was admitted to Flechsig's clinic. In mid-November '93 the hallucinatory phenomena began, the spoken communications which he attributes to different grades in this fantasmatic world, consisting of two levels of divine reality, the anterior and posterior realms of God, and of all sorts of entities that are in a more or less advanced stage of reabsorption into this divine reality.

These entities, the souls, move in an opposite direction to what he calls the *world order,* a fundamental notion in the structuring of his delusion. Instead of moving towards the reintegration of the absolute Other, they move on the contrary in the direction of attaching themselves onto him, Schreber, in forms that vary over the delusion's course of development. At the outset we see the phenomenon of introjection expressed openly, in his lived experience, when he says that Flechsig's soul enters him here and that it resembles the threads of a spider's web, that it's big enough to be unassimilable by him, and that it 247
comes out again through his mouth.[6] Here we have a sort of lived schema of introjection, which will become attenuated later on, be polished into a much more spiritualized form.

In fact Schreber will become increasingly integrated into this ambiguous speech with which he becomes as one, and to which, with all his being, he

[6] Mem, 82–83.

…s a response. He literally loves it like himself. This phenomenon can …dly be described as an internal dialogue since it's precisely around the existence of the other that the meaning of the preeminence of the signifying game revolves, increasingly emptied of meaning.

What is the meaning of this invasion by the signifier that tends to drain itself of signified as it occupies more and more place in the libidinal relation and invests all the moments, all the desires, of the subject?

I paused at a series of those repetitive texts, which it would be tedious to unfold for you here. Something struck me – even when the sentences may have a meaning, one never encounters anything that resembles a metaphor.

But what is a metaphor?

2

I am introducing you here to an order of inquiry never pointed out.

Metaphor is not the easiest thing in the world to speak about. Bossuet says it's an abridged simile [*comparaison*]. Everyone is aware that this is not entirely satisfactory, and I believe that in fact no poet would accept it. I say *no poet* because a definition of poetical style could be to say that it begins with metaphor, and that where metaphor ceases poetry ceases also.

His sheaf was neither miserly nor spiteful – Victor Hugo. That's a metaphor. It's certainly not a latent simile, it's not – *just as* the sheaf was willingly dispersed among the needy, *so* our character was neither miserly nor spiteful. There's not a comparison but an identification. The dimension of metaphor must be less difficult for us to enter than for anyone else, provided that we recognize that what we usually call it is identification. But that's not all – our
248 use of the term *symbolic* in fact leads us to restrict its sense, to designate only the metaphorical dimension of the symbol.

Metaphor presupposes that a meaning is the dominant datum and that it deflects, commands, the use of the signifier to such an extent that the entire species of preestablished, I should say lexical, connections comes undone. Nothing in any dictionary usage can suggest for one instant that a sheaf is capable of being miserly, and even less of being spiteful. And yet it's clear that the use of a language is only susceptible to meaning once it's possible to say, *His sheaf was neither miserly nor spiteful,* that is to say, once the meaning has ripped the signifier from its lexical connections.

Here we have the ambiguity of the signifier and the signified. Without the signifying structure, that is, without predicative articulation, without the distance maintained between the subject and its attributes, the sheaf cannot be qualified as miserly or spiteful. It's because there is a syntax, a primordial order of the signifier, that the subject is maintained as separate, as different from its qualities. It's completely out of the question that an animal could create a metaphor, even though we have no reason to think that it doesn't also have an intuition of what is generous and what can easily and abundantly grant it what it desires. But insofar as it doesn't possess the articulation, the discursive – which is not just meaning, with all that this entails about attraction and repulsion, but an alignment of signifiers – metaphor is unthinkable within the animal psychology of attraction, appetite, and desire.

This phase of symbolism that is expressed in metaphor presupposes similarity, which is exhibited uniquely by position. It's by virtue of being the subject of *miserly* and *spiteful* that the sheaf can be identified with Booz in his lack of avarice and in his generosity. It's by virtue of the similarity of position that the sheaf is literally identical to the subject Booz. This dimension of similarity is, surely, the most striking thing about the significant use of language, which so dominates the apprehension of the workings of symbolism as to mask from us the existence of the other dimension, the syntactic. However, this sentence would lose all sense if we disturbed the word order.

This is what gets neglected when symbolism is discussed – the dimension linked to the signifier's existence, its organization.

3

What, on this basis, cannot fail to occur to one, and which occurred to a
linguist friend of mine. Roman Jakobson, is that the distribution of certain 249
disorders known as aphasias can be reconsidered in the light of the opposition between on the one hand the relations of similarity, or substitution, or choice, and also of selection or concurrence, in short, all that is of the order of synonymy, and on the other hand the relations of contiguity, alignment, signifying articulation, syntactic coordination.[7] From this perspective the classical opposition between sensory and motor aphasia, which has been criticized for a long time, becomes strikingly coordinated.

You are all familiar with Wernicke's aphasia. The aphasic links together a sequence of sentences of an extraordinarily developed grammatical nature. He will say – *Yes, I understand. Yesterday, when I was up there, already he said, and I wanted, I said to him, that's not it, the date, not exactly, not that one . . .*

The subject thereby demonstrates complete mastery of everything articulated, organized, subordinated, and structured in the sentence, but what he says is always wide of what he wants to say. Not for an instant can you be in any doubt that what he wants to say is present, but he never manages to give verbal incarnation to what he is aiming at in the sentence. He constructs

[7] See Roman Jakobson, "Two Aspects of Language and Two Types of Aphasic Disturbances."

around it an entire fringe of syntactic verbalization, the complexity and level of organization of which are far from indicating a loss of attention to language. But if you ask him for a definition, an equivalent term, even without wanting to go so far as a metaphor, if you confront him with the use of language that logic calls metalanguage, or language about language, he can't follow you.

There's no question of making the slightest comparison between a disorder of this type and what happens to our psychotics. But when Schreber hears *Factum est,* which then stops, a phenomenon certainly manifests itself here at the level of the relations of contiguity. The relations of contiguity dominate, following the absence or failure of the function of meaningful equivalence by means of similarity.

We, too, have to take account of this striking analogy by introducing an opposition under the two rubrics of similarity and contiguity into what happens in hallucinatory delusional subjects. One could not make the dominance of contiguity in hallucinatory phenomena more evident than by pointing out the effect of interrupted speech – and of interrupted speech precisely as it's given, that is, as invested and, let's say, libidinized. What imposes itself on the subject is the grammatical part of the sentence, the one that exists only by virtue of its signifying character and by being articulated. This is what becomes a phenomenon imposed within the external world.

The aphasic I was speaking of is incapable of coming to the point. Hence
250 an apparently empty discourse, which, curiously, even in the most experienced subjects, in neurologists, always sets off nervous laughter. Here you have this character who employs enormous, extraordinarily articulate bla-bla-bla, but who can never get to the heart of what he has to communicate. The imbalance in the phenomenon of contiguity that comes to the fore in the hallucinatory phenomenon, and around which the whole delusion is organized, is not unlike this.

Typically, it's always the signified that we draw attention to in our analyses, because it's undoubtedly what is the most seductive, and it's what at first sight appears to be the true dimension of symbolic investigation by psychoanalysis. But in misrecognizing the primordial mediating role of the signifier, in misrecognizing that it's the signifier that in reality is the guiding thread, not only do we throw the original understanding of neurotic phenomena, the interpretation of dreams itself, out of balance, but we make ourselves absolutely incapable of understanding what is happening in the psychoses.

While a later part of analytic investigation, one concerning identification and symbolism, is on the side of metaphor, let's not neglect the other side, that of articulation and contiguity, with what is here sketched out that is initial and structuring in the notion of causality. The rhetorical form that is the opposite of metaphor has a name – it's called metonymy. It involves substitution for something that has to be named – we are in fact at the level of the name. One thing is named by another that is its container, or its part, or that is connected to it.

If, using the technique of verbal association as it's practiced at the level of the laboratory, you give a subject a word like *hut,* he has more than one way to respond. Certain responses will be in the register of contiguity. *Hut – Burn it.* Also, the subject may say *hovel* or *cabin* to you – there we already have the synonymous equivalent, a little bit further on we move into metaphor, in saying – *burrow,* for example. But there is also another register. If for example the subject says *thatch,* no longer is it quite the same thing. It's a part of the hut that enables it to be designated as a whole – it's possible at a pinch to talk of a village composed of three thatches, to mean three little houses. Here it's a question of evoking. The subject may also say *dirtiness* or *poverty.* We no longer have metaphor, we have metonymy.

The opposition between metaphor and metonymy is fundamental, since what Freud originally drew attention to in the mechanisms of neurosis, as 251
well as in the mechanisms of the marginal phenomena of normal life or of dreams, is neither the metaphorical dimension nor identification. It's the contrary. In general what Freud calls condensation is what in rhetoric one calls metaphor, what he calls displacement is metonymy. The structuration, the lexical existence of the entire signifying apparatus, is determinant for the phenomena present in neurosis, since the signifier is the instrument by which the missing signified expresses itself. It's for this reason that in focusing attention back onto the signifier we are doing nothing other than returning to the starting point of the Freudian discovery.

Next week we shall return to this question by studying why in psychosis these workings of the signifier end up totally preoccupying the subject. The issue in this case is not the mechanism of aphasia — it's a certain relationship to the other as lacking, deficient. It's by proceeding from the subject's relation to the signifier and to the other, with the different levels of otherness, imaginary other and symbolic Other, that we can articulate this psychical intrusion, this invasion by the signifier, called psychosis.

2 May 1956

253

XVIII

Metaphor and metonymy (II): Signifying articulation and transference of the signified

SENSORY APHASIA AND MOTOR APHASIA

THE POSITIONAL LINK

ALL LANGUAGE IS METALANGUAGE

DETAIL AND DESIRE

In introducing the opposition between similarity and contiguity here, I'm not saying that I consider that psychosis is in any way comparable to aphasia.

I would say more than this. What I retain from the two levels of disorder that have been distinguished in aphasia is that there is the same opposition between them as the one that appears, no longer in a negative but in a positive way, in metaphor and metonymy.

I was told that this opposition had thrown some of you into great perplexity, and that you have been telling yourselves – *Metaphor has indeed shown us the importance of opposition, disagreement, and confusion*.

The opposition between signifier and signified isn't a simple substitute for the famous and no less inextricable opposition between idea, or thought, and word. Someone, an outstanding grammarian, has written a remarkable work in which there is only one fault, its unfortunate subtitle, *Words for thought*.[1] This way of putting it is, I hope, no longer sustainable for any of you.

1

We clearly show the constant life of metaphor in these transferences of signified, an example of which I gave you last time with *His sheaf was neither miserly nor spiteful*.

Here you have an example of metaphor. One may say, in a sense, that meaning dominates everything, that it's all of a sudden the meaning that imprints on the subject, *his sheaf*, this value that shows it generously dispers-
254 ing itself, as if of its own accord. However, the signifier and the signified are always in a relationship that may be described as dialectical.

This isn't a rehash of the relation upon which the notion of expression

[1] *"Des mots à la pensée"*: the subtitle of Damourette and Pichon, *Essai de grammaire*.

rests, where the thing, that which one refers to, is expressed by a word regarded as a label. My discourse is intended precisely to destroy this idea.

You must have heard aphasics spoken about, and you are aware of their extraordinarily lively and rapid, apparently fluid speech, at least up to a point. They express themselves admirably on a theme without being able to utter the word, while using an entire, extremely subtle syntactic articulation to get at something whose name or precise indicator they have on the tip of their tongue, but they are only capable of going round it in circles.

What is enthralling here is the persistence of the subject's intentionality despite this localized verbal impotence.

People have claimed to have brought out a kind of intellectual deficit of a predemential order as its correlative. This is a step forward which nuances the initial massive notion according to which it's a question of an incapacity to passively grasp verbal images, a step that indicates that the disorder is much more complex than appears at first sight. But whatever deficits the subject may display if we set him a specific task, according to the modes that characterize the position of the tests, nothing will be solved as long as we are ignorant of their mechanism and their origin.

One can see the subject protest against a reading of an observation that conveys a given precise historical detail, concerning a date, an hour, a form of behavior. This is when the subject trots out his discourse, however disturbed and jargonaphasic its character. Should he make a mistake, it's still in relation to a definite historical detail he possessed just five minutes earlier that he begins to enter the dialogue. Here one can grasp the presence and intensity of the intentionality at the heart of the deployment of discourse, which never manages to catch up with it again.

From the phenomenological viewpoint the sensory aphasic's language is a language of paraphrases. His jargonaphasia – the word is a bit too strong – is characterized by an abundance and ease of articulation and expression of sentences, however segmented they may ultimately become.

Paraphrase is the direct opposite of metaphrase, if by this is meant everything of the order of literal translation. This means that if you ask him to translate, to give a synonym, to repeat the same sentence, the same one he has just uttered, he can't do it. He is able to hook onto your discourse or 255
onto his own, but he has the greatest difficulty in commenting on a discourse. You will get from him replies that are so lively, so pathetic in his desire to make himself heard, as to border on the comical. You have to be interested in the phenomenon itself if you are not to laugh.

Therefore, there is a similarity disorder here, which is that the subject is incapable of metaphrase, and what he has to say lies entirely within the domain of paraphrase.

Alongside sensory aphasia there is what is broadly called motor aphasia. It ranges from disorders of agrammatism, well-known by now, to an extreme reduction of his stock of words – its immortal image is the famous *pencil* that he is unable to get out. This other dimension of aphasic deficit can be very well ranged within the order of contiguity disorders.

Here it's essentially the articulation, the syntax of language, which, progressively along the scale of cases and in the evolution of certain subjects, deteriorates to the point of making them incapable of articulating in a compound sentence what they are nevertheless able to name correctly. They retain the nominative capacity, but lose the propositional capacity. They are unable to construct propositions.

Owing to the properties of the signifier and the signified, the constant temptation to which linguists themselves, and *a fortiori* those who aren't linguists, succumb is to consider that it's what is the most obvious in the phenomenon that says it all.

Up to a point linguists have fallen victim to this illusion. The emphasis they place, for example, on metaphor, which has always been studied much more than metonymy, is proof of this. In full and living language it's what is the most gripping, but also the most problematical – how does it happen that language is at its most effective when it manages to say something by saying something else? It's enthralling indeed, and it's even thought that this is the way to the crux of the phenomenon of language, in opposition to a naive notion.

The naive notion has it that there is a superimposition, like a tracing, of the order of things onto the order of words. It's thought that a great step forward has been made by saying that the signified only ever reaches its goal via another signified, through referring to another meaning. This is only the first step, and one fails to see that a second is needed. It has to be realized that without structuring by the signifier no transference of sense would be possible.

A number of you rightly saw last time that this is what I meant in emphasizing the role of the signifier in metaphor.

256 **2**

The deficit, if we approach things from this angle, has two sides.

The first is the dissolution of the link between intentional meaning and the apparatus of signifiers. The latter is on the whole retained by the subject, who nevertheless fails to master it in relation to his intention. The second is the dissolution of the link internal to the signifier. Here the fact is emphasized that there is a sort of regressive decomposition, which is sufficiently well explained by the Jacksonian theory according to which functions decompose in the inverse order of their acquisition, not in development – language isn't reducible to the ideally primary language of the infant – but through a veritable *turning*.[2]

For my part, is that what I wanted to emphasize?

I say – *No, it's not*. According to a type of general law of illusion concerning what goes on in language, it isn't what appears in the foreground that is important. What's important is the opposition between two sorts of links that are themselves internal to the signifier.

First, the positional link, which is the foundation of the link that I earlier called propositional. This is what in a given language sets up that essential dimension which is the order of words. To understand this it suffices to recall that in French *Pierre bat Paul* isn't equivalent to *Paul bat Pierre*.

Concerning the second form of aphasic disorders, notice the strict coherence there is between maintaining the positional function of language and maintaining an adequate stock of terms. This is an absolutely incontestable clinical phenomenon and shows us the fundamental binding of the signifier.

What appears at the grammatical level as characteristic of the positional link reappears at all levels and sets up the synchronic coexistence of terms.

The verbal locution is its highest form. At a lower level there is the word, which has the air of a stability that, as you know, has been rightly challenged. While the independence of the word manifests itself from certain angles, it can't be regarded as radical. The word can in no way be regarded as a unit of language, even though it constitutes a privileged elementary form. At an even lower level you find the phonematic oppositions or couplings which characterize the ultimate radical element that distinguishes one language from another.

In French for example *boue* and *pou* are opposed to one another, whatever your accent. Even if, because you live near a border, you tend to pronounce 257
boue like *pou*, you will pronounce the other *pou* differently, because French is a language in which this opposition is valid. In other languages there are oppositions totally unknown in French. This binding of opposites is essential to the functioning of language. It must be distinguished from the link of similarity, implicated in the functioning of language, which is tied to the indefinite possibility of the function of substitution, which is conceivable only on the basis of the positional relation.

The mainspring of the metaphor isn't the meaning, which is supposed to be transposed from Booz onto the sheaf. I readily admit that someone might object to me that Booz's sheaf is metonymic, not metaphorical, and that underlying this magnificent poetry, and never named directly, there is Booz's royal penis. But that isn't what gives this sheaf its metaphorical quality, it's that the metaphor is placed in the position of subject, in Booz's place. It's a phenomenon of signifiers that is involved.

[2] In English in the original.

Let's move to the limit of poetic metaphor, which you wouldn't hesitate to describe as surrealist, even though we didn't have to wait for the surrealists to make metaphors. You are unable to say whether it makes sense or not. I won't say that this is the best way of putting things, but, in any case, it's near enough.

Take an expression that we can agree is indeed a metaphor. You will see whether it's the sense that sustains it.

Love is a pebble laughing in the sun .

What does this mean? It's indisputably a metaphor. It's likely enough that if it was born, it's because it contains a sense. As for finding one . . . I could do a whole seminar on it. This seems to me to be an indisputable definition of love, and I shall say that it's the last I paused at, because to me it appears indispensable if one wants to avoid falling endlessly into irremediable confusions.

In short, a metaphor is above all sustained by a positional articulation. This can be demonstrated even in its most paradoxical forms.

None of you has, I believe, failed to hear of the exercise that a poet of our day has carried out under the rubric of *Un mot pour un autre* [one word for another]. It's a little comedy in one act by Jean Tardieu. It concerns a dialogue between two women. One is announced, the other goes up to her and says:

My dear, my dearest, how many pebbles is it since I have had the apprentice to sugar you?

258 *Alas, my dear,* answers the other, *I myself have been extremely unvitreous, my three littlest oil-cakes,* etc.

This is confirmation that, even if it's in a paradoxical form, not only is the sense maintained, but that it tends to manifest itself in a particularly fortunate and metaphorical manner. It may be said that the sense is in some way renewed. Whatever effort the poet may have made to push it in the direction of a demonstration, one is at every instant a hair's breadth from a poetic metaphor. It belongs to a register that is no different from what arises as natural poetry as soon as a powerful meaning is involved.

The important thing isn't that the similarity should be sustained by the signified – we make this mistake all the time – it's that the transference of the signified is possible only by virtue of the structure of language. All language implies a metalanguage, it's already a metalanguage of its own register. It's because potentially all language is to be translated that it implies metaphrase and metalanguage, language speaking of language. The transference of the signified, so essential to human life, is possible only by virtue of the structure of the signifier.

Do get it into your heads that language is a system of positional coherence, and secondly that this system reproduces itself within itself with an extraordinary, and frightful, fecundity.

It's not for nothing that the word *prolixity* is the same word as *proliferation. Prolixity* is the frightening word. All use of language incurs fright, which stops people and finds expression in the fear of intellectuality. *He intellectualizes too much,* people say. This serves as an alibi for the fear of language. In fact, you can observe that there is verbalism wherever one makes the error of granting too much weight to the signified, whereas it's by heading further in the direction of the independence of the signifier and the signified that all operations of logical construction adopt their full effect.

At least for the phenomena that interest us, one always falls into verbalism by further adhering to what I call the mythology of significance [*mythologie significative*]. Mathematics on the other hand uses a language of pure signifier, a metalanguage *par excellence.* It reduces language to its systematic function upon which another system is built, grasping the former in its articulation. The efficacity of this way of doing things isn't in doubt in its own register.

3 259

When one reads the rhetoricians, one realizes that they never get to an entirely satisfactory definition of metaphor, or of metonymy.

This results in, for example, the formula that metonymy is an impoverished metaphor. One might say that the thing is to be taken in exactly the opposite sense – metonymy exists from the beginning and makes metaphor possible. But metaphor belongs to a different level than metonymy.

Let's study the most primitive phenomena, and let's take an example that for us analysts is particularly alive. What is more primitive as the direct expression of a meaning – that is of a desire – than what Freud relates about his youngest little daughter, the one who has since occupied such an interesting place in analysis, Anna?

Anna Freud asleep – things are, you see, in their pure state – she talks in her sleep – *Big strawberries, raspberries, cakes, porridge.*[3]

There's something here that looks like the signified in its pure state. And it's the most schematic, the most fundamental form of metonymy. There's no doubt that she desires these strawberries, these raspberries. But it isn't self-evident that these objects should all be there together. The fact that they are there, juxtaposed, coordinated in this articulated naming is due to the positional function that places them in a situation of equivalence. This is the essential phenomenon.

[3] *Interpretation of Dreams,* SE 4:130.

If there is anything that shows indisputably that it's not purely and simply a question here of a phenomenon of expression that a psychology, say Jungian, could get us to see as an imaginary substitute for the object appealed to, it's precisely the fact that the sentence begins with what? With the name of the person, *Anna Freud*. She's an infant of nineteen months, and we are at the level of naming, of equivalence, of nominal coordination, of signifying articulation as such. It's only within this framework that the transference of meaning is possible.

This is the heart of Freud's thought. His work begins with the dream, its mechanisms of condensation and displacement, of figuration – these are all of the order of metonymic articulation, and it's on this foundation that metaphor is able to intervene.

It's even more apparent at the level of the erotization of language. If there is an order of acquisition, it's certainly not what makes it possible to say that
260 children begin with such and such an element of the verbal stock rather than by some other. There is the greatest diversity. One doesn't take hold of language by one end, like certain painters who start their paintings at the left-hand corner. For language to be born, it must always already be grasped as a whole. On the other hand, for it to be able to be grasped as a whole, it has to be grasped at the outset by means of the signifier.

People speak of the concrete nature of language in children. This is something that, contrary to appearances, refers to contiguity. Someone recently confided to me what had been said by his child, a boy, who at the age of two and a half had grabbed his mother as she was leaning over him to say goodnight and said to her – *My big girl full of bottom and muscles*.

This language is obviously not the same as that of *His sheaf was neither miserly nor spiteful*. The child doesn't do that yet. Nor does he say that *love is a pebble laughing in the sun*. We are told that children understand surrealist and abstract poetry, which would be a return to childhood. This is stupid – children detest surrealist poetry and find repugnant certain stages of Picasso's painting. Why? Because they're not yet up to metaphor, but only metonymy. And when they do appreciate certain things in Picasso's paintings it's because metonymy is involved.

We can also see metonymy in certain passages in Tolstoy, where whenever a woman approaches you see the shadow of a fly, a spot on the upper lip, etc., emerge in place of her – the metonymic process of a great stylist. In general metonymy animates this style of creation called the realist style, as opposed to the symbolic style and to poetic language. The promotion of detail that characterizes it is no more realist than anything else. Only quite specific paths can make a detail the guide of the desiring function – not just any detail can be promoted as equivalent to the whole.

The proof of this is the trouble we go to to emphasize certain of these details, through a series of significant transferences, in our experiments with mazes designed to bring out what we call the intelligence of animals. Call it intelligence if you wish – it's merely a question of definition. It's a matter of the extension of the field of the real in which we can include the animal with its current capacities of discrimination, provided that it's instinctually, libidinally, interested.

The supposed realism of describing the real by details is only conceivable in the register of an organized signifier, due to which, by virtue of the fact that the mother is *my big girl full of bottom and muscles,* the child will evolve 261
in a certain way. It's clearly as a function of his early metonymic abilities that at a certain moment the bottom can become an equivalent of the mother for him. Whatever the sense by which we can conceive the sensitization on the vital level, it alters absolutely nothing in the problem.

It's on the basis of the metonymic articulation that this phenomenon is able to take place. The coordination of signifiers has to be possible before transferences of the signified are able to take place. The formal articulation of the signifier predominates with respect to transference of the signified.

How do we now raise the question of the repercussions on the function of language of disturbances in the relationship to the other? Just as metaphor and metonymy are opposed to one another, so the fundamental functions of speech are opposed to one another – foundational speech and passwords.

Why are they both fundamentally necessary? What distinguishes them? This is something that arises in relation to a third term. If it's necessary for man to use speech to make discoveries or to get his bearings, it's as a function of his natural propensity to decompose in the presence of the other.

In what way does he compose and recompose himself? We shall come back to this on another occasion, but in the phenomena that Schreber presents you can already grasp the use we can make of these categories.

I spoke to you last time of the interrupted sentences, but there is also question and reply. This has to be understood as having the value of being opposed to the dimension of foundational speech, where one doesn't ask the other for his opinion. The function of question and reply, insofar as it is given value through initiation into language and is its complement and its root, lays bare the signifying foundation of foundational speech in relation to what is profoundly significant in such speech. The delusional phenomenon lays bare, at all levels moreover, the signifying function as such.

I shall give you another example. You know these famous equivalences that the delusional Schreber gives as having been formulated by the birds from the sky parading in the twilight. One finds assonances here – *Santiago or Carthago, Chinesenthum or Jesum-Christum.*[4] Is the absurdity of this all that

[4] Mem, 210.

is to be retained? What strikes Schreber is the fact that the birds from the sky are brainless. On this Freud is in no doubt – they are young girls.[5]

But what's important isn't the assonance, it's the term-by-term correspondence between closely neighboring elements of discrimination, which only
262 have importance for a polyglot like Schreber within the linguistic system of German.

Schreber, with all his perspicacity, once again shows that what is being sought is of the order of the signifier, that is, of phonematic coordination. The Latin word *Jesum-Christum* here is, as we know, an equivalent of *Chinesenthum* only insofar as in German the ending *tum* has a particular sound quality.

Promoting the signifier as such, the emergence of this always hidden substructure that is metonymy, is the condition of any possible investigation of the functional disorders of language in neurosis and psychosis.

9 May 1956

[5] "Case of Paranoia," SE 12:36.

XIX 263

An address: Freud in the century

The session is opened by Professor Jean Delay.

For the centenary of Freud's birth, who was born May 16, 1856, commemorative occasions have been organized in Paris.

It's appropriate to recall that it was in Paris, while following Charcot's teaching at la Salpêtrière when he was only twenty-nine years old, that Freud found his calling. And in the article in the edition of his complete works he himself stressed all he owed to the teaching at la Salpêtrière.

This filiation in no way detracts from his obvious, brilliant originality, since it's really to him that we owe the method and doctrine of psychoanalysis. One can, indeed one must, have reservations about certain theoretical and practical aspects of psychoanalysis. But it remains no less true that in highlighting the role of affective conflicts and instinctual disorders in the neuroses he has made a very important contribution to psychiatry. Moreover, by highlighting the role of the unconscious in all manifestations of mental life it can be said that his contribution goes beyond the framework of medical science and is applicable to all human sciences.

This is why I thought it necessary on the occasion of this centenary to ask Jacques Lacan, who is the director here, with Daniel Lagache and Mme Favez-Boutonier, of the Société française de psychanalyse, to address us on Freud and his influence in the century. I believe he is particularly well qualified for this since he has an admirable knowledge of the life and work of Freud.

Here I am, then, today entrusted by Professor Jean Delay with a commis- 264
sion that, through being different from the teaching that under his patronage takes place here on this same day each week, greatly honors me – namely, to speak about Freud to an audience, new to the subject, of students in their

psychiatry course, with the intention of commemorating the centenary of his birth.

I have a twofold aim here, which will perhaps give my talk some sort of double vision, that of instructing through honoring, of honoring through instructing – and I should have to apologize for it were I not hoping to adapt the aim of this talk to making the man's arrival in the world coincide with his arrival at the supreme sense of his work.

This is why my title, *Freud in the century,* is intended to suggest more than a chronological reference.

1

I wish to begin by saying what, while appearing under Freud's name, extends beyond the time of his appearance and conceals its truth even in its very unveiling – that Freud's name signifies *joy*.

Freud himself was conscious of this, as is demonstrated by a good number of things – an analysis of a dream that I could adduce, dominated by a sum of composite words, more especially by a word of ambiguous resonance, both English and German at the same time, and in which he enumerates the charming little spots in the environs of Vienna.[1]

If I pause at this name, it's not that my procedure is panegyrical. I'm anticipating what I shall articulate in my discourse by recalling that his family, like all the families of Moravia, of Galicia, of the outlying provinces of Hungary, owing to an edict of 1785 by Joseph II, had to choose this name from a list of first names – it's a feminine first name, in fairly frequent use at the time. But this name is a much older Jewish name which throughout history one already finds translated differently.

This is well suited to remind us that this recurrence of a purely literal tradition persists through the cultural assimilation of hidden signifiers and takes us very close to the heart of the structure with which Freud answered his questions. To be sure, to grasp this properly we would immediately need to evoke the extent to which he acknowledged belonging to the Jewish tradition and its literal structure which, he says, goes so far as to imprint itself
265 upon the structure of language. Freud could make the striking observation in a message addressed to a confessional community on the occasion of his seventieth birthday that he acknowledges that this was where his most intimate identity lay.[2]

There is, to be sure, a contrast between this acknowledgment and his early rejection – offensive, almost insulting, for those close to him whom he had

[1] SE 4:298.

[2] "Address to the Society of B'nai B'rith" was read on Freud's behalf at a meeting of the Society on May 6, 1926 in honor of his seventieth birthday; see SE 20:271–4.

the most reason to spare – of the religious faith of his fathers. Perhaps this is the angle from which we might be best introduced to what would help us understand how questions were raised for Freud.

However, this isn't how I shall be going about it. For, in point of fact, it's not always the simplest approaches that seem the clearest. In a word, they aren't the ones we are the best prepared for. And it's certainly not for nothing that we often have to take a more complex route to make truths heard.

Nor is it in Freud's biography that we shall find the source of the subversion brought about by his discovery.

It does not seem that a touch of neurosis, which can certainly help us understand Freud, has ever guided anyone before him down the same path. Nothing is less perverse, it seems to me, than the life of Freud. If this were where one had to seek the price of his daring, neither his poverty as a student nor his years of struggle as the father of a large family seems sufficient to me to explain something that I would call an abnegation of love relations, which one really has to point out when it concerns the person who renewed the theory of Eros.

Recent revelations, the letters to his fiancée, the great attraction of a recent biography,[3] seem to me to be complemented by a certain something which I shall call a touching egocentrism that consisted of demanding from the other an unreserved compliance with the ideals of his beautiful soul and of being torn apart at the thought of the favors shown to another the unforgettable evening that he received from her the first token of her love. All this comes down to what I should call the rawness of a virgin, which we may excuse him for, on discovering its equally indiscreet equal in the same published letters to a fiancée of our own Hugo.

This disclosure, quite opportune in the final analysis, prevents me from dwelling on the dignity of a union where what Freud himself confides indicates mutual respect and attention to parental tasks – in short, the high tradition of Jewish family values. For what one cannot fail to detect in his early letters is some kind of reduction to the smallest common denominator of a petit-bourgeois convention of a love the sentimental extravagance of which
doesn't exclude reserve or Freud's long-held rancor towards his fiancée for 266
having caused him, through an ill-timed journey, to miss the glory of having been the inventor of the surgical use of cocaine. This is indication enough of a relationship of psychical forces for which the term of ambivalence, employed without rhyme or reason, would be entirely inappropriate.

In point of fact, we shall not follow the geography of these ravages over time.

One day I heard Freud spoken of in these terms – *without ambition and*

[3] Ernest Jones's biography, *Sigmund Freud: Life and Work* was partially completed at the time Lacan is speaking.

without needs. The thing is comical if one thinks of the number of times throughout his work that Freud confessed his ambition which, while undoubtedly quickened by all sorts of obstacles, is much more extensive in his unconscious, as he was able to show. To make you appreciate this, must I depict for you – as Jung, speaking to me personally, did one day – the scene of Freud's reception at the University he placed on the world's stage? I mean, depict the stream, whose symbolic meaning he was the first to have shown, blossoming out into a growing stain on his pale trousers?

Shall I say it? This isn't the point from which I would like to throw light upon the figure of Freud, for really it seems that nothing can go beyond what he disclosed in his long autobiography that his first works constitute – *Die Traumdeutung, The Psychopathology of Everyday Life* and *Der Witz*.[4] Nobody, in a sense, has ever taken the confession so far, at least within the limits that a man's concern for his authority imposes on him. And this isn't to diminish its importance, far from it. The sigh at which these confidences stop perhaps gives us the feeling of a barrier, but nothing ever since has enabled us to cross it – even the most indiscreet hypothesis makers have never managed to add anything to what he himself disclosed to us.

There is something here worth dwelling on, which is well suited to make us feel the value of a critical method I shall surprise you with by saying that someone's work is to be judged by the standard of its own criteria.

If the discovery of psychoanalysis really is to have reintegrated into science an entire objectifiable field of man and to have shown its supremacy, and if this field is the field of sense, why seek the genesis of this discovery outside the meanings that its inventor encountered within himself along the path leading him to it? Why look elsewhere than in the register to which this discovery must, if one is to be rigorous, be limited? If we must have recourse to some other source foreign to the field discovered by our author, and by nobody else, to explain what it is, the prevalence of this field becomes null and void, through having been made subordinate.

To suppose the supremacy, and not the subordination, of sense as efficient
267 cause is apparently to repudiate the principles of modern science. In fact, for the positive science to which Freud's masters, this Pleiad that Jones quite rightly mentions at the beginning of his study, belonged, the entire dynamics of sense can, question-beggingly, be neglected — it is all fundamentally superstructure.[5] It's therefore a revolution in science that Freud introduces, if this science has the value he claims for it.

Does it have this value? Does it have this meaning?

[4] I.e., *Jokes and their Relation to the Unconscious.*
[5] Jones, *Sigmund Freud* 1:45.

2

I want to pause here to try to restore the point of view, currently effaced, from which Freud's work can be viewed in its proper light.

I shall ask you straightaway to be prepared for a contrast between what Freud's work authentically signifies and what is currently being offered as the sense of psychoanalysis. For many of you, the students, as you draw nearer to things in the mental sphere, psychoanalysis is, it's said, first of all a means to a better understanding of the mentally ill.

I can't recommend too highly that those of you who have the opportunity to become acquainted with the analytic literature – and God knows how enormous, almost diffuse, it has become – combine this reading with an at least equivalent measure of Freud himself. The difference will leap out at you.

The term *frustration,* for example, has become the *leitmotiv* of the prolific mothers of analytic literature in English, with the abandonism and relationship of dependence it comprises. Now, this term is quite simply absent from Freud's work. The simplistic use of notions taken out of context, like that of reality testing, or of bastardized notions like that of the object relation, the recourse to the ineffability of affective contact and of lived experience – all of this is strictly foreign to the inspiration behind Freud's work.

This style has for some time tended to descend to the level of a foolish optimism which stems from an equivocal moralism and is founded on an equally crude schematism, which really is the most superficial image ever given to man to apply to his own development – the famous sequence of so-called pregenital phases of the libido. The reaction has not failed to make itself felt, so much so that we have now got to the pure and simple restoration of an orthopedics of the ego, which only a hundred years ago everyone would have laughed at as being the most simplistic question begging.

This rather improbable slide is due, I believe, to the fact that there is a 268
profound misrecognition in thinking that analysis is meant to be used as a bridge for gaining access to a sort of intuitive penetration and easy communication with the patient. If analysis had only been an improvement in the doctor-patient relation, we would literally have no need of it.

Just recently, reading an old text by Aristotle, the *Nicomachean Ethics,* with the intention of rediscovering the origin of Freudian themes on pleasure in it – it makes salubrious reading – I came across a curious term that means something like *fearful.* And this explained many things to me, in particular why it's sometimes the best minds among young psychiatrists that rush headlong down this mistaken path by which they seem to be captivated. I think as a matter of fact that paradoxically they are the best, dreadfully intelligent young men. They're afraid to be so, they frighten themselves – *Where would we be if we gave way to our fine intelligence?* And so they enter analysis where they're taught that their intellectualization is a form of resistance. Once they have finished they're delighted, they've encountered at first hand this famous intellectualization, which for so long had been an obstacle for them. At this stage my discourse can no longer address them.

By contrast, what is at issue in Freud's work? What stands out in it? What, in a word, is its style? Freud's own style would alone suffice to characterize its significance. To see this, I ask you to refer to another form of resistance, which hasn't been much better appreciated than the one I alluded to just before.

For a long time it was thought that the main resistance encountered by Freud's work was due to the fact that he was touching on sexual matters. Good God, why would sexual matters have been any less welcome at that time than in our own, where they appear to be the delight of everyone?

Besides, we have had to wait until our own day for some well intentioned scholar to point out the kinship between Freud's work and the *Naturphilosophie* that prevailed in Germany at the beginning of the nineteenth century. This time was far from having been as fleeting and contingent as Jones represents it to us from an Anglo-Saxon perspective, nor were we in France, above all at the time Freud began to become known here, lacking certain irrationalist or intuitionist tendencies that were advocating recourse to an affective, or sentimental, effusion to understand man or, even, natural phenomena – I don't need to mention the name of Bergson. Why did honest and
269 cultivated people suddenly see in Freud's work some kind of excessive scientism? Why didn't the scholars themselves, who seemed repelled by the results and the originality of the method whose status they didn't immediately identify, ever think of referring Freud to the vitalist or irrationalist philosophy that was much more alive then?

As a matter of fact, nobody was taken in by it. Psychoanalysis does in fact manifest something of the positive spirit of science *qua* explanatory. Psychoanalysis is as far removed as is possible from any form of intuitionism. It has nothing to do with this hasty, short-circuited understanding that so simplifies and limits its significance. To put it back into its proper perspective, one only has to open Freud's work and see the place that a particular dimension, which has never been really emphasized, has there. The value of this for opposing the current evolution of analysis can now be recognized, named, and orientated towards a real reform of analytic studies.

I shall light my lantern and I'll tell you what this is in a way that attempts to be both rapid and striking.

Open *The Interpretation of Dreams*. You will find nothing there resembling this graphology of children's drawings that has ended up becoming the paradigm of analytic interpretation, none of these ascending and descending manifestations of the waking dream. If there is anything this resembles, it's deciphering. And the dimension in question is that of the signifier. Take any of Freud's dreams and you will see that a word, such as *Autodidasker,* predominates.[6] This is a neologism. From here we get *Lasker,* plus a number of other memories. The very form of the word is absolutely essential where interpretation is concerned. An initial interpretation, an orientation or a dichotomy, will direct us towards *Lassalle.* Here one discovers Alex, Freud's brother, through the intermediary of another, purely phonetic and verbal transformation. Freud finds in his recollection a novel by Zola in which a character by the name of *Sandoz* appears. In the way Freud reconstructs it, Zola constructed *Sandoz* out of *Aloz,* the ananym of his name, by replacing *Al,* the beginning of *Alexander,* by the third syllable *sand.* Thus, just as it was possible to make *Sandoz* from *Zola,* so *Alex* is included in the *Lasker* that Freud dreamed as the last part of the word *Autodidasker.*

I'm telling you what Freud did. I'm telling you how his method proceeds. And, as a matter of fact, one only has to open any page of the book, *Die Traumdeutung,* to find an equivalent. I could have taken any other dream, the one for example where he speaks of jokes that have been made on his name, or the one that features a swimming bladder.[7] You will always find a sequence of homonyms or metonyms, of onomastic constructions that are absolutely 270
essential to an understanding of the dream and without which it dissipates, vanishes.

M. Emil Ludwig wrote a book against Freud, almost defamatory in its unfairness, in which he evokes the impression of delusional alienation that one is supposed to get from reading him.[8] I should almost say that I prefer such a testimony to the wearing down of the angles, to the softening, reductive smoothing out being brought about by analytic literature claiming to follow Freud. The incomprehension, the refusal, the shock displayed by Emil Ludwig – whether he's being honest or acting in bad faith doesn't matter to us much – is greater testimony than the disintegration of Freud's work that is being achieved in the decadence analysis is sliding into.

How has it been possible to omit the fundamental role of the structure of the signifier? Of course, we understand why. What is expressed within the apparatus and the play of signifiers is something that comes from the bowels of the subject, which can be called his desire. As soon as this desire is caught up in the signifier it's a signified desire. And thus we are all fascinated by the meaning of this desire. And we forget, despite Freud's reminders, the apparatus of the signifier.

Freud emphasizes, however, that the elaboration of the dream is what makes

[6] *The Interpretation of Dreams,* SE 4:298–302.
[7] SE 4:298 & 206.
[8] *Doctor Freud, an Analysis and a Warning.*

the dream the leading model of symptom formation. Now, this elaboration bears a strong resemblance to a logical and grammatical analysis, just slightly more erudite than what we did at school. This register is the normal level of Freudian work. It's the very register that makes linguistics the most advanced of the human sciences, provided one is simply prepared to acknowledge that what is distinctive about positive science, modern science, isn't quantification but mathematization and specifically combinatory, that is to say linguistic, mathematization which includes series and iteration.

This is what stands out in Freud's work. Without it nothing of what he subsequently develops is so much as thinkable.

I'm not alone in saying this. We have recently published the first volume of the journal in which we inaugurate our attempt to renew the Freudian inspiration, and you can read there that at the bottom of the Freudian mechanisms one rediscovers these old figures of rhetoric which over time have come to lose their sense for us but which for centuries elicited a prodigious degree of interest. Rhetoric, or the art of oration, was a science and not just an art. We now wonder, as if at an enigma, why these exercises could have captivated whole groups of men for such a long time. If this is an anomaly
271 it's analogous to the existence of psychoanalysts, and it's perhaps the same anomaly that's involved in man's relationships to language, returning over the course of history, recurrently, with different ramifications and now presenting itself to us from a scientific angle in Freud's discovery. Freud encountered it in his medical practice when he came upon this field in which the mechanisms of language can be seen to dominate and organize the construction of certain so-called neurotic disorders, unbeknown to the subject, outside his conscious ego.

Here's another example Freud gives at the beginning of *The Psychopathology of Everyday Life*, and which I've given a commentary on in my seminar.[9] Freud can't recall the name *Signorelli* and a series of other names present themselves to him, *Boticelli*, *Boltraffio*, *Trafoi*. How does Freud construct his theory of this memory lapse? During a journey in *Bosnia-Herzegovina* he is talking to someone when he has this kind of name loss. There's also the beginning of a sentence uttered by a peasant – *Herr, what is there left to say now?* It's about the death of a patient, in the face of which a doctor can do nothing. So here we have *Herr*, and death, which is hidden, since Freud, any more than the rest of us, doesn't have any particular reason to linger over the thought of it. What is the other place where Freud has already had occasion to reject the idea of death? It's a place that isn't far from Bosnia, where he received very bad news about one of his patients.

That's the mechanism. Its schema, analogous to that of a symptom, suf-

[9] SE 6:1–7.

fices to demonstrate the essential importance of the signifier. It's insofar as *Signorelli* and the series of names are equivalent words, translations of one another, metaphrases if you like, that the word is linked to repressed death, refused by Freud. He bars them all, even those within the word *Signorelli*, which has only the most distant of links with it – *Signor, Herr*.

What takes its place in response? The other does, he who both is Freud and isn't Freud, the other who is on the same side as the memory lapse, the other from whom Freud's ego has withdrawn and who answers in its place. He doesn't give the reply, since he is forbidden to speak, but he gives the beginning of the telegram, he answers, *Trafoi* and *Boltraffio*, which he makes the intermediary of the metonymy, the intermediary of the slide between *Herzegovina* and *Bosnia*. Freud has exactly the same conception of this mechanism as the one I'm expounding here. Verify it.

Similarly, everything lucid, unique that Freud has contributed on the subject of *Witz* is conceivable only on the basis of the signifying material involved.

That is what, beyond all the determinisms and all the formations, beyond
all the presentiments, Freud encountered after turning forty. Of course, he 272
had a father and a mother like everyone else. His father died and everyone knows that that never passes unnoticed, but all the same these facts must not cause us to underestimate the importance of the discovery of the positive order of the signifier for which something in him had undoubtedly prepared him, the long literary, literalist, tradition from which he came.

The discovery he made in dealing with dreams is to be radically distinguished from any intuitive interpretation of dreams, such as it had been possible to practice before him. Moreover, he had a heightened awareness of how crucial to his thought this adventure that *Die Traumdeutung* was, and in writing to Fliess he mentions it with a kind of fervor, he calls it something like *my garden plant*, by which he meant a new species that had emerged from his stomach.

3

Freud's originality, which disconcerts our sentiment but alone enables the effect of his work to be understood, is his recourse to the letter. This is the spice in Freud's discovery and in analytic practice. If some of this hadn't fundamentally remained, there would have been nothing left of psychoanalysis a long time ago. Everything stems from here. Who is this other who speaks in the subject, of whom the subject is neither the master nor the counterpart, who is the other who speaks in him? Everything is here.

It's not enough to say that it's his desire, for his desire is libido, which, let's not forget, above all means whim [*lubie*], unbounded desire, due to the fact that he speaks. If there were no signifiers to support this rupture, these fragmentations, displacements, transmutations, perversions, this insulation of human desire, the latter would have none of these characteristics that make up the substance of the signifying material provided by analysis.

Nor is it enough to say that this other is in some way our counterpart, on the pretext that he speaks the same language as what we may call common discourse, which is thought to be rational and which, as it happens, sometimes is. For in this discourse of the other what I take to be me is no longer a subject but an object. It's a function of mirage, in which the subject refinds himself only as misrecognition and negation.

It's on this basis that the theory of the ego is best understood.

Freud produced it in a number of stages, and one would be wrong to think that it must date from *Das Es*.[10] Perhaps you've already heard mention of the
273 famous Freudian topography. I fear that you've heard only too much mention of it, since the way it's interpreted goes in a sense contrary to Freud's reason for introducing it. It was in 1914, with his major article "On Narcissism," which is prior to this topography that has now come to the foreground, that Freud constructed a theory of the ego.

The main, unique reference of contemporary analytic theory and practice, namely the famous so-called pregenital stages of the libido which are thought to date from the beginning of Freud's work, date from 1915. "On Narcissism" dates from 1914.

There can be no mistaking Freud's intentions in emphasizing the theory of the ego. It was a question of avoiding two traps. The first is dualism. There is a kind of mania in some analysts which consists in turning the unconscious into another ego, a bad ego, a double, a symmetrical counterpart to the ego – whereas the theory of the ego in Freud is on the contrary designed to show that what we call our ego is a certain image we have of ourselves, which gives us a mirage, of totality no doubt. These leading mirages don't at all orientate the subject in the direction of so-called profound – an adjective I personally don't care for – self-knowledge. The ego's function is explicitly designated in Freud as analogous in every way to what in the theory of writing is called a determinative.

Not all forms of writing are alphabetic. Some are ideophonetic and contain determinatives. In Chinese a thing like this means *something more or less just*, but if you add this, which is a determinative, it becomes *to govern*. And if instead of putting in this determinative you put in a different one it means *illness*. The determinative emphasizes in a particular way, inserts into a class of meanings, something that already has its phonetic individuality as a signifier. Well then, for Freud the ego is precisely a sort of determinative whereby certain of the subject's elements are associated with a special function that

[10] I.e., *The Ego and the Id*.

appears on the horizon of his theory at that moment, namely aggressiveness, considered as characteristic of the imaginary relationship with the other in which the ego constitutes itself through successive and superimposed identifications. Its variable value, its value as a sign, essentially distinguishes it from the entity of the organism as a whole. And, indeed, this is the other trap that Freud was avoiding.

As a matter of fact, even as Freud rallies the personality that speaks in the unconscious around a center, he wanted to avoid the mirage of the famous *total personality* that hasn't failed to regain the upper hand throughout the entire American school which continues to relish the term, promoting the restoration of the primacy of the ego. This is a complete misrecognition of 274
Freud's teaching. The total personality is precisely what Freud intends to characterize as fundamentally foreign to the function of the ego as it has been regarded by psychologists until now.

There is a twofold alienation in the movement of Freudian theory.

There is the other as imaginary. It's here in the imaginary relation with the other that traditional *Selbst-Bewusstsein* or self-consciousness is instituted. There is no way that the unity of the subject can be brought about in this direction. The ego isn't even the place, the indication, the rallying point, the organizing center of the subject. It's profoundly dissymmetrical to it. Although it is in this sense that he is going to begin by getting one to understand the Freudian dialectic – I can in no way expect to attain my accomplishment and my unity from the recognition of an other who is caught up with me in a relation of mirage.

There is also the other who speaks from my place, apparently, this other who is within me. This is an other of a totally different nature from the other, my counterpart.

That's what Freud contributes.

If this still required confirmation, we would only have to observe the way in which the technique of the transference is prepared. Everything is designed to avoid the relation of ego to ego, the imaginary relation that could be established with the analyst. The subject isn't face to face with the analyst. Everything is designed to efface the entire dual, counterpart-to-counterpart relation.

On the other hand, analytic technique derives from the necessity for an ear, an other, a listener. The analysis of a subject can only be brought about with an analyst. This is a reminder to us that the unconscious is essentially speech, speech of the other, and can only be recognized when the other sends it back to you.

Before I finish I would still like to speak about what Freud added towards the end of his life, when he had already left his troop of followers behind him a long time before. I'm unable to doubt for one instant, merely from the evidence of the style and tone of Freud's dialogue with all around him, that he had a profound notion of their radical inadequacy, of their total incomprehension. There is a period in Freud's work, between 1920 and 1924, when he quite simply broke off. He knew that he didn't have very long to live – he died at 83 years of age, in 1939 – and he went straight to the heart of the problem, namely the compulsion to repeat [*automatisme de répétition*].

This notion of repetition is so perplexing for us that one tries to reduce it
275 to a repetition of needs. If on the contrary we read Freud we see that the compulsion to repeat was based, as it always had been from the beginning of his entire theory of memory, on the question raised for him by the insistence of speech which returns in the subject until it has said its final word, speech that must return, despite the resistance of the ego which is a defense, that is, the adherence to the imaginary misconstrual of identification with the other. Repetition is fundamentally the insistence of speech.

As a matter of fact, the final word of Freudian anthropology concerns what possesses man and makes him, not the support of the irrational – Freudism isn't a form of irrationalism, on the contrary – but the support of a form of reason of which he is more victim than master and by which he is condemned in advance.

This is the final word, the red thread that passes through all of Freud's work. From beginning to end, from the discovery of the Oedipus complex to *Moses and Monotheism*, via the extraordinary paradox from the scientific point of view of *Totem and Taboo*, Freud only ever asked himself, personally, one question – how can this system of signifiers without which no incarnation of either truth or justice is possible, how can this literal logos take hold of an animal who doesn't need it and doesn't care about it – since it doesn't at all concern his needs? This is nevertheless the very thing that causes neurotic suffering.

Man is in fact possessed by the discourse of the law and he punishes himself[11] with it in the name of this symbolic debt which in his neurosis he keeps paying for more and more.

How can this have taken hold, how does man enter into this law which is foreign to him and which as an animal he has nothing to do with? It was to explain this that Freud constructed the myth of the murder of the father. I'm not claiming that this is an explanation, but I'm showing you why Freud fomented this myth. Man must become involved in it as guilty. This remains in Freud's work to the end and confirms what I'm presenting to you here and teach elsewhere.

Henceforth, what is the Freudian discovery's center of gravity. What is its philosophy? Not that Freud was doing philosophy. He always repudiated the claim that he was a philosopher. But to ask oneself a question is already to

[11] *"il se châtie":* alternatively, he mortifies himself.

be a philosopher, even if one is unaware that this is what one is doing. What, then, does Freud the philosopher teach? To keep the positive truths that Freud has contributed in proportion, to leave them in their place, let's not forget that his inspiration is fundamentally pessimistic. He denies any tendency towards progress. He is fundamentally anti-humanist to the extent that there is in humanism this romanticism which would like to make the mind the flower of life. Freud is to be situated in a realist and tragic tradition, 276
which explains why it is that it's in the light of Freud that we are today able to understand and read Greek tragedy.

But for us, workers, scholars, doctors, technicians, what direction does this return to the truth of Freud indicate?

It is the direction of a positive study whose methods and forms are given to us in this sphere of the so-called human sciences, which concerns the order of language, linguistics. Psychoanalysis should be the science of language inhabited by the subject. From the Freudian point of view man is the subject captured and tortured by language.

Psychoanalysis introduces us to a psychology, to be sure, but which one? Psychology properly so-called is effectively a science of perfectly well-defined objects. But, undoubtedly, by virtue of the significant resonances of the word, we slide into confusing it with something that refers to the soul. One thinks that everyone has *his own* psychology. One would be better off, in this second usage, to give it the name it could be given. Let's make no mistake – psychoanalysis isn't an egology. From the Freudian perspective of man's relationship to language, this *ego* isn't at all unitary, synthetic. It's decomposed, rendered complex in various agencies – the ego, the superego, the id. It would certainly be inappropriate to make each of these terms a little subject in its own right, which is a crude myth that makes no advance, illuminates nothing.

Freud could not have been in any doubt about the dangers confronting his work. When, in 1938, he took up his pen for his final preface to *Moses and Monotheism* he added a very curious note – *I do not share,* he says, *the opinion of my contemporary Bernard Shaw, who claims that man would be capable of achieving something only if he could live to be three hundred years old. I do not believe this prolongation of life would have any advantages unless,* as the translation goes, *the conditions of the future were totally transformed.* There you have the sad nature of these translations. In German, this has quite a different sense – *many other things would have to be profoundly altered, at the base, at the root, in the determinations of life.*[12]

This note by Freud written when he was old, continuing to pursue his meditation before leaving his message to decompose, to me appears to echo

[12] SE 23:54 n.2. This is the first of two prefatory notes Freud added in 1938.

the terms in which the chorus accompanies the final steps of Oedipus towards the little wood of Colonus. Accompanied by the wisdom of the people, he meditates upon the desires that bring man to pursue shadows, he indicates that it's his having strayed that makes him unable even to know where the
277 woods are. I'm astonished that nobody – except for someone who rendered this into Latin reasonably well – has ever managed to translate properly the *mé phunaï* that the chorus then utters.[13] It's reduced to the value of a verse that says it's better *not to have been born,* whereas the sense is absolutely clear – the only way to overcome all this business of logos, the only way to be rid of it all, would be *not to have been born like this*. This is the very sense accompanying the gesture of the old Freud, when he rejected with his hand any wish that his life be prolonged.

It's true that somewhere in his work on the *Witz,* in other words on the quip, he indicates a reply – *Much better not to have been born – unfortunately, this happens barely once in two hundred thousand.*[14]

I give you this reply.

16 May 1956.

[13] *Oedipus at Colonus,* 1388.
[14] SE 8:57.

THE ENVIRONS OF THE HOLE

XX 281

The appeal, the allusion

THE ONSET OF PSYCHOSIS

SPEAKING OUT

THE MADNESS OF LOVE

THE EVOLUTION OF DELUSION

If we reflect that the means of representation in dreams are principally visual images and not words, we shall see that it is even more appropriate to compare dreams with a system of writing than with a language. In fact the interpretation of dreams is completely analogous to the decipherment of an ancient pictographic script such as Egyptian hieroglyphs. In both cases there are certain elements which are not intended to be interpreted (or read, as the case may be) but are only designed to serve as "determinatives," that is to establish the meaning of some other element. The ambiguity of various elements of dreams finds a parallel in these ancient systems of writing; and so too does the omission of various relations which have in both cases to be supplied from the context. If this conception of the method of representation in dreams has not yet been followed up, this, as will be readily understood, must be ascribed to the fact that psychoanalysts are entirely ignorant of the attitude and knowledge with which a philologist would approach such a problem as that presented by dreams.[1]

This passage is clear enough. The apparent flagrant contradiction that you can draw from it on the basis of Freud's remark that dreams are expressed in images rather than otherwise is restored and resituated as soon as he shows the sort of images in question – namely, images that occur in writing, that is not even for their literal sense since there is a number of them that will not be there to be read, but simply to contribute an exponent without which this would remain enigmatic.

The other day I wrote some Chinese characters on the board. I could just as easily have written some ancient hieroglyphs – the first person pronoun, for example, which is drawn as two little signs that have a phonetic value and may be accompanied by a more or less fleshed-out image which is there to

[1] Sigmund Freud, "The Claims of Psycho-Analysis to Scientific Interest," SE 13:177.

give the other signs their sense. But the other signs are no less autographic than the little fellow[2] and have to be read in a phonetic register.

The comparison with hieroglyphs is rendered all the more valid and certain by the fact that it's dispersed throughout *Die Traumdeutung* and that Freud returns to it constantly.

282 Freud wasn't unaware of what hieroglyphic writing really is. He was in love with everything touching on the culture of ancient Egypt. Very often he would make reference to the style, to the signifying structure, of hieroglyphs and to the sometimes contradictory, superimposed, way of thinking of the beliefs of the ancient Egyptians. And he readily refers to this to give, for example, an image expressive of a certain way in which contradictory concepts coexist in neurotics.

At the end of this passage he evokes the language of symptoms and speaks of the specificity of the signifying structuration in the different forms of neuroses and psychoses. Then suddenly, in a striking summary, he compares the three great neuropsychoses. *For instance,* he says, *what a hysteric expresses by vomiting an obsessional will express by painstaking protective measures against infection, while a paraphrenic will be led to complaints or suspicions that he is being poisoned. These are all of them different representations of the patient's wish to become pregnant which have been repressed into the unconscious, or of his defensive reaction against that wish.*[3]

That was to set us going.

1

Let's return to our subject.

We're not far away from it with the theme of procreation, which lies at the heart of the symptomatology in the Schreber case. But even today we shall not get there immediately.

I would like, from yet another angle, and concerning what you heard on Monday evening from our friend Serge Leclaire, to raise once again the issue of what I call the ultimate signifier in neurosis.

Even though it's essentially a signifier, it of course isn't a signifier without meaning. I stress this fact that it doesn't depend on meaning but is the source of meaning.

The two sides, male and female, of sexuality are not given data, are nothing that could be deduced from experience. How could the individual situate himself within sexuality if he didn't already possess the system of signifiers, insofar as it institutes the space that enables him to see, at a distance, as an

[2] Presumably a reference to one of the characters drawn.
[3] "Claims of Psycho-Analysis to Scientific Interest," SE 13:178.

enigmatic object, the thing that is the most difficult of access, namely his own death? This is no more difficult of access, if you think about it, if you think precisely of the long dialectical process necessary for an individual to accomplish it and of the extent to which our experience consists of too much and too little in one's access to the male and female poles – a reality that may 283
make us wonder whether it's so much as graspable outside the signifiers that isolate it.

The notion we have of reality as that around which the setbacks and obstacles of neurosis revolve must not deflect us from remarking that the reality with which we are concerned is upheld, woven through, constituted, by a tress of signifiers. We have to bring out the point of view, the plane, the particular dimension, of the human being's relationship to the signifier if we are to know even what we are saying when for example we say that in psychosis something becomes lacking in the subject's relation to reality. As a matter of fact it's a question of a reality structured by the presence of a particular signifier that is inherited, traditional, transmitted – but how? Of course, by virtue of the fact that all around the subject people speak.

If we now admit as a fact of common experience that not to have undergone the trial of Oedipus, not to have seen its conflicts and its dead ends open before one, and not to have resolved it, leaves the subject with a certain defect, in a certain state of inability to bring about the correct distance that is called human reality, this is because we hold that reality implies the subject's integration into a particular play of signifiers. Here I'm only formulating what everyone admits, in a kind of implicit way, in analytic experience.

We have indicated in passing that what characterizes the hysterical position is a question that refers precisely to the two signifying poles of male and female. The hysteric addresses it with all his being – how can one be either male or female? – which implies that the hysteric nevertheless has reference to it. The question is this – what is it that the entire structure of the hysteric, with his fundamental identification with the individual of the sex opposite to his own by which his own sex is questioned, is introduced into, suspended from, and preserved in? The hysterical manner of questioning, *either . . . or . . .*, contrasts with the obsessional's response, negation, *neither . . . nor . . .*, neither male nor female. This negation comes about against a background of mortal experience and of hiding his being from the question, which is a way of remaining suspended from it. The obsessional is precisely neither one nor the other – one may also say that he is both at once.

I shall move on, since that was only intended to situate what happens in the psychotic, who contrasts with the position of each of the subjects of the two great neuroses.

In my talk on Freud a fortnight ago I spoke of language insofar as it's inhabited by the subject who to a greater or lesser extent speaks out in lan- 284 guage with all his being, that is, in part unknowingly. How can one fail to see in the phenomenology of psychosis that everything from beginning to end stems from a particular relationship between the subject and this language that has suddenly been thrust into the foreground, that speaks all by itself, out loud, in its noise and furor, as well as in its neutrality? If the neurotic inhabits language, the psychotic is inhabited, possessed, by language.

What comes to the foreground reveals that the subject is subjected to a trial, to the problem of some fault concerning the permanent discourse that supports the everyday, the miscellany, of human experience. Something detaches itself from the permanent monologue and appears as some kind of music for several voices. It's worthwhile dwelling on its structure so as to ask ourselves why it's made in this way.

This is, at the level of the phenomena, something that immediately gives us the impression of being structured. Don't forget that the very notion of structure is borrowed from language. To misrecognize this, to reduce it to a mechanism, is as conclusive as it is ironic. What is it that Clérambault has isolated under the name of the elementary phenomena of psychosis – the repeated, contradicted, commanded thoughts – if it's not this discourse that is augmented, recapitulated in antitheses? But on the pretext that there is an entirely formal structuration here – and Clérambault is absolutely right to insist upon this – the conclusion he draws is that we are dealing with simple mechanical phenomena. This is totally inadequate. It's much more promising to think of it in terms of the internal structure of language.

The merit of Clérambault is to have shown its *ideationally neutral* nature, which in his language means that it's in total discord with the subject's mental state, that no mechanism of the affects adequately explains it, and which in ours means that it's structural. The weakness of the etiological or pathogenic deduction is of little concern to us in comparison with what he stresses, namely that the nucleus of psychosis has to be linked to a relationship between the subject and the signifier in its most formal dimension, in its dimension as a pure signifier, and that everything constructed around this consists only of affective reactions to the primary phenomenon, the relationship to the signifier.

The subject's relation of exteriority to the signifier is so striking that all clinicians have emphasized it in one way or another. The syndrome of influence still leaves some things vague, but the syndrome of action from without, as naive as it appears, does underline the essential dimension of the phenomenon, the psychotic's exteriority in relation to the entire apparatus of language. Hence the question arises whether the psychotic has really entered language.

285 Many clinicians have shown an interest in the psychotic's prior history.

Helene Deutsch has emphasized a certain *as if* that appears to mark the first stages of development in those who at some moment sink into psychosis. They never enter the game of signifiers, except through a kind of external imitation.[4] The non-integration of the subject into the register of the signifier indicates the direction from which the question of the preconditions of psychosis arises – which is undoubtedly soluble only through analytic investigation.

It sometimes happens that we take prepsychotics into analysis, and we know what that produces – it produces psychotics. The question of the contraindications of analysis would not arise if we didn't all recall some particular case in our practice, or in the practice of our colleagues, where a full-blown psychosis – a hallucinatory psychosis, I'm not speaking of a precipitated schizophrenia – is triggered during the first analytic sessions in which things heat up a bit, at which point the poor analyst rapidly becomes the transmitter who makes known to the analysand [*analysé*] what he must do and must not do.

Aren't we here touching on what in our very own experience, without our having to look any further, lies at the heart of the reasons for the onset of psychosis? It's one of the most difficult things that can be proposed to a man, with which his being in the world doesn't confront him all that often – it's what is called speaking out [*prendre la parole*], I mean speaking out one's own speech, which is quite the opposite of saying *yes, yes* to the speech of one's neighbor. This isn't necessarily put into words. The clinic shows that, provided one knows how to discern it at very different levels, it is at precisely this moment that psychosis breaks out.

It's sometimes a question of a tiny spot of speaking out, whereas previously the subject had been living in his cocoon like a moth-worm. This is the form that Clérambault characterized very well under the name of the mental automatism of old maids. I'm thinking of the marvelous richness characteristic of his style – how could Clérambault have failed to dwell on the facts? There was really no reason to pick out these unfortunate beings, forgotten by everybody, whose existence he describes so well and in whom, at the slightest provocation, mental automatism emerges from this discourse that had always remained latent and unexpressed in them.

If we allow that the failing [*défaillance*] of the subject on encountering real speech locates his entry, his sliding, into the critical phenomenon, the inaugural phase, of psychosis, then we can begin to see how this comes to link up with what we have already expounded.

[4] See "Some Forms of Emotional Disturbance and their Relationship to Schizophrenia."

286 **2**

The notion of *Verwerfung* indicates that there must already have been something in the relation to the signifier previously lacking here in the initial introduction to fundamental signifiers.

This is, quite clearly, an absence undiscoverable by experimental research. There is no way of grasping something that lacks at the time it lacks. In the case of President Schreber this would have been the absence of the primordial male signifier to which for years he was able to appear to be equal – he looked as if he, like everyone else, were upholding his role as a man and of being somebody. Virility does signify something for him, since it's equally the object of his very lively protestations at the time the delusion erupts, which initially presents itself in the form of a question over his sex, an interpellation [*appel*] that comes to him from outside, as in the fantasy – *how nice it would be to be a woman undergoing intercourse.* The delusion's development expresses the fact that for him there is no other way of realizing himself, of affirming himself as sexual, than through admitting he is a woman, transformed into a woman. This is the axis of the delusion. For there are two planes to distinguish.

On the one hand, the course of the delusion reveals the need to reconstruct the cosmos, the world's entire organization, around the fact that there is a man who can only be the wife of a universal god. On the other hand, let's not forget that in his common discourse up to the critical period of his existence this man appeared to know just like everyone else that he was a man, and what he somewhere calls his manly honor cries out aloud when he happens suddenly to be aroused a bit too strongly by the enigma of the absolute Other entering into play, which emerges with the first signs of the delusion.

In short, we are led here to the distinction that is the thread running through everything we have until now deduced from the very structuration of the analytic situation – namely, what I have called the little other and the absolute Other.

The former, the other with a small o, is the imaginary other, the otherness in a mirror image, which makes us dependent upon the form of our counterpart. The latter, the absolute Other, is the one we address ourselves to beyond this counterpart, the one we are forced to admit beyond the relation of mirage, the one who accepts or is refused opposite us,[5] the one who will on occasion deceive us, the one of whom we will never know whether he is deceiving us,
287 the one to whom we always address ourselves. His existence is such that the fact of addressing ourselves to him, of sharing something like language with

[5] *. . . celui qui accepte ou qui se refuse en face de nous . . .*

him, is more important than anything that may be placed at stake between him and us.

Misrecognizing the distinction between these two others in analysis, where it's present throughout, lies at the origin of all the false problems, and in particular of the one that appears now that the primacy of the object relation is being emphasized.

Indeed, there is an obvious discrepancy between the Freudian position according to which the newborn, on entering the world, is in a so-called autoerotic relation, that is, a relation in which the object doesn't exist, and the clinical observation that from the beginning of life we undoubtedly have every indication that all sorts of objects exist for the newborn. The solution to this difficulty can only be found by distinguishing between the imaginary other insofar as he is structurally the originary form of the field in which a multiplicity of objects is structured for the human newborn, and the absolute Other, the Other with a big O, which is surely what Freud was driving at – and which analysts have subsequently neglected – when speaking of the non-existence, originally, of any Other.

There is a good reason for this, which is that this Other lies entirely within itself, Freud says, but at the same time entirely outside itself.

The ecstatic relation to the Other is an issue that didn't arise yesterday, but because it has been left in the background for several centuries it's worth our while, for we analysts who are constantly dealing with it, to reexamine it.

In the Middle Ages a distinction was drawn between what was called the physical theory and the ecstatic theory of love. This is the way the question of the subject's relation to the absolute Other was raised. Let's say that in order to understand the psychoses we have to make the love relation with the Other qua radically Other, and the mirror situation, everything of the order of the imaginary, *animus* and *anima,* which is located according to the sexes at one or other of the places, overlap in our little schema.

Where does the difference between someone who is psychotic and someone who isn't come from? It comes from the fact that for the psychotic a love relation that abolishes him as subject is possible insofar as it allows a radical heterogeneity of the Other. But this love is also a dead love.

It may seem to you that it's a curious and unusual detour to resort to a medieval theory of love in order to introduce the question of psychosis. It is, however, impossible to conceive the nature of madness otherwise.

Think about, sociologically, the forms of enamoration, of falling in love, 288
attested in culture.

Psychologists only ever put the question of *patterns* on the agenda. In certain cultures things have become so worn out that it's extremely awkward to know how to give form to love – the crisis begins the moment one takes the classic orchid, worn as a corsage, to the first rendezvous. Let's take as a reference point the technique, for it was a technique, or the art, of love – say, the practices of the love relation that prevailed for a time down in our Provence or in our Languedoc. There is an entire tradition there that was followed by the Arcadian novel along the lines of *L'Astrée,*[6] as well as by romantic love, in which one can observe a degradation in love patterns, which became increasingly uncertain.

Undoubtedly, over the course of this historical evolution passionate love becomes, to the extent that it's practiced in the style called platonic or passionate idealism, an increasingly ridiculous thing, or what is commonly called, quite rightly, a form of madness. The tone has been lowered, the thing has fallen into derision. We undoubtedly play upon this alienated and alienating process, but in an increasingly external manner upheld by an increasingly diffuse mirage. The thing, if it no longer takes place with a beautiful woman or with a lady, is accomplished in a darkened cinema with an image on the screen.

It's something of this order that I want to bring into prominence. This dimension tends in the direction of the madness of pure mirage insofar as the original style of the love relation has been lost. It strikes us as comical, this total sacrifice of one being for another, systematically pursued by people who had the time to do nothing but this. It was a spiritual technique that had its own modes and registers that we can barely grasp, given the distance that separates us from these things. We analysts would find plenty to interest us in this mixture of sensuality and chastity that was technically sustained, so it would appear, over the course of a singular concubinage with no physical relationship, or at the very least with deferred relations.

The characteristic of alienating degradation, of madness, that connotes the remnants of this practice which have been lost at the sociological plane provides us with an analogy with what takes place in the psychotic and gives meaning to the sentence from Freud I quoted to you the other day, namely that the psychotic loves his delusion like himself.[7]

The psychotic can only apprehend the Other in the relation with the sig-
289 nifier, he lingers over a mere shell, an envelope, a shadow, the form of speech. The psychotic's Eros is located where speech is absent. It is there that he finds his supreme love.

Many things become clear if we take them in this register – for example, the curious onset of Schreber's psychosis with the curious expression *soul murder* he employs, a most unusual echo, you'll agree, of the language of love

[6] Seventeenth-century novel by Honoré d'Urfé.
[7] See above, chap. 17, p. 214.

in the technical sense I have just been highlighting for you, love at the time of the *Carte de Tendre*.[8] This sacrificial and mysterious symbolic soul murder is formed at the onset of psychosis according to the precious language.

What can we discern concerning the onset of psychosis – at the least, that an imaginary abundance of modes of beings that are as many relations to the little other, an abundance supported by a certain mode of language and speech, is produced proportionate to a certain interpellation to which the subject is unable to respond?

3

From the outset I've emphasized the intrusion of what Schreber calls the fundamental language, which is affirmed as a sort of particularly full signifier.

This ancient German, he says, is full of resonances by virtue of its nobility and simplicity. There are passages where things go much further than this – Schreber attributes the misunderstanding with God to the fact that the latter does not know how to draw the distinction between what expresses the real feelings of the little souls, and thus of the subject, and the discourse in which he commonly expresses himself over the course of his relations with others. A distinction is thus literally traced out between the unconscious discourse that the subject expresses with all his being and common discourse.

Freud says it somewhere – there is more psychological truth in Schreber's delusion than in the psychologists.[9] This is Freud's wager. Schreber is more true than anything psychologists may say about him, he knows a lot more about human mechanisms and feelings than psychologists do. If God doesn't stop at man's daily needs, if he understands nothing of man, it's because he understands him only too well. The proof of this is that he also introduces into the fundamental language what happens while man sleeps, that is, his dreams. Schreber emphasizes this as if he had read Freud.

Opposed to this from the outset is a side of the signifier that is given to us
for its qualities, its particular density – not for its meaning, but for its meaningfulness. The signified is empty, the signifier is retained for its purely for- 290
mal properties, which are used for example to form series. This is the language of the birds from the sky, the discourse of the young girls, which
Schreber grants the privilege of being without meaning.

The register in which the onset of psychosis is played out is located between these two poles – the word of revelation, which opens up a new dimension and gives a feeling of ineffable understanding, which corresponds to nothing previously experienced, and on the other hand the refrain, the same old song.

[8] Best known part of Madeleine de Scudéry's novel *Clélie*.
[9] See Freud's remarks at the end of the Schreber case, SE 12:78–79.

Beginning with what I call the first sign of the onset of psychosis, the world sinks into confusion, and we can follow, step by step, how Schreber reconstructs it in an attitude of gradual, ambiguous, reticent, *reluctant* as they say in English, consent. He admits bit by bit that the only means of escape, of preserving a certain stability in his relations with the invasive, desiring entities that for him are the supports of the unleashed language of his internal uproar, is to accept his transformation into a woman. Isn't it better, after all, to be a spirited woman than a cretinous man?[10] His body is thus progressively invaded by images of feminine identification to which he opens the door; he lets them take over, he has himself possessed, remodeled, by them. In a note somewhere there is the notion of his permitting images to enter himself.[11] And it's at this point that he recognizes that the world doesn't appear to have changed all that much since the beginning of his crisis – the return of a certain, no doubt problematic, sense of reality.

Concerning the delusion's evolution, it's worth observing that initially full manifestations of speech are produced and that they are satisfactory to him. But while his world is being reconstructed on the imaginary plane, there is a proportionate withdrawal of sense to other places. Speech is initially produced in what he calls *the anterior, prior realms of God*. Then God withdraws to a distance, remoteness, and that which corresponds to the first great signifying intuitions slips further and further away. At the same time as he reconstructs his world, that which is close to him and which he deals with, the speech of this anterior god with whom he has this unusual relation, which is an image of copulation, as is shown by the first dream of psychotic invasion, this god enters the universe of the learning by rote, of the refrain, of empty sense, and of objectification. In the vibrant space of his introspection what he calls *writing-down* henceforth permanently connotes, records, and ratifies his thoughts. There is a displacement here in the subject's relation to speech.

291 The spoken hallucinatory phenomena that for the subject have a sense in the register of interpellation, irony, defiance, allusion, always allude to the Other with a big O, as if it were a term that is invariably present but never seen and never named except indirectly. These considerations will lead us to some linguistic remarks relating to a fact that is within your reach but which you never grasp. I have in mind the two distinct types of usage of personal pronouns.

There are personal pronouns that decline, *je* [I], *me* [me], *tu* [you], *te* [you], *il* [he], *le* [him or it], *etc*. In the register *me* [me], *te* [you], *le* [him or it], the

[10] Mem, 178.
[11] Mem, 231–37.

personal pronoun is liable to be elided. In the other me, *moi* [me], *toi* [you], *lui* [him], it isn't elided.

Do you see the difference? *Je le veux* [*I want it* or *I want him*] and *Je veux lui* or *elle* [*I want him* or *her*] aren't the same thing.

We'll stop there for today.

30 May 1956

293 # XXI

The quilting point

SENSE AND SCANSION

THE FULL CIRCLE AND SEGMENTATION

"*YES*, I COME INTO HIS TEMPLE . . ."

THE FEAR OF GOD

THE FATHER, A QUILTING POINT

Does the subject hear with his ears something that exists or something that doesn't exist? It's quite obvious that it doesn't exist and that consequently it's of the order of a hallucination, that is, of a false perception. Is this adequate for us?

This massive conception of reality leads to the quite mysterious explanation, advanced by analysts, according to which a so-called refusal to perceive produces a hole and there then appears in reality a drive that has been rejected by the subject. But why should something as complex and architectured as speech appear in this hole? This is what we are not told.

To be sure, such an explanation already constitutes progress over the classical conception, but we can go further. In short, we can expect that the phenomenon of psychosis will enable us to restore the proper relationship, increasingly misunderstood in analytic work, between the signifier and the signified.

1

I remind you that at the end of the period during which the external world disintegrated for Schreber, with its roots in that period, there appeared in him a structuration of the relations between the signifier and the signified that is presented thus – there are always two planes.

They are without doubt indefinitely subdivided within themselves. But
294 Schreber's efforts always to locate an anterior plane and a plane beyond is obviously imposed on him by his experience, and this guides us towards something that is really deep-seated in psychotic structure. I have sometimes got you to feel this in an immediate way in my presentations.

On one of these planes phenomena are produced that are above all ones the subject regards as neutralized, as signifying less and less a true other – phrases, he says, learned by rote, drummed into the birds from the sky who repeat them to him, who don't know what they are saying. This term *birds* leads to the parrot – it's a question of the transmission of something empty that wearies and exhausts the subject. At their first appearance these phenomena are situated at the limit of meaning, but they soon turn into quite the contrary – residue, refuse, empty bodies.

I have already mentioned these interrupted sentences that suggest a continuation. They teach us a great deal about the unity that prevails at the level of the signifier – in particular, that the latter isn't isolatable.

These unfinished sentences are in general interrupted at the point at which the full word that would give them their meaning is still lacking but is implied. I've already picked out more than one example of this. For instance, the subject hears – *Do you still speak . . .* , and the sentence stops. This means – *Do you still speak . . . foreign languages?*[1]

The said *conception of souls* is this dialogue, which is much fuller than the drummed-in words the souls exchange with him, in teaching him an entire psychology of thoughts, on the subject of himself. What first of all manifested itself at the beginning of the delusion, like an ineffable and vigorous form of expression, withdraws to a distance, becomes enigmatic, passes into the *posterior realms of God,* at the level of which the intrusive and absurd voices multiply. Even further beyond these voices there are other voices which express themselves in striking formulas.

I remind you of one that is not the least striking of them – *Lacking now is . . . the leading thought.*[2] They also speak to him of *Gesinnung,* which can mean either conviction or faith. *Gesinnung,* they explain, is something we owe any good man, even the blackest of sinners, subject to the demands of purification inherent in the order of the universe, something we owe him in exchange [*dans l'échange*], in the name of that which must regulate our relations with human beings. It is indeed faith that is in question, that minimum of good faith implied by recognition of the other.

A certain period of his hallucinations goes much further still. We have the most unusual expression [. . .]. It's a rare word, extremely difficult to translate. After consulting with people who know about these things, I had arrived at the idea that it was a question of nothing other than what I call the base word, the key, the ultimate linchpin, rather than the solution. It has a tech- 295
nical connotation, in fact, in the art of hunting – it would be what hunters call the *fumées,* that is, the traces of big game.

The essential aspect seems to me to be the withdrawal or migration of sense, its flight onto a plane that the subject is led to situate as the background. Two styles, two levels, are opposed to one another. On the one hand

[1] Mem, 311 n.114.
[2] Mem, 218.

scansion, which plays on the properties of the signifier, with the implicit questioning that scansion contains and which extends to coercion. On the other hand sense, the nature of which is to take flight, to define itself as something that flees, but which at the same time presents itself as an extremely full sense, the fleeing of which draws the subject in towards what would be the core of the delusional phenomenon, its navel. You know that Freud uses this term *navel* to designate the point at which the sense of a dream appears to culminate in a hole, a knot, beyond which it is to the core of being that the dream appears to be attached.[3]

This description is no more than phenomenological. Try to get as much out of it as possible for what is at issue here, which is to find an explanation, a mechanism. We devote ourselves to the work of scientifically analyzing phenomena whose ways of manifesting themselves are familiar to us doctors, practitioners – the condition of familiarity is essential if we are not to lose the sense of analytic experience. The phenomenal relationship I am speaking of remains entirely within the distinction I've stressed a hundred times between the signifier and the signified.

You must undoubtedly end up saying to yourselves – *In the end, don't we know that within the meanings that orient analytic experience this signifier is given by one's own body? And, conversely, that when he speaks of this signifier a given element of which happens to be missing, doesn't he, by means of one of these sleight-of-hand tricks that he holds the secret to, place meaning at the summit of the signifier? There is always a three-card trick from one register to another, according to the needs of the demonstration.*

Well then, I shall happily grant you that there is in fact something of this sort, and this is just what I would like to explain to you today.

The problem is to give you a vivid sense of what you should have a general intuition of anyway, and which last year I showed you concerning a given neurotic phenomenon, by means of a game of letters that some of you recall, and this year concerning psychosis – the elementary meanings we call desire, or feeling, or affectivity, these fluctuations, these shadows, these resonances even, have certain dynamics that can be explained only at the level of the signifier insofar as it is structuring.[4]

296 The signifier doesn't just provide an envelope, a receptacle for meaning. It polarizes it, structures it, and brings it into existence. Without an exact knowledge of the order proper to the signifier and its properties, it's impossible to understand anything whatsoever, I don't mean about psychology – it

[3] Freud refers to the dream's navel at SE 5:525 and also at 4:111 n.1. The expression "core of our being," "*Kern unseres Wesens,*" occurs at SE 5:603.

[4] Cf. chaps. 15 – 16, Sem 2:175–205.

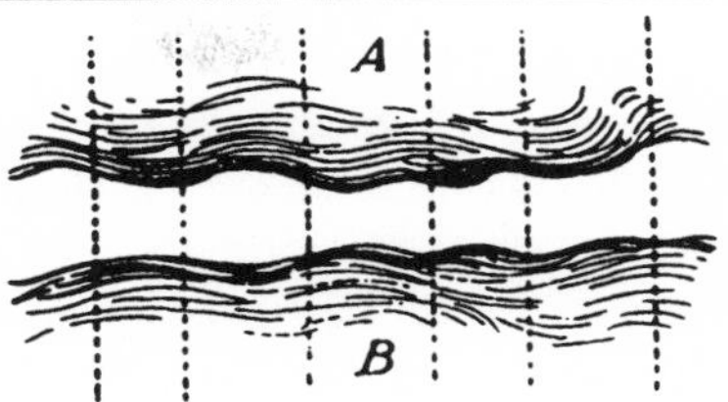

Saussure's schema

suffices that one restrict it in a certain way – but certainly about psychoanalytic experience.

This is what I would like to show you today.

The opposition between the signifier and the signified lies, as you know, at the basis of Ferdinand de Saussure's linguistic theory. It has been expressed in the famous schema of the two curves.[5]

At the upper level Saussure locates the series of what he calls thoughts – without the slightest conviction, since his theory consists precisely in reducing this term to that of the signified insofar as it is distinct from both the signifier and the thing – and he insists above all upon the aspect of amorphous mass. It's what, for our part, we shall provisionally call the sentimental mass of the current of discourse, a confused mass in which appear units, islands, an image, an object, a feeling, a cry, an appeal. It's a continuum, whereas underneath is the signifier as a pure chain of discourse, a succession of words, in which nothing is isolable.

How can I show you this through an experience?

I have to tell you that I spent a week looking for something in the area of the personal pronoun that would give you an image in French of the difference between *je*, *I*, and *moi*, *me*, in order to explain to you how the subject can lose mastery of them, if not contact with them, in psychosis. But concerning the person of the subject and the way it functions, it isn't possible to stop at this pronominal embodiment – it's the structure of the term as such that is involved, at least for our languages. I'm only saying this to secure the steps that I want to get you to follow today.

Come last night, then, I had a mountain of documents. But the ways linguists go about things are so diverse, so contradictory, and would require so many different levels to show you what is meant, that I once again found myself reproducing this double flow of discourse on a piece of paper.

This is indeed the impression we get. The relationship between the signi- 297
fied and the signifier always appears fluid, always ready to come undone. Analysts know better than anyone what is ungraspable in this dimension and

[5] *Course*, 112.

how much they themselves may hesitate before taking the plunge. A step forward has to be taken in order to give what is involved here a sense that is really usable in our experience.

Saussure tries to define a correspondence between these two flows that would segment them. But the sole fact that his solution is inconclusive, since it leaves the locution and the whole sentence problematic, clearly shows both the sense and limitations of his method.

Well then, I think to myself – *What does one start with?* And I go about looking for a sentence, a bit like this pseudo-Shakespeare stuck for inspiration, who paces up and down, repeating – *To be or not . . to be or not . . .*, stuck until he discovers that he can continue by starting at the beginning again – *To be or not . . . to be.* I start with a *Yes.* And, since French, not English, is my language, what comes to me next is – *Yes, I come into his temple to worship the Eternal Lord.*[6]

This means that no signifier is isolable.

It's very easy to see it immediately. Stop at *Yes, I* – why not? If your ear really was like a machine, at each instant the unfolding of the sentence would be followed by a sense. *Yes, I* does have a sense, which probably even constitutes the significance of the text.

Everyone wonders why the curtain rises on this *Yes, I come . . .*, and they say – *There is a conversation going on.* It's initially because this makes sense. The initial *yes* does indeed have a sense, linked to a species of ambiguity that remains in the word *yes, oui,* in French. It's not necessary to be involved with a woman of the world to be aware that *Yes* sometimes means no and that *No* sometimes means perhaps. The *oui* appeared late in French, it appeared after the *si,* after the *da,* which we agreeably rediscover in our time in the *dac.*[7] Because it comes from something that means, *How good that is,* the *oui* is in general a confirmation and at the very least a concession. Most often a *Oui, mais, Yes, but,* is just the type of thing.

Yes, I come into his temple. . . . Don't forget who this character is who is introducing himself here, being a little bit forward. It's the said Abner. He is an officer of the Queen, the said Athaliah, who gives the story its title and who sufficiently dominates everything that takes place as to be its main character. When one of the soldiers begins by saying, *Yes, I come into his temple . . .*, we have no idea where it might be taking us. It could well end up anywhere. *I come into his temple . . . to arrest the High Priest,* for example. It does have to be completed for one to know what is going on. The sentence

[6] *"Oui, je viens dans son temple adorer l'Eternel,"* the opening line of Racine's *Athaliah.*

[7] *Dac* is a familiar abbreviation of *d'accord, okay.* In contemporary French *si* is an affirmative response to a negative question.

only exists as completed and its sense comes to it retroactively. We need to 298
have got right to the end, that is to say, to this famous *Eternal Lord*.

We are, here, in the order of signifiers, and I hope I have made you feel what the continuity of the signifier is. A signifying unit presupposes the completion of a certain circle that situates its different elements.

3

That is where I had paused momentarily. But this modest beginning has a much greater interest. It made me appreciate that the entire scene gives a very nice opportunity to get you to sense what brings psychologists to a standstill, because their function is to understand something of which they understand nothing, and what linguists don't extend to, despite the marvelous method they have in their hands. As for us, we shall go a bit further.

If we return to the scene, who is there listening to the said Abner? Jehoiada is, the High Priest who is engaged in cooking up the little conspiracy that will end with the accession to the throne of his son whom he rescued from massacre at the age of two and a half months and raised in a distant refuge. You can imagine the sentiment in which he listens to this declaration by the officer – *Yes, I come into his temple to worship the Eternal Lord*. The old man may well say to himself, in response – *What is he doing here, then?* The theme continues –

> *Yes, I come into his temple to worship the Eternal Lord,*
> *I come, according to ancient and hallowed custom,*
> *To celebrate with you the glorious day*
> *When on Mount Sinai we received the law.*

In short, they have a chat. And once the Eternal Lord has been left there in the lurch, he won't be spoken of again until right at the end of the play. They start reminiscing. Those were the good old days, *masses of holy people streamed in through the gates*, but now, how things have changed, *scarcely a handful of zealous worshippers*.

Here we start to understand what this is all about. *Scarcely a handful of zealous worshippers* – here's a character who thinks that this is the moment to join the Resistance. Here we are at the level of meaning – while the signifier goes on its merry way, *zealous worshippers* indicates what's at issue, and the ear of the High Priest does not, we can well imagine, fail to pick up this *zeal*
in passing. *Zeal* comes from the Greek and means something like emulation, 299
rivalry, mimicry, because in this game one only wins by doing what suits, by looking like the others.

The climax appears at the end of the first discourse, namely that

I tremble with fear, to hide nothing from you, that Athaliah
Should have you ripped from the altar
And wreak upon you her dreadful revenge,
Shedding the remnants of a forced respect.

Here we see a word emerge that has a great deal of importance – *tremble*. It's etymologically the same word as *craindre, fear,* and *fear* is going to appear. There is something here that reveals the significant climax of the discourse, that gives an indication that has two senses. Here we are placed at the level of the upper register, that is, of what Saussure calls the amorphous mass of thoughts – it may be inherently amorphous, but it isn't merely that, because the other has to guess it.

Abner is there in effect, undoubtedly zealous, but when later the high priest virtually grabs him by the throat and says to him – *Stop the chatter. What's this all about? How does one recognize those who are anything other than zealots?*, one is going to realize how hard times are. It's a long time since God has given anything much in the way of proof of his power, whereas the power of Athaliah and her followers has up till now always proved to be triumphant. Consequently, when he mentions this new threat we don't see what he is driving at very well. It's double-edged. It's equally a warning, a piece of good advice, a counsel of prudence, or even of what's called discretion.

The other's responses are much briefer. He has many reasons for this, and principally that he is the more powerful, he holds the trump card, as it were – *Where,* he simply replies, *does this dark foreboding come from today?* And the signifier sticks perfectly to the signified. But you can see that he gives absolutely nothing away, all he does is make a retort, send back to the subject a question about the sense of what he has to say.

Thereupon, Abner elaborates further and begins to penetrate a bit further into the significant game. It's a mixture of flattery – *Do you believe you can be holy and just with impunity?* and informing, which consists of recounting that there is a certain Mattan who is, in any case, indomitable. He doesn't pursue
300 very far his denunciation of the proud Athaliah, who is after all still his Queen. There happens to be a scapegoat, which is extremely convenient for continuing to lay the bait.

It's still not clear what the point of all this is, unless it's this –

Do believe me, the more I think about it, the less I am able to doubt
That upon you her wrath is about to break.

This displays the moving nature of the characters well. The less he is able to doubt . . . this doubt doesn't make such a disagreeable pillow, but it's no longer quite the moment to relax.

Yesterday I observed her . . .

Here we are at the level of the intelligence officer.

> *. . . and I saw her eyes*
> *At the holy place throw furious glances.*

I would like you to observe that after all the courtesy that Abner has pledged over the course of the exchange, nothing will have happened by the end if we remain at the level of meaning. At this level everything can be summed up in a few words. They both know a bit more than they are prepared to say. Jehoiada is the one who knows the most, but in order to go out and meet what the other claims to know, he makes only one allusion to the fact that there is something in the wind, in other words an Elician in the sanctuary.

But you have the striking evidence of the speed with which the said Abner jumps on this – *She made a mistake,* he says later, that is to say –*Did she botch part of the massacre? What if there remains someone from this famous family of David?* This contribution shows well enough that the reason Abner has gone into the temple is that he is attracted by the smell of fresh blood. But in the final analysis he knows neither more nor less at the end of the dialogue than at the beginning, and this first scene in its meaningful fullness could be summed up in these words –

> – *I have come to the Festival of the Lord.*
> – *Very well,* says the other. *Take part in the*
> *procession and no talking in the ranks.*

It's not this at all, on the one condition that you are aware of the role of the signifier. If you are, you will see that there are a number of key words underlying the discourse of the two characters and that they partly coincide. There 301
is the word *tremble,* the word *fear,* the word *extermination. Tremble* and *fear* are used by Abner first, who takes us to the point I have just indicated, that is, to the point at which Jehoiada truly starts to speak out.

> *He who can still the raging seas*
> *can also thwart the wicked in their plots.*
> *In respectful submission to His holy will,*
> *I fear God, dear Abner, and have no other fear.*

I fear God, you say . . . , he replies, whereas Abner had never said this,

> *. . . his truth touches me.*
> *Here is how the Lord answers you out of my mouth.*

And we see the word I pointed out to you at the beginning, *zeal,* appear here –

> *By zeal for my law,*
> *By sterile vows do you think to honor me?*

What is the fruit for me of all your sacrifices?
The blood of your Kings cries out, and is not heard.
Break off all your pacts with impiety.
From the midst of my people extinguish the crimes
And then you will immolate your victims in my name.

You mustn't think that these are innocent victims in more or less fixed form in appropriate locations. When Abner observes that *the Holy Ark is mute and gives no more oracles,* he gets this lively response –

Ungrateful race. What? Will the greatest marvels
strike your ears but never move your heart?
Must I, Abner, must I recall the series
Of wondrous prodigies accomplished in our time?
Of Israel's tyrants the celebrated disgrace,
And God found faithful in all his threats;
The impious Ahab destroyed, and drenched with his blood
The field that by murder he had usurped;
302 *Near this fatal field Jezebel immolated,*
Under the horses' hooves this Queen was crushed,
In her inhuman blood the dogs slaked their thirst,
And her hideous body dismembered;
. . .

So we know what sort of victim will be involved.

In short, what is the role of the signifier here? Fear is something that is particularly ambivalent. We others, we analysts, aren't unaware of this – it's as much something that drives you on as something that holds you back, it's something that makes you a double being and that, when you express it before a character with whom you want to play at being afraid together, will always place you in the position of a reflection. But there is something else, which looks homonymous – *the fear of God.*

This isn't the same thing at all. It's the signifier, itself rather rigid, that Jehoiada trots out precisely at the moment he is alerted to the danger.

The fear of God is an essential expression in a certain line of religious thought which you would be wrong to think of as simply the general line. The fear of *the gods,* from whom Lucretius wants to free his little friends, is something altogether different, a multiform, confused feeling, one of panic. The fear of *God,* on the other hand, on which a tradition that goes back to Solomon is based, is the principle of wisdom and the foundation of the love of God. Moreover, this tradition is precisely our own.

The fear of God isn't a signifier that is found everywhere. Someone had to invent it and propose to men, as the remedy for a world made up of manifold terrors, that they fear a being who is, after all, only able to exercise his cruelty through the evils that are there, multifariously present in human life. To have replaced these innumerable fears by the fear of a unique being who has no other means of manifesting his power than through what is feared behind these innumerable fears, is quite an accomplishment.

You will say to me – *That really is a curate's idea!* Well, you're wrong. The curates have invented absolutely nothing in this genre. To invent a thing like this you have to be a poet or a prophet, and it's precisely insofar as this Jehoiada is one to some extent, at least by the grace of Racine, that he can use as he does this major and primordial signifier.

I have only been able to briefly mention the cultural history of this signifier, but I have sufficiently indicated to you that it's inseparable from a particular structuration. It's the signifier that dominates the thing, since as far as the meanings are concerned they have completely changed.

This famous fear of God completes the sleight of hand that transforms, 303
from one minute to the next, all fears into perfect courage. All fears – *I have no other fear* – are exchanged for what is called the fear of God, which, however constraining it may be, is the opposite of a fear.

What has happened by the end of the scene is precisely this – the said Jehoiada has handed the fear of God onto the other, and in the proper way, the right way round, painlessly. And straightaway Abner departs completely trustworthy, with this word that echoes *God found faithful in all his threats.* It's no longer a question of zeal, he will join the faithful troops. In short, he himself has become the support of the bait that will hook the Queen. The play is already played out, it's over. It's insofar as Abner doesn't say a word to her about the real risks she is running that the Queen will take the bait he henceforth represents.

The power of the signifier, the effectiveness of this word *fear*, has been to transform the *zeal* at the beginning, with everything that is ambiguous, doubtful, always liable to be reversed, that this word conveys, into the *faithfulness* of the end. This transmutation is of the order of the signifier as such. No accumulation, no superimposition, no summation of meanings, is sufficient to justify it. The entire progress of this scene, which would otherwise be worthy of the *Deuxième Bureau*,[8] resides in the transmutation of the situation through the intervention of the signifier.

Whether it be a sacred text, a novel, a play, a monologue, or any conversation whatsoever, allow me to represent the function of the signifier by a spatializing device, which we have no reason to deprive ourselves of. This point around which all concrete analysis of discourse must operate I shall call a quilting point.

[8] The French Secret Service.

When the upholsterer's needle, which has entered at the moment of *God found faithful in all his threats,* reappears, it's all over, the chap says, *I'm going to join the faithful troops.*

Were we to analyze this scene as a musical score, we should see that this is the point at which the signified and the signifier are knotted together, between the still floating mass of meanings that are actually circulating between these two characters and the text. It's due to this admirable text, and not to the meaning, that *Athaliah* is not a piece of boulevard theatre.

The quilting point is the word *fear,* with all these trans-significant connotations. Everything radiates out from and is organized around this signifier, similar to these little lines of force that an upholstery button forms on the
304 surface of material. It's the point of convergence that enables everything that happens in this discourse to be situated retroactively and prospectively.

4

The schema of the quilting point is essential in human experience.

Why does this minimal schema of human experience which Freud gave us in the Oedipus complex retain its irreducible and yet enigmatic value for us? And why privilege the Oedipus complex? Why does Freud always want to find it everywhere, with such insistence? Why do we have here a knot that seems so essential to him that he is unable to abandon it in the slightest particular observation – unless it's because the notion of father, closely related to that of the fear of God, gives him the most palpable element in experience of what I've called the quilting point between the signifier and the signified?

Perhaps I've spent a long time explaining this to you, but I nevertheless believe that this creates an image and enables you to grasp how it can happen, in psychotic experience, that the signifier and the signified present themselves in a completely divided form.

One can think that in a psychosis everything is there in the signifier. It looks as if everything is there. President Schreber seems to understand perfectly well what it is to be screwed by Professor Flechsig and by a number of others who become his substitutes. What is vexatious is precisely that he should say so, and in the clearest possible way – why, henceforth, should this provoke, as people explain to us, such profound disorders in his libidinal economy?

No, it's in another register that what happens in psychosis has to be explored. I don't know how many there are, but it isn't impossible that one should manage to determine the minimal number of fundamental points of insertion between the signifier and the signified necessary for a human being to be

called normal, and which, when they are not established, or when th
way, make a psychotic.

What I'm proposing is still altogether crude, but it's the point from which we can begin next time to examine the role of the *personization* of the subject, namely the manner in which in French *je* and *moi* are differentiated.[9]

Of course, no particular language has any privilege in the order of signi- 305
fiers, the resources of each are extremely different and always limited. But equally, any one of them covers the entire field of meanings.

Where in the signifier is the person? How does a discourse hang together? Up to what point can a discourse that seems personal bear, on the level of the signifier alone, a sufficient number of traces of impersonalization for the subject not to recognize it as his own?

I'm not saying that this is the source of the mechanism of psychosis, I'm saying that the mechanism of psychosis manifests itself here. Before outlining this mechanism we must make an effort to recognize at the different stages of the phenomenon the points at which the quilting is omitted. A complete catalogue of these points would enable us to discover some surprising correlations and appreciate that it isn't just in any old way that the subject depersonalizes his discourse.

In this respect there is an experience within hand's reach. Clérambault recognized it. He alludes somewhere to what happens when all of a sudden we are gripped by an event from our past that we find difficult to tolerate being affectively evoked. When it's not a question of commemoration but of the resurgence of affect, when, recollecting being angry, we are very close to being angry, when, recollecting a humiliation, we relive the humiliation, when, remembering the destruction of an illusion, we feel the need to reorganize our equilibrium and our meaningful field, in the sense in which one speaks of social field – well then, this is the most favorable moment, Clérambault notes, for the emergence, which he himself calls purely automatic, of scraps of sentences sometimes taken from one's most recent experience, and which have no kind of meaningful relationship with the matter at hand.

These phenomena of automatism are in fact admirably observed – but there are many others – and having the adequate schema is sufficient for one to situate oneself in the phenomenon in a way that is no longer purely descriptive but properly explanatory. There you have the order of things that an observation such as that of President Schreber, which is no doubt unique in the annals of psychopathology, must convey to us.

[9] Damourette and Pichon define "personization" as the distribution of verbs on the "delocutory" plane (i.e., in the indicative, subjunctive, and conditional moods) and on the "locutory" plane (i.e., in the imperative mood).

Next time I shall pick things up at the *je* and the *tu*.

There is no need for these to be expressed in a sentence for them to be there. *Come on!* is a sentence and implies an *I* and a *you*.

306 In the schema I have given you, where are the *I* and the *you?* You imagine perhaps that the *you* is here, at the level of the big Other, do you? No, not at all. This is where we shall begin – the *you* in its verbalized form does not at all coincide with this pole that we have been calling big O.

6 June 1956

XXII

"Thou art the one who wilt follow me"

THE OTHER IS A LOCUS
THE *YOU* OF THE SUPEREGO
DEVOLUTION AND OBSERVATION
THE VOICE
INTERPELLATION OF THE SIGNIFIER

I'm much more myself. Before, I was a para-me who thought of myself as the true one, and who was absolutely false.

In any case, I want to point out that there is a lot of us, those who gave our support to the Popular Front.[1]

These sentences, which are attested, I have selected from Damourette and Pichon's *Grammaire,* a substantial and highly instructive work, even if only because of the enormous quantity of very intelligently classified documents, whatever errors it contains as a whole and in its details.

These two sentences, one spoken and one written, show us that what I am going to get you to think about today is not a forged artifact, a misplaced literary subtlety.

The first sentence obviously comes from a patient in analysis. Pichon indicates this by her initials, Mme X, such and such a date. *I'm much more myself,* she says, no doubt very satisfied with progress accomplished in her treatment, *Before, I was a para-me who thought of myself as. . . .* Thank God that the French language, which is often ambiguous when spoken, here, owing to the encounter between a silent consonant and an initial vowel, enables what is in question to be clearly discerned.[2] The verb is in the first person singular, it's I *who thought of myself as. . . .* Through the relative pronoun, the first person has been transmitted to the relative clause.

You'll tell me – *This is obvious!* That was the response of a charming woman

[1] *"Je suis beaucoup plus moi. Avant, j'étais un paramoi qui croyais être le vrai, et qui était absolument faux.*

"En tout cas, je veux préciser que nous sommes nombreux ceux qui avons soutenu le Front populaire."

[2] With most verbs the difference between the first and third person singular would not normally be heard in French, but when, as here, the following word begins with a vowel, the final consonant of the verb may be pronounced. The first and third persons can then be differentiated in spoken language.

308 whom I tried recently to interest in these issues by propounding to her the problem of the difference between *I am the woman who will not abandon you* and *I am the woman who shall not abandon you.*[3] I have to say that I was unsuccessful. She refused to show any interest in this nuance whose importance you have nevertheless already felt.

Usage makes this sufficiently clear, since in the same sentence Mme X continues – *I am much more myself. Before, I was a para-me who thought of myself as the true one, and who was absolutely false.*

I think that no sentence is more appropriately expressed. It *was absolutely false,* this para-me. An *I* in the first part of the sentence, it has become an *it* in the second.

There are a few of them like that in Pichon, equally quite pertinent and still of interest – *In any case, I want to point out that there is a lot of us, those who gave our support to the Popular Front, voted for its candidates, and who thought of themselves as having a totally different ideal to follow, a totally different action, and a totally different reality,* etc.[4]

If you pay attention you can collect these examples by the bucketful. The issue is whether or not the personization that is in the principal clause crosses the screen, the lens, at the entrance to the relative clause. The screen is obviously neutral, it won't vary. It is therefore a question of knowing what the penetrative power, as it were, of the antecedent personization consists in.

We shall see that this minor linguistic point can also be found in other languages in a manner that is very much alive. But obviously one would have to look in other syntactic forms. We shall come back to this later on.

1

Last time I left you at the point of examining what new light the advances we have made concerning the function of the signifier can contribute to the burning question, which has been made topical in a confused way by the function of the object relation and made present as much by the structure as by the phenomenology of psychosis, of the other.

Until now I have been showing you the duality of this other, between the imaginary other and the Other with a big O, this Other that I discussed in the small piece I read out to you in the last session of last year, and which

[3] *"Je suis la femme qui ne vous abandonnerai pas"* and *"Je suis la femme qui ne vous abandonnera pas."* The relative verb is in the second person in the first example and in the third person in the second example. The old or regional distinction in English usage between *shall* and *will* seems to capture much of the sense of the distinction that Lacan draws.

[4] *"En tout cas je veux préciser que nous sommes nombreux ceux qui avons soutenu le Front populaire, voté pour ses candidats, et qui croyaient à un tout autre idéal poursuivi, à une tout autre action et à une tout autre réalité."*

has just been published in *Evolution psychiatrique* under the title of *La Chose freudienne.*[5]

I apologize for quoting myself, but what's the use of polishing up one's propositions if one is not to use them? I say – *the Other is, therefore, the locus* 309
in which is constituted the I who is speaking with him who hears.[6] I say this following some remarks on the fact that there is always an Other beyond all concrete dialogue, all interpsychological play. This proposition that I quote has to be taken as a starting point, the issue is to find out where it leads to.

I would like you to be aware of how much difference there is between such a perspective and the one that is confusedly accepted today. Saying that the Other is the locus in which is constituted he who is speaking with him who hears is something quite different from setting out from the idea that the other is a being.

We have been intoxicated for some time in analysis by themes that have indisputably come from so-called existentialist discourse, where the other is the *thou,* the one who can respond, but in a symmetrical mode, one of complete correspondence, the alter ego, the brother. One forms a fundamentally reciprocal idea of intersubjectivity. Add to this the sentimental confusions that come under the rubric of personalism, plus Martin Buber's book on the I and the thou,[7] and the confusion will be definitive and irremediable unless one returns to experience.

Far from having made any contribution whatsoever that would throw light on the foundation of the existence of the other, all the existentialist experience has done is to suspend it, in an increasingly radical way, from the hypothesis of projection – upon which you of course all live – according to which the other is barely more than a certain human semblance, animated by an *I* that is the reflection of my own.

Animism and anthropomorphism are there, always liable to emerge and in fact impossible to refute, as are the summary references to the experience of language at the time of one's first babbling. It's brought to our attention that the child doesn't immediately acquire mastery of *you* and *I,* but the acquisition is ultimately summed up in the child's being able to say *I* when you have said *you* to him, in his understanding that when he is told *you're going to do this* he has to say in his register *I'm going to do this.*

In analysts this symmetrical conception culminates in a number of first truths, in extraordinary statements such as the following, which I heard from the mouth of someone who belongs to what one calls the other group – *One can't analyze someone for whom the other doesn't exist.*

5 See "The Freudian Thing," E, 401-36 / 114-45.
6 E, 431 / 141.
7 Martin Buber, *I and Thou.*

ıder what it means to say that *the other doesn't exist.* I wonder whether ression has any value whatsoever, even as an approximation. What is at issue? A lived experience? An irreducible feeling? Take the case of Schre-
310 ber, for whom all humanity was at one time in the state of fleeting-improvised-men – well then, there is indeed an other for him, a singularly accentuated other, an absolute Other, an entirely radical Other, an Other who is neither a place nor a schema, an Other who he says is a living being in his own way, and who he stresses is capable, when threatened, of egoism like other living beings. God, finding himself in a position in which his independence is threatened by this disorder for which he is primarily responsible, manifests spasmodic defense relations. He nevertheless retains an otherness such that he is a stranger to living things and, more particularly, is deprived of all understanding with respect to the vital needs of our Schreber.

That there is for Schreber an other who is worthy of the name is adequately indicated by the singularly pointed, witty beginning of one of the chapters of his *Memoirs,* where he says he is in no way a paranoiac. A paranoiac is someone who relates everything to himself, he's someone whose egocentrism is invasive – he's read Kraepelin – but *as for me,* he says, *it's quite different, it's the Other who relates everything to me.*[8] There is an Other, and this is decisive, structuring.

Thus, before speaking of the other as something that is either placed or not placed at a certain distance, which we are either capable or incapable of embracing, of clasping, or even of consuming in more or less rapid quantities, one would have to know whether the very phenomenology of things as they present themselves in our experience doesn't necessitate a different approach – precisely the one I adopt in saying, before seeing how it will be more or less brought about – that the Other must first of all be considered a locus, the locus in which speech is constituted.

Persons – since this is what we are interested in today – must come from somewhere. They come first in a signifying, by which I mean formal, manner. Speech is constituted for us by an *I* and a *you.* These are two counterparts. Speech transforms them, by giving them a certain appropriate relationship, but – and this is what I want to insist upon – a distance that's not symmetrical, a relationship that isn't reciprocal. In fact, the *I* is never there where it appears in the form of a particular signifier. The *I* is always there in the name of a presence that supports the discourse as a whole, whether in direct or indirect speech. The *I* is the *I* of him who is pronouncing the discourse. Underneath everything that is said there is an *I* who pronounces it. It's within this enunciation that the *you* appears.

These are first truths, so much so that you are liable to look further than

[8] Mem, 262.

the end of your nose. There is nothing more to understand than what I have just observed. That the *you* is already within discourse is obvious. There has 311
never been a *you* anywhere else than where one says *you*. Let's start from there.

As for the *I*, is it, too, a coin, a fiduciary element circulating in discourse? I hope to answer this a little later, but I raise the question now so that you won't lose sight of it and so that you will know what I'm getting at.

2

The *you* is far from being addressed to an ineffable person, to that species of beyond whose leading accent the sentimentalist tendency in the manner of existentialism would like to show us. It's something quite different in its usage.

The *you* isn't always the full *you,* of which so much is made and which, as you know, I myself occasionally evoke in some leading examples. *You are my master, you are my woman* – I make a great deal of such expressions for getting the function of speech understood.

It is a question today of recentering the significance attached to this *you,* which is far from always having this full employment.

I return to some linguistic observations.

The second person is far from always being employed with this emphasis. When it is said in quite ordinary usage – *One can't go for a walk in that place without someone's accosting you,*[9] it isn't about any *you* in reality. The *you* is almost the reflexive of the *one,* it is its correspondent.

Something even more significant – *When you have attained this degree of wisdom, all that remains is to die.*[10] Here again, what *you* is involved? I am certainly not addressing myself to no one in particular in this utterance. I ask you to take the sentence as a whole because there is no sentence that can be detached from the fullness of its meaning. What *you* is alluding to is so far from being an other that I should say it is alluding to those left behind who would persist in living after this discourse – if wisdom says that there is no end to anything other than death, then all that remains is to die. This shows you well enough that the function of the second person on this occasion is precisely to allude to what is nobody, to what is depersonalized.

In fact, this *you* that one kills here is the one that is perfectly familiar to us from the phenomenology of psychosis, as well as from common experience.[11]
It's the *you* that says *you* in us, this *you* that always makes itself more or less 312

[9] *"On ne peut pas se promener dans cet endroit sans qu'on vous aborde."*
[10] *"Quand on en vient à ce degré de sagesse, il ne vous reste plus qu'à mourir."*
[11] *"Tu,"* "you," and *"tue,"* "kill," are homophonic.

discreetly heard, this *you* that speaks alone, and says *You see!* to us, or, *You're always the same*. As in Schreber's experience, this *you* doesn't need to say *you* in order to be the *you* that speaks to us. A tiny bit of disintegration suffices – Schreber had more than his fair share – for things like, *Don't surrender to the first inducement* to emerge.[12]

This is an allusion to something that isn't named and that we reconstruct as being Schreber's homosexual tendency, but it is possibly something different, since invitations, injunctions, are not rare but constant. This sentence is in fact the rule of conduct for many people – *Don't surrender to your initial reaction, it might be the right one,* as they say.[13] And what are you taught, if it isn't precisely never to surrender to the first inducement? Here we recognize our good old friend the superego, who suddenly appears before us in his phenomenal form, rather than in amiable genetic hypotheses. This superego is indeed something like the law, but it's a law without dialectic, and it's not for nothing that it is recognizable, more or less correctly, in the categorical imperative, with what I would call its maleficent neutrality – one author calls it the internal saboteur.

We would be wrong if we misunderstood that this *you* is also present as an observer – it sees everything, hears everything, notes everything. This is indeed what takes place in Schreber, and it's his mode of relation to it that is expressed in him by this remorseless, incessant *you,* which provokes him into responses devoid of any kind of sense.

I am tempted to quote the old expression, *Nobody suspects a thing,*[14] that used to be displayed in the pages of the telephone directory concerning a private detective agency. One senses to what extent an ideal is involved here. How happy everybody would be if in fact nobody did suspect a thing! But hide as one may behind a curtain, there is always a big pair of shoes that stick out. It's the same for the superego. But it doesn't suspect anything. Nothing is less doubtful than whatever appears to us through the intermediary of this *you*.

It is incredible that we should be liable to forget this major obstacle, which our analytic experience makes manifest – that the *you* is present as a foreign body. An analyst, Mr. Isakower, went so far as to compare it with what takes place in a little crustacean of the prawn genus that has the unusual property of having, at the beginning of its existence, its vestibular chamber, the organ that governs balance, open to the marine environment.[15] The vestibular chamber subsequently closes and includes a number of small particles prev-

[12] "Not at the first demand," Mem, 164.

[13] *"Ne cédez pas à votre premier mouvement, ce pourrait être le bon."* Talleyrand is reputed to have said, *"Méfiez-vous des premiers mouvements, parce qu'ils sont les bons."* Mistrust your initial reactions because they are the right ones.

[14] *"Nul ne s'en doute."*

[15] Otto Isakower, "On the Exceptional Position of the Auditory Sphere."

alent in the environment that will make it easier for it to adopt a vertical or horizontal position. At the beginning of their existence these little animals 313
themselves gently introduce small grains of sand into their shell, then, by a physiological process, the chamber closes up. If you substitute small particles of iron filings for these grains of sand you can lead these charming little things to the end of the earth with an electromagnet or make them swim upside down.

This is the function of the *you* in man according to Mr. Isakower, and I would be happy to make an apologue of this in order to get the experience of the *you* understood, but at its lowest level. One totally misrecognizes its function if one neglects that it leads to the *you* as signifier.

Analysts – the path I'm following here isn't a solitary one – have emphasized yet another point. I can't dwell upon the relation that exists between the superego, which is nothing other than the function of the *you,* and the sentiment of reality. I don't need to insist on this for the simple reason that it's stressed on every page of President Schreber's observation. If the subject doesn't doubt the reality of what he hears, it's because of this characteristic of foreign body that the intimation of the delusional *you* presents. Need I invoke the philosophy of Kant, who recognizes a fixed reality only in the starry skies above our heads and the voice of conscience within?[16] This foreignness, like the character Tartuffe, is the true possessor of the house who readily says to the ego – *You will have to leave.* When the feeling of foreignness, strangeness, strikes somewhere, it's never on the side of the superego – it's always the ego that loses its bearings, it's the ego that enters the state of *you,* it's the ego that thinks it is in the state of the double, that is, expelled from the house, while the *you* remains the possessor of things.

That's our experience. We don't have to stop there all the same. But ultimately we have to be reminded of these truths if we are to understand where the structural problem lies.

It may seem strange to you that I mechanize things in this way, and perhaps you will imagine that I'm working with an elementary notion of the discourse I teach, that everything is contained within the relation between the *I* and the *you,* between the ego and the other.

This is what linguists – not to mention psychoanalysts – start mumbling about whenever they investigate the question of discourse. One may even regret seeing that Pichon, in the quite remarkable work I have mentioned, finds it necessary to remind us that for the basis of his definition of verbal distributories[17] – as he puts it – one has to set out from the idea that discourse is always addressed to an other, to the allocutor.[18] And so he begins

[16] Conclusion, *Critique of Practical Reason,* 258.

[17] *"répartitoire."* Damourette and Pichon define a "distributory" as a system of grammatical classification involving number, voice, person, etc.

[18] Damourette and Pichon define the "allocutor" as the second person singular.

314 with the simple locutory plane[19] found in the imperative, *Come here!* There's no need to say much about this – *Come here!* presupposes an *I*, it presupposes a *you*. There is moreover a narrative plane that is delocutory,[20] on which there's always I and you, but on which one is alluding to something else.

We can only think that one is not fully satisfied with such a distribution, since a new problem arises concerning the interrogative, which we shall introduce with a dissymmetry that forms a symmetry provided we regard the number three as the best.

If the narrative is *He's coming*, the interrogative is *Vient-il?*, *Is he coming?* But it's not so simple in this function. The proof is that one says *Le roi vient-il?*, *Is the King coming?*, which clearly shows that *t-il* is not quite the same subject in the interrogative as in the narrative. This may mean *there is a King*, *let the King come*, or *if the King comes*. The question becomes much more complex as soon as one approaches the concrete usage of language. The imperative *Viens!*, *Come here!*, creates the illusion of a symmetrical, bipolar presence of an *I* or a *you*. But are the *I* or the *you* also present when reference is made to this third object called a third person?

The said third person doesn't exist. I tell you this in passing so as to begin to unsettle some principles that are, certainly, very tenacious in your minds, owing to the elementary teaching of grammar. There is no third person, M. Benveniste has demonstrated this conclusively.[21]

Let's pause for a moment in order to place the question that the subject asks himself, or more exactly the question that *I* ask myself about what *I* am or may hope to be.

In our experience we only ever find it expressed by the subject outside himself and without his knowledge. It's a fundamental question, however, since it lies at the foundation of neurosis, which is where we have grabbed it by the ears.

We can see that this question, when it crops up, decomposes remarkably. It crops up in forms that have nothing interrogative about them, like *Puissé-je y arriver!*, *Would that I succeed!*, but which are in between an exclamation, a wish, an expression of doubt. If we want to give this a little bit more consistency, to express it in the delocutory and narrative register, in the indicative, notice how we quite naturally say – *Penses-tu réussir?*, *Do you really think you'll succeed?*

In short, I would like to convey to you a distribution of the functions of language other than by rambling on about the locution, the delocution, and

[19] The "locutory plane" is defined as "the state of language when the attention is focused on the state of mind of the person speaking." Glossary, *Essai de grammaire* 7:10.

[20] The "delocutory plane" is the state of language when the expression is focused on the thing being spoken of.

[21] See Emile Benveniste, "The Nature of Pronouns" and "Relationships of Person in the Verb."

the allocution – and to do it as a function of the question that is always latent, never raised.

If it is brought to light, if it emerges, it's always in connection with a mode
of appearance of speech that we may in various ways call a mission, a man- 315
date, a delegation, or a devolution, in reference to Heidegger. It's the foundation or foundational speech – *You are this, my woman, my master,* a thousand other things. This *You are this,* when I receive it, makes me in speech other than I am.

Who utters it? Is this *you* the same as the *you* swimming at large in the examples I have given you? Is this mission phenomenally primary or secondary in relation to the question?

The question tends to emerge when we have to answer to a mission. The third party at issue here – I point this out to you in passing – is nothing resembling an object. It's always the discourse itself to which the subject is referring. To the *you are my master* a certain *what am I?* responds – *What am I if that's what I am, if indeed I am it at all?* This *it* isn't the master taken as an object, it is the entire enunciation of the sentence that says *I am your master,* as if *your master* had a sense solely through the homage I receive from it. *What am I, if I'm what you've just been saying I am?*

There is a very nice prayer in Christian practice called the *Ave Maria.* Moreover, nobody suspects that this begins with the three letters that buddhist monks murmur all day long, AUM, there must be something radical in the order of the signifier here – but it's not important. *I salute you, Mary* and – according to another popular saying – *You will have a son without a husband,* as the song goes.[22] Moreover, this is not at all unrelated to the subject of President Schreber. The response is not at all, *I am what?*, but, *I am the maid-servant of the Lord, that it be done unto me according to your word. I am the maid-servant* simply means, *I abolish myself. What am I if I am she who you say I am? But that it be done unto me according to your word.*

Such is the order of response at issue in speech at its clearest. When the devolution presents itself in a sufficiently advanced manner, we can study the reciprocal relationships between the *you,* a foreign body, and the signifier that pins down, quilts, the subject.

I ask you to consider with me today some examples whose linguistic significance is completely tangible to us French.

3

What is the difference between *Thou art the one who wilt follow me everywhere* and *Thou art the one who will follow me everywhere?*[23]

22 *"Je vous salue Marie / Vous aurez un fils sans mari."*
23 *"Tu es celui qui me suivras partout"* and *"Tu es celui qui me suivra partout."* In

316 We have a principal clause in the second person, *Thou art the one*. *Who* is the screen. Will it or will it not let the *thou* pass into the relative? You see immediately that it is absolutely impossible to separate the *thou* from the sense of the signifier that follows. The permeability of the screen doesn't depend on the *thou,* but on the sense of *to follow* and on the sense that I place upon it, I who am speaking – this I who is speaking isn't necessarily me, it is perhaps whoever hears that with the echo that lies underneath the whole sentence – on the sense placed on this sentence.

Thou art the one who wilt follow me everywhere is at the very least an election, perhaps unique, a mandate, a devolution, a delegation, an investment. *Thou art the one who will follow me everywhere* is an observation, which we are inclined to feel as being on the side of a sorrowful observation. Of this *thou* who *will follow me everywhere* we shall rapidly have had a stomach full if this really is determinative in character. If in one case this tends towards the sacrament, in the other it would move fairly quickly over to the side of the persecution included in the very term *to follow*.

You will tell me yet again that the signifier in question is precisely a meaning. My retort is that the meaning of *secution* that is in question when I say *thou art the one who will follow me everywhere* to the one whom I recognize as my companion, and which may be the response to *you are my master* that we are always going on about, implies the existence of a certain mode of signifier. I shall materialize this for you immediately.

Suivre, to follow, may be ambiguous in French. It may not carry quickly enough in itself the mark of the signifying originality of the dimension of the true *suivre*. Follow what? This is what remains open. And this is precisely what I want you to observe – that it remains open. Follow your being, your message, your word, your group, what I represent? What is it? It's a knot, a point of contraction in a bundle of meanings, whether acquired by the subject or not. If the subject hasn't acquired it, he will hear *Tu es celui qui me suivra partout, Thou art the one who will follow me everywhere,* what the other has said to him *suivras, wilt follow,* that is, in quite a different sense, which changes even the significance of the *thou*.

The presence of the *thou,* in the *wilt follow,* affects the personization of the subject to whom one is addressing oneself. When I say, in a tangible example, *Thou art the woman who will not abandon me,* I display a much greater certainty concerning the conduct of my partner than when I say *Thou art the woman who wilt not abandon me*. To make you feel the difference which [in French] isn't heard, in the first case I exhibit a much greater certainty and in

the first of these two sentences the subordinate verb is in the second person singular, in the second it is in the third person singular. For what follows it is important to bear in mind that the two French sentences sound the same.

the second a much greater trust. This trust presupposes precisely a looser
link between the person who appears in the *thou* of the first part of the sentence and the one who appears in the relative. It's precisely because this link 317
is loose that it appears in a special form of originality with respect to the signifier and because it presupposes that the person knows what sort of signifier is at issue in this *to follow,* that she assumes it. This also means that she may not follow.

I am going to select a reference that touches on the most radical characteristic of the relations between the *I* and the signifier. In the old Indo-European languages, and in certain remnants in living languages, there is what is called the middle voice. The middle voice is distinguished from the active and the passive in that, this is an approximation one learns at school, the subject performs the action in question for himself. There are for example two different forms for saying *I sacrifice,* according as one performs the sacrifice or offers the sacrifice.

Let's not enter into the nuances of the middle voice concerning verbs that have the three voices, because, not using it ourselves, our feel for it will always be poor. What is instructive is the verbs that have only a middle voice. Selecting them from an article by M. Benveniste on this subject in the *Journal de psychologie normale et pathologique* of January–March 1950, dedicated entirely to language, the following are middle verbs – to be born, to die, to follow or embrace a movement, to be master, to be lying down, to return to a familiar state, to enjoy or benefit, to suffer, to be patient, to be mentally agitated, to take measures – which is the *medeor* that is invested in you as doctors – to speak.[24] In short, this is the entire register at work precisely in analytic experience.

These verbs exist only in the middle voice in a number of languages. What do they have in common? It emerges on investigation that what they have in common is that the subject is constituted as such in the process or the state expressed by the verb.

Don't attach any importance to the terms *process* or *state* – the verbal function isn't easily apprehended in a category. The verb is a function in the sentence, nothing else. There is no difference between the name and the verb other than their function within the sentence. Substantives are able to express a process or state also. The implication of the subject is absolutely unchanged by the fact that the process or state concerned is expressed in verbal form. If it's expressed in verbal form, this is because it is the support of a number of signifying accents that place the sentence as a whole in a temporal mode.

The existence of distinct forms for the verbs in which the subject is constituted as such, as *I,* like the Latin *sequor* which, by virtue of the full sense of

[24] See "Active and Middle Voice in the Verb," 148.

318 the verb *to follow,* implies the presence of the *I* in the *secution,* gives us a clue to what is involved in the fact that in French the verb in the relative clause agrees or doesn't agree with the *thou* of the main clause. It will agree or not agree with the *thou,* depending on the way in which the *I* in question is involved, captivated, pinned down, caught up in the quilting I spoke of the other day, depending on the way in which, in the subject's total relationship to the discourse, the signifier latches on.

The entire context of *Thou art the one who wilt follow me* changes according to the accent placed on the signifier, according to the implications of the *wilt follow,* according to the mode of being that lies behind this *wilt follow,* according to the meanings the subject has coupled to a certain signifying register, according to the baggage with which the subject departs into the indetermination of the *what am I?* – and it matters little whether this baggage is primordial, acquired, secondary, defensive, fundamental, its origin matters little. We live with a number of responses, in general highly suspect, to *what am I?* If *I am a father* has a sense, it's a problematic sense. If it is common usage to tell oneself, *I am a professor,* this leaves completely open the question *professor of what?* If one tells oneself, among a thousand other identifications, *I am a Frenchman,* this presupposes the bracketing of everything the notion of belonging to France may represent. If you say *I am a Cartesian,* in most cases you haven't got a clue about what M. Descartes said because you have probably never opened him. When you say *I am the one who has clear ideas,* one has to ascertain why. When you say *I am the one who has character,* the whole world may rightly ask *which one?* And when you say *I always tell the truth,* well then, you're not afraid.

It's this relation to the signifier that determines the accent that the first part of the sentence, *Thou art the one who . . . ,* will have for the subject according as the signifying part has been conquered and assumed or on the contrary *verworfen,* rejected by him.

I still want to give you some more examples before I leave you.

If I say to someone *tu es celui qui dois venir, thou art the one who must come,* the background of signifiers that this presupposes is no longer there if I say *Tu es celui qui doit arriver, Thou art the one who must arrive,* since this is simply to say that *you will arrive,* and this leaves it to be supposed – *Yes, but in what state!*[25]

Tu es celui qui veux ce qu'il veut, Thou art the one who wantst what he wants, means *You are an obstinate little person. Tu es celui qui veut ce qu'il veut, Thou art the one who wants what he wants,* means *You are the one who knows how to*

[25] The subordinate clauses in the two examples are in the second and third person respectively.

want. It is not necessarily a question of being the one who wilt foll
not follow me, thou art the one who will follow his path to the end.

Tu es celui qui sais ce qu'il dit, Thou art the one who knowst what he is saying, isn't *the one who will follow his path to the end*.

The importance of these distinctions is to show that the change of empha- 319
sis, the fullness that *thou* confers on the other, which is also what he gets back, is essentially linked to the signifier.

4

What happens when the signifier in question, the organizing center, the point of significant convergence that it constitutes, is evoked but fails to appear [*fait défaut*]?

We can both deduce this from this approach and see it confirmed in our experience.

It's enough to situate our formula on the schema I have given you as being that of speech.[26] *Thou art the one who wilt follow me everywhere*. Naturally, the S and the O are always reciprocal, and insofar as the message we receive is that of the other that founds us, the O is at the level of the *thou*, the little *o'* at the level of *who . . . me,* and the S at the level of *wilt follow*.

What happens if the signifier which gives the sentence its weight and the *thou* its emphasis is lacking? if this signifier is heard, but nothing in the subject is able to respond to it? The function of the sentence is then reduced solely to the significance of the *thou,* a free signifier that is nowhere pinned down. There is no elective *thou*. The *thou* is precisely he to whom I address myself, nothing else. If I say *Thou art*, the *thou* is the one who dies.[27] This is exactly what one observes in Schreber's interrupted sentences, which stop precisely at the moment at which a signifier that remains problematic is on the point of emerging, charged with a definite meaning, but one doesn't know which – a paltry, derisory meaning, which indicates the gap, the hole, where nothing meaningful is able to respond in the subject.

It is precisely insofar as this signifier is interpellated, evoked, involved, that there emerges around it the pure and simple apparatus of the relation to the other, the empty muttering – *Thou art the one who*. . . . This is the very model of the interrupted sentence of President Schreber who, of course, produces the other's presence, made all the more radical, all the more radically other, by the fact that there is nothing that places him at a level of the signifier with which the subject would in any way be in harmony. Schreber states

[26] See above, chap. 1, p. 14.
[27] *"Tu es,"* "you are," and *"tuez,"* "kill," are homophonic.

it – if the Other abandons him for one instant, drops him, a veritable decomposition occurs. This decomposition of the signifier occurs around a point of interpellation constituted by the lack, the disappearance, the absence of a certain signifier to the extent that at a given moment it is interpellated as such.

320 Let's suppose that it's a question of *wilt follow me*. All meanings nearby will be evoked, there will be *I shall be ready, I shall be obedient, I shall be dominated, I shall be frustrated, I shall be whisked away, I shall be alienated, I shall be influenced*. But the *wilt follow* in the full sense won't be there.

Which meaning is it that, in the case of President Schreber, has been drawn near to like this? Which signifier has thus been interpellated, the lack of which has produced such an upheaval in a man who till then had come to terms with the apparatus of language perfectly well, insofar as he establishes a normal relation with his fellows? Which is the signifier whose absence can explain how this constant repetition of speech becomes for him the elective mode of relating to another, how otherness is reduced to the unique register of absolute otherness, breaking, dissipating the otherness of all the other beings in his surroundings?

This is the question we shall stop at today.

I point out to you here and now, so as not to leave you completely up in the air, the direction in which we shall be looking. The key words, the signifying words of Schreber's delusion, *soul murder, nerve-contact, voluptuousness, blessedness*, and a thousand other terms, revolve around a fundamental signifier, which is never mentioned and whose presence is in command, is determinant. He says it himself. I shall give you an indication and, to reassure you by showing you that we are in our own domain, I shall tell you that in Schreber's entire work his father is cited only once.

This is on the subject of his most well-known, if not his most important, work, which is called *Manual of Bedroom Gymnastics*.[28] It's a book that I did everything to obtain, full of little diagrams. The only time Schreber mentions his father by name is when he goes and looks in this book to see whether what the voices tell him about the typical position of men and women when they make love really is true. You will admit that it is an amusing idea to go in search of this in a *Manual of Bedroom Gymnastics*. Everyone knows that love is an ideal sport, but all the same.

However amusing this way of approaching it may be, this must nevertheless put you on the track of what, after having approached, from the direction of the coherence of the sentence, the problem of what results from a certain lack at the level of the signifier, I shall bring along for you next time.

13 June 1956

[28] I.e., *Medical Indoor Gymnastics*. See Mem, 166.

XXIII 321

The highway and the signifier "being a father"

Thou art the one who followowst me the best.
Thou art the one who follows me like a little dog.
Thou art the one who did follow me that day.
Thou art the one who didst follow me through trials.
Thou art the one who followst the law . . . the text.
Thou art the one who follows the mob.
Thou art the one who didst follow me.
Thou art the one who did follow me.
Thou art the one who art.
Thou art the one who is.[1]

1

Your trade of psychoanalyst is well worth your pausing for a moment at what speaking means.[2] Though it's of a slightly different nature, this is an exercise that borders on mathematical games, which are never given enough attention, for they have always been used for training the mind.

Here, this goes beyond a bit of entertainment. This isn't something that can be totally objectified, formalized. This is at the level of what conceals itself, it's here that you pause the least willingly, and yet it's here that is found the essential in what happens when you are in a relationship with the discourse of another.

Let's pick up from where we had got to last time, with the future tense of the verb *to follow* – *Thou art the one who wilt follow me, Thou art the one who will follow me.*

We began to punctuate the genuine double senses that arise according as 322
one passes through the screen of *the one who* or not. The demonstrative is nothing other than the famous third person. In all languages this person is made out of demonstratives, and this is the reason it's not a person of the verb. There remain the two other persons, the *thou* to whom I address myself and in the background the presence of an ego more or less presenced – I would even say invoked, provided we give this term its full sense.

[1] *"Tu es celui qui me suis le mieux," "Tu es celui qui me suit comme un petit chien," "Tu es celui qui me suivait ce jour-là," "Tu es celui qui me suivais à travers les épreuves," "Tu es celui qui suis la loi . . . le texte," "Tu es celui qui suit la foule," "Tu es celui qui m'as suivi," "Tu es celui qui m'a suivi," "Tu es celui qui es," "Tu es celui qui est."*

[2] *"ce que parler veut dire";* this also means the exact value of what is said.

I emphasized the opposition that exists between the character of inevitability, the simple observation, of *Thou art the one who will follow me* in the third person, and the mandate, the delegation, the interpellation, that can be heard in *Thou art the one who wilt follow me*. I could equally have contrasted prediction and foresight, a difference that is perceptible only in a sentence embodying the message. If we abstractify, prediction becomes something different.

Thou art the one who didst follow me and *Thou art the one who did follow me* offer an analogous divergence. The tense of the verb isn't solely reducible to the consideration of past, present, and future, it's involved in quite a different way when the second person is there. I should say that in the former case, where the *didst follow me* is in the second person, an action in time is involved, a temporalized action, considered in the act of being accomplished. In the other, *Thou art the one who did follow me*, it's a perfect tense, a completed thing, so much so that one may even say that it borders on a definition – *Of the others, thou art the one who did follow me*.

There is without any doubt a rule here, but one needs to give numerous examples of it if one is to succeed in grasping it. The difference between *Thou art the one who followst me the best* and *Thou art the one who follows me like a little dog* is there to enable you to have a go at the exercises that follow, what it is appropriate to put in the spaces.

Thou art the one who did follow me that day. Thou art the one who, at one time, didst follow me through trials. Between these two expressions there is all the difference that there is between constancy and faithfulness. Let's even say, if the word *constancy* is perhaps ambiguous, all the difference between permanence and faithfulness.

The *me* doesn't need to be there. *Thou art the one who followst the law, Thou art the one who followst the text* seem to me to be inscribed differently from *Thou art the one who follows the mob*, while being perfectly valid sentences from the point of view of the signifier, that is, as organic groups whose significant value is organized from the beginning to the conclusion.

MR. PUJOL – *They're not identified phonetically, but only orthographically.*

323 These grouped examples don't seem to me to be too contrived to be valid. These differences don't exist without a reason.

M. PUJOL – *In* Tu es celui qui m'as suivi, Thou art the one who didst follow me, *it's the other who inserts the* s, *it's not the speaker.*

Here you've come to the heart of the matter, in taking up what I've just indicated – that this *thou* to whom I address myself from the place I myself am in as Other with a big O is in no way my pure and simple correlate. These examples demonstrate that there is something else beyond the *thou*, which is the *ego* that sustains the discourse of the one who follows me when he follows my speech, for example. It's precisely the greater or lesser intensity, the greater or lesser presence of this *ego*, that decides between the two forms. Of course, it's he who sanctions, and it's because the sanctioning depends on him that we're applying ourselves to these examples. This *ego* is beyond this *thou art the one*, which is the mode in which he is called to orientate himself. In one case it's *he* who is going to follow, and in effect the words *the one* becomes null and void – he will follow, *he* will follow, it's *he* who will follow. In the other, it's not *he* who is in question, it's *I*.

In a word, it's a matter of showing you that the support of this *you*, whatever form it takes in my experience, is an *ego*, the ego expressing it, but that the *ego* can never be taken to sustain it completely. Whenever I make an appeal to the other via this message, this delegation, whenever I explicitly designate him as the one who must act, the one who is to act, but even more, as the one to whom I announce what he is going to be, no doubt I sustain him but there remains something completely uncertain and problematic in this fundamental communication, which is the announcement, not to say the annunciation.

The *I* is essentially fleeting in nature and never entirely sustains the *thou*.

2

Indeed it's one of the most profound characteristics of the mental foundation of the Judaeo-Christian tradition that against it speech clearly profiles the being of the *I* as its ultimate ground. On all the essential questions the subject always finds himself in a position, summoned, to justify himself as *I*. The *I* who says, *I am the one who am*, this *I*, absolutely alone, is the one who radically sustains the *thou* in his interpellation. That's all the difference there is between the god of the tradition we come from and the god of the Greek tradition. I wondered whether the Greek god is capable of proffering himself 324
in the mode of any *I*. Would he say, *I am the one who is?* This is out of the question, however. The super-attenuated form of the Greek god isn't something that there is any reason to laugh at, or to believe that it's situated on the path to the atheistic disappearance of God. It's rather the god Voltaire was interested in to the point of regarding Diderot as a cretin, the god of deism, who is of the half-flesh, half-fish order of the *I am the one who is*.

Your minds won't readily dwell on the god of Aristotle, because this has become unthinkable for us. But still, try to get yourselves to meditate – a mode of this *medeor* I was speaking to you about last time, and which is the original verb of your medical function – for a second on what the relationship to the world might have been for a disciple of Aristotle's for whom God was the most immutable sphere in the sky. He isn't a god who announces himself through the word, like the one we were evoking a second ago. He is that part of the starry sphere that includes the fixed stars, he is that sphere in the world that doesn't move. This obviously involves a relationship to the other that to us is foreign and unthinkable and much more distant than the one put into play, for example, in the punitive fantasm [*la fantaisie punitive*].

Nobody dwells on this – it's because at the heart of the religious thought that has formed us there is the idea of making us live in fear and trembling, that the coloration of guilt is so fundamental in our psychological experience of the neuroses, without its being possible for all that to prejudge what they are in another cultural sphere. This coloration is even so fundamental that it was by its means that we explored the neuroses and noticed that they were structured in a subjective and intersubjective mode. This is why there is every reason to wonder whether the tradition that announces itself in the expression which is, we're told, flanked by a little tree on fire – *I am the one who am*, doesn't fundamentally bear upon our relationship to the other. We're not so far from our subject matter. It's a question of this in President Schreber – of a mode of constructing the Other-God.

The word *atheism* has quite a different sense for us from that which it could have had in a reference to the Aristotelian divinity, for example, where it's a question of a relationship to a superior entity [*étant*], to the supreme entity. Our own atheism is located in another perspective – it's linked to this always elusive aspect of the *I* of the other.

An other who announces himself as *I am the one who am* is by virtue of this sole fact a god beyond, a hidden god, and a god who under no circumstances unveils his face. Precisely from the Aristotelian perspective it could be said
325 that our own point of departure is already atheistic. This is an error, but from that perspective it's strictly true, and in our experience it's no less so. Whatever announces itself as *I am the one who am* is totally problematic, not sustained, and almost unsustainable, or only sustainable by an idiot.

Think about the *I am* of *I am the one who am*. This is what makes for the problematic nature of the relation to the other in our own tradition. It's also what in its own right characterizes our relationship to entities, to objects, and our own science – much more profoundly than its so-called experimental nature. The ancients didn't experiment any less than we do, they experimented on what interested them. This isn't the issue. It's in the way in which we place others, little others, in the light of the ultimate, absolute Other that we are distinctive in the way we fragment the world, break it down into pieces. The ancients on the other hand approached it as something that was graded on a scale of consistency of entities. Our position radically calls into question the very being of what announces itself as *being*, and not as an *entity*.[3]

We are no longer in a position to reply to him who says, *I am the one who*

[3] "*être*" and "*étants*," the standard translations of Heidegger's "*Sein*" and "*Seiendes*," which were translated in *Being and Time* as *being* and *entities*.

am. What are we to be able to reply to *the one who am?* We know only too well. A birdbrain – in fact we get lots of flights of these birdbrains coming in from the other side of the Atlantic – whom I met recently remarked to me – *But still, all the same, I am me!* To him that seemed to be the ultimate certainty. I assure you that I didn't instigate this, and that I wasn't there to make anti-psychological propaganda.

As a matter of fact, if there is one minimal thing that is obvious in experience – I won't say analytic experience, but simply in anyone's internal experience – it's that we are certainly even less the ones who are,[4] for being well aware what a racket, what frightful chaos permeated by various objurgations, we experience within ourselves at every turn, at every instant.

I've guided you by the hand long enough for you to perceive that speech, and especially this essential form of speech in which we announce ourselves as a *thou,* is a complex mode that is far from reducible to the intuition of two centers exchanging signals. As the relation of subject to subject is structured in a complex mode by the properties of language, the specific role the signifier plays in it has to be located therein.

I would like to return to some simple properties of the said signifier. The radicalism I showed you on the subject of the relation of subject to subject extends to an investigation proceeding in the direction of the Other as such, which shows that strictly speaking it cannot be grasped – it doesn't sustain, it can never totally sustain, the wager that we offer it. Inversely, the point of 326
view I am trying to maintain before you involves a certain materialism of the elements in question, in the sense that the signifiers are well and truly embodied, materialized, they are words that wander about and as such they play their role of fastening together.

To give you a rest, I shall now offer an analogy. An analogy is not an argument,[5] but the examples I have used have been of a rigorous quality, like this first scene of *Athaliah,* where I showed you that the development consisted in substituting for the interlocutor, Abner, *the fear of God,* which has no more of a relationship to the fears and the voice of Abner than has the *didst follow me*.

An aside. I recently happened to read an article in English on Racine which defines the originality of his tragedy by the claim that he had the art, the skill, to introduce into this setting, almost without his public's knowledge, characters of high whoredom.[6] You see the distance between Anglo-Saxon

[4] "*sommes,*" first-person plural.

[5] "*Comparison n'est pas raison,*" a French proverb.

[6] See "The Agency of the Letter in the Unconscious or Reason Since Freud," E, 503 n.1 / 176 n.17. The reference is to a book review by Geoffrey Brereton, "Keeping up with Racine," *New Statesman and Nation,* Saturday May 19, 1956, p. 575. Brereton's term is "extreme bitchery."

culture and our own. The fundamental mark of *Andromaque, Iphigénie,* etc. is whoredom. It is pointed out in passing that Freudians have made an extraordinary discovery in Racine's tragedies. I haven't yet noticed this, I'm sorry to say. It's true that in the wake of Freud one has sought exemplification of a certain number of analytic relations in the plays of Shakespeare, and not without some self-satisfaction. But as for our own cultural references, they have been slow to appear. It may be time to start, one might perhaps find something to illustrate, as I did last time, the problems that have arisen over the use of the signifier.

Let's turn to an example I want to give you to get you to understand the gravity, the inertia specific to the signifier in the field of relations with the Other.

3

The road, now there's a signifier worth taking as such – the road, the highway you travel down in your various means of locomotion, the road that goes from Mantes to Rouen, for example. I won't say *Paris,* which is a special case.

The existence of a highway between Mantes and Rouen is a fact that all on its own presents itself to the researcher's meditation.

Suppose that – as happens in the south of England, where you have these
327 highways only in an exceedingly parsimonious way – to get from Mantes to Rouen you have to go via a series of minor roads, such as the one that goes from Mantes to Vernon, then from Vernon to wherever. Having had this experience is enough to make one aware that a succession of minor roads and a highway are not at all the same thing. Not only does it slow you down in practice, but it completely changes the meaning of your behavior concerning what happens between the point of departure and the point of arrival – *a fortiori*, if you imagine an entire region covered by a network of minor roads without a highway anywhere.

The highway is something that exists in itself and is immediately recognizable. When you emerge from a path, a thicket, a shoulder, or a minor local road, you know immediately that you have come to a highway. The highway isn't something that extends from one point to another, it's a dimension spread out in space, the presencing of an original reality.

If I take the highway as an example, it's because, as Monsieur de la Palice would say, it's a path of communication.[7]

[7] *Une vérité de Monsieur de la Palice* is a purely formal truth which is amusing because self-evident.

You may get the impression that there is a banal metaphor here, that the highway is only a means of going from one point to another. Mistake.

A highway is not at all the same as the track made by the movement of elephants through an equatorial forest. As important, so it seems, as these tracks are, they are nothing other than the passage of elephants. Undoubtedly this isn't nothing, since it's supported by the physical reality of elephantine migrations. Moreover, this passage has a direction. I don't know whether these pathways lead, as is sometimes claimed, to cemeteries, which appear to be quite mythical – it seems that they're rather bone depots – but the elephants certainly don't languish about their roads. The difference between the highway and the elephant track is that we stop along ours – and the Parisian experience comes to the foreground – we stop along the way to the point of forming agglomerations and rendering these places of passage so viscous as to be virtually impassable.

A great many other things occur on highways.

It sometimes happens that we take a trip down the highway intentionally and on purpose so as then to turn around and come back again. This movement of departure and return is also quite essential, and it puts us on the track of the evident fact that the highway is a site around which not only all sorts of dwellings, of places of abode, agglomerate but which also, qua signifier, polarizes meanings.

Houses are built alongside the highway, and they rise up and spread out 328
with no other function than to be looking out at the highway. It's precisely because the highway is an undeniable signifier in human experience that it marks a stage in history.

The Roman road, the road taken and named as such, has in human experience quite a different consistency from those paths, those trails, even the ones with staging posts, of rapid communication, that in the East succeeded for a time in holding empires together. Everything touched by the Roman road adopted a style that goes much further than what is immediately accessible as an effect of the highway. Wherever it went, it left traces that are practically irremovable. Roman imprints, with everything that developed around them, are essential – as are, moreover, interhuman relationships of law, the mode of transmitting the written thing, as well as the mode of promoting the human appearance, statues. M. Malraux may rightly say that there is nothing to retain in Roman sculpture from the point of view of the eternal art museum, it remains no less true that the very notion of a human being is linked to the vast diffusion of statues in Roman sites.

The highway is thus a particularly tangible example of what I'm saying when I speak of the function of the signifier insofar as it polarizes meanings, hooks onto them, groups them in bundles. There is a real antinomy between the function of the signifier and the induction it exerts on the grouping of ıgs. The signifier polarizes. It's the signifier that creates the field of ngs.

npare three maps in a large atlas.

On a map of the physical world you will see things inscribed in nature, ready to play a role, certainly, but still in their natural state. Compare a political map – there you will find, in the form of traces, of alluvion, of sediments, the entire history of human meanings maintaining themselves in a kind of equilibrium and tracing out these enigmatic lines that are the political boundaries of lands. Take a map of the major paths of communication and see how a road that runs through countries linking one river basin to another, one plain to another, crossing a mountain chain, crossing bridges, organizing itself, has been traced out from South to North. You will notice that it's this map that best expresses the role of the signifier in man's relationship to the land.

Don't act like the person who marvelled at the fact that water courses pass precisely through towns. It would be proof of analogous foolishness not to see that towns have formed, crystallized, been established at road junctions.
329 It's where they cross, with a bit of fluctuation moreover, that what becomes a center of meanings, a human agglomeration, a town, comes about historically, with all that is imposed upon it by this dominance of the signifier.

What happens when we don't have a highway and we are forced to combine minor paths, more or less separate modes of grouping meaning, with one another when we go from one point to another? To go from this point to that point we shall have a choice between different components of the network, we can take this route, or that route, for various reasons – for the sake of convenience, in order to roam, or simply because of a mistake at a crossroads.

Several things can be deduced from this, which explain Schreber's delusion to us.

Which signifier is it that is in abeyance in his inaugural crisis? It's the signifier *procreation* in its most problematic form, the one that Freud himself evokes in relation to obsessionals, which isn't the form *being a mother* but the form *being a father*.

This is an appropriate place to pause for a moment to think about the fact that the function of *being a father* is absolutely unthinkable in human experience without the category of the signifier.

What can it mean *to be a father?* You are familiar with the learned discussions, ethnological or other, one immediately enters into to establish whether primitives who say that women conceive when they're placed in such and such a spot possess the scientific notion that women become fertilized once they have duly copulated. These inquiries have nevertheless seemed to some to be perfectly foolish, since it's difficult to conceive of human animals stupid enough to fail to notice that when one wants to have kids one has to copulate. This is not the point. The point is that the sum of these facts – of copulating with a woman, that she then carries something within her womb for a certain period, that this product is finally expelled – will never lead one to constitute the notion of what it is *to be a father*. I'm not even speaking about the entire cultural cluster implied in the term *being a father*, I'm simply speaking of what it is *to be a father* in the sense of procreation.

A rebound effect is necessary for the fact that man copulates to receive the sense it really has, but to which no imaginary access is possible, that the child is as much his as the mother's. And for this effect of action in return to occur, the elaboration of the notion of *being a father* must have been raised by work that has taken place through an entire cluster of cultural exchanges to the state of major signifier, and this signifier must have its own consistency and status. The subject may well know that copulating is *really* at the origin of procreation, but the function of procreation as a signifier is something else.

I grant you that I haven't yet completely lifted the veil – I'll leave that for 330
next time. In order for procreation to have its full sense there must also be, in both sexes, an apprehension, a relation with the experience of death, which gives the term *to procreate* its full sense. Moreover, paternity and death are two signifiers that Freud links in relation to obsessionals.

The signifier *being a father* is what creates the highway in sexual relations with a woman. If the highway doesn't exist, one finds oneself faced with a number of elementary minor paths, copulation and then the woman's pregnancy.

To all appearances President Schreber lacks this fundamental signifier called *being a father*. This is why he had to make a mistake, become confused, to the point of thinking of acting like a woman. He had to imagine himself a woman and bring about in pregnancy the second part of the path that, when the two were added together, was necessary for the function of *being a father* to be realized.

The experience of the couvade, as problematic as it seems to us, may be located as an uncertain, incomplete assimilation of the function of *being a father*. It does effectively answer to a need imaginarily – or ritually or otherwise – to realize the second part of the path.

To take my metaphor a little bit further I shall say to you – what do those who are called road-users do when there is no highway and it's a question of taking minor roads to go from one point to another? They follow the signs erected by the side of the road. That is, where the signifier isn't functioning, it starts speaking on its own, at the edge of the highway. Where there is no road, written words appear on signs. This, perhaps, is the verbal function of auditory verbal hallucinations – they are the signs along their little path.

If we suppose that the signifier continues on its way alone whether we pay

attention to it or not, we must admit that within us, more or less eluded by the maintenance of the meanings that interest us, there is a kind of buzzing, a veritable pandemonium, which we have been bewildered by ever since childhood. Why not imagine that, at the precise moment at which the link between what Saussure calls the *amorphous mass* of the signifier and the amorphous mass of meanings and interests comes apart and is revealed to be deficient, the continuous current of the signifier once again assumes its independence? And then, in this buzzing that people who are hallucinating so often depict to you on this occasion, in this continuous murmur of these
331 sentences, of these commentaries, which are nothing but the infinity of these minor paths, the signifiers begin to talk, to sing on their own. The continuous murmur of these sentences, of these commentaries, is nothing other than the infinity of these minor paths.

There's still a chance that they will vaguely indicate the right direction.

Next time I shall try to show how everything that in delusion is orchestrated and organized according to different spoken registers reveals, in its layering and in its texture, the fundamental polarization of the suddenly encountered, suddenly observed, lack of a signifier.

20 June 1956

XXIV 333

"Thou art"

FORMS OF GAPS

THE VERB *TO BE*

FROM THE *THOU* TO THE OTHER

THE TORTOISE AND THE TWO DUCKS

THE ONSET OF PSYCHOSIS

I shall begin my little weekly discourse by telling you off – but when all is said and done, when I see you there, all so kindly lined up so late in the year, it's rather this verse that comes to mind – *It's you who are the faithful ones.* . . .

I shall nevertheless resume my plan again, which is related to the last meeting of the Société [française de psychanalyse].

It's clear that while the paths I take you down lead somewhere, they're not so well beaten that you have no difficulty in showing that you recognize the place where someone is moving along. Nevertheless this is no reason to keep quiet – even if it were only to show that you have some idea of the question. By speaking you might display some confusion, but you gain nothing from remaining silent. You will tell me that what you gain from it is that it's as a group that you act like duffers and that when all is said and done it's much more bearable in this form.

On this subject one can't but be struck by what certain philosophers, who are precisely those of the moment and to whom from time to time I discreetly refer, have formulated – that man, of all entities, is an open entity. The openness of being fascinates anyone who begins to think. This kind of panic statement that defines our time cannot fail to appear at certain moments as a balance to and a compensation for what the colloquial term *bouché, duffer,* expresses, namely, as is sententiously observed, a divorce between the prejudices of science where man is concerned and the experience of man in what is supposed to be his authenticity. These people strive to rediscover that 334
surely what is at the bottom of thought isn't the privilege of thinkers, but that in the slightest act of his existence the human being, however much he may err as to his own existence, nevertheless remains, precisely when he wishes to articulate something, an open being.

This is the level at which those who really think, who say it, are said to maintain themselves. Rest assured in any case that I'm not at this level, even though certain people try to circulate the contrary idea. At the very least, this isn't the level at which the reality in question is situated and conceptualized when we are exploring analytic matters.

No doubt it's impossible to say anything sensible about this, unless one resituates it in what we shall call the gaps of being. But these gaps have assumed certain forms, and this is where there is something valuable in analytic experience – it's surely in no way closed to the radically questioning and questionable side of the human position, but it contributes some determinants. Of course, to take these determinants as determined is to propel psychoanalysis down the path of the prejudices of science, which lets the entire essence of human reality escape. But by simply maintaining things at this level, and not placing them too high, either, it is possible to give our experience the right tone of what I call mediocre reason.

Next year – François Perrier's lecture propelled me into this, as I wasn't sure what I would do – I shall take as the theme of the seminar the object relation or purported relation. Perhaps I shall introduce this by a comparison between the objects of phobia and fetishes, two series of objects. You can already see straight off how different they are in their catalogue.

For today we shall pick things up again where we left them last time.

1

Regarding the way I have introduced these lessons on the signifier someone said to me – *You start from a long way off, no doubt, it's tiring, one doesn't properly see what it is that you're driving at, but still, retrospectively, one can see that there was some relationship between what you started with and where you ended up*. This way of putting things proves that nothing is lost in going back over the same ground one more time.

The question is restricted. I'm not claiming to be covering the entire subject of a thing as enormous as the case of President Schreber, or, *a fortiori*,
335 the field of paranoia in its entirety. I claim to be throwing light on only a small field. I'm applying myself to certain phenomena without reducing them to a mechanism foreign to them, without forcing them into the categories currently in use, into the *Psychology* chapter of the philosophy program. I'm trying to refer them to slightly more elaborate notions concerning the reality of language. I claim that this effort is of a kind to allow the question of origins, in the precise sense of the determinism of or of the occasion for the onset of psychosis, to be raised otherwise, which will ultimately include entirely etiological determinations.

I ask the question – what is required in order that it speak [*ça parle*]?

This is in effect one of the most essential phenomena of psychosis. Expressing it thus is already of a kind to remove some false problems, namely those that are raised when one says that in psychosis the id [*le ça*] is conscious. We increasingly dispense with this reference, about which Freud always said that, literally, no one knew where to place it. From the economic point of view nothing is more uncertain than its effect – it's entirely contingent. We are therefore placing ourselves squarely in the Freudian tradition in saying that after all the only thing that we have to think through is that it [*ça*] speaks.

It speaks. But why does it speak? Why is it that, for the subject himself, it speaks? Why is it that it presents itself as speech, and that it, not he, is this speech? We've already raised this question at the level of the *thou,* of the distant *thou* as someone pointed out to me, which I was getting at in trying to symbolize the signifier through the example of the highway. We shall return to this *thou* point once again, since it was also upon this that the progress we made last time, as well as certain of the objections that were made to me, were centered.

Let's pause at this *thou,* if there is any truth whatsoever in my claim that the originary apprehension of what I am leading you towards and asking you to give some reflection to must be located around a thorough study of its function.

Last time someone made the grammatical objection to me that there was something arbitrary in bringing together *Thou art the one who wilt follow me* and *Thou art the one who will follow me,* the elements not being homologous. It's not the same *the one* in question in the two cases, since the former could also be elided, leaving *Thou wilt follow me*.

One may make the initial observation that *Thou wilt follow me* is a commandment. *Thou art the one who wilt follow me,* if we understand it in its full sense, isn't a commandment but a mandate. It implies, in the presence of the other, something expanded that presumes presence. An entire universe insti- 336
tuted by discourse is presumed here, within which *thou art the one who wilt follow me*.

Let's begin by pausing first at this *thou,* making the remark, which looks self-evident but is rather rare, that the said *thou* has no literal meaning.

This isn't merely because I address it indifferently to everyone – as a matter of fact I address it to myself as well as to you, and virtually to all kinds of things, I may thou something that is as foreign as is possible to me, I can say thou to an animal, I can say thou to an inanimate object – this isn't the point. Look closely at the formal, grammatical aspect of the thing. This is, moreover, what every kind of usage of the signifier comes down to for you. You will place meanings there despite yourselves. One may say that you believe in grammar! Your entire schooling amounts, as intellectual gain, to your having been made to believe in grammar. To be sure, you weren't told as much, since the aim would not have been achieved.

Let's therefore pause at some sentences like the following – *If you poke your nose outside you'll get shot down*. Or again – *When you see the bridge you turn right.*[1] Here the *you* doesn't have the subjective value of any reality of the other whatsoever, it's entirely equivalent to a site or a point – it introduces a condition or temporality, it has the value of a conjunction.

This may seem rash to you, but I assure you that if you spoke a bit of Chinese you would be convinced of it. One can have a lot of fun with Chinese characters, with this one for example, which is the sign for a woman and the sign for a mouth. The *you* is someone one addresses oneself to in giving him an order, that is, as befits speaking to women. One may say a thousand other things, so let's not delay, and let's stay with the *you*. The *you* may be used in this form to formulate the expression *as if,* and in another form it's used unambiguously to formulate a *when* or an *if,* introducing a conditional.

If this thing is less apparent in our languages, and if we have some resistance to understanding it and to acknowledging it in the examples I've just given, this is solely a function of the prejudices of grammar, which prevent you from hearing. The artifices of etymological and grammatical analysis force you to insert the second person singular into this *you*. Of course, it is the second person singular, but it's a matter of knowing what it's used for. In other words, our *you* is related to elements existing in languages that are
337 described as having no inflection and that for us have the advantage of serving to open up our minds a bit. They do in fact have particles at their disposal, which are the curious signifiers whose usage, like that of our *you*, is singularly multiple and sometimes so broad as to create a degree of confusion in our descriptive grammars. Moreover, one would only need to write the least bit phonetically to observe that differences in tonality or accent of the signifier *you* have effects that go entirely beyond the identification of the person and are completely different from this from the point of view of meaning.

Attributing autonomy to the *you* as signified isn't without its difficulties. Let's say that in general it has the value of an introduction, of a protasis as we say, that which is placed before. This is the most general way of designating what precedes the statement [*énoncé*] of what it is that gives the sentence its importance.

There would be many other things to say about this if we went into the details. Much use would have to be made of expressions like this *you've only got to . . .* which we use to get rid of our interlocutor. It's something that has so little to do with *only* that the lapsus quite spontaneously slides into *to do this*. It's turned into something that declines, that is inflected – the *you've only got to . . .* does not have the value of reducing this something that allowed some very enlightening semantic remarks.

What's important is that you grasp that the *you* is a long way from having

[1] *"Si tu risques un oeil au-dehors, on va te descendre"* and *"Tu vois le pont, alors tu tournes à droite."*

a univocal value and is therefore a long way from permitting us to hypostatize the other. The *you* is in the signifier what I call a way of hooking the other, of hooking him in discourse, of fastening meaning to him. It should in no way be confused with the allocutor, that is, he to whom one is speaking. This is obvious, as it's very often absent. In imperatives, where the allocutor is implied in the most manifest of ways, and around which a certain register of language known as the *simple locutory* has been defined, the *you* doesn't appear. There is a sort of limit that begins at the signal – I mean the articulated signal. *Fire!* is undeniably a sentence, and one only has to utter it to appreciate that this is something that provokes a reaction. Then there is the imperative *Come here!* which necessitates nothing. One stage further on and the *you* is implicated, for example, in that order in the future tense I was speaking about before, this *you* which is a hooking-up [*accrochage*] in discourse, a way of situating it in the curve of meaning that Saussure represents for us, parallel to this curve of the signifier.[2] The *you* is the hooking of the other in the waters of meaning.

In the final analysis, if we pursue our apprehension, or our metaphor, to its radical end, this term that is used to identify the other at a point in these waters is a form of punctuation.

Reflect on this fact, which is made particularly evident in unsectioned lan- 338
guages, that punctuation is what plays the most decisive role of hooking up, so much so that a classical text may vary in its entirety according as you place it at one point or another. I would even say that this variability is used to increase the richness of interpretation, the variety in the sense of a text. All those interventions known as commentaries in relation to traditional texts play precisely upon the way punctuation is apprehended or fixed in any given case.

The question is this – if the *you* is a signifier, a punctuation by which the other is secured at a point of meaning, what is required to elevate it to subjectivity? This *you*, unsecured in the substratum of discourse, in its pure carriage – this *you*, which by itself isn't so much what designates the other as what enables us to act upon him, but which also is always present in us in a state of suspension, comparable in every way to these otoliths I spoke about the other day, which enable us, with a bit of guile, to conduct little crustaceans about at will with an electromagnet[3] – this *you* which for us, insofar as we leave it free and in suspension within our own discourse, is always liable to exercise this conduction about which we can do nothing but oppose it and respond to it – what is required to elevate this *you* to subjectivity so that, in its form as signifier, present in discourse, it becomes the supposed support

[2] See above, chap. 21, p. 261.
[3] See above, chap. 22, p. 276.

of something that is comparable to our *ego* and yet isn't our *ego,* that is to say, the myth of an other?

This is the question that interests us, since it isn't so astonishing to hear people speaking their internal discourse out loud in the manner of psychotics, a little bit more than we do ourselves. The phenomena of flight of ideas were observed long ago. They're comparable to the testimony we gather from a psychotic in every way, except that the subject doesn't believe himself to be under the influence of a scrambling device.

We shall simply say that this *you* presupposes an other who, in short, is beyond him. How does this come about? Our next step should be situated around an analysis of the verb *to be.*[4]

2

We can't exhaust everything proposed to us concerning the analysis of this
339 verb *to be* by the philosophers who have centered their meditation on the question of *Dasein,* and especially Mr. Heidegger, who has begun to consider it from the grammatical and etymological angle in texts that are quite faithfully expounded in several articles that Monsieur Jean Wahl has recently devoted to them.

Mr. Heidegger attaches a great deal of importance to the signifier at the level of the analysis of the word and of conjugation, as it's usually called – let us more accurately say declension. In German as in French this famous verb *to be* is far from being a simple verb and even from being one single verb. It's evident that the form *suis, am,* doesn't come from the same root as *es, art, est, is, êtes,* [*you*] *are,* and as *fut,* [*it*] was, nor is there any strict equivalence to the form *été, been.* Whereas *fut* has an equivalent in Latin, as does *suis* and the series of *est, été* comes from another source, from *stare.* The distribution is equally different in German where *sind,* [*they*] *are,* is grouped with *bist, art,* whereas in French the second person is grouped with the third. Three roots have been more or less uncovered for all the European languages, those that correspond to *sommes,* [*we*] *are, est* and *fut,* which has been compared with the root *phusis* in Greek, which is related to the idea of life and growth. As to the others, Mr. Heidegger insists upon the two aspects, *Sten* which would be closer to *stare,* to stand alone, and *Verbahen,* to last, to endure, this sense being nevertheless attached to the source *phusis.* According to Mr. Heidegger, the idea of standing erect, the idea of life and the idea of lasting, enduring, is therefore what an etymological analysis combined with a gram-

[4] *"être"* is both a substantive and an infinitive. The substantive is translated into English as *being,* the infinitive as *to be*

matical analysis yields, and it's out of a kind of reduction or of indetermination cast over these senses as a whole that the notion of being emerges.

I summarize, so as to give you some idea of the thing. I must say that an analysis of this order is rather inclined to elide, to mask, what Mr. Heidegger is trying to initiate us into, namely that which is absolutely irreducible in the function of the verb *to be,* the copulatory function pure and simple. One would be mistaken to think that this function is disclosed through a gradual shift in direction of these various terms.

We raise this question – at what moment and by what mechanism does the *you,* such as we have defined it as a form of punctuation, as an indeterminate signifying mode of hooking on, achieve subjectivity? Well then, I believe that it's essentially when it's taken in the copulatory function in pure form and in the ostensive function. And it's for this reason that I chose the exemplary sentences that we started with – *thou art the one who. . . .*

Which element is it that, elevating the *you,* makes it go beyond its indeterminate function of boredom and begins to turn it, if not into subjectivity, then at least into something that constitutes a first step towards the *Thou art the one who wilt follow me?* It is the *It is thou who will follow me.* This is ostension, which in fact implies the presence of the assembly of all those who, whether or not united into a community, are supposed to form its body, to 340
be the support of the discourse in which ostension is inscribed. This *it is thou* corresponds to the second formula, namely, *thou art the one who will follow me.*

Thou art the one who will follow me presupposes, I am saying, the imaginary assembly of those who are the supports of the discourse, the presence of witnesses, indeed, of the tribunal before which the subject receives the warning or the opinion that he is called upon to reply to. As a matter of fact, unless he replies *I follow you,* that is, unless he complies, there is at this level no other response open to the subject than to maintain the message in the very state in which it was sent to him, at the very most modifying the person, than to inscribe it as an element of his internal discourse, which whether he likes it or not is what he has to reply to in order not to follow it. It would strictly speaking be necessary that he precisely not follow this indication at all onto the terrain where it calls on him to reply, that is, that he refuse to hear. He is taken there as soon as he hears. The refusal to hear is a force that no subject, without special gymnastic training, is really capable of. It's in this register that the particular force of discourse becomes apparent.

In other words, at the level we have come to the *you* is the other such as I cause him to be seen [*le fais voir*] by means of my discourse, such as I designate him or denounce him, he is the other insofar as he is captured in ostension in relation to this *everybody* that the universe of discourse presupposes. But by the same token I bring the other out of this universe, I objectify him within it, I may even designate his object relations for him, should he so much as ask me to, as is characteristic of the neurotic. That may go quite a long way.

Notice that it's not entirely useless to give people what they ask for. It's just a question of whether it's beneficial. In fact, if this has any incidental effect, it's insofar as it helps him to complete his vocabulary. Those who operate with object relations believe they are actually designating them, and consequently it's only rarely, and then by pure chance, that any beneficial effect is produced. Completing his vocabulary may enable the subject to extract himself from the signifying entanglement that constitutes the symptomatology of his neurosis. This is why things worked better whenever this addition to the vocabulary, this *Nervenanhang,* to use the vocabulary of our delusional, had still retained some of its freshness. Since then, what we have at our disposal in our little exercise books as *Nervenanhang* has greatly fallen in value and doesn't quite fill the function that one might hope for concerning the resubjectification of the subject, by which I designate the operation of extracting oneself from this signifying entanglement in which we have out-
341 lined the essence and very forms of the neurotic phenomenon. To handle this object relation correctly, one would need to understand that in this relation it's the neurotic who is ultimately the object. It's even for this reason that he got lost as subject and seeks himself as an object.

We have come to the point at which there is no common measure between ourselves and this *you* such as we have brought it out. There is ostension necessarily followed by reabsorption, injunction followed by disjunction. In order to have an authentic relationship with the other at this level and on this plane, he must answer, *Thou art the one whom I follow*. Here we are on his wavelength, and it's he who guides our desire.

Tu es celui que je suis lends itself to a play on words.[5] It's the relationship of identification with the other that is involved, but if we in fact guide one another in our reciprocal identification towards our desire, we shall necessarily encounter one another there, and we shall encounter one another in an incomparable way, since it's insofar as I am you that I am – here the ambiguity is complete. *Je suis* isn't only to follow, it's also *Je suis, et toi, tu es, I am and thou art,* and also, *toi, celui qui, thou, the one who,* to the point of encountering, *me tueras, wilt kill me*. When the other is captured as an object in the relation of ostension, we can only encounter this relation as a subjectivity equivalent to our own on the imaginary plane, the plane of the *moi ou toi, I or thou,* one or the other, all confusion is possible concerning the object

[5] "Thou art the one whom I follow," "Thou art the one who I am," "Kill the one whom I follow," and "Kill the one who I am."

relation. The object of our love is only ourselves, it's the *tu es celui qui me tues, thou art the one who kilst me.*

Observe the fortunate opportunity that the signifier offers us in French, with the different ways of understanding *tu es.*[6] One can make use of it indefinitely. If I were to say to you that we do this all day long – instead of saying, *To be or not . . . to be or. . .* ,[7] one may say, *Tu es celui qui me . . . tu es. . .* , *Thou art the one who . . . me . . . thou art. . .* , etc. This is the foundation of the relationship with the other. In all imaginary identification, the *tu es, thou art,* ends in the destruction of the other, and vice versa, because this destruction is simply there in the form of transference and hides itself in what we shall call *thouness.*

In this respect I could have brought you a particularly disheartening and stupid analysis of the type to be found in the famous *Meaning of Meaning,* which elevates this kind of drivel to giddy heights.[8] Similarly for this famous passage in which it's a matter of urging people who have the beginnings of virtue to have at least the consistency to finish the job. One of them says something like this – *Toi qui ne peux supporter le tu, tue-moi, Thou who canst not bear the thou, kilst me.* This is a reasonable idea – if you can't bear the truth of the *thou,* you can always be designated for what you are, namely a scoundrel. If you want your neighbors' respect, raise yourself to the notion of normal distances, that is, to a general notion of the other, the order of the world, and the law. This *thou* seems to have disconcerted commentators, and as a matter of fact I think that today's *thouness* will familiarize you with the 342
register in question.

Let's take the next step. It concerns the other's being recognized as an other. What, then, is required for the other to be recognized as an other? What is this other? He is the other insofar as he figures in a sentence of mandate. We have to pause at this for a moment.

Recognition of the other doesn't constitute an unattainable limit, since we have also seen that the disappearing otherness of the ego's imaginary identification only encounters the you at an extreme point at which neither is able to subsist together with the other. The Other, with a big O, has to be recognized beyond this relationship, even reciprocal relationship, of exclusion. It has to be recognized in this disappearing relation as being just as elusive as I. In other words, it must be invoked as what it is unaware of about itself. This is indeed the sense of *Thou art the one who wilt follow me.*

If you examine this closely, if *Thou art the one who wilt follow me* is a

[6] "Thou art" and "Kill."
[7] In English in the original.
[8] C. K. Ogden and I. A. Richards, *The Meaning of Meaning.*

delegation, indeed a consecration, then it's insofar as the response isn't a play on words but an *I follow you, I am,*[9] *I am what thou hast just said*. There is a usage of the third person that is absolutely essential to discourse in that it designates what its very subject matter is, that is, what has been said. *Je le suis, ce que tu viens de dire, I am it, what thou hast just said,* which as it happens means exactly – *I am very precisely what I am ignorant of, since what thou hast just said is absolutely indeterminate, I don't know where thou wilt lead me*. The full response to the *Thou art the one who wilt follow me* is *I am it*.

You know the fable of the tortoise and the two ducks.[10] The tortoise turns up at the crucial moment when the ducks have offered to take him with them to America, and everybody is waiting to see this little tortoise stuck onto the traveler's staff – *The Queen?* says the tortoise, *Oui, vraiment, je la suis, Yes, really, I am she*. Pichon asks himself huge questions to discover whether it's a question of a queen in the abstract or a concrete queen and speculates, in a disconcerting way for someone who had a bit of finesse in grammatical and linguistic matters, on the question of whether she ought not to have said, *Je suis elle*. Had the tortoise been speaking of an existing queen, she could have said any number of things, for example, *Je suis la reine, I am the Queen,* but since she says *Je la suis,* in referring to what you have just spoken of, there is no distinction to be made, it suffices to know that this *la, her,* concerns what is implied in the discourse.

What is implied in the discourse is indeed what is at issue. We must pause for a moment at this inaugural speech of the dialogue and take stock of the enormity of the *Thou art the one who wilt follow me*. It's to the *thou* itself, as the unknown, that we address ourselves. This is what gives it its naturalness,
343 and its force as well, and also what makes it pass from *thou art* into the *wilt follow* of the second part, where it persists. It persists there precisely because in the meantime it may decline there. In this formula it's therefore not an I, insofar as I cause it to be seen, that I address myself to, but all the signifiers that make up the subject opposite me. I say *all* the signifiers he possesses, his symptoms included. We address ourselves both to his gods and to his demons, and for this reason this way of stating the sentence I have until now been calling the mandate I shall now call the invocation, with this term's religious connotations.

An invocation isn't an inert formula. It's that by which I get that faith which is mine to pass into the other. In good authors, perhaps in Cicero, an invocation in its original religious form is a verbal formula by means of which, before combat, one tries to make favorable to oneself what I was just calling the gods and demons, the enemy's gods, the signifiers. It's to them that the

[9] *"Je te suis, je suis."*
[10] La Fontaine, "The Turtle and the Two Ducks," 97.

invocation is addressed, and this is why I think that the term *invocation* is suited to designate the most elevated form of the sentence, where all the words I pronounce are true words, evocative voices to which each of these sentences must reply, the insignia of the veritable other.

You have just seen how it is that the *you* depends upon the signifier as such. It's on the level of the vociferated signifier that depend the quality and the nature of the *thou* that is interpellated to respond. Henceforth, when the latter lacks the signifier that carries the sentence, the *I am the one* that replies to you can only play the part of an eternal interrogation. *Thou art the one who* . . . what? The limiting case is the reduction to the preceding signifier – *Thou art the one who. . . , thou art the one who. . .* , etc., *Thou art the one who . . . kilst me.*[11] The *thou* reappears indefinitely. This is how it is whenever, in the appeal proffered to the other, the signifier falls into the field which for the other is excluded, *verworfen,* unattainable. The signifier at this point produces a reduction, but an intensified one, to the pure imaginary relation.

3

This is precisely the point at which this so singular phenomenon is located that has had all the commentators on President Schreber scratching their heads – the puzzling *soul murder,* as he calls it.

This phenomenon, which for him is the signal of the onset of psychosis, may for the rest of us, the commentator-analysts, adopt all sorts of meanings, but it cannot be placed anywhere else than in the imaginary field. It relates 344
to the short-circuiting of the affective relation, which makes the other a being of pure desire who henceforth can only be, in the register of the human imaginary, a being of pure interdestruction. There is a purely dual relation here, which is the most radical source of the very register of aggressiveness. Freud didn't miss this, moreover, but he discussed it in the homosexual register. This text offers us a thousand proofs of what I am putting forward, and this is perfectly coherent with our definition of the source of aggressiveness and its emergence when the triangular, oedipal relation finds itself to be short-circuited, when reduced to its dual simplification.

Undoubtedly we lack the elements in the text that would enable us to get a better grasp of Schreber's relations with his father, with a certain presumed brother, whom Freud also makes a great deal of. But we don't need anything more to understand that it's necessarily via the purely imaginary relation that the register of the *you* must pass at the moment at which it's evoked, invoked, interpellated from the Other, from the field of the Other, by the emergence of a signifier that is primordial but excluded for the subject. I named this

[11] *"Tu es celui qui me tues."*

signifier last time – *Thou art the one who is,* or who will be, *a father*. As a signifier it can in no way be received, insofar as the signifier represents an indeterminate support around which there is grouped and condensed a number, not even of meanings, but of series of meanings, which come and converge by means of and starting from the existence of this signifier.

Before the Name-of-the-Father there was no father, there were all sorts of other things. If Freud wrote *Totem and Taboo,* it was because he thought he could glimpse what there was, but before the term *father* was instituted in a certain register historically there was certainly no father. I am only giving you this perspective as a pure concession, for it interests me in no manner or degree. I'm not interested in prehistory, except to indicate that it's fairly likely that Neanderthal man lacked a certain number of essential signifiers. There's no point in searching so far back, for we can observe this lack in subjects within our reach.

Observe this crucial moment carefully and you will be able to pick out this passage in the onset of every psychosis – it's the moment at which from the Other as such, from the field of the Other, there comes the interpellation of an essential signifier that is unable to be received.

In one of my case presentations I happened to show a West Indian whose family history brought out the problematics of the original ancestor. This was a Frenchman who had gone and introduced himself over there, a sort of pioneer, who had led an extraordinarily heroic life, involving all sorts of high-
345 points and lowpoints in his fortunes, and who had become an ideal for the entire family. Our West Indian, extremely deracinated from the region of Detroit where he had been leading quite a comfortable life as a craftsman, found himself one day in possession of a woman who announced to him that she was going to have a baby. It wasn't known whether it was his or not, but nevertheless within several days his first hallucinations declared themselves.

Barely had it been announced to him, *You are going to be a father* when a character appeared to him telling him, *You are Saint Thomas*. It must have been, I think, Saint Thomas the Doubter and not Saint Thomas Aquinas. The annunciations that followed leave no room for doubt – they came from Elizabeth, the one to whom it was announced very late in life that she was going to bear a child.

In short, this case demonstrates very well the connection between the register of paternity and the blossoming of revelations, of annunciations regarding generation, namely, precisely what the subject is literally unable to conceive – and it's not by chance that I use this word. The question of generation, a term of alchemical speculation, is always there ready to emerge as a response by detour, as an attempt to reconstitute what isn't receivable for the psychotic subject, for the *ego* whose power is invoked without his being strictly speaking capable of a response.

Henceforth, beyond every signifier able to be significant for the subject, the only response can be the permanent and, I would say, constantly sensitized employment of the signifier as a whole. We can in fact observe that the memorizing commentary accompanying all human acts immediately finds itself revived, spoken out loud in the emptiest and the most neutral of forms, and becomes the ordinary mode of relation of an *ego* unable to find its respondent in the signifier at the level from which it's interpellated.

Precisely because he is interpellated on terrain where he is unable to respond, the only way to react that can reattach him to the humanization he is tending to lose is to make himself permanently present in this slender commentary on the stream of life that constitutes the text of mental automatism. The subject who has crossed this limit no longer has the customary significant security, except through the accompaniment of a constant commentary on his gestures and acts.

These phenomena present an exceedingly rich character in the case of President Schreber, but they are not specific to him since they enter into the very definition of mental automatism. This justifies the use of the word *automatism,* of which so much use has been made in mental pathology without one's really knowing what one was saying. The term has a fairly precise sense in neurology where it characterizes certain phenomena of liberation, but its employment by analogy in psychiatry remains problematic at the very least. It's nevertheless the most appropriate word in de Clérambault's theory if you 346
think of the distinction, completely forgotten today, that Aristotle makes between *automaton* and fortune.[12] If we go straight to the signifier, that is to say on this occasion with all the reservations that such a reference comprises, straight to etymology, we see that *automaton* is what really thinks by itself without any link to that beyond, the *ego,* which gives thought its subject. If language speaks all alone, the occasion to use the term *automatism* is now or never, and this is what gives the term de Clérambault used its resonance of authenticity, its satisfying side for us.

What we have just been emphasizing will enable us next time to see what is lacking in each of the two points of view developed by Freud and Mrs. Ida Macalpine.

Freud posits a latent homosexuality that is supposed to imply a feminine position – this is where the leap is. He speaks of a fantasy of fertilizing impregnation, as if the thing were self-evident, as if every acceptance of the feminine position implied in addition this register that is so developed in Schreber's delusion and that ends up making him into the wife of God. Freud's theory is that the only way for Schreber to avoid what results from the fear of castration is *Entmannung,* unmanning, or simply emasculation, transfor-

[12] Aristotle, *Physics.*

mation into a woman – but after all, as Schreber himself observes somewhere, isn't it better to be a spirited woman than a poor unfortunate man, oppressed, or even castrated?[13] In short, the solution to the conflict introduced by latent homosexuality is found in an enlargement to the size of the universe.

On the whole, Freud's theory is the one that best respects the balance of the psychosis's progress. It's nevertheless certain that Mrs. Macalpine's objections are a worthy reply to Freud, even a worthy complement to a part of his theory.[14] She emphasizes, as being determinant in the process of psychosis, a fantasy of pregnancy, thus evoking a rigorous symmetry between the two great lacks that can manifest themselves as neuroticizing in each sex. She goes a long way in this direction and says some very amusing things to which the text lends support, including in the background the evocation of a heliolithic civilization where the sun, regarded as feminine and incarnated in stones, is said to be the fundamental symbol matching the promotion of the phallus in classical theory. There is a correspondence in the very name of the town in which Schreber is hospitalized, Sonnenstein.[15]

In the concrete analyses of the least neurotic of people we are constantly
347 encountering this mischievous mockery by the signifier, where unusual homonyms from all the corners of the horizon strangely intersect and appear to give a unity, sometimes ungraspable by any other means, both to the entire destiny of a subject and to his symptoms. It's surely less appropriate here than elsewhere to retreat from this investigation where the moment of onset of psychosis is concerned.

Before I finish I would like to draw your attention to the significant, indeed unfortunate, words that Flechsig said to Schreber on the occasion of his relapse when the latter arrived for his consultation in an extremely disturbed state. Flechsig had already been elevated for him to the value of an eminent paternal character. The function of paternity had previously already been put on alert or in suspension. We know from his testimony that he had hoped to become a father, that over the period of eight years separating the first from the second crisis his wife had had several spontaneous abortions. Now, Flechsig said to him that since the previous occasion enormous progress has been made in psychiatry and that they are going to give him one of those short sleeps that will be very fertile.[16]

[13] See above, chap. 20, p. 256.

[14] Ida Macalpine and Richard A. Hunter, "Translators' Analysis of the Case."

[15] "Translators" Analysis of the Case," 379. Both *Heliolithic* and *Sonnenstein* literally mean sun-stone.

[16] "He . . . gave me hope of delivering me of the whole illness through one prolific sleep." Mem, 39. The verb, lacking in the original, has been supplied by the translators. See Lacan's comment in "Preliminary Question," E, 545 n.1 / 222 n.10.

Perhaps this was just the thing not to say. From this moment our Schreber no longer slept and that night he tried to hang himself.

The relation of procreation is in fact implicated in the subject's relationship to death.

I shall keep this for next time.

27 June 1956

349

XXV

The phallus and the meteor

PREVALENCE OF CASTRATION

IDA MACALPINE

NATURAL SYMBOLIZATION AND SUBLIMATION

THE RAINBOW

INSERTED IN THE FATHER

I'm not sure what to begin with to end this course. On the off chance, I've put two small schemas on the board for you.

The first is an old one. It's a sort of grid which I used at the start of this year to try to show you how the problem of delusion is raised if we want to structure it insofar as it appears to be a relation in some way linked to speech. The second of these schemas is entirely new and I will have occasion to refer to it shortly.

1

What I have put forward this year has been centrally concerned with placing the emphasis back upon the structure of delusion. Delusion may be regarded as a disturbance of the object relation and is therefore linked to a transference mechanism. But I wanted to show you that all its phenomena, and I even think I can say its dynamics, would be clarified in reference to the functions and structure of speech. This will also free this transference mechanism from all kinds of confused and diffuse object relations.

By hypothesis, whenever one deals with a disturbance regarded overall as immature, one refers to a linear developmental series derived from the immaturity of the object relation. Now, experience shows that this unilinearity leads to impasses, to inadequate, unmotivated explanations that superimpose themselves on one another in a way that does not enable cases to be differ-
350 entiated and, first and foremost, obliterates the difference between neurosis and psychosis. The mere experience of partial delusion mitigates against speaking of immaturity, or even of regression or simple modification of the object relation.

The same thing goes if one refers to the neuroses alone. Next year we shall see that the notion of object relation isn't univocal, when I begin by contrasting the object of phobias with the object of perversions. This will be to take up again, at the level of the category of *object,* the problem of the relations between the subject and the other, two terms which, regarding the psychoses, are opposed.

I left you last time with two opposed descriptions, Freud's and that of a psychoanalyst who is far from being without merit and, while representing the most modern tendencies, has at least the advantage of doing so very intelligently.

Let's briefly summarize Freud's position on the subject of Schreber's delusion and the objections brought against him, and let's see if anything like a better solution has even begun to be outlined.

For Freud, we're told, Schreber's delusion is linked to the irruption of a homosexual tendency. The subject negates it, defends himself against it. In his case, which isn't the case of a neurotic, this negation ends in what we might call divine erotomania.

You know how Freud divides up the various denials [*dénégations*] of the homosexual tendency. He starts from a sentence that symbolizes the situation – *I love him, a man.*[1] There is more than one way of introducing denial into this sentence. One may say for example, *It's not I who love him* or, *It's not him I love* or again, *For me there's no question of love, I hate him.* Moreover, he tells us, the situation is never simple and isn't limited to a simple symbolic reversal. For reasons that he takes to be implied sufficiently, but upon which as a matter of fact he doesn't insist, an imaginary reversal of the situation occurs in only a part of the three terms, namely *I hate him* is for example transformed through projection into *He hates me.* In our case, *It's not him I love, it's someone else,* a big He, God himself, is inverted into *He loves me,* as in all erotomania. It is clear that Freud is indicating that the final result of defense against the homosexual tendency can't be understood in the absence of a very advanced reversal of the symbolic apparatus.

Everything may therefore appear to revolve around defence. It must undoubtedly be very intense indeed to propel the subject into trials that extend to nothing less than the derealization, not only of the external world in general, but of the very people around him, even those he is closest to, including the other as such. This necessitates an entire delusional reconstruction, fol- 351
lowing which the subject gradually resituates, though in a profoundly disturbed way, a world in which he is able to recognize himself, in an equally disturbed way, as destined – at a time projected into the uncertainty of the future, at a date that is indeterminate but that certainly cannot be delayed – to become the subject par excellence of a divine miracle, that is, to be the

[1] SE 12:63–65.

ort and feminine receptacle of the recreation of all humanity. Schreber's sion in its final state presents with all the megalomaniacal characteristics of delusions of redemption in their most highly developed form.

How do we account for the intensity of the defense? Freud's explanation looks like it is contained entirely within the reference to narcissism. The defence against the homosexual tendency begins with a narcissism under threat. The megalomania represents that by which the narcissistic fear expresses itself. The ego's enlargement to the dimensions of the world is a fact of libidinal economy which is apparently located entirely on the imaginary level. Making himself the supreme being's love object, the subject can henceforth abandon that which, of all that he was going to save, initially seemed most precious to him – namely the mark of his virility.

But ultimately, and I stress this, the pivot, the point of convergence of the libidinal dialectic that the mechanism and development of neurosis refer to in Freud, is the theme of castration. It's castration that conditions the narcissistic fear. To accept castration the subject must pay as elevated a price as this reworking of the whole of reality.

Freud stuck by this prevalence. In the material, explanatory order of Freudian theory, from beginning to end, this is an invariable, a prevalent invariable. He never subordinated or even relativized its place in the theoretical conditioning of the subjective interplay in which the history of any psychoanalytic phenomenon whatsoever is inscribed. It was around Freud, within the analytic community, that one wanted to give it symmetrical or equivalent things. But in his work the phallic object occupies the central place in libidinal economy, in both man and woman.

This is an altogether essential fact, characteristic of all the theorizing given and maintained by Freud – whatever reworking he brought to his theorizing, throughout all the phases of the schematization he was able to give of psychic life, the prevalence of the phallic center was never modified.

If there is some truth in Mrs. Macalpine's remarks – and this is however
352 the only thing that she doesn't really make evident – it's that, effectively, in Schreber castration is never an issue. The Latin term that is used in German, *eviratio – Entmannung,* means in the text *transformation,* with all that this word conveys of transition, *into a woman* – it's not castration at all.[2] This doesn't matter, Freud's analysis makes the entire dynamics of the subject Schreber revolve around the theme of castration, of the loss of the phallic object.

We must remark that despite certain weaknesses in his argument, which are due to the use of terms that only have their place in the imaginary dialectic of narcissism, the virile object is the essential element at play in the con-

[2] "unmanning" in Mem.

flict. It alone enables us to make sense of and to understand the different stages of the delusion's evolution, its phases, and its final construction. Furthermore, we may note in passing all sorts of subtleties that have not been developed or completely explored. Freud shows us for example that projection alone cannot explain delusion, that it is not a matter of a mirror image of the subject's feeling, but that it is indispensable to determine stages in it and, at a certain moment as it were, a loss of the tendency, which ages. Over the course of the year I have greatly insisted upon the fact that what has been repressed within reappears without, re-emerges in the background – and not in a simple structure but in a position that is, as it were, internal, which makes the subject himself, who in the present case happens to be the agent of persecution, ambiguous, problematic. He is initially only the representative of another subject who not only permits but undoubtedly acts, in the final analysis. In short, the otherness of the other is spread out. It's one of the problems to which as a matter of fact Freud does lead us, but he stops there.

Ida Macalpine, after others, but in a much more coherent way than others, objects that nothing permits us to think that this delusion presupposes the genital maturity, if I may call it that, that would explain the fear of castration. The homosexual tendency is far from manifesting itself as primary. What we see from the start are symptoms, initially hypochondriacal, which are psychotic symptoms.

At the outset one finds this particular something which is at the heart of the psychotic relation, such as the psychosomatic phenomena that this clinician has especially worked on, and which certainly for her are the means of access to the phenomenology of this case. It is here that she might have directly apprehended phenomena that are structured quite differently from what takes place in the neuroses, namely, where there is some sort of direct imprint or inscription of a characteristic and even, in certain cases, of a conflict upon what may be called the material picture that the subject presents as a corpo- 353
real being. A symptom such as a facial eruption, which can be variously characterized dermatologically, will be mobilized in response to a given anniversary for example, directly, without any intermediary, without any dialectic, without any interpretation's being able to indicate any correspondence with anything from the subject's past.

This is no doubt what drove Ida Macalpine to raise the most unusual problem of direct correspondences between the symbol and the symptom. The apparatus of the symbol is so absent from the mental categories of the contemporary psychoanalyst that the sole way such relations can be conceived is through the intermediary of a fantasy. Furthermore, her entire argument consists in relating the development of the delusion to a fantasmatic theme, to an originary – original [*originelle*] according to the usual word today – pre-oedipal fixation, emphasizing that what sustains desire is essentially a theme of procreation, but one that is pursued for its own sake, is asexual in form, and only induces conditions of devirilization, of feminization, as a sort of *a posteriori* consequence of the requirement in question. The subject is conceived as born into the sole child-mother relation, prior to any constitution of a triangular situation. This is when he would have seen a fantasy of desire born within himself, a desire to equal the mother in her ability to create a child.

This is Mrs. Macalpine's entire argument, which I have no reason to pursue here in all the richness of its detail, since it is within your reach in the substantial preface and postface to the English edition of Schreber's text she has done. It is important to see that this construction is connected with a certain reorientation of the entire analytic dialectic which tends to make the imaginary economy of fantasy, the various fantasmatic reorganizations, disorganizations, restructurations, and destructurations, the hub of all comprehensive progress as well as of all therapeutic progress. The schema that is currently so widely accepted, frustration-aggressiveness-regression, is at the base of everything in this delusion that Mrs. Macalpine thinks she can explain.

She goes a long way in this direction. There is, she says, a decline, a twilight of the world, and at one point a quasi-confusional disorder of the apprehensions of reality, only because the world has to be recreated.[3] She thus introduces, at the most profound stage of the mental confusion, a sort of teleology. The entire myth was only constructed because it is the only way for the subject Schreber to satisfy himself in his imaginary requirement of childbirth.

354 Ida Macalpine's point of view can no doubt enable us to understand the putting into play, the imaginary impregnation, of the subject to be reborn – I'm copying here one of Schreber's themes which is, as you know, the *picturing*.[4]

But from such a point of view, in which only imaginary fantasies are involved, what enables us to understand the prevalence that Freud gives to the function of the father?

Whatever certain of the weaknesses in Freud's argument concerning psychosis may be, it is undeniable that the function of the father is so exalted in Schreber that nothing less than God the father – in a subject for whom up to this point this has had no sense – is necessary for the delusion to attain its culminating point, its point of equilibrium. The prevalence, in the entire evolution of Schreber's psychosis, of paternal characters who replace one another, grow larger and larger and envelop one another to the point of

[3] Mem, 387–88.
[4] In English in the original. Mem, 231–37.

becoming identified with the divine Father himself, a divinity marked by the properly paternal accent, is undeniable, unshakable, and destined to make us raise the question once again – how come something that confirms that Freud is so right is only investigated by him in certain modes that leave a lot to be desired?

In reality, everything in him is balanced, and everything remains inadequate in Mrs. Macalpine's rectification. It's not only the vastness of the fantasmatic character of the father that prevents us from being in any way satisfied with a dynamics founded on the irruption of a pre-oedipal fantasy. There are many more things, including what in both cases remains enigmatic. Freud, much more than Mrs. Macalpine, comes close to the preponderant, crushing, proliferating aspect of the phenomena of verbal auditivation, the formidable captivation of the subject in the world of speech, which is not only copresent with his existence, which constitutes not only what last time I called a spoken accompaniment of acts, but also a perpetual intimation, solicitation, summation even, to manifest itself on this plane. Not for one instant must the subject cease testifying, at the constant inducement of the speech that accompanies him, that he is there present, capable of responding – or of not responding, because perhaps, he says, one wants to compel him to say something silly. By his response, as by his nonresponse, he has to testify that he is always awake to this internal dialogue. Not to be so any longer would be the signal of what he calls a *Verwesung*, that is, as it has been correctly translated, a decomposition.

This is what we have drawn attention to this year and what we have insisted upon, in order to say that it's what gives the pure Freudian position its value. Despite the paradox presented by certain manifestations of psychosis if one 355
refers them to the dynamics that Freud recognized in neurosis, psychosis nevertheless happens to be explored in a more satisfactory manner from his point of view.

His point of view. Freud never completely elucidated it, but it's what makes his position tenable in relation to this kind of leveling-off, as it were, of instinctual signs that psychoanalytic dynamics have tended to be reduced to since Freud. I am speaking of the terms that he never abandoned, that he requires for any possible analytic understanding, even where it hangs together only approximately, for it hangs together all the better in this way – namely, the function of the father and the castration complex.

It can't be a question purely and simply of imaginary elements. What one finds in the imaginary in the form of the phallic mother isn't homogeneous, as you are all aware, with the castration complex, insofar as the latter is integrated into the triangular situation of the Oedipus complex. This situation is not completely elucidated by Freud, but by virtue of the sole fact that it is always maintained it is there ready to lend itself to elucidation, which is only possible if we recognize that the third element, central for Freud, which is the father, has a signifying element that is irreducible to any type of imaginary conditioning.

2

I'm not saying that the Name of the Father is the only one of which we can say this.

We can uncover this element whenever we apprehend something that is of the symbolic order properly so-called. On this subject I reread, once again, Ernest Jones's article on symbolism.[5] I shall take up one of the most notorious examples in which this master's brat tries to grasp the phenomenon of the symbol. It concerns the ring.

A ring, he tells us, doesn't enter into play as an analytic symbol insofar as it represents marriage, with all that is cultural and developed, even sublimated – since this is how he expresses himself – that this conveys.[6] The ring as a symbol of marriage is to be sought somewhere in sublimation – we couldn't care less about all that, it drives us up the wall, we're not people to speak to about analogies. If a ring signifies something it's because it is a symbol of the female sexual organ.

356 Doesn't this kind of declaration give you cause to wonder, when we know that the putting into play of the signifier in the symptom has no link with anything of the order of a tendency? You would really have to have the oddest idea of natural symbolization to believe that a ring is the natural symbolization of the female sexual organ.

You are all familiar with the theme of the *Ring of Hans Carvel*, a fine story from the Middle Ages of which La Fontaine made a tale and which Balzac used again in his *Contes drolatiques*. This fellow, who is colorfully depicted and is sometimes said to be a priest, dreams that he has a ring on his finger and on waking finds that he has his finger inside the vagina of his companion. To put this in a way that dots the *i*s and crosses the *t*s – how could the experience of penetrating this orifice, since it is an orifice that is in question, resemble in any way at all that of putting on a ring, if one didn't already know in advance what a ring is?

A ring isn't an object one encounters in nature. If there is anything in the order of penetration that resembles the more or less tight-fitting penetration of a finger inside a ring, it is certainly not – I appeal, as Marie-Antoinette used to say, not to all mothers, but to all those who have ever put their finger

[5] Ernest Jones, "The Theory of Symbolism." Lacan examined this paper in "*A la mémoire d'Ernest Jones: sur sa théorie du symbolisme,*" E, 697–717.

[6] "Theory of Symbolism," 128–29.

in a certain place – it's certainly not penetrating this place which is, my God, more like a mollusk than anything else. If something in nature is designed to suggest certain of the properties of a ring [*anneau*] to us, it is restricted to what language has dedicated the term *anus* to, which in Latin is spelt with one *n*, and which in their modesty ancient dictionaries designated as the ring that can be found behind.

But to confuse one with the other on the basis of the fact that it may be a question of natural symbolization, one must really have had in the order of these cogitative perceptions. . . . Freud himself must have really despaired of you not to have taught you the difference between the two, and regarded you as irredeemable little idiots.

Mr. Jones's lucubration is designed to show us that a ring is introduced into a dream, indeed a dream that culminates in a sexual action, only because we thereby signify something primitive. Cultural connotations frighten him and this is where he is mistaken. He doesn't imagine that the ring already exists as a signifier, independently of its connotations, that it's already one of the essential signifiers by which man in his presence in the world is capable of crystallizing many things other than marriage. A ring isn't a hole with something around it, as Mr. Jones seems to think, in the manner of these people who think that to make macaroni one takes a hole and surrounds it 357
with flour. A ring above all has a signifying value.

How else can we explain that a man is able to understand something, what is called understanding, of the simplest formulation to be inscribed in language, the most elementary utterance – *That's it* [*c'est cela*]? For a man, this expression nevertheless has an explanatory sense. He has seen something, anything, which is there, and *that's it*. Whatever the thing is he is in the presence of, whether it be a question of the most unusual, the most bizarre, or even the most ambiguous, *that's it*. It is now located somewhere other than where it was beforehand, which was nowhere, now it's – *that's it*.

I would for a moment like deliberately to take a phenomenon that is exemplary because it's the most inconsistent of that which can present itself to man – the meteor.[7]

By definition the meteor is *that* [*cela*], it's real and at the same time it's illusory. It would be quite wrong to say that it's imaginary. The rainbow, *that's it*. You say that the rainbow is *that*, and then you search. People racked their brains for some time until M. Descartes came along and completely reduced the whole affair. There is a region that becomes iridized in little drops of water in suspension, etc. Fine. And so what? There is the ray on

[7] Besides the current meaning of *mass from space made luminous by the earth's atmosphere*, "meteor" has the older, generic meaning of any atmospheric phenomenon. This earlier meaning is clearly intended in the current context.

one side and the condensed drops on the other. *That's it.* It was only an appearance – *that's it.*

Notice that the question is not at all settled. A ray of light is, as you know, a wave or a corpuscle and a little drop of water is a curious thing, since ultimately it's not really in gaseous form, it's condensation which is falling in a liquid state, but in a suspended fall, between the two, in the state of an expansive pool, as water.

When we say, then, *That's it,* we imply that that's all it is, or that that's not what it is, namely, the appearance that we had stopped at. But this proves to us that everything that has subsequently emerged, the *that's all it is* as well as the *that's not what it is,* was already implied in the *that's it* at the beginning.

A rainbow is a phenomenon that has no kind of imaginary interest, you will have never seen an animal pay one any attention, and as a matter of fact man pays no attention to an incredible number of related manifestations. Various iridizations are exceedingly widespread in nature and, gifts of observation or some special research aside, nobody pauses at them. If on the contrary rainbows exist, it's precisely in relation to the *that's it.* That's why we have named them rainbows and why when one speaks of them to someone
358 who hasn't yet seen one there is a point at which one says to him – *That's what a rainbow is.* And this *that's what it is* presupposes the implication that we are going to carry on until we have run out of breath, to discover what lies hidden behind it, what its cause is, to which we shall be able to reduce it. Notice that what has characterized the rainbow and the meteor from the beginning – and everybody knows this since this is why it's called a meteor – is precisely that nothing is hidden behind it. It exists entirely in this appearance. What makes it nevertheless subsist for us, to the point where we do not stop asking ourselves questions about it, stems uniquely from the original *that's it,* that is, the naming as such of the rainbow. There is nothing besides this name.

In other words, to pursue this further, this rainbow doesn't speak, but one could speak in its place. Nobody ever speaks to it, this is quite striking. The aurora is interpellated, and so are all sorts of other things. The rainbow retains the privilege, along with a number of other manifestations of the same kind, that nobody speaks to it. No doubt there are reasons for this, namely that it is quite particularly insubstantial. But let's say that one speaks to it. If one speaks to it, one can make it speak. One can make it speak to whomever one wants. This could be to the lake. If the rainbow has no name, or if it doesn't want to hear anything of its name, if it doesn't know that it's called the rainbow, the only resource this lake has is to show it the thousand little mirages of the sunshine upon its waves and the rising vapor. It may well attempt to join up with the rainbow, but it will never join up with it, for the simple reason that the little fragments of sun that dance on the surface of the lake, like the vapor that wafts away, have nothing to do with producing the rainbow which begins at a certain angle of inclination of the sun and at a certain density of the droplets in question. There is no reason to search for either the inclination of the sun or for any of the indices that determine the phenomenon of the rainbow, so long as it is not named as such.

If I've just carried out this lengthy study concerning something that has the characteristic of a spherical belt, able to be unfolded and refolded, it's because the imaginary dialectic in psychoanalysis is of exactly the same kind. Why are the mother-child relationships, to which there is a tendency to limit it more and more, inadequate? There is really no reason.

We're told that a mother's requirement is to equip herself with an imaginary phallus, and it's very clearly explained to us how she uses her child as a quite adequate real support for this imaginary prolongation. As to the child, there's not a shadow of doubt – whether male or female, it locates the phallus very early on and, we're told, generously grants it to the mother, whether or 359
not in a mirror image, or in a double mirror image. The couple should harmonize symmetrically very well around this common illusion of reciprocal phallicization. Everything should take place at the level of a mediating function of the phallus. Now, the couple finds itself on the contrary in a situation of conflict, even of respective internal alienation. Why? Because the phallus is, as it were, a wanderer. It is elsewhere. Everyone knows where analytic theory places it – it's the father who is supposed to be its vehicle. It's around him that in the child the fear of the loss of the phallus and, in the mother, the claim for, the privation of, or the worry over, the nostalgia for, the phallus is established.

Now, if affective, imaginary exchanges between mother and child are established around the imaginary lack of the phallus, then that which makes it the essential element of intersubjective coaptation in the Freudian dialectic, the father, has his own and that's that, he neither exchanges it nor gives it. There is no circulation. The father has no function in the trio, except to represent the vehicle, the holder, of the phallus. The father, as father, has the phallus – full stop.

In other words, he is that which in the imaginary dialectic must exist in order for the phallus to be something other than a meteor.

3

So fundamental is this that if we try to situate on a schema what it is that makes the Freudian conception of the Oedipus complex cohere, it is not a question of a father-mother-child triangle, but of a triangle (father)-phallus-mother-child. Where is the father in this? He is in the ring that holds all this together.

The notion of father can only be supposed as provided with an entire series of signifying connotations which give it existence and consistency and which are a very long way indeed from merging with those of the genital, from which it is semantically different across all the linguistic traditions.

I shan't start quoting Homer and Saint Paul to tell you that invoking the father, whether it be Zeus or someone else, is entirely different from purely and simply referring to the generative function. An indefinite number of beings can issue from a woman. They could all be women —moreover, we shall soon reach this point, since every day the newspapers tell us that parthenogenesis is on the way and that soon women will beget daughters without anyone's assistance. Well then, notice that if any masculine elements intervene here,
360 they will play a role of fecundation without being anything other than an indispensable lateral circuit, as in animals. There will be the begetting of women by women, with the aid of lateral abortees that can be used to set the process off again but will not structure it. It's only when we seek to inscribe descendence as a function of males that any innovation in the structure intervenes. It's only when we speak of descendence from male to male that a cut intervenes, which is the difference between generations. The introduction of the signifier of the father introduces henceforth an ordering in the descendants, the series of generations.

We're not here to develop all the facets of this function of the father, but I am pointing out one of the most striking of them, which is the introduction of an order, of a mathematical order, whose structure is different from the natural order.

We've been trained in analysis through the experience of the neuroses. The imaginary dialectic may suffice if, within the framework of this dialectic that we have sketched out, there already exists this implied signifying relation for the practical use one wants to put it to. In two or three generations no doubt no one will understand it at all anymore, a cat won't be able to find its kittens, but for the moment, on the whole, the continued presence of the theme of the Oedipus complex preserves the notion of signifying structure, which is so essential for finding one's way about the neuroses.

But where the psychoses are concerned, things are different. It's not a question of the subject's relation to a link signified within existing signifying structures, but of his encounter under elective conditions with the signifier as such, which marks the onset of psychosis.

Look at the point in his life at which President Schreber's psychosis declares itself. On more than one occasion he was in the situation of expecting to become a father. Here he is, all of a sudden, invested with a socially eminent function, one that has great value for him – he becomes President of the Court of Appeal. I should say that within the administrative structure in question it is something like the Conseil d'Etat.[8] Here he is admitted to the top of the legislative hierarchy, among men who make laws and are all twenty years older than he is – a disturbance in the order of generations. Following what? Following an explicit call from the ministers. This promotion of his nominal existence solicits a renewing integration from him. Ultimately the question is whether or not the subject will become a father. The question of the father centers all Freud's research, all the points of view he has introduced into subjective experience.

This is entirely forgotten, I'm well aware. Recent analytic technique is 361
clouded by the object relation. The supreme experience that is described, this famous distance taken in the object relation, ultimately consists in fantasizing the sexual organ of the analyst and imaginarily absorbing it. Make filiation the equivalent of fellatio? Indeed there is an etymological relationship between these two terms, but this isn't a sufficient reason for deciding that analytic experience is a sort of obscene chain that consists in the imaginary absorption of an object that has finally been extracted from fantasies.

In any case, it is impossible in the phenomenology of psychosis to misunderstand the originality of the signifier as such. What is perceptible in the phenomenon of everything that takes place in psychosis is that it is a question of the subject's access to a signifier as such and of the impossibility of that access. I shan't go back over the notion of *Verwerfung* I began with, and for which, having thought it through, I propose to you definitively to adopt this translation which I believe is the best – *foreclosure*.

There follows a process whose first stage we have called an imaginary cataclysm, namely that no longer can anything in the mortal relation, which is in itself the relation with the imaginary other, be held on lease. Then there is the separate deployment and bringing into play of the entire signifying apparatus – dissociation, fragmentation, mobilization of the signifier as speech, ejaculatory speech that is insignificant or too significant, laden with non-meaningfulness, the decomposition of internal discourse, which marks the entire structure of psychosis. After the encounter, the collision, with the inassimilable signifier, it has to be reconstituted, since this father cannot be simply a father, a rounded-out father, the ring of just before, the father who is the father for everybody. And President Schreber does in fact reconstitute him.

Nobody is aware of being inserted into the father. Nevertheless, I would like to point out to you before leaving you this year that to be doctors you may be innocent, but that to be psychoanalysts you should nevertheless meditate from time to time on a theme such as this, even though neither the sun

[8] The supreme juridical body of the French State.

nor death can look itself in the face. I shan't say that the slightest little gesture to arouse an evil creates possibilities for a greater evil, it *always* entails a greater evil. This is something that a psychoanalyst should become accustomed to, because I believe that he is absolutely incapable in all conscience of conducting his professional life without it. Having said this, it won't take you very far. The newspapers are always saying that God only knows whether the progress of science is dangerous, etc., but for us this is neither here nor
362 there. Why not? Because you are all, myself included, inserted into this major signifier called Father Christmas. With Father Christmas things always work out and, I would add, they work out well.

What is at issue in the psychotic? Suppose someone unthinkable for us, one of these gentlemen who, we are told – if indeed any have ever existed, don't believe I attribute any importance to such hearsay – was capable of such self-discipline that he no longer believed in Father Christmas and was able to convince himself that everything good that one does entails an equivalent evil and that consequently one mustn't do it. Admitting this, even for an instant, is sufficient for you to understand that all sorts of things which are fundamental at the level of the signifier may depend on it.

Well then, compared to you the psychotic has this disadvantage, but also this privilege, of finding himself a little bit at odds with, askew in relation to, the signifier. Once he is summoned to harmonize with these signifiers, he has to make a considerable effort of retrospection, which culminates in these extraordinarily bizarre things that constitute what is called the development of a psychosis. This development is quite particularly rich and exemplary in the case of President Schreber, but I have shown you in my case presentations that things become a bit clearer once one possesses this point of view, even in the most common illnesses. The most recent case I have shown you was of someone who was very, very strange, on the verge of mental automatism, though not quite there. For him everyone was suspended in an artificial state whose coordinates he defined well. He had observed that the signifier dominates the existence of beings, and his own existence appeared to him to be much less certain than anything that presented itself with a certain signifying structure. He stated it quite crudely. You noticed that I put this question to him – *When did all this begin? During your wife's pregnancy?* He was a bit astonished for a moment, then answered me – *Yes, that's true* – adding that it had never occurred to him.

From the imaginary point of view, what we say in passing, in analysis, has strictly no importance, since it's solely a question of frustration or of no frustration. One frustrates him, he is aggressive, he regresses, and we continue like that until the most primordial fantasies emerge. Unfortunately, this isn't the correct theory. One has to know what one's saying. It isn't sufficient to bring signifiers into play in this way – *I tap you on the shoulder . . . You're*

really a nice person . . . You had a bad daddy . . . Things will work out. One has to use them in full knowledge, make them resonate otherwise, and at least know how not to employ certain of them. The negative indications con- 363
cerning certain contents of interpretation are highlighted by such a point of view.

I leave these questions open. The year ends in dialect, why should it end in any other way?

In conclusion I would like to move to a different genre of style from my own. Several weeks back I promised myself to end on a very pretty page by an admirable poet called Guillaume Apollinaire. It comes from the *Enchanteur pourrissant*.

At the end of one of the chapters there is the enchanter who is rotting away in his tomb, and who, like any good cadaver, I won't say speaks drivel, as Barrès would say, but enchants and speaks very well. There is also the Lady of the Lake seated on her tomb – it was she who had got him to enter the tomb by telling him that he could get out again easily, but she, too, had her tricks, and the enchanter is there, rotting away, and from time to time speaks. This is where we are when a number of madmen appear in the middle of various funeral processions, along with a monster whom I hope you are going to recognize. This monster is the one who found the analytic key, the active force of men, and especially in the relation of the father-child to the mother.

> *I mewed, I mewed, said the monster, I encountered only owls who assured me that he was dead. I shall never be prolific. However, those who are have qualities. I confess that I do not recognize any in me. I am alone. I am hungry, I am hungry. Here I discover a quality of my own; I am famished. Let's look for something to eat. He who eats is no longer alone.*[9]

4 July 1956

[9] *L'Enchanteur pourrissant*, 49.

BIBLIOGRAPHY

Abraham, Karl. "The Psycho-Sexual Differences between Hysteria and Dementia Praecox." In *Selected Papers of Karl Abraham,* 64–79. Translated by Douglas Bryan and Alix Strachey. 1927. Reprint. London: Maresfield Library, 1988.

Apollinaire, Guillaume. *L'Enchanteur pourrissant.* Paris: Gallimard, 1972.

Aristotle. *Nicomachean Ethics.* Translated by W. D. Ross. 1925. Reprint. Oxford: Oxford Univ. Press, 1954.

——. *Physics.* Books 1 and 2. Translated by W. Charlton. Oxford: Oxford Univ. Press, 1970.

Baumeyer, Franz. "The Schreber Case." *International Journal of Psycho-Analysis* 37 (1956):61–74.

Benveniste, Emile. "Active and Middle Voice in the Verb." In *Problems in General Linguistics,* 145–51. Translated by Mary Elizabeth Meek. Coral Gables, Florida: Univ. of Miami Press, 1971.

——. "The Nature of Pronouns." In *Problems in General Linguistics,* 217–22. Translated by Mary Elizabeth Meek. Coral Gables, Florida: Univ. of Miami Press, 1971.

——. "Relationships of Person in the Verb." In *Problems in General Linguistics,* 195–204. Translated by Mary Elizabeth Meek. Coral Gables, Florida: Univ. of Miami Press, 1971.

——. "Remarks on the Function of Language in Freudian Theory." In *Problems in General Linguistics,* 65–75. Translated by Mary Elizabeth Meek. Coral Gables, Florida: Univ. of Miami Press, 1971.

Blondel, Charles. *The Troubled Conscience and the Insane Mind.* Translated by F. G. Crookshank. London: Kegan Paul & Co., 1928.

Boehme, Jakob. *Signature of All Things: And Other Writings.* Greenwood, SC: Attic Press, 1969.

Buber, Martin. *I and Thou.* Translated by Walter Kaufmann. New York: Charles Scribner's Sons, 1970.

Cicero. *The Nature of the Gods.* Translated by Horace C. P. McGregor. Harmondsworth: Penguin, 1972.

Claudel, Paul. *Le soulier de satin, ou, le pire n'est pas toujours sûr.* Paris: Gallimard, 1920. Translated by John O'Connor, under the title *The Silk Slipper: or the Worst Is not the Surest.* New York: Sheed and Ward, 1945.

Clérambault, Gaëtan Gatian de. "Les délires passionnels; érotomanie, revendication, jalousie." In *Oeuvre psychiatrique*, 1:337–46. Edited by Jean Fretet. 2 vols. Presses universitaires de France, 1942.

——. "Psychoses à base d'automatisme." Two articles. In *Oeuvre psychiatrique*, 2:528–44 & 544–76. Edited by Jean Fretet. 2 vols. Presses universitaires de France, 1942.

Damourette, Jacques, and Edouard Pichon. *Des mots à la pensée: Essai de grammaire de la langue française*. 7 vols. Paris: Bibliothèque du français moderne, 1932–51.

Descartes, René. *Meditations on First Philosophy, with Selections from the Objections and Replies*. Translated by John Cottingham. Cambridge: Cambridge Univ. Press, 1986.

Deutsch, Helene. "Some Forms of Emotional Disturbance and their Relationship to Schizophrenia." In *Neuroses and Character Types: Clinical Psychoanalytic Studies*, 262–81. Edited by John D. Sutherland and M. Masud R. Khan. London: Hogarth Press, 1963.

d'Urfé, Honoré. *L'Astrée*. 5 vols. 1607–28. New edition. Edited by H. Vaganay. Geneva: Slatkine Reprints, 1966.

Eisler, Michael Josef. "Analyse eines Zwangssymptoms." *Internationale Zeitschrift für Psychoanalyse* 8 (1922):462–70.

Erasmus, Desiderius. *Praise of Folly and Other Writings*. Translated by Robert M. Adams. New York: Norton, 1988.

Festugière, André Marie Jean. *Epicurus and his Gods*. Translated by C. W. Chilton. Oxford: Blackwell, 1955.

Fontaine, Jean de La. "The Turtle and the Two Ducks." In *Fifty Fables of La Fontaine*, 97. Translated by Norman R. Shapiro. Urbana: Univ. of Illinois Press, 1988.

Freud, Sigmund. "Address to the Society of B'nai B'rith." SE 20:271–74.

——. "The Antithetical Meaning of Primary Words." SE 11:155–61.

——. "The Claims of Psycho-Analysis to Scientific Interest." SE 13:165–90.

——. *The Complete Letters of Sigmund Freud to Wilhelm Fliess 1887–1904*. Translated and edited by Jeffrey Moussaieff Masson. Cambridge, MA: Harvard Univ. Press, 1985.

——. "The Dissolution of the Oedipus Complex." SE 19:173–79.

——. *The Ego and the Id*. SE 19:12–59.

——. "Female Sexuality." SE 21:225–43.

——. "Fetishism." SE 21:152–57.

——. "Fragment of an Analysis of a Case of Hysteria." SE 7:7–122.

——. "From the History of an Infantile Neurosis." SE 17:7–122.

——. "Further Remarks on the Neuro-Psychoses of Defence." SE 3:162–85.

——. *The Interpretation of Dreams*. SE 4& 5.

——. *Jokes and their Relation to the Unconscious*. SE 8.

——. *Moses and Monotheism*. SE 23:7–137.

——. "The Neuro-Psychoses of Defence." SE 3:45–61.

——. "A Note upon the 'Mystic Writing-Pad'." SE 19:227–32.

——. *The Origins of Psycho-Analysis. Letters to Wilhelm Fliess, Drafts and Notes 1887–1902*. Edited by Marie Bonaparte, Anna Freud, and Ernst Kris. Translated by Eric Mosbacher and James Strachey. New York: Basic Books, 1954.

——. "Psycho-Analytic Notes on an Autobiographical Account of a Case of Paranoia (Dementia Paranoides)." SE 12:9–82.

——. "Repression." SE 14:146–58.

——. "Sexuality in the Aetiology of the Neuroses." SE 3:263–85.

——. "Some Psychical Consequences of the Anatomical Distinction between the Sexes." SE 19:248–58.

——. *Standard Edition of the Complete Psychological Works of Sigmund Freud*. 24 volumes. Translated and edited by James Strachey in collaboration with Anna Freud, assisted by Alix Strachey and Alan Tyson. London: The Hogarth Press, 1953–74.

——. *Three Essays on the Theory of Sexuality*. SE 7:130–243.

Génil-Perrin, Georges. *Les Paranoïaques*. Paris: Norbert Maloine, 1926.

Gracián, Baltasar. *El Criticón*. 1651–1657. Translated by Paul Rycaut, under the title *The Critick*. London, 1681.

Heidegger, Martin. *Being and Time*. Translated by John Macquarrie and Edward Robinson. New York: Harper & Row, 1962.

——. "Logos (Heraclitus Fragment B 50)." In *Early Greek Thinking*, 59–78. Translated by David Farrell Krell and Frank A. Capuzzi. New York: Harper & Row, 1975.

Hugo, Victor. *Booz endormi*. In *La légende des siècles*, 82. Paris: Hachette, 1921.

Isakower, Otto. "On the Exceptional Position of the Auditory Sphere." *International Journal of Psycho-Analysis* 20 (1939): 340–48.

Jakobson, Roman. "Two Aspects of Language and Two Types of Aphasic Disturbances." In Roman Jakobson and Morris Halle, *Fundamentals of Language*, 53–87. The Hague: Mouton, 1956.

Jaspers, Karl. *General Psychopathology*. Translated from the 7th German edition (1959) by J. Hoenig and Marian W. Hamilton. Manchester: Manchester Univ. Press, 1962.

Jones, Ernest. *Sigmund Freud: Life and Work*. 3 vols. New York: Basic Books, 1953–57.

——. "The Theory of Symbolism." In *Papers on Psycho-Analysis*, 87–144. 5th edition. Baltimore: Williams & Wilkins, 1948.

Kant, Immanuel. *Critique of Practical Reason and Other Writings in Moral Philosophy*. Translated by Lewis White Beck. Chicago: Univ. of Chicago Press, 1949.

——. "Versuch, den Begriff der negativen Grö*β* en in die Weltweisheit einzuführen." *Werke*, 1:775–819. 6 vols. Wiesbaden: Insel Verlag, 1960.

Katan, Maurits. "Further Remarks about Schreber's Hallucinations." *International Journal of Psycho-Analysis* 33 (1952):429–32.

——. "Schreber's Delusions of the End of the World." *The Psychoanalytic Quarterly* 18 (1949):60–66.

——. "Schreber's Hallucinations about the 'Little Men'." *International Journal of Psycho-Analysis* 31 (1950):32–35.

——. "Schreber's Prepsychotic Phase." *International Journal of Psycho-Analysis* 34 (1953):43–51.

——. "Structural Aspects of a Case of Schizophrenia." *The Psychoanalytic Study of the Child* 5 (1950) :175–211.

Kraepelin, Emil. *Clinical Psychiatry*. Translated from the 7th German edition (1903–

1904) by A. R. Diefendorf. New York: Scholars' Facsimiles and Reprints, 1981.

Kris, Ernst. "Ego Psychology and Interpretation in Psychoanalytic Therapy." *Psychoanalytic Quarterly* 20 (1951) :15–30.

Lacan, Jacques. "The Agency of the Letter in the Unconscious or Reason Since Freud." In *Ecrits: A Selection*, 146–78. Translated by Alan Sheridan. New York: Norton, 1977.

——. "Au-delà du 'principe de réalité'." *Ecrits*, 73–92. Paris: Editions du Seuil, 1966.

——. *De la psychose paranoïaque dans ses rapports avec la personnalité, suivi de premiers écrits sur la paranoïa*. Paris: Editions du Seuil, 1975.

——. "De nos antécédents." *Ecrits*, 65–72. Paris: Editions du Seuil, 1966.

——. "The Direction of the Treatment and the Principle of its Power." *Ecrits: A Selection*, 226–80. Translated by Alan Sheridan. New York: Norton, 1977.

——. "The Freudian Thing, or the Meaning of the Return to Freud in Psychoanalysis." In *Ecrits: A Selection*, 114–45. Translated by Alan Sheridan. New York: Norton, 1977.

——. "The Function and Field of Speech and Language in Psychoanalysis." *Ecrits: A Selection*, 30–113. Translated by Alan Sheridan. New York: Norton, 1977.

——. "Intervention on the Transference." In *Feminine Sexuality*, 61–73, edited by Juliet Mitchell and Jacqueline Rose. Translated by Jacqueline Rose. London: Macmillan, 1982.

——. "Réponse au commentaire de Jean Hyppolite sur la *Verneinung* de Freud." *Ecrits*, 381–99. Paris: Editions du Seuil, 1966.

——. *The Seminar. Book I. Freud's Papers on Technique, 1953–1954*. Edited by Jacques-Alain Miller. Translated by John Forrester. Cambridge: Cambridge Univ. Press, 1988.

——. *The Seminar. Book II. The Ego in Freud's Theory and in the Technique of Psychoanalysis, 1954–1955*. Edited by Jacques-Alain Miller. Translated by Sylvana Tomaselli. Cambridge: Cambridge Univ. Press, 1988.

Lacan, Jacques, J. Lévy-Valensi, and P. Migault. "Ecrits 'inspirés': Schizographie." In Jacques Lacan, *De la psychose paranoïaque dans ses rapports avec la personnalité, suivi de premiers écrits sur la paranoïa*, 365–82. Paris: Editions du Seuil, 1975.

Laforgue, René. "Verdrängung und Skotomisation." *Internationale Zeitschrift für Ärtzliche Psychoanalyse* 12 (1926) :54–65.

——. *Relativité de la réalité*. Paris: Denoël et Steele, 1932.

Lorenz, Konrad. *King Solomon's Ring*. Translated by Marjorie Kerr Wilson. London: Methuen, 1961.

Ludwig, Emil. *Doctor Freud, an Analysis and a Warning*. New York: Hellman & Williams, 1947.

Macalpine, Ida, and Richard A. Hunter. "Translators' Analysis of the Case." In Daniel Paul Schreber, *Memoirs of My Nervous Illness*, 369–411. Translated by Ida Macalpine and Richard A. Hunter. 1955. 2nd edition. Cambridge, MA: Harvard Univ. Press, 1988.

Merleau-Ponty, Maurice. *The Phenomenology of Perception*. Translated by Colin Smith. London: Routledge & Kegan Paul, 1962.

Molière. *Les Précieuses ridicules*. In *Oeuvres complètes*. Paris: Gallimard, Pléiade, 1965.

Odier, Charles. "Une névrose sans complexe d'Oedipe." *Revue Française de Psychanalyse* 6 (1933) :298–343.

Ogden, Charles K., and Ivor A. Richards. *The Meaning of Meaning: A Study of the Influence of Language upon Thought and of the Science of Symbolism*. 10th edition. San Diego: Harcourt Brace Jovanovich, 1989.

Pascal, Blaise. *Pensées*. Translated by A. J. Krailsheimer. Harmondsworth: Penguin, 1970.

Piéron, Henri. *The Sensations: Their Functions, Processes and Mechanisms*. Translated by M. H. Pirenne and B. C. Abbott. New Haven: Yale Univ. Press, 1952.

Plotinus. *The Enneads*. Translated by S. MacKenna. 3rd edition. London: Faber, 1956.

Racine, *Athaliah*. In *Britannicus, Phaedra, Athaliah*. Translated by C. H. Sisson. Oxford: Oxford Univ. Press, 1987.

Sartre, Jean-Paul. *Being and Nothingness: An Essay on Phenomenological Ontology*. Translated by Hazel E. Barnes. New York: Philosophical Library, 1956.

Saussure, Ferdinand de. *Course in General Linguistics*. Edited by C. Bally and A. Sechehaye in collaboration with A. Reidlinger. Translated by Wade Baskin. New York: McGraw-Hill, 1966.

Schreber, D. G. M. *Medical Indoor Gymnastics*. Translated from the 26th German edition by Herbert A. Day. New York, 1899.

Schreber, Daniel Paul. *Memoirs of My Nervous Illness*. Translated by Ida Macalpine and Richard A. Hunter. 1955. 2nd edition. Cambridge, MA: Harvard Univ. Press, 1988.

Scudéry, Madeleine de. *La Carte du Tendre*. Vol. 2 of *Clélie, histoire romaine*. 1654–1661.

Séglas, Jules. *Leçons cliniques sur les maladies mentales et nerveuses (Salpêtrière, 1887–1894)*. Paris: Asselin et Houzeau, 1895.

Sérieux, Paul, and J. Capgras. *Les Folies raisonnantes: le délire d'interprétation*. Reprint. Marseille: Laffitte, 1982.

Silberer, Herbert. "Spermatozoenträume." *Jahrbuch für psychoanalytische und psychopathologische Forschungen* 4 (1912):141–61.

——. "Zur Frage der Spermatozoenträume." *Jahrbuch für psychoanalytische und psychopathologische Forschungen* 4 (1912):708–40.

——. "Zum Thema: Spermatozoenträume." *Zentralblatt für Psychoanalyse und Psychotherapie* 3 (1913):211.

Somaize, Baudeau de. *Le dictionnaire des précieuses*. New York: Kraus Reprint, 1970.

——. *Le grand dictionnaire historique des précieuses*. Geneva: Slatkine Reprints, 1972.

Sophocles. *Oedipus at Colonus*. In *The Three Theban Plays*. Translated by Robert Fagles. New York: Viking Press, 1982.

Spinoza, Baruch. *The Ethics*. In *The Collected Works of Spinoza*, 1:408–617. Edited and translated by Edwin Curley. 2 vols. Princeton, N.J.: Princeton Univ. Press, 1985–.

Tardieu, Jean. *Un mot pour un autre*. In *Le professeur Froeppel: nouvelle édition revue et augmentée de Un mot pour un autre*. Paris: Gallimard, 1978.

Tomkins, Silvan S. "Consciousness and the Unconscious in a Model of the Human Being." Address delivered at the 14th International Congress of Psychology and published in French in *La Psychanalyse* no. 1 (1956):275–86.

Trésor de la langue française: dictionnaire de la langue du XIXe et du XXe siècles (1789–1960). Edited by Paul Imbs. Paris: Editions du Centre National de la Recherche Scientifique, 1971–.

INDEX

Abel, Karl, 108
Abraham, Karl, 20
acting out, 79–81
aggressiveness, 93–95, 205, 240–41, 314
  in Schreber, 305
alienation, 40–42
  in Freudian theory, 241
  in psychosis, 204–5
allocutor
  distinguished from *you*, 299
anal preoccupations in a case of hysteria, 171
analysis, *see* psychoanalysis
analyst, *see* psychoanalyst
analytic relation, *see* psychoanalytic relation
animal psychology and mirror stage, 93–96
Anna O., 103
aphasia, 219–221, 223–224
Apollinaire, Guillaume, *L'Enchanteur pourrissant*, 323
appeal, *see* interpellation
Aristotle, 14, 64–65, 174, 187, 307
  and god, 287–88
  Nicomachean Ethics, 235
"as if" mechanism, 192–93
Augustine, Saint, 32, 137
autoerotism, 147, 253

Balzac, Honoré de, *Contes drolatiques*, 316
behaviorism, 114
being, 137–39, 148–49, 300
Bejahung [judgment], 12, 46, 81–84
Benveniste, Emile, 27, 32, 108–09, 278, 281–82
Bergson, Henri, 111, 118, 236
between-I, 193–95
bisexuality, 83
Bleuler, Eugen, 4, 135
Blondel, Charles, 21–22
  La Conscience morbide, 118
Boehme, Jakob, *Signatura rerum*, 184
Bossuet, Jacques Bénigne, 218
Breuer, Josef, 103
Buber, Martin, *I and Thou*, 273

call, *see* interpellation
Capgras, J., 17–18
castration
  in aetiology of Schreber's illness, 30
  as central for Freud, 312, 315
  and feminine position, 204
  and narcissism, 312
  in Oedipus complex, 176
  in psychoanalysis since Freud, 105–06
  refusal of, by Wolf Man, 13
  in Schreber's delusion, 89, 307–08
  and *Verwerfung*, 12
categorical imperative, 276
causality, 197–98
censorship, 60
certainty and reality, 74–76

Charcot, Jean, 231
Cicero, 183, 186, 304–05
  The Nature of the Gods, 115
Clérambault, Gaëten Gatian de, 5–6, 18
  and mental automatism, 269, 307
communication, 187–89
communication theory, 37
condensation, 83, 221, 228
consciousness, 181
  and memory, 153–54
contiguity, 220–21
contradiction in the unconscious, 202
conviction, passional and delusional, 190–91
couvade
  and being a father, 293
  in ethology, 212–213
  and masculine procreation, 179

Damourette, Jacques, 271–72, 277–79
Dasein, 300–01
death
  and procreation, 293
  and symbolic, 179
deciphering
  and dream interpretation, 236–37, 247
  and paranoia, 10–11
decompensation, psychotic, 204–05
defense, 154, 202
  and delusion, 79, 311–12
  and ego, 105
  Freud on, 102–03
  against homosexuality, 30
  Kris on, 80–81
  and paranoia, 50, 144
  and real, 86
déjà vu, 111
Delay, Jean, 231
delusion
  and castration, 312–13
  classification of, 16–28
  as defense, 79, 311–12
  dialectic of, 40
  discourse and, 33–34
  and elementary phenomenon, 19
  and fantasies, 87–88
  Freud on, 41–43, 215–16
  and imaginary, 9, 21, 87–88
  interpretation, 18, 22–23
  Kraepelin on, 17–18
  and language, 31–34, 36
  and latent discourse, 209
  litigious, 18, 49
  and Oedipus complex, 212–13
  onset of, 86–87
  paranoid, 44–56
  partial, 38
  of persecution, 42, 46, 120
  of presumption, 92
  and projection, 42
  psychiatric approaches to, 34–36
  and psychoanalysis, 132
  and psychosis, 44–56
  and real, 21
  of reference, 9, 18
  and regression, 104
  subject in, 35–36
  and symbolic, 21
  voices in, 123
  see also hallucination
delusional intuition, 33
dementia praecox
  Abraham on, 20
  and paranoia, 17, 77
  and paraphrenia, 135
denial [*Verneinung,* negation] and homosexuality, 41–43, 311
Descartes, René, 64, 66, 186, 317
desire, 227
  and delusion, 104
  and imaginary, 197
  object of, 39–40, 84–85, 177–78
  and the signifier, 239–40
Deutsch, Helene, 192–93, 251
diachrony, 54, 119
dialectic
  imaginary, 40–41
  in psychosis, 22–23
Diderot, Denis, 287
Disavowal, *see Verleugnung*
discourse, 136–39
  as diachronic, 54
  of freedom, 132–35
  internal, 110, 209, 299–300
  and language, 53–54

of the law, 242
meaning of term, 51
in neurosis and psychosis, 132
of the psychotic, 33–34, 250
in Schreber's delusion, 121–123, 130, 139–41
and science, 63–64
and verbal hallucination, 113
displacement, 221, 228
Dolto, Françoise, 163
Dora, see Freud, works referred to
dream interpretation, 10, 236–38
deciphering and, 236–37, 247
dreams
and writing, 247–48
of punishment, 62
drive
and defense, 105
in neurosis, 86
in psychosis, 73, 258
duality of signifier and signified, 119–20
d'Urfé, Honoré, *L'Astrée,* 254

ego
and aggressiveness, 93, 241, 303
as alienated, 85
and analyst's intervention, 80
conflict-free sphere of, 166
as constituted through identification, 241
and defense, 105
in delusions, 42–43, 52, 56
and discourse of reality, 132, 134, 145
in *Dora,* 175
Freudian theory of, 240, 243
function of, 240; in cure, 14
healthy part of, 131
and ideal ego, 144
in imaginary relation, 205
and internal discourse, 113, 135
and interpellation, 307
and misrecognition, 239–40
and narcissism, 240
in neurosis, 177–78
official, 154–55
orthopedics of, 235
and other, 22, 39, 146, 194–95
in projection, 76–77
and psychiatry, 36
in psychosis, 14, 144, 312
and reality testing, 174
and schema L, 14, 74, 161–62
in Schreber's fantasy, 62
and soul-murder, 208–09
strengthening of, 174
and subject, 14
and superego, 277
and *thou,* 286, 300
ego psychology, 166, 173, 196
Einstein, Albert, 64, 184, 187
Eisler, Michael Josef, 168–72, 212–13
elementary phenomenon, 14, 22, 34, 75, 121
definition of, 5n
and interpretation, 21
Lacan on, 19
and language, 250
and understanding, 10
emasculation and feminine function, 86
enjoyment, 40
epicurianism, 125–26
Erasmus, Desiderius, *Praise of Folly,* 16
erotism and aggressiveness, 93–95
erotomania, 42–43, 49
ethology, 9, 177
évolution psychiatrique (group), 39
Evolution psychiatrique (journal), 273
existence and signifier, 179–80
existentialism and subjectivity, 273–74

fantasy
in delusion, 88
and ego, 174
as imaginary, 15, 174
Macalpine on, 313–15
of pregnancy, 86; in case of male hysteria, 168–72, 178–79, 212–13; in Schreber's delusion, 252, 308
in psychosis, 45; and in neurosis, 144, 193
in Schreber, 46, 61, 69, 307–08

father
in Freud's work, 215, 321
function of, 212–13
in hysteria, 171–72, 178–79
murder of, 215, 242
in Oedipus complex, 96, 175–76, 204, 315–16, 319
and phallus, 319–20
and quilting point, 268
as signifier, 285–94
see also name-of-the-father
Father Christmas, 322
feminine position
in Oedipus complex, 176–77
in Schreber, 85–86, 307–08
Ferenczi, Sandor, 25
fertile moment, 17, 103
in Schreber, 191
fixation
homosexual, 50
pre-oedipal, 313–14
in psychosis, 142, 199
Flechsig, Professor Paul Emil, 107, 268
in Schreber's delusion, 97–98, 108, 126, 194, 217
Schreber's homosexual attachment to, 61, 85–86, 99
Schreber's Open Letter to, 26
as seducer, 194
treatment of Schreber, 25, 308–09
flight of ideas, 300
foreclosure [*Verwerfung*, rejection], 321
fort-da, 81
foundational speech, 229
fragmented body, 39, 56
in paranoia, 52
in Schreber's delusion, 87
freedom, discourse of, 132–35
and delusion, 145
Freud, Sigmund, 231–44
cases and dreams cited: Anna Freud's dream, 227; "Autodidasker," 237; Dream of Irma's injection, 193, 195; "Signorelli," 238–39
as decipherer, 10
on double meaning of primary words, 27, 108
genius of, 10–11
jewishness, 232
name, 232
and *Naturphilosophie*, 236
on paranoia, 10; and schizophrenia ("paraphrenia"), 3–4, 135
personality, 232
pessimism, 243
and scientism, 236
sense of mystery in, 216
style, 236
teaching, 8
on the unconscious, 119
on varieties of paranoia, 41–43, 311
work, distortion of, 235
works referred to: "The Antithetical Meaning of Primary Words," 27; *Beyond the Pleasure Principle*, 179; "The Claims of Psycho-Analysis to Scientific Interest," 281; "The Dissolution of the Oedipus Complex," 175; *Dora* ["Fragment of an Analysis of a Case of Hysteria"], 90–92, 171–72, 174–75, 178, 180; *The Ego and the Id*, 240; "Female Sexuality," 175; "Fetishism," 156; *The Interpretation of Dreams [Die Traumdeutung]*, 10, 62, 84, 153, 234, 236–37, 239, 248; *Jokes and their Relation to the Unconscious*, 37, 166, 234, 239, 244; Letter 46, 180; Letter 52, 143, 151–54, 156, 181–82; "The Loss of Reality in Neurosis and Psychosis," 44; *Moses and Monotheism*, 214, 242–43; "On Narcissism," 240; "Negation" *[Die Verneinung]*, 12, 46, 88; "Neurosis and Psychosis," 44; "Some Psychical Consequences of the Anatomical Distinction between the Sexes," 175; *The Psychopathology of Everyday Life*, 166, 180, 234, 238; Schreber case ["Psycho-Analytic Notes on an Autobiographical Account of a Case of Paranoia (Dementia Para-

noides)"], passim; *Totem and Taboo,* 242, 306; Wolf Man case ["From the History of an Infantile Neurosis"], 12–13, 45–46, 85, 156, 169
frustration, 235

Génil-Perrin, Georges, 5
God, 287–88
  nondeceiving, 64–66, 186
  as quilting point, 265–68
Griaule, Marcel, 151, 200
guilt, 242
  in neurosis, 288

hallucination, 44–56, 69–70, 110, 206–07, 293
  as defense, 144, 203–04
  ego and, 105
  and internal discourse, 162
  and judgment of existence, 150
  in Letter 52, 182
  in psychosis, 23, 36
  and reality, 14, 75, 136, 141–42, 258
  Séglas on, 24
  and signifier, 293–94
  and subject, 14
  in Wolf Man, 13, 45–46
  see also delusion
hallucinatory
  confusion in Schreber, 107
  phenomenon, in Dora, 92; in Schreber, 125, 217
Hegel, G. W. F., *Phenomenology of Mind,* 40
Heidegger, Martin, 124, 279, 300–01
  "Logos," 175
Heraclitus, 124
history and symbolic, 111
Hoff, Dr., 71
hole in symbolic, 283
  and female sex, 176
  in psychosis, 45, 156–57, 201, 202–03
Homer, 320
homosexuality
  in a case of traumatic hysteria, 170
  and Oedipus complex, 196–97
  in psychosis, 193, 204
  in Schreber, 30, 61, 307–08, 311–14
Hugo, Victor, 218–19, 222–25, 233
  Booz endormi, 228
hypnoid states, 103
hypochondria in Schreber, 107
Hyppolite, Jean, 12, 46, 82, 150
hysteria, 60, 190
  in *Dora,* 90–92
  masculine and feminine, 178, 249
  traumatic, 168–72, 212–13

I and *thou*
  in language, 274, 277–84, 286–87
id, 14, 80
  in psychosis, 296–97
  and reality, 204
  scotomization of, 44–45
ideal ego and ego, 144, 146
identification
  feminine, in Schreber, 63
  imaginary, 177–78, 302–03
  and metaphor, 218
  in mirror stage, 39–40
  narcissistic, 92–93
  and Oedipus complex, 198–99
  in psychosis, 205
  and speech, 282
  symbolic, 171
image
  in dreams, 247
  of the father in psychosis, 205
  and preverbal, 165
  specular, 95–96
imaginary
  and animal ethology, 7–9
  assembly, supporting discourse, 301
  compensation, 193
  dialectic, 60
  in human behavior, 95
  identification, 178; in Schreber's delusion, 98–99
  and language, 53–54
  and meaning, 63
  in *Memoirs,* 69
  phallus, 319
  and preverbal, 165
  in psychosis, 106, 146, 162–63

imaginary (*continued*)
and real, 39
recognition of, in analysis, 15
and schema L, 161–62
in Schreber's delusion, 70, 97, 209
and specular alienation, 204–05
and specular image, 95–96, 144–45
and symbolic, 9, 177
symbolism and, 173
imaginary relation, 51
between egos, 14
with the father, 205
of *I* and *thou,* 302–03
and narcissism, 92–93
and Oedipus complex, 96
to one's own body, 11
to other, 56, 241, 253
in Schreber's delusion, 68–70, 305
inmixing of subjects, 193–94
instinct, 147–48, 189
insult, 55
in delusions, 49–50, 100
intellectualization, 235–36
inter-I, 216
interlocutor in Schreber's delusion, 124
interpellation, 286–87, 304–05
in psychosis, 252, 254–55, 283–84, 305–07
interpretation in psychoanalysis, 22, 80–81
intersubjectivity
in delusions, 193
as reciprocal, 273
introjection, 212, 217
Isakower, Otto, 276–77

Jakobson, Roman, 219
Jaspers, Karl, 6–7
jealousy, 39, 42
projective & delusional, 46, 76, 145–46
John of the Cross, Saint, 77–78
Jones, Ernest, 234, 236, 316–17
judgment of attribution and of existence, 150–51
Jung, Carl, 185, 234

Kant, Immanuel, 4, 110
and negative magnitudes, 122, 156
and schema-ideas, 165
and superego, 277
Katan, Maurits, 61, 105, 211–12
on defense in Schreber, 102
on hallucination, 203–04
and prepsychotic period, 191–92
Kleinian conception of analysis, 146–47
knowledge *[connaissance]*
as paranoid, 177–78
Kraepelin, Emil, 135
cited by Schreber, 125, 274
on paranoia, 17–19, 23
Kretschmer, Ernst, 18
Kris, Ernst, 79–80, 166

Lacan, Jacques
case presentations, 31–32, 47–53, 59–60, 75, 202, 306–07, 322
as psychiatrist, 5
works referred to: "The Freudian Thing, Or the Meaning of the Return to Freud in Psychoanalysis," 71, 72, 273; *De la psychose paranoïaque dans ses rapports avec la personnalité* [Lacan's thesis], 4–5, 19
Laënnec, René, 115
La Fontaine, Jean de, 304, 316
Lagache, Daniel, 231
language
of the delusional, 32–34
and preconscious, 164–67
in psychosis, 161–62
in Schreber's delusion, 99–101, 142
and speech, 53–56
and subject, 249–50
law
and Oedipus complex, 83
and Schreber, 70
Leclaire, Serge, 248
Leibniz, Wilhelm Gottfried, 35
lived experience of psychotic, 118
Lorenz, Konrad, 94–95
love, 55
and the Other, 253–55

Macalpine, Ida, 307–09, 310—15
madness
  common usage of term, 16
  cure of, 131
  and psychoanalytic treatment, 15
  and psychosis, 4–5
  reasonable, 21, 23
Malraux, André, 291
mandate, 280, 304
master-slave dialectic, 40, 132
maternal relation, 319
  and pre-oedipal relations, 84–85
meaning, 119
  anticipation of, in discourse, 137
  fascination of, 237–38
  as imaginary, 63
  as ineffable, 55
  in language, 53, 198
  and preverbal, 165
  in psychoanalysis, 196
  in Schreber's delusion, 85
megalomania in Schreber's delusion, 69, 126, 312
memory
  disturbances of, 104
  Freud's theory of, 152–55, 181
mental automatism, 34, 251, 296
  definition of, 5–6
  and interpellation, 307
Merleau-Ponty, Maurice, *Phenomenology of Perception*, 75
message, received in inverted form, 52
metalanguage, 226
metaphor, 218–21, 222–230
metonymy, 218–21, 222–230, 239
middle voice, 281
mirror stage
  identification and, 39
  and narcissism, 93
  and schema L, 161
  and Schreber's delusion, 87
misrecognition
  of dialectical dimension, 23
  of Freud's teaching, 241
  of history, 104
  in the imaginary, 240
  of nature of psychoanalysis, 235
Montpensier, Mlle de, 111
mother-child relationship, 319

name-of-the-father
  and foreclosure, 193, 306
  in Oedipus complex, 96
  see also father
narcissism
  and defense, 312
  and delusion, 89
  and imaginary, 92–93
  and psychosis, 104, 146
nature, as nondeceptive, 64–66
negation [denial, *Verneinung*]
  of homosexual tendency, 311
  in imaginary, 240
  in language, 155–56
  in psychosis, 41–43
  and *Verwerfung*, 13
neologism in psychosis, 32–33
Nerval, Gérard de, 78
neuropsychoses, 248
neurosis
  as compromise, 87
  and defense, 79
  as discourse, 155
  and guilt, 288
  and language, 167–68
  and prepsychosis, 191–92
  projection in, 42
  and psychosis, 11–12, 44–47, 60–61, 63, 85, 86–88, 104–05, 132, 156–57, 192, 199, 202, 250
  as question, 174–75, 178–80
  repression in, 81, 84
  symbolic debt in, 242
nihilation, symbolic, 148

object
  as object of the other's desire, 39
  refinding of, 84–85
object relation, 272, 302
  in *Dora*, 90
  as dual relation, 14–15
  and imaginary, 165–66
  and psychoanalytic technique, 321
  in psychosis, 310–11

obsessional neurosis
and death, 179–80
paternity and death in, 293
and procreation, 292
and repression, 60
Oedipus complex
father in, 212
Freud and Klein on, 147
and imaginary relation, 96
and the law, 83
phallus in, 319–20
and quilting point, 268
and sexualization, 172, 175–77
and signifier, 189–90
and the subject, 198–99
other
and alienation, 241
in delusion, 52–53
as imaginary, 302–03
and Other, 40, 50–51, 252–53, 272–73
in speech, 38
and subject, 239–40
Other
and being, 288
image of, 209
as nondeceptive, 64
and onset of psychosis, 193
in psychosis, 43, 52–53, 162
and recognition, 50–51, 168, 303
and Schema L, 14, 52–53, 56
in Schreber's delusion, 69, 135, 256, 284
and signifier, 290–94
in speech, 37–38, 41
and subject, 52, 74
testimony and, 40
overdetermination, 119–20

paranoia, 3–5, 10, 16–21, 23, 28
combinatory, 23
and defense, 144
and *dementia praecox* and paraphrenia, 77
etiology of, 312
Freud on, 10
insult in, 49–50
in Letter 52, 156
and libido, 105
pathogenesis of, 29–31
and *Verwerfung,* 150
of Wolf Man, 13
paranoiac
as bearing witness, 41
paranoid knowledge, 39
paraphrenia
Freud on, 4
and paranoia and *dementia praecox,* 77
Pascal, Blaise, 16
password, as fundamental to speech, 229
paternal
function, 212–13
imago, 209
paternity
in aetiology of Schreber's illness, 30
and onset of psychosis, 306–07
perception, and memory, 154
perplexity
in psychosis, 49, 53, 194; linked to certainty, 157
in Schreber's delusion, 192
Perrier, François, 296
persecution
in Dora, 91
in paranoia, 90
person, in language, 270–71
personality, sane part of, 38
personization, 269, 280
phallus
father and, 319–20
imaginary, 319
and Oedipus complex, 176, 319–20
Picasso, Pablo, 228
Pichon, Edouard
Grammaire, 271–72, 277–78, 304
translator of Schreber, 97
Piéron, Henri, 9
Pierson, Dr., 109
pleasure principle
and memory, 153
and reality principle, 85, 197
Plotinus, 121
positional link in language, 225
précieuses, les, 114–15, 117–18
preconscious

and language, 164–65, 167
in Schreber, 61–62
pregenital stages, 189, 240
pre-oedipal relations, 84–85
prepsychotic phase, 56, 202–03
in Schreber, 61–62, 191–93, 217
preverbal communication
and preconscious, 164–65
primitive phenomenon, 53
procreation
and being a father, 292–93
Macalpine on, in Schreber, 313–14
and symbolic, 179
projection, 42, 50, 76–77
delusional, 45–47, 145–46, 313
imaginary, 145
Proust, Marcel, 78
Psychanalyse, La (journal), 150
psychiatry, and psychosis, 7, 16–21, 23–24, 34–36
psychoanalysis
and common discourse, 134–35
and language, 243
and psychogenesis, 7
and subjectivity, 186
psychoanalyst
in schema L, 161–62
psychoanalytic interpretation, 11
psychoanalytic relation
and onset of psychosis, 15
as structuring Freudian experience, 8
psychology
defined as the ethological, 7–8
psychosis
chronic hallucinatory, 206, 208
compared with aphasia, 222
délire à deux, 47–53
diagnosis, 92
Freud's approach to, 3–4
and imaginary, 106
and lack of signifier, 201, 322
and language, 11–12, 32–33, 250
lived experience and, 67
meaning of term, 4–5
mechanism of, 63
and neurosis, 11–12, 44–47, 60–61, 63, 85, 86–88, 104–05, 132, 156–57, 192, 199, 202, 250
onset of, 87, 251, 254–55, 305–06, 320–21
passional, 22–23
prehistory of, 86–87
and quilting point, 268
treatment of, 163
triggered by analysis, 15, 251
and understanding, 21–22
psychosomatic phenomena in psychosis, 313
psychotic phenomenon, 85
punctuation, role of, 299

quilting of *I*, 281–82
quilting point, 258–70

Racine, Jean, *Athaliah*, 262, 267, 289–90
real, 86, 107, 189
as discourse, 63
and foreclosed, 81
and hallucination, 46, 50, 51, 81–82, 86, 135–36
and imaginary, 39, 63–64, 83, 129, 197
language and, 118
and objectivity, 186
philosophy and, 110
in psychosis, 12–14
and reality principle, 85
reappearance of non-symbolized in, 86, 88, 190–91
signifier in, 130–32, 139, 201
subjectivity in, 186, 193–94
and symbolic, 9, 63–64, 82–83
reality
and certainty, 76
and hallucination, 50–51, 75, 84
human beings' access to, 147
in neurosis, 44–45
in psychosis, 44–45, 204
relation to, 47
and signifier, 249
and symbolic nihilation, 148
reality principle
and pleasure principle, 85, 197
and *Verneinung*, 84
reality, sense of, 111

recognition
of the other, 303–05
by the other, in Schreber, 78
and true speech, 51
regression, 154–55
rejection [*Verwerfung*, foreclosure], 12–13, 45–46, 81, 85, 150–51
repetition, 242
repression [*Verdrängung*], 182
and language, 59–60, 63, 84
in Schreber, 46
and *Verwerfung*, 12–13, 86–87
in Wolf Man, 46
resistance, 48–49
Richards, I. A. and C. K. Ogden, *Meaning of Meaning*, 303
rivalry, imaginary, 40

Saint-Amant, Marc-Antoine Girard, 114, 117
Sartre, Jean-Paul, *Being and Nothingness*, 94
Saussure, Ferdinand de, 53, 54, 181, 264
schema of, 261
on signifier and signified, 119, 261–62, 294, 299
schema L [or Z-shaped schema], 74, 87, 98, 253, 283, 310
and analytic discourse, 161–62
and hallucinations, 14, 52
schizophrenia, 135
and paranoia, 3–4
Schreber, Daniel Paul
and adapted delusion, 56
and *Aufklärung*, 124
chronology of illness, 106–09
compared to philosopher, 55
and existence of other, 274
on external reality, 133
and foundational speech, 279
and God, 67, 69, 90
as God's woman, 192
and hallucination, 85
and homosexuality, 29–30, 106
and interpellation, 307
on Kraepelin, 125, 274
Lacan's method concerning, 60–61, 296
and masturbation, 61
onset of his illness, 30
and paternity, 30–31
projection in, 46
as psychologist, 255
symbolic analysis of, 11
as writer, 78
Schreber's delusion, 26–28, 56, 78, 216–17
of being forsaken, 126–27
bellowing miracle, 140
call for help, 140
Cassiopeia, 98–99
and castration, 312–13
of his own death, 97
decomposition, 315
divine rays, 26, 32, 67
evolution of, 62–63, 120, 256
father in, 213, 314, 321
fleeting-improvised-men, 53, 79, 97, 210, 274
flight of sense, 259–60
fringe phenomena, 139, 157, 205
and God, 67–70, 87, 106, 113, 140–41, 210, 217, 259
hallucinated discourse, 121–22
interrupted sentences, 100–01, 113–14, 123, 141, 216, 259, 283–84
of the little men, 69, 211–12
miracled birds, 115, 141, 229–30, 255, 258–59
mirror relationship, 97
natural world order, 56
nerves, 26–27, 32–33, 54, 66, 78, 210, 284; of God, 108, 140; of intellect, 66
otherness in, 56
perplexity in, 192
phrases learned by rote, 114, 258–59
progression of, 26
and psychoanalytic theory, 27–28
question and reply in, 229
rays, 26–27, 100, 108, 113, 141
realms of God, 99, 121
reconciliation, 77
refrain, 33, 114

Schreber as wretch, 99
signified in, 258–60
signifier in, 255–60
soul murder, 54, 76, 208–09, 254–55, 305
souls in, 107, 217; conception of, 259; tested souls, 32, 97–99
speech phenomena in, 139–42
stabilization of, 86
terminal state of, 118
transformation into a woman, 252
twilight of the world, 61, 107, 205, 217
tying-to-celestial-bodies, 98
unmanning, 307
Unsinn, 122, 124, 141
voices, 114, 121
writing-down system, 128, 130–31, 256
Schreber's fantasy
of intercourse as a woman, 61, 192
Schreber's father, 76, 284, 305
in aetiology of Schreber's illness, 30–31, 89, 308
Schreber's fundamental language, 11, 26–27, 32–33, 55, 68, 87, 98, 100, 108, 211, 255
Schreber's God
Ahriman and Ormuzd, 99, 108
nature of, 67–70, 79, 106, 108, 124–26, 127—28, 130–31, 135, 255–56, 314–15
realms of, 107
relationship to, 62, 77–78, 87, 89–90, 100–01, 126, 162, 194, 252, 274, 307, 311
Schreber's illness, history of, 25
Schreber's little studies, 109
Schreber's *Memoirs,* 25–26, 30, 66–69, 76, 78, 97, 113, 206, 208, 210–11, 274
writing of, 109
Schreber's psychosis
onset of, 254–55, 320
terminal state of, 120
Schreber, D. G. M., *Medical Indoor Gymnastics,* 284
science, modern, 63–65, 184–85
final cause in, 187
and human experience, 295
and subjectivity, 186
scotomization, of reality, 44–45
Scudéry, Madeleine de, *Carte de Tendre,* 255
Seelenmord, see Schreber's delusion, soul-murder
Séglas, Jules, *Leçons cliniques,* 23–24
self-consciousness, 241
Sérieux, Paul, 17
sexuality
and law, 83
and Oedipus complex, 170
and signifier, 248–49
Shakespeare, William, 290
Shaw, George Bernard, 243
sign and signifier, 167, 188–89
signified
and signifier, 119
and structure of language, 53
signifier
autonomy of, 197
and communication, 188–89
function of, 291
as material of language, 32
and meaning, 54, 198
in Oedipus complex, 176
primordial, 151, 156, 200
in psychosis, 199
pure, 199–200
in real, 139, 201
and science, 184–85
and sign, 167, 188–89
and signified, 119–20, 262–63
as signifying nothing, 185
and structure, 53, 183–84
and symbol, 316–17
in the unconscious, 119
Silberer, Herbert, 212
similarity
in delusions, 220
and metaphor, 219
Société française de psychanalyse, 231, 295
Somaize, Baudeau de, 114–16, 117
Sophocles, *Oedipus at Colonus,* 244
speech, 36–38

speech (*continued*)
foundational, 37
full, 14, 36–37
lying, 37, 51
as mission, 279
as pact, 39–40
in psychosis, 36, 101
subjectivity in, 289
true, 40, 51, 52–53
Spinoza, Baruch, 48, 66, 210,
stickleback, 93–95
subject
in discourse, 51–52
and disturbances of memory, 104
and imaginary, 56
and language, 37, 249–50
and Other, 52, 74, 239–40
and person, 55–56
and primitive *Bejahung*, 83
and schema L, 14, 161
and signifier in psychosis, 190, 250
in speech, 38, 54
and truth, 37
of the unconscious, 41
and voices, 123
and other, 74
subject-to-subject relation, 37
subjectivity
in language, 271–74
in the real, 186
and science, 188–89
and *you*, 299
superego, 190
and ego, 277
as law, 276
in the Oedipus complex, 190
suppression, 46
symbol, Jungian and Freudian, 173
symbolic
articulation, 111
compared with imaginary and real, 8–10, 53, 63
debt, 242
and imaginary, 9, 177
and language, 53–54
and object relation, 15
in Oedipus complex, 96, 212
and remembering, 104
and signifier, 63–64, 96–97
and subject, 179
use of term by Freud, 45
symbolization, 81–83
failure of, 81, 86
origin of, 46
of woman, 176–77
symptom
hysterical, 178
as language, 60
in neurosis and psychosis, 45
and signifier, 119–20
synchrony, 54
syndrome of influence, 250

talking cure, 103
Tardieu, Jean, 226
testimony
Schreber's, 60, 76–78
in speech, 38–39
third person in language, 278, 285
thou and *I*, 279–80, 282–84, 285–87, 297, 301–4, 305–06
thought, magical, 200
thought-echo, 35–36
Tolstoy, Leo, 228
Tomkins, Silvan S., 187
total personality, mirage of, 241
trace, 167
transference, 180, 241
in Schreber, 30–31
transitivism, 39, 145
traumatism, 44, 103
truth, 214–15
of the thing, 204
Tardieu, Jean, *Un mot pour un autre*, 226

unconscious
and common discourse, 255
as discourse of the Other, 56, 112
as language, 11, 119, 166
in Letter 52, 181
mechanisms, 238
and preconscious, 166–67
in psychosis, 11–12, 143–44
signifier in psychosis, 142

understanding, 20–22, 191
  Jaspers on, 6–7
unity of the personality, 8
Unterdrückung [suppression], 46
utterance
  as move in a game, 51

Verdichtung [condensation], 83
Verdrängung [repression], 84, 150
  in Letter 52, 182
  in Schreber, 46
Verleugnung [disavowal] and *Verwerfung*, 150
Verneinung [negation, denial], 12, 46, 82, 83–84, 150, 155
  and *Verwerfung*, 62, 86–87
  in Letter 52, 156
  in psychosis, 87, 132
Verwerfung [foreclosure, rejection], 12–13, 142, 282, 305
  and *Bejahung*, 81–82
  Lacan's translation of, 321
  as lack in signifier, 203, 252
  and paranoia, 149—50
  and primordial signifier, 156
  and projection, 47
  and the real, 190
  and *Verneinung*, 86
Vogel, R. A., 4
Voltaire, 7–8, 287
Vorbewusstsein [preconscious], 181–82

Wahrnehmung [perception], 181
Wernicke, Karl, 18
Wernicke's asphasia, 219
Wiener, Norbert, 37
woman
  question of, 175–78
  Schreber as, 77, 293

you, in language, 274–78, 298–302

Zurich school, 3–4